AF600454

COMPELLING GOD

Theories of Prayer in Anglo-Saxon England

Compelling God

Theories of Prayer in Anglo-Saxon England

STEPHANIE CLARK

UNIVERSITY OF TORONTO PRESS
Toronto Buffalo London

Toronto Buffalo London
www.utorontopress.com

ISBN 978-1-4875-0198-3

Library and Archives Canada Cataloguing in Publication

Clark, Stephanie, 1975–, author
Compelling God : prayer in Anglo-Saxon England / Stephanie Clark.

(Toronto Anglo-Saxon series ; 26)
Includes bibliographical references and index.
ISBN 978-1-4875-0198-3 (cloth)

1. English literature – Old English, ca. 450–1100 – History and criticism. 2. Christian literature, Latin (Medieval and modern) – England – History and criticism. 3. Prayer – Christianity – History – To 1500. 4. Prayers, Early Christian – England. 5. Prayer in literature. 6. Spirituality in literature. 7. Bede, the Venerable, Saint, 673–735. 8. Alfred, King of England, 849–899. 9. Aelfric, Abbot of Eynsham. I. Title. II. Series: Toronto Anglo-Saxon series ; 26

PR179.P73C63 2018 829.09'3824832 C2017-904295-5

University of Toronto Press acknowledges the financial assistance to its publishing program of the Canada Council for the Arts and the Ontario Arts Council, an agency of the Government of Ontario.

Canada Council for the Arts Conseil des Arts du Canada

Funded by the Government of Canada
Financé par le gouvernement du Canada
Canada

Lean sceal, gif we leogan nellað, þam þe us þas lisse geteod.

(Return must be made, if we do not wish to deceive, to him who granted us these favors.)

– *Maxims II*, l. 70

Contents

Acknowledgments

Gratias ago vobis, who have read and commented on parts of this manuscript, or who have listened to me talk about its ideas for these many years. Thank you for sharpening and refining those ideas through your conversation, comments, and questions.

To Charles D. Wright, my most long-standing debt of gratitude. Without his guidance and support this project would never have come to be. Through his generosity and love of study, Charlie models all that is best about academic life. My thanks also to Renée R. Trilling for first pointing me in the direction of gift theory, and to Thomas D. Hill and Martin Camargo for early feedback on the project.

To Shannon Godlove, with whom I was so fortunate to go through graduate school, who has turned what might have been competition into friendship, and whose encouragement, advice, and straightforward critique I can always count on.

To my colleagues at the University of Oregon, for their collegiality and encouragement, most especially James Earl, Anne Laskaya, Martha Bayless, Warren Ginsberg, Heidi Kaufman, Paul Peppis, and Karen Ford, who, as department head, was exceptionally helpful to me in really practical ways. Thanks also to Timothy Hannon, Francesca Gentile, and Katie Jo LaRiviere for research aid.

To the Office for Research, Innovation, and Graduate Education, University of Oregon, whose summer research fellowship enabled me to write the chapter on Alfred. In addition, to the Oregon Humanities Center and the University of Oregon Department of English and College of Arts and Sciences for their generous help with subvention funding (and to David Vázquez for helping arrange it). To Mount Angel Abbey Library, for use of their patristic resources. And to Leslie Lockett, for her kind correspondence on the Alfredian authorship question.

To the two anonymous readers for University of Toronto Press for their helpful and sensible suggestions for revision, to Suzanne Rancourt for her logistical help throughout the publishing process, and to Catherine Plear for catching so many inconsistencies and infelicities during the copy edit.

To the many friends in Texas, Illinois, and Oregon, who have shown their friendship by interest in my work, among them Dayspring Brock, Jessica White, Monica Ashour, Amanda White, William and Aurelia Drake, Amity Reading, Jeff Love, Janine Giordano-Drake, Elizabeth Hoiem (who suggested the title of this book), Carol James, and Fran Pecor. Recognition also to my most constant companions, the sitters on books Nokomis, Theophanu, and Origen (not the theologian). *Orant etiam aves.* Cats too, probably.

To my grandmother, Louise Glover, whose love of learning and study still inspires, and my mother, Marjorie Glover Clark, whose commitment to freedom and self-direction shaped my early education.

And especially to my father, Byron Clark, one of my earliest teachers, who had the idea that a high-school education should include Augustine's and Pelagius's writings on the controversy over grace and other unusual things. Dad, there won't be a movie; you'll have to make do with this.

COMPELLING GOD

Introduction

"[S]eek the Lord abundantly provided with the gift of spiritual prayers,"[1] says the Venerable Bede in his Homily 2.10. Such a statement, likening prayers to gifts, or comparing prayer to other kinds of exchanges, is not unusual within the context of Christian prayer. Exchange language suffuses prayer. In prayer, personal identity is formed through the exchanges imagined between God and humanity, the community, and the individual person. Through prayer, its practitioners place themselves in an exchange relationship with God, sometimes characterized by obligation, at other times freedom; sometimes by the language of commerce or labour, at other times, gift and gratuity. Yet scant consideration has been given to what it means that prayer itself, the exchange between humans and God, might be understood as a gift economy and how the terms of that economy might shift over time, from place to place and even (perhaps) according to social class. This book examines the way Anglo-Saxon teachings on prayer represent exchange between humans and God (and humans and humans), and the way particular forms of selfhood and visions of community are bound up in particular forms of exchange.

Anglo-Saxon spirituality is largely left out "of the grand narratives of devotion and mysticism in the Middle Ages,"[2] including the history of prayer.

1 Paraphrased from this sentence: "Decet autem nos sicut operum bonorum luce fulgidos ita etiam spiritalium orationum gratia refertos dominum quaerere," *Opera. Pars III, Opera homiletica. Pars IV, Opera rhythmica*, ed. David Hurst and J. Fraipont, CCSL 122 (Turnhout: Brepols, 1955), 247, ll. 21–2. Chapter 2 spells out the logic of understanding *gratia* as gift (to God).

2 Allen J. Frantzen, "Spirituality and Devotion in the Anglo-Saxon Penitentials," in *EMS* 22 (2005), 117.

Yet the Anglo-Saxons were not only important synthesizers and disseminators of the Western prayer tradition in early medieval Europe, they were also innovators. Anglo-Saxonists are often understandably irked at being left out of the "Middle Ages" by those who study post-Conquest periods,[3] but attempts to recuperate Anglo-Saxons by inserting them into narratives of spirituality are apt to misrepresent Anglo-Saxon England in order to assert its value. Those who have attempted to find a place for Anglo-Saxon prayer in such narratives notice individually oriented devotion and the sort of personal creativity and affectivity found in the prayers of Anselm and the later mystical tradition, thereby reading the Anglo-Saxon evidence in light of later developments.[4] Such a focus ignores the dominant medieval approach to prayer, which was predicated not on spontaneous or even wordless "communion" with the Divine more broadly, and not on an understanding of the praying self as a unique individual communing with God, but on petition, which includes ritual action, and formal prayers.

"[P]rayer," says Roy Hammerling, "is at the heart of all religious practice and belief."[5] Religion, before scientific empiricism assumed the role,

3 See, for instance, Joyce Hill's fine rant in her review of *The Cambridge History of Medieval English Literature*, ed. David Wallace: "[F]or all its anxiety to be inclusive – of the various languages and literatures of the British isles, of 'literature' as most broadly defined, and of its institutional as well as its authorial production – [the book] begins (at least as far as England is concerned) at 1066. Why should this be so? And what will be the effect of this implicit but seemingly authoritative pronouncement about what counts as 'medieval' within the English literary tradition? If Old English and Anglo-Latin literature are not part of 'medieval English literature,' then what are they part of? Or are they – as the *Cambridge History* seems to wish – to be consigned to oblivion?" in *Review of English Studies* n.s. 51.201 (2000), 101.

4 Frantzen's "Spirituality and Devotion" introduces Scott DeGregorio, "Affective Spirituality: Theory and Practice in Bede and Alfred the Great," and Christina M. Heckman, "*Imitatio* in Early Medieval Spirituality: The Dream of the Rood, Anselm, and Militant Christology," both in *EMS* 22 (2005). Similarly focusing on spirituality and the individual devotional tradition are Benedicta Ward, *High King of Heaven: Aspects of Early English Spirituality* (Kalamazoo: Cistercian Publications, 1999), and Thomas H. Bestul in several publications; e.g., "Continental Sources of Anglo-Saxon Devotional Writing," in *Sources of Anglo-Saxon Culture*, ed. Paul Szarmach and Virginia Darrow Oggins (Kalamazoo: MIP, 1986), "St. Anselm and the Continuity of Anglo-Saxon Devotional Traditions," in *Annuale Mediaevale* 18 (1977), and "St. Anselm, the Monastic Community at Canterbury, and Devotional Writing in Late Anglo-Saxon England," in *Anselm Studies* 1 (1983).

5 Roy Hammerling, "Introduction," in *A History of Prayer: The First to the Fifteenth Century*, ed. Roy Hammerling (Leiden: Brill, 2008), 2. Hammerling also quotes Benedicta Ward, "Prayer is spirituality"; however, this is a much more problematic

was at the heart of the way people ordered and interpreted the world. Ritual practices of prayer stood at the centre of the way Anglo-Saxons structured time, the self, and social reality. Prayer mediated between individual and community, devotee and divinity, nature and spirit, interior and exterior, imagination and concrete action. And prayer was everywhere in Anglo-Saxon England. As far as can be determined, everyone prayed, from monks who structured their lives around the *opus dei*, to cooks who timed eggs with the Paternoster, to uneducated laymen who desired healing. Prayer is represented in nearly every kind of document, both verse and prose: not only in the expected places, especially in the liturgical manuscripts that comprise more than a third of extant Anglo-Saxon manuscripts,[6] but also in sermons, in saints' lives, in treatises, in letters, in charters, in charms and recipes, in colophons, and in marginalia. Yet in spite of (or perhaps because of) prayer's ubiquity, Anglo-Saxon and other early medieval writers seldom explicitly specify a theory or theology of prayer: what they understood people to be doing when they pray, or how they understood prayer to work, either upon practitioners or upon God.[7]

This is not to say that prayer in Anglo-Saxon England has been completely ignored. The textual aspects of prayer – prayerbooks and other manuscripts – have been an object of ongoing interest, especially insofar as the prayerbooks seem to reflect early traditions of private prayer.[8] In addition, liturgical studies, which often focus on manuscripts, sources issues, and chains of transmission, sometimes encompasses performance contexts

statement, partially because "spirituality" is such a vaguely defined term, and partially because the values reflected in "spirituality" are rooted in modernity. See the "Note on 'Spirituality'" in Cheslyn Jones et al., eds., *The Study of Spirituality* (New York: Oxford University Press, 1986), xxiv–xxvi, and Gordon Mursell's brief history of the term in *English Spirituality from the Earliest Times to 1700* (Westminster: John Knox Press, 2001), 3–4. These authors all write specifically about Christianity. Writing from an anthropological perspective on religion more generally, Marcel Mauss also calls prayer "one of the central phenomena of religious life," *On Prayer*, ed. W.S.F. Pickering, trans. Susan Leslie (New York: Durkheim Press/Berghahn Books, 2003), 21.

6 According to a count from the index to Gneuss and Lapidge, *Anglo-Saxon Manuscripts* (Toronto, University of Toronto Press: 2014).

7 Chapter 1 gives an overview of the early Christian treatises and teaching on prayer, plus the types of Anglo-Saxon textual evidence.

8 I discuss the prayerbooks and the scholarship on them towards the end of chapter 1.

as well.[9] Devotional poems, most especially *The Dream of the Rood*, have seen a great deal of study, although only a small portion is on the devotional aspects of the poems.[10] Insofar as prayer and exchange has garnered attention, the focus is on exchange among humans and the work prayer does in the human economy.[11] But very little notice has been given to how Anglo-Saxons themselves use exchange language, and what work there is has focused on the way poems like *The Dream of the Rood* represent God as a Germanic lord. As Frantzen laments, those writing histories of spirituality have paid little attention to Anglo-Saxon "spirituality"[12] – the subjective aspects of prayer – but this perhaps reflects the fact that there is very little study of "spirituality" within the field – and for good reason, as this introduction seeks to clarify. There is also little attention paid to how Anglo-Saxons themselves understood prayer. In fact, the scholarship that most approaches conceptual understanding of prayer is work on charms, where the definitional difference between prayer and charms becomes a more pressing issue.[13]

9 The Henry Bradshaw Society publishes many print editions of liturgical manuscripts. See also Henry Mayr-Harting, *The Coming of Christianity to Anglo-Saxon England*, 3rd ed. (London: Batsford, 1991). In addition, Jesse D. Billett, *The Divine Office in Anglo-Saxon England, 597–c. 1000* (London: Boydell, 2014), and M.J. Toswell, *The Anglo-Saxon Psalter* (Turnhout: Brepols, 2014), give excellent studies of, respectively, the monastic cycle of prayer and of psalters, which were often used as prayerbooks.

10 Studies of *The Dream of the Rood* are much too extensive to rehearse here. Éamon Ó Carragáin, *Ritual and the Rood: Liturgical Images and the Old English Poems of the Dream of the Rood Tradition* (Toronto: University of Toronto Press, 2005), gives a thorough recent study of the larger context of the poem. For an example study of the devotional poems, see Barbara Raw, *The Art and Background of Old English Poetry* (London: Edward Arnold, 1978), chapter 8, "Private Poetry." However, much of the work on the minor devotional poems focuses on other types of issues. For instance, a good share of the work on *Resignation* focuses on the question raised by Alan Bliss and Allen J. Frantzen of whether it is one poem or two, "The Integrity of *Resignation*," in *Review of English Studies* 27 (1976). Liturgical context gains attention for poems such as *Christ I*, *Gloria*, and the *Lord's Prayer*.

11 Far more work has been done on this topic in Carolingian France. For examples, see the works mentioned in n. 71 below.

12 See n. 5, above, for the problematic nature of this word in historical studies.

13 Although the definitions are often made using modern categories of thought. Karen Louise Jolly usefully challenges this in *Popular Religion in Late Saxon England: Elf Charms in Context*, 2nd ed. (Chapel Hill: University of North Carolina Press, 1996).

But the most explicit places where Anglo-Saxons themselves theorize prayer have been, as a body, largely overlooked.[14] Thus, this book focuses on the work of several English authors who addressed prayer most explicitly and extensively. The period is bookended by the sermon series of Bede (d. 735) and Ælfric (d. 1010). Bede wrote in Latin for monks, while Ælfric wrote in Old English for a mixed audience of laypeople and religious. The variety of texts produced in the circle of King Alfred (d. 899) provides another window into Anglo-Saxon conceptions of prayer: Asser's representation of Alfred at prayer in his biography is illuminated by the particular focus of the prayer beginning the *Soliloquies* and the theory of prayer represented in the introductions to the prose translation of the Psalms. The writings of the Alfredian circle and of Ælfric are fundamental to understanding the religious reforms that took place in their lifetimes; both were influenced by Bede and Alcuin's innovations in prayer practice. Thus, this book examines the work of authors from three major periods of Anglo-Saxon history: Bede in seventh century Northumbria, reflecting an early monastic perspective influenced by both Rome and Ireland; Alfred in ninth century Wessex, reflecting Carolingian developments among high-ranking laypeople; and Ælfric around the turn of the millennium in southern England, reflecting the type of teaching on prayer produced for laypeople by one of the major figures associated with the Benedictine Reform of the late tenth century.

All of these authors imagine[15] prayer as exchange with God, and for all of them, this exchange forms and constitutes the person and the community

14 The major exception to this is Scott DeGregorio's dissertation, which studies many of the same texts, although from the perspective of spirituality studies rather than exchange: "Explorations of Spirituality in the Writings of the Venerable Bede, King Alfred, and Abbot Ælfric of Eynsham" (PhD diss., University of Toronto, 1999). Three excellent articles adapted from the dissertation were published: "The Venerable Bede on Prayer and Contemplation," in *Traditio* 54 (1999); "Texts, *Topoi* and the Self: A Reading of Alfredian Spirituality," in *EME* 13.1 (2005); and "Ælfric, *Gedwyld*, and Vernacular Hagiography: Sanctity and Spirituality in the Old English Lives of SS Peter and Paul," in *Ælfric's Lives of Canonized Popes*, ed. Donald Scragg (Kalamazoo: MIP, 2001).

15 Throughout this book I speak of the imagined relationship between humans and God. By this I mean that because God, in the Christian tradition, is in his truest being invisible and incomprehensible to bodily senses, the relationship is one that precators imaginatively enter into. However, even though the relationship between human and God is imagined by individual precators, God is not a product of the individual imagination. The invisible, ineffable being that is God is concretized and anthropomorphized

in varying ways. In understanding prayer as a gift the Anglo-Saxons are not unique.[16] However, people's expectations of prayer are formed by the economic systems they are embedded within. Thus, for instance, when post-Reformation writers refer to prayer as a gift they invoke a different structure of expectations and values than do medieval writers.[17] The remainder of this introduction will consider the issues at stake in considering prayer as a gift, and the sorts of questions and problems that the gift raises as people imagine exchange with God. As will become clear, one reason Anglo-Saxon prayer has been overlooked in the grand narratives of spirituality is because its ritualized performance and the economic structures that underlie it make it hard to fit within the definitional concerns of spirituality or devotion. To highlight issues at stake I begin by considering theories of prayer latent in prayer studies. I will then give an overview of the central principles of gift theory that subsequent chapters will build on, and I will show that there is substantial overlap between conceptual problems caused by imaging prayer as a gift that mediates between humans and God and gifts as objects that mediate between people.

---

through a particular community's beliefs and practices as well as through individual understanding. See Gavin Flood, *The Truth Within: A History of Inwardness in Christianity, Hinduism, and Buddhism* (Oxford: Oxford University Press: 2013), 7–8.

16 I am avoiding the formulation "gift of prayer" because that is a specific Reformation-era development that sees prayer as a gift *from* God *to* humans, given as an assurance of salvation. Interestingly, this "gift" was understood through metaphors of contract and earnest. See Lori Branch, "The Rejection of the Liturgy, the Rise of Free Prayer, and Modern Religious Subjectivity," in *Restoration* 29.1 (2005), 7, and the passage she cites from David Zaret, *The Heavenly Contract: Ideology and Organization in Pre-Revolutionary Puritanism* (Chicago: University of Chicago Press, 1985), 175–6. In early Christianity prayer is more usually seen as a gift from humans to God, and even if the directionality were reversed, prayer still does not fulfil the same function to assure salvation, since those anxieties were specifically products of Reformation-era changes in belief.

17 For two widely divergent uses of the concept of prayer as a gift, note the treatise on the subject by John Wilkins, one of the founders of the Royal Society and a clergyman, *A Discourse Concerning the Gift of Prayer, Shewing What it is, wherein it Consists, and how far it is Attainable by Industry* (London, 1704), and the numerous references to prayer as a gift throughout Bruce Ellis Benson and Norman Wirzba, eds., *The Phenomenology of Prayer* (New York: Fordham University Press, 2005).

Theories of Prayer

Prayer in the Western tradition is widely defined as "communion with God." For instance, early in the Christian era Clement of Alexandria (d. ca. 215) says, "Prayer is, then, to speak more boldly, converse [Greek *homilia*, converse, companionship] with God."[18] Theodulf of Orléans (d. 821), a younger contemporary of Alcuin of York, repeats the by-then commonplace idea: "Adsidue si ores, tibi sit si lectio crebra, / Ipsa deo loqueris, et deus ipsi tibi"[19] (If you pray continually, if abundant reading is yours, you yourself will speak to God, and God himself to you). The modern era gives many variants. Marcel Mauss, writing from an anthropological perspective and meaning something slightly different, says, "Prayer is speech."[20] More traditionally, Ann and Barry Ulanov state, "Prayer above all else is conversation with God."[21] The psychologist Mary Whiton Calkins says, "prayer ... as communion with God, may take on any form of personal intercourse."[22] She then quotes Clement's definition, translating *homilia* as "conversation and intercourse." But even this apparently transhistorical definition does not account for different understandings of communion and community. In fact, notice the way the language above slips between "speech" and "communion," from mere words to something beyond words, from words that must be given over and received to a shared state of being, from a reciprocal economy to an ideal of union outside of any economy. In addition, the focus on prayer as speech elides any understanding of prayer as action, disassociating it from any ritual actions that might accompany it, further removing it from the exterior body, to the word, and then to the interior mind or spirit.[23] Nor does this definition

18 Clement of Alexandria, *The Stromata*, ed. Kevin Knight, trans. William Wilson, ANF 2 (Buffalo: Christian Literature Publishing, 1885), 7.7.

19 Theodulf of Orleans, Carmen 43, "Carmen LXIII, Ad Gislam," MGH, Poetarum Latinorum Medii Aevi, Tomus I: Poetae Latini aevi Carolini, 541, ll. 17–18.

20 Mauss, *On Prayer*, 22.

21 Ann Ulanov and Barry Ulanov, "Prayer and Personality: Prayer as Primary Speech," in Jones et al., *The Study of Spirituality*, 24.

22 Mary Whiton Calkins, "The Nature of Prayer," in *The Harvard Theological Review* 4.4 (1911), 491.

23 Stanley J. Tambiah notes the tendency to divide words from deeds in studies of magic to differentiate prayers from charms or spells: "Some of us have operated with the concept of 'magic' as something different from 'religion'; we have thought of 'spell' as acting mechanically and as being intrinsically associated with magic; we have opposed 'spell' to 'prayer' which was thought to connote a different kind of communication with the

account for cultural changes in its fundamental elements: in ideals of selfhood as formed and performed by the praxis of prayer; in concepts of God and his relationship with the material world; and in values formed by economic assumptions that govern what sorts of transactions are idealized. Without careful attention to changing definitions and theories of prayer, we tend to import our own assumptions and values to its study.

It is hardly possible to summarize modern theories of prayer comprehensively. Prayer inhabits many different religious or spiritual environments, and even those within the Christian tradition, which is the focus of this book, can have only the most basic elements in common. With this caveat, then, and asking some measure of indulgence for the inevitable simplifications that follow, let me sketch a modern Western theory of prayer, rooted in individualism, influenced by Protestantism's suspicion of forms and ritual, and dominated by secularism, with its premises of objectivity and its materialist bias.[24] This modern theory has shaped the academic study of prayer and, from the turn of the twentieth century on, determined the contours of its study as scholars adopt or resist it.

I begin with an extreme case, an implicit theory of prayer found in a scientific 2006 meta-analysis of fourteen double-blind studies on the question of whether prayer "works" as an alternative medical treatment.[25] The study concluded that there was no scientifically discernible effect of distant intercessory prayer on the healing of hospital patients. In this study, "distant" meant that the patients did not know that they were being prayed for or even (in some cases) that they were participating in a study at all.[26] Distance removed the possibility that prayer could have either a subjective

divine," "The Magical Power of Words," in *Man* n.s. 3.2 (1968), 176. Chapter 4 will further address the difference between charms and prayers.

24 See Stanley J. Tambiah, *Magic, Science, Religion, and the Scope of Rationality* (Cambridge: Cambridge University Press, 1990), 17ff, for a concise summary of the relationship between Protestantism and secularism in the context of anthropological attempts to distinguish between science, magic, and religion. A distinctive development in Protestantism was the breaking apart of secular and sacred, of political and religious power. This allowed space for individual conscience in religious conviction as well as for tolerance of divergent religious practice. The secular came to dominate the public arena, while religion was increasingly seen as a private matter.

25 Kevin S. Masters et al., "Are There Demonstrable Effects of Distant Intercessory Prayer? A Meta-analytic Review," in *Annals of Behavioral Medicine* 32.1 (2006).

26 Masters et al., "Distant Intercessory Prayer." "[M]any believe that prayer is effective in and of itself ... This point is significant as an important feature of the studies to be examined in this meta-analysis is that the participants (mostly patients) did not know

effect, which is possible when people pray for themselves;[27] an objective placebo effect, which might come about when people know that they are being prayed for; or even a social effect, brought about by the correlation between being prayed for and the strength of a patient's social network. To study prayer objectively, scientists must reduce the question "What is prayer?" to questions surrounding prayer's objective efficacy or effect (and thus, testability). As the authors of the study, Masters et al., note, "the [intercessory prayer] literature also lacks a theoretical or theological base."[28] That is, the scientific literature removes such prayer from the system (the culture or religion) that gives the practice meaning, placing it within a different system – scientific empiricism – in which it is revealed to have no meaning; that is, no practical efficacy. The experimental system reflects the understanding (or the theory) that prayer is utilitarian, materially efficacious, and centred on precators'[29] desires.

In response to the reductive absurdity of imagining that prayer's only function is to get what the precator wants,[30] modern practitioners might claim, as pseudo C.S. Lewis does all over the Internet, "I do not pray because it changes God; I pray because it changes me."[31] In this case, prayer's efficacy is turned inward; it is subjectively efficacious. The subjective understanding of prayer can also give something for the scrutiny of the scientific gaze: brain-imaging studies look at the effects of prayer states

if they were receiving prayer, that is, they were blind as to whether they were in the prayer or control group. Likewise, their health care providers were also blind to prayer condition ... By implementing these rigorous methodological procedures, the authors of these studies removed known psychological processes or placebo effects from the set of possible explanatory mechanisms that could account for significant findings," 21–2.

27 Masters et al., "Distant Intercessory Prayer," 21.

28 Masters et al., "Distant Intercessory Prayer," 21.

29 Modern English does not have a good term for "the one praying"; therefore, I have borrowed Hugh A.G. Houghton's term "precator" (which he borrowed, in turn, from pre-classical Latin) from "The Discourse of Prayer in the Major Apocryphal Acts of the Apostles," in *Apocrypha* 15 (2004), 172. For the purposes of my study, I prefer this to Susan Boynton's "orant," *Libelli precum* in the Central Middle Ages," in Hammerling, *A History of Prayer*, 270, because the root of precator is in *preces*, prayers, petition.

30 To clarify: Masters et al. do not make this claim. It is rather more common among the New Atheists and their followers.

31 Medievalists know this phenomenon: a phrase or idea becomes attached to a prominent figure in order to authorize it. I have found no evidence that the real C.S. Lewis actually made this statement; rather, it was said by the character played by Anthony Hopkins in the 1993 movie *Shadowlands*, dir. Richard Attenborough (Savoy Pictures, 1993).

on the brain.[32] The results of these studies might then be interpreted to support (or not) the existence (or not) of God,[33] although they need not necessarily be – all that studies of the subjective efficacy of prayer show is that the discipline of praying (here grouped with meditational practices from a variety of faith traditions) changes the brain's chemistry and electromagnetism; they are silent as to matters beyond the material. That is, these studies reflect a theory of prayer essentially identical to the study by Masters et al., mentioned above. The scientific approach determines value only through questions of material usefulness and efficacy.

The context of the scientific gaze of emerging modernism – of which the Masters study is but a late example – brings into focus the preoccupations of two of the foundational books on the study and psychology of prayer. Both William James's *Varieties of Religious Experience* (1902) and Friedrich Heiler's *Prayer: A Study in the History and Psychology of Religion* (1919) define prayer in just such a way as to avoid materialist reductionism.[34] James explicitly addresses the attacks of empiricism upon prayer:

---

32 See, for instance, the various recent works of Dr. Andrew Newberg, a neuroscientist who uses brain imaging to study mental states, especially religious and spiritual experience.

33 An entertainingly naïve example of such extrapolation is found at the end of a brief article by self-identified sceptic and emeritus professor of neurology, David C. Haas. Haas asks whether a supernatural being could "read" electromagnetic currents in the brain caused by praying silently. Haas concludes, "… generic translations from neural patterns to verbal thoughts in any language would be impossible. A supernatural being would need to instantly surmount these difficulties – for multitudes of concurrent supplicants – in order to grasp the informational content of a mental prayer. Moreover, such a being would, logically, need to be with each supplicant while he or she is rotating with Earth at 1,038 miles per hour (if at the equator), orbiting around the Sun at 18.5 miles per second, rotating around the center of the Milky Way at about 150 miles per second, and moving through space with our galaxy at some thousands of miles per second," "Prayer: A Neurological Inquiry," in *CSI: The Committee for Skeptical Inquiry*, April 2007, http://www.csicop.org/si/show/prayer_a_neurological_inquiry/. Aside from Haas's rather literal rendering of the problems such a "supernatural being" would face in reading electromagnetic impulses in individuals' brains, and the staunchly materialist way he sends it hurtling through time and space, the very idea of a "supernatural being," by definition operating beyond the laws of nature, would seem to be the wildcard in his calculations. Once you have posited such a being it makes no sense to limit its actions in the way Haas does.

34 Evelyn Underhill's book *Mysticism: A Study in the Nature and Development of Man's Spiritual Consciousness* (New York: Dutton, 1911) is also a product of this particular moment; however, her focus is on mystical experience more generally, which is only one aspect (and not a universal one) of the phenomenon of prayer. In addition to reacting against scientific reductionism, they might perhaps be resisting the theology of

> We have heard much talk of late against prayer, especially against prayers for better weather and for the recovery of sick people. As regards prayers for the sick, if any medical fact can be considered to stand firm, it is that in certain environments prayers may contribute to recovery, and should be encouraged as a therapeutic measure. Being a normal factor of moral health in the person, its omission would be deleterious. The case of the weather is different … every one now knows that droughts and storms follow from physical antecedents, and that moral appeals cannot avert them. But petitional prayer is only one department of prayer; and if we take the word in the wider sense as meaning every kind of inward communion or conversation with the power recognized as divine, we can easily see that scientific criticism leaves it untouched.[35]

Like Masters et al., James understands that "petitional" prayer is utilitarian and should be (but often is not) efficacious. While he denies its efficacy with weather, he observes that prayer for the sick "may contribute to recovery," although his wording indicates that its efficacy rests upon praxis and the moral system that gives it meaning, not upon the power of a divine being invoked through prayer. In defending the practice of prayer against "scientific criticism," James devalues petitionary prayer, indicating its status as a lesser form. He goes on to quote at length from the 1897 work of Auguste Sabatier, a French Protestant theologian, borrowing his definition of prayer:

> Prayer is no vain exercise of words, no mere repetition of certain sacred formulae, but the very movement itself of the soul, putting itself in a personal relation of contact with the mysterious power of which it feels the presence … Wherever this interior prayer is lacking, there is no religion; wherever, on the other hand, this prayer rises and stirs the soul, even in the absence of forms or of doctrines, we have living religion.[36]

---

prayer found in early- and mid-twentieth-century Christian Fundamentalism (in the historical sense of the term rather than the way it is commonly used today), in which answered prayer was seen as "proof" against scepticism (for a later example of the genre, see John R. Rice, *Prayer: Asking and Receiving* (1942, rprnt. Wheaton, IL: Sword of the Lord Publishers, 1945). The Fundamentalists, for their part, are adopting the language of objective proof to defend faith against what Rice calls "modernism."

35 William James, *The Varieties of Religious Experience: A Study in Human Nature* (1902, rprnt. New York: Mentor, 1958), 351–2.

36 James, *Varieties*, 352.

"It seems to me," James then says in his own voice, "that the entire series of our lectures proves the truth of M. Sabatier's contention."[37] The kind of prayer James values sheds the forms – the *corpora* or *materia*, we might suspect – of words and ritual, allowing the movement of the pure, ungendered soul itself so that the precator personally experiences the "mysterious power," unmediated by specific doctrine or religious belief, the presence of which is attested by subjective individual feeling. In addition, Sabatier seems to imagine prayer as the breath or the spirit that animates religion, forms, or doctrines that are dead without "interior" prayer.[38] That is, *mere* ritual prayer, *mere* petitionary prayer – utilitarian, centred on the concerns of the precators – is lifeless without this wordless and subjective feeling of contact that is *true* prayer. Such a definition places prayer beyond the reach of the scientific gaze, even while admitting the *magisterium* of science within the lesser realm of the material and bodily petitionary prayer.

Friedrich Heiler similarly defines "genuine prayer" as "the free, spontaneous expression of one's own experience, or at least the fruit of what one has experienced and gained in struggle."[39] For Heiler, "genuine" prayer is *only* spontaneous and, in its truest form, leaves words behind.[40] In the section of his introduction called "Sources for the Study of Prayer," he denies that written prayers give knowledge of the "individual devotional life," except insofar as the "free, creative and profound prayer of distinct personalities is unmistakably revealed"[41] – this poses a problem for people

37 James, *Varieties*, 353.

38 I suspect that Sabatier (or James translating Sabatier) is using "religion" in the old sense of "piety" rather than the later sense of a system of belief and practice. See Wilfred Cantwell Smith, *The Meaning and End of Religion: A New Approach to the Religious Traditions of Mankind* (New York: Macmillan, 1963), chapter 2, for the historical development of the term. James himself seems to struggle with the dual sense of the term, since he is inquiring into "religious experience," the "religious phenomenon" as an objective observer, but one for whom the subjective nature of religious experience stands as an important bulwark against "materialists and atheists." Thus he at times separates out "genuine" or "living" religion – experience of the divine and the pious response such experience calls forth; see *Varieties*, 353.

39 Friedrich Heiler, *Prayer: A Study in the History and Psychology of Religion*, trans. Samuel McComb (New York: Oxford University Press, 1958), xxiii. In Heiler's statement we might hear a distant echo of Wordsworth's preface to *Lyrical Ballads* (1880): "[A]ll good poetry is the spontaneous overflow of powerful feelings."

40 Heiler, *Prayer*, xvii–xviii.

41 Heiler, *Prayer*, xxii.

interested in Anglo-Saxon spirituality! Except for "some" of the prayers of Anselm, no medieval prayers apparently meet his criteria (Heiler was a Lutheran minister). Thus, even more than James, Heiler roots prayer within the experiences of the individual. Like James, for Heiler genuine prayer is beyond the reach of the scientific gaze; it "conceals itself in delicate modesty from the eyes and ears of the profane."[42]

Both of these men's definitions of prayer (and their projects as a whole) were shaped by the concerns of their own day: they resist a modernist materialist mindset that in their own era was dismissive of the spiritual world and spiritual experience. As a tool of their resistance, they followed in the prayer tradition coming out of the Reformation, which tended towards suspicion of set prayer, preferring individual, spontaneous prayer as "true" prayer and conceptualizing prayer as something a person does within himself, as an interior activity or discipline.[43] Feeding into this discourse of spirituality is the type of selfhood preferred from the Romantic period on, rooted in interiority, individualism, genuine emotional experience, and spontaneity-marked sincerity. Thus, in opposition to a theory of prayer as utilitarian, objectively efficacious (and therefore falsifiable), and centred on the will of the precators, James and Heiler both insist on a theory in which prayer – *genuine* prayer – centres on a subjective experience of the divine validated by individual feelings and stripped of words, form, and ritual, thus preserving a value that goes beyond mere efficacy and transcends mere doctrine, even while it is sourced in the "deepest need and innermost yearning of the human heart."[44]

Within academia, it is this understanding of prayer that has driven the study of spirituality and devotion: it reflects a recognizable subjectivity and puts individual creativity (especially valued by literary scholars) at the

42 Heiler, *Prayer*, xvii.

43 See Branch, "Rejection of Liturgy." It should also be noted that this sense of "true" prayer was grafted onto ideas of progressive evolution, so that the more ritualistic forms of prayer were seen as less evolutionarily developed than more "spiritual" interior forms of prayer. Mauss, for instance, writing in 1909, summarizes the development: "At first completely mechanical and effective only through the production of certain sounds, prayer finished by being completely mental and interior. Having at one time been only minimally cerebral, it has ended up by being no more than thought and an outpouring of the spirit. At first strictly collective, said in common or at least according to forms rigidly fixed by the religious group, sometimes even forbidden, prayer becomes the domain of the individual's free converse with God," *On Prayer*, 24.

44 Heiler, *Prayer*, xviii.

centre. The focus presents a problem for the study of Anglo-Saxon prayer, however, in that most prayers left in the historical record are written records of traditional set prayers – not prayer at all, according to Heiler. Indeed, as the corpus of scholarship on Anglo-Saxon prayer shows, the study of *prayer* is just as often the study of texts and sources, and only rarely of subjectivities. The present book argues that the text-based nature of Anglo-Saxon prayer is not a mere vagary of historical preservation: the forms of prayer idealized in Anglo-Saxon England were text-based and ritually performed.

James and Heiler do not describe the concerns or practice of Anglo-Saxon prayer. And why should they? Anglo-Saxon Christianity never faced the challenges of scientific empiricism and therefore never faced the need to define prayer in such a way as to escape empirical falsification. If the discourse of prayer reflects ongoing anxieties and debates in the culture that produces it, the challenge Anglo-Saxon Christianity did, at times, face was from Germanic paganism. Unlike Greco-Roman Christianity, Anglo-Saxon Christianity was not, early on, shaped against any native philosophical system that might offer a plausible alternative to Christian belief. While the Anglo-Saxons certainly inherited a Roman Christianity formed against but also through those pre-Christian philosophical systems, that these influences had little meaning for them is evident in the way they often adapt their sources to remove the finer philosophical distinctions.[45] The system that *did* offer an alternative was their native religion ("paganism," from the Christian point of view), later reintroduced by the Danes. Little is known about this religion, but if it was anything like the Roman religions,[46] it was not a system of belief in particular doctrines or dogma and was not philosophically oriented, but was rather oriented towards praxis and loyalty. As Stanley J. Tambiah says, "religion as a system of

45 Each of the following chapters give examples of this, as each author adapts Augustine, and Ælfric adapts Gregory. As chapter 1 addresses, Greco-Roman philosophy influenced some early discussions of prayer – I think especially of Cassian's oft-cited "fiery prayer" – towards a sort of Neoplatonic or gnostic mysticism that has a cursory similarity to the descriptions of prayer that James and Heiler give (indeed, my earlier point was not to deny that such prayer exists – and that it exists at various times and in various cultures – but rather to note that the value both men give it is a product of their particular cultural moment).

46 Jörg Rüpke, *Religion of the Romans*, trans. Richard Gordon (Cambridge: Polity, 2007).

ideas and beliefs, as a doctrine" was a product of Protestantism.[47] Thus, it is no surprise that a major tension in Anglo-Saxon Christian sources is between competing loyalties to God or to pagan gods, defined within the Christian system as disguised devils. It is again no surprise that the Anglo-Saxon discourse of prayer has failed to capture the imagination of scholars of spirituality and devotion – the superiority of Christianity to "paganism" is no longer a live topic of debate or even interest in an environment that strives towards tolerant pluralism.[48] The topic that is of interest – the growth of affective piety and the formation of the modern Western individual – is not one to which the Anglo-Saxon evidence speaks strongly.[49]

To illustrate the importance of an orientation towards praxis and loyalty for understanding a theory of prayer, we might look at the Royal Prayerbook, one of the earliest Anglo-Saxon collections of prayers.[50] Patrick Sims-Williams has delineated the contents of the prayerbook, especially noting the way they mix devotion and magic, with prayers "rang[ing] from personal, Augustinian devotions, which explore the theology of

47 Tambiah, *Magic, Science, Religion*, 5. As will be seen, the Anglo-Saxon evidence supports the contention that faith is not necessarily intellectual assent to particular doctrines. As chapter 4 discusses, the Creed is often used as a performance of loyalty to a particular god (the Christian one).

48 Polemics such as Ælfric's *De auguriis*, in *Ælfric's Lives of Saints*, vol. 1, ed. Walter W. Skeat (London: Trübner, 1881), 364–83 I.17 or *De falsis diis*, in *Homilies of Ælfric: A Supplementary Collection*, vol. 2, ed. John C. Pope (London: Oxford University Press, 1968), 667–724, are now of interest primarily for what they can tell us about paganism, not Christianity. There are also those theorists of religion who do posit that Christianity presents unique solutions to problems posed by polytheistic religions (René Girard) or the materialist excesses of secularism (Slavoj Žižek, Terry Eagleton, Jean-Pierre Dupuy).

49 See, however, Frantzen, "Spirituality and Devotion," DeGregorio, "Affective Spirituality," and Bestul, "St. Anselm and Continuity" for other opinions.

50 The Royal Prayerbook, BL Royal 2.A.xx, dated to the eighth century, is minimally edited in the appendix of Arthur Benedict Kuypers, *The Prayer Book of Aedeluald the Bishop* (Cambridge: Cambridge University Press, 1902), 200–25. Birch also provides a description and summary of its contents in Appendix A of *An Ancient Manuscript of the Eighth or Ninth Century: Formerly Belonging to St. Mary's Abbey, or Nunnaminster, Winchester* (1889, rprnt. from the collections of the University of California Libraries), 101–13. Patrick Sims-Williams gives the fullest discussion of its contents, noting sources, analogues, and derivatives of many of the prayers in the chapter "Prayer and Magic," in *Religion and Literature in Western England, 600–800* (Cambridge: Cambridge University Press, 1990), 276–327. He analyses the Harley Fragment along with Royal, but for simplicity's sake, I focus only on Royal.

Grace, to medical charms ... "[51] The charms Sims-Williams refers to are three: two against bleeding (nos. 11 and 40 in Walter de Gray Birch's appendix to *An Ancient Manuscript of the Eighth or Ninth Century*) and no. 35, which is an exorcism.[52] As Sims-Williams says, Royal returns "again and again to the theme of protection against illness, death and supernatural adversity."[53] He notes that the compiler seems to show an awareness of the difference between prayers and charms insofar as the charms appear at the "peripheries ... at the beginning or end, or at the end of quires," and that such materials disappear almost entirely from the ninth-century Continental prayerbooks.[54] He further shows the difficulty of divining which elements in the manuscript could be considered magical and which devotional: Royal contains the opening and closing lines of the four Gospels, which may seem unambiguously "devotional." In some other manuscripts the Gospel incipits "seem intended to represent the gospels as a whole, functioning as atropaic [*sic*] or healing amulets rather than as texts for serious study," and he cites several instances of their magical use in farm spells and such like.[55] Yet, as he goes on to note, the incipits were also used in the preparations for baptism. The baptismal rite includes exorcisms, and in it the catechumens renounce the devil and all his works.[56] Including the incipits in a manuscript like Royal (or even wearing them like an amulet) could be intended to invoke the rite of baptism, in which those baptized enter into the protection of the Church, reminding the individual person,

---

51 Sims-Williams, *Religion and Literature*, 327.

52 The three items Sims-Williams draws our attention to are not differentiated from the more conventional prayers. Number 11 follows three prayers commonly used in the liturgy: the Magnificat, the "Song of Zechariah," and the "Song of the Three Youths," and precedes "The Prayer of St. Hugbald the Abbot." The latter does not have the same status as the liturgical prayers but is a prayer of confession that contains a long invocation of various holy persons. Number 35, the exorcism, follows several penitential prayers and a lorica-like prayer for protection and precedes prayers attributed to Mary and Augustine. Number 40, another charm against hemorrhage and distinctive in its use of Greek, follows, invoking Beronice (the woman healed of the issue of blood in the Gospel account). That charm is followed by two abecedarial hymns that end the book, both of which Birch attributes to Sedulius, and one of which is quite common.

53 Sims-Williams, *Religion and Literature*, 286.

54 Sims-Williams, *Religion and Literature*, 301–2. This statement refers to Anglo-Saxon prayerbooks generally; it is not true of Royal.

55 Sims-Williams, *Religion and Literature*, 292.

56 See Henry Ansgar Kelly, *The Devil at Baptism: Ritual, Theology, and Drama* (Ithaca: Cornell University Press, 1985), especially chapter 6 on the development of the renunciation formula.

any devils lurking about, and perhaps God himself that the person is under God's protection. If the function is essentially memorial, it is not magic, although it certainly shows a faith in the material efficacy of God's protection and makes less of a distinction between natural and spiritual worlds than we are inclined to do.

If we adopt an attitude of naturalistic rationalism, Royal's mixing of devotional prayer and charms points to the imperfect Christianization of eighth-century Mercia, a society in which coercive magical rites existed alongside more theologically sophisticated devotional prayers in a confused and incoherent way.[57] However, Stanley J. Tambiah reminds us that in pre-modernity the distinction between religion and magic is not so easy to make.[58] While ancient Greece distinguished between the natural and spiritual worlds in a way that is familiar to us in the scientific era (although the lines between them seem eccentric to us), and while early Christianity adopted this distinction to some extent (as Pseudo-Augustine's sermon *De auguriis* witnesses),[59] it was not native to polytheistic Germanic peoples.[60] As the Anglo-Saxons Christianized, healing was a potent metaphor for salvation – the word for healing and salvation (*hæl*) is the same in Old English – and there was no clear line separating natural and demonic causes of

57 This characterization is unsatisfactory for another reason: the blood-staunching charms are almost certainly introduced from Greek sources (perhaps through intermediaries), which means that they are a product of learned clerical or monastic culture.

58 See also Jolly's argument in *Popular Religion* that elf charms are not evidence of continuing paganism because belief in elves was not seen to be at odds with Christian belief. The whole thrust of Jolly's argument reminds us that the lines between Christian and pagan, prayer and magic, natural and spiritual were not drawn in the same places then as now.

59 This sermon is now attributed to Caesarius of Arles. It is printed as Pseudo-Augustinian sermon 268 in PL 39, cols 2268–71, and as number 54 in *Sancti Caesari Arelatensis Sermones*, ed. D.G. Morin, CCSL 103 (Turnhout: Brepols, 1953), 235–40. See Audrey Meaney, "Ælfric's Use of His Sources in His Homily on Auguries," in *English Studies* 6 (1985): 477–95. Anglo-Saxon medical books also largely bear witness to a naturalistic understanding of human disease (the Lacnunga is, I believe, the major exception). It should be remembered that medical books like Bald's Leechbook were not the products of the superstitions of the uneducated masses, but rather memorialize monastic practice, often heavily influenced by Mediterranean medicine.

60 See Tambiah's explanation of the difference between a polytheistic orientation towards nature, in which there is a bond between the gods and the natural world because they share in the same substance, and the monotheistic (developed in Judaism), in which God is entirely other than the created universe. The polytheistic view thus sees no strong distinction between natural and spiritual, *Magic, Science, Religion*, 6–7.

illness. In the absence of such a distinction, the early medieval understanding of magic relies on what sort of power was being called on, whether God or devils.[61] Appealing to devils was seen to be equally as efficacious as appealing to God; Ælfric says as much in *Catholic Homilies* I.31.[62] Such appeals were forbidden not because they were inefficacious, but because, as chapter 4 on Ælfric reveals, such an appeal was an acknowledgment of loyalty on the part of the appellant. Whichever power the precator appealed to "owned" the appellant's soul. In that case, the Royal charms are merely a type of prayer, different in genre but not in essence, in a collection invoking the protective power of God and, we might add, making known the precator's loyalty to him.

Sims-Williams cites a further definition of magic (quoted from Keith Thomas's *Religion and the Decline of Magic*) that points us towards a tension regarding the will within Anglo-Saxon prayer: religion appeals for divine aid whereas magic coerces natural or supernatural forces.[63] Such a definition reflects an understanding of God's omnipotence and human dependence that Christians would recognize as orthodox. It makes an important distinction between the ego-oriented nature of magic, centred on the practitioner's will, and the other-oriented nature of prayer, open to another's will. Yet this distinction simplifies what is, in practice, a tension within the practice of prayer, and it points towards an important issue that Anglo-Saxon prayer grappled with: the lines between appeal and coercion become very fine indeed once humans are imagined as participating in a gift exchange with God.

Indeed, the Anglo-Saxons studied in this book had a profoundly relational conception of God, and prayer was understood in terms of the gift. We tend to take the language of gift within prayer, pervasive as it is, as conventional and perhaps calcified, but, as reading Bede, Alfred, and Ælfric shows, these authors were very careful with the implications of exchange

61 "Magic" tends to be the label for taboo practices. Pagans use it to characterize Christian miracles; Christians use it to characterize pagan supernatural acts. There was also a distinction, both inside Christian belief and outside it, between harmful antisocial magic and harmless healing magic.

62 *Ælfric's Catholic Homilies: The First Series*, ed. Peter Clemoes, EETS s.s. 17 (Oxford: Oxford University Press, 1997).

63 Sims-Williams, *Religion and Literature*, 302n121. Keith Thomas says, "[P]rayer … was a form of supplication: a spell was a mechanical means of manipulation," *Religion and the Decline of Magic* (1971, rprnt. London: Penguin Global, 2012), 46.

paradigms. Thus, shifting focus from questions of spirituality to exchange causes all sorts of interesting things to come into focus, not the least of which is the way people in a market capitalist economy regularly understand gift exchange as utilitarian, self-interested transactionality. That is, as careful as we are in the study of historical forms of selfhood, and as much as we try to avoid bringing anachronisms to the study of the Middle Ages, we often import a modern *homo economicus* – an individual acting in his[64] own self-interest – to the gift economy of prayer.[65] However, in using the term "economy," I do not merely mean to denote the discipline that has to do with money and commodities, but rather "circulation" and patterns of exchange more broadly. Economy as circulation allows us to think about the way that exchange relates entities (people, gods) to each other, and the way people understand themselves as socially embedded or autonomous through economic structures.[66] The broader understanding also more clearly reveals overlapping concepts between the reciprocity inherent to acts of gift giving and acts of communication. Prayer shares characteristics of both.

The Anglo-Saxon practice of prayer ritualistically enacts a relationship between God and humans that, when properly performed, serves either to transform or guarantee the character and intention of the precator before

---

64 I use the masculine pronoun intentionally. As Marilyn Strathern's *The Gender of the Gift: Problems with Women and Problems with Society in Melanesia* (Berkeley: University of California Press, 1988) makes apparent, the model of the modern (Western) individual is gendered masculine, though Western feminism seeks the same sort of independence for women (largely focused on reproductive and economic issues) that men already have. Strathern, an anthropologist, criticizes feminist anthropology for imposing the Western "commodification" of gender on the study of Melanesian tribal societies; see chapter 11.

65 The bedrock idea for modern economic theory, that the basic unit of the economy is the individual transacting in his own self-interest, originates with Adam Smith, *The Wealth of Nations* (London, 1776).

66 In this, I loosely follow Catherine Clarke, who defines economy as "patterns of exchange, mutual obligation and reciprocity between individuals or groups," *Writing Power in Anglo-Saxon England: Texts, Hierarchies, Economies* (Woodbridge: Boydell and Brewer, 2012), 3. Robert Bjork argues, in the context of *Beowulf*, that language is a "less obvious manifestation of the gift economy," tracing an economics of meaning that falls apart as the poem progresses; "Speech as Gift in *Beowulf*," in *Speculum* 69 (1994), 995. Jacques Derrida, too, in *Given Time I: Counterfeit Money*, trans. Peggy Kamuf (Chicago: University of Chicago Press, 1994), is more interested in the gift as a phenomenon of language than in actual gift giving practices.

God.[67] Its practice works out tensions between obligation and freedom of action, the desire to control God or be controlled by him, embedded within the ability to know intention. Even though exchange practices between humans do not always map neatly onto the relationship imagined between humans and God, Anglo-Saxon theories of prayer replicate and expose issues contained within early medieval practices of gift exchange.

Theories of the Gift

I will not attempt here to give an exhaustive review of gift theory or scholarship on the medieval gift;[68] my purpose is to clarify some common confusions and highlight some of the key principles the following chapters will develop. Gift theory, which grew out of the discipline of anthropology, has been usefully applied to the Middle Ages, often to analyse ceremonial exchange and the social relationships and networks of power created through such exchanges.[69] Prayer itself was often ceremonial (think of Bede's account of Augustine of Canterbury's *plein air* approach

67 The practice also lends itself to the temptation of misuse, misrepresentation, and manipulation on the part of precators to get what they desire and to secure the future.

68 Marcel Mauss's *The Gift*, first published as "Essai sur le don, forme et raison de l'échange dans les sociétés archaïques," in *L'Année Sociologique* 1 (1925): 30–186, and translated by W.D. Halls, *The Gift: The Form and Reason for Exchange in Archaic Societies* (New York: W.W. Norton, 1990), is the foundation of gift studies and has produced such a sprawling and fruitful field of research and study that it would be impossible to rehearse it here. However, Mark Osteen's introduction to *The Question of the Gift: Essays across Disciplines*, ed. Mark Osteen (New York: Routledge, 2002), gives a very accessible introductory overview of the field and the types of issues at stake. Arnoud-Jan Bijsterveld, *Do ut des: Gift Giving, Memoria, and Conflict Management in the Medieval Low Countries* (Hilversum: Uitgeverij Verloren, 2007), also gives an overview of the post-Maussian scholarship for the benefit of medievalists reading his book.

69 See, for example, Clarke, *Writing Power*; Andrew Cowell, *The Medieval Warrior Aristocracy: Gifts, Violence, Performance, and the Sacred* (Cambridge: D.S. Brewer, 2007); Arnoud-Jan Bijsterveld, "Gift Exchange, Landed Property, and Eternity: The Foundation and Endowment of the Premonstratensian Priory of Postel (1128/1138–1179)," in *Land and Ancestors: Cultural Dynamics in the Urnfield Period and the Middle Ages in the Southern Netherlands*, ed. Frans Theuws and Nico Roymans (Amsterdam: Amsterdam University Press, 2004), and *Do ut des*; as well as two anthologies, Wendy Davies and Paul Fouracre, eds., *The Languages of Gift in the Early Middle Ages* (Cambridge: Cambridge University Press, 2010), and Gadi Algazi et al., eds., *Negotiating the Gift: Pre-Modern Figurations of Exchange* (Göttingen: Vandenhoeck & Ruprecht, 2003).

to King Ethelbert of Kent, for one striking example),[70] and it was often a "thing" exchanged between people. As studies of medieval prayer and gift giving show, prayer had real value in the medieval economy. These studies reveal the way prayer as a gift exchanged between people created or strengthened social relationships, was involved in transfers of property, and contributed to secular and ecclesiastical power.[71] Such studies reveal both the ways that massive transfers of wealth took place outside market forms of exchange, and also the way religious belief had very real effects on the medieval economy. Work on almsgiving and donation further shows that many medieval people imagined a basic fungibility between material and spiritual goods – material wealth could be transferred to the spiritual realm by being given away.[72] In the process, social relationships were created and sustained. Yet, with the exception of the striking ways transactional language was used for the spiritual economy in formulations like *munera/remuneratio*[73] or *sacrum commercium*,[74] scholars have not applied gift theory to the way early medieval people use exchange language in a spiritual context, and have not fully noticed the way that

70 Bede, *Historia Ecclesiastica gentis Anglorum*, ed. Michael Lapidge (Paris: Les Éditions du Cerf, 2005), 1:198–204, book 1, ch. 25.

71 For instance, Arnold Angenendt, "*Donationes pro anima*: Gift and Countergift in the Early Medieval Liturgy," in *The Long Morning of Medieval Europe: New Directions in Early Medieval Studies*, ed. Jennifer R. Davis and Michael McCormick (Aldershot: Ashgate, 2008), and "Sacrifice, Gifts, and Prayers in Latin Christianity," in *Early Medieval Christianities, c. 600–c. 1100*, ed. Thomas F.X. Noble and Julie M.H. Smith (Cambridge: Cambridge University Press, 2008); Barbara Rosenwein, *To Be the Neighbor of Saint Peter: The Social Meaning of Cluny's Property, 909–1049* (Ithaca: Cornell University Press, 2006), and Mayke de Jong, "Carolingian Monasticism: The Power of Prayer," in *The New Cambridge Medieval History, c. 700–900*, ed. Rosamond McKitterick (Cambridge: Cambridge University Press, 1995).

72 Boniface Ramsey, "Almsgiving in the Latin Church: The Late Fourth and Early Fifth Centuries," in *Theological Studies* 43.1 (1982); Eliana Magnani, "Almsgiving, *Donatio pro anima*, and Eucharistic Offering in the Early Middle Ages," in *Charity and Giving in Monotheistic Religions*, ed. Miriam Frenkel and Yaakov Lev (Berlin: Walter de Gruyter, 2009).

73 Bernhard Jussen, "Religious Discourses of the Gift in the Middle Ages: Semantic Evidences (Second to Twelfth Centuries)," in Algazi et al., *Negotiating the Gift*.

74 Martin Herz, *Sacrum Commercium: Eine begriffsgeschichtliche Studie zur Theologie der Römischen Liturgiesprache* (München: Kommissionsverlag Karl Zink, 1985). The work by Angenendt, already cited, and David Ganz, "Giving to God in the Mass: The Experience of the Offertory," in Davies and Fouracre, *The Languages of Gift*, stand as further examples.

the language of one type of exchange is sometimes used metaphorically to describe an exchange of a different kind (chapter 2 touches on this).

Within Anglo-Saxon studies, scholarship on *Beowulf* dominates the discussion of the gift;[75] therefore, the focus of gift exchange within the field tends to be on heroic literature and the kind of social performance usually limited to aristocratic men.[76] A few studies bring gift exchange into

75 See, for example, Peter Baker, *Honour, Exchange and Violence in "Beowulf"* (Cambridge: D.S. Brewer, 2013); Leslie Lockett, "The Role of Grendel's Arm in Feud, Law, and the Narrative Strategy of *Beowulf*," in *Latin Learning and English Lore: Studies in Anglo-Saxon Literature for Michael Lapidge*, vol. 1, ed. Katherine O'Brien O'Keeffe and Andy Orchard (Toronto: University of Toronto Press, 2005); Jos Bazelmans, "Beyond Power: Ceremonial Exchange in *Beowulf*," in *Rituals of Power: From Late Antiquity to the Early Middle Ages*, ed. Frans Theuws and Janet L. Nelson (Leiden: Brill, 2000), based on his dissertation, published as *By Weapons Made Worthy: Lords, Retainers, and Their Relationship in "Beowulf"* (Amsterdam: Amsterdam University Press, 1999), and "One for All, All for One: The Old English *Beowulf* and the Ritual and Cosmological Character of the Relationship between Lord and Warrior-follower in Germanic Societies," in *Method and Theory in Historical Archaeology: Papers of the Medieval Europe Brugge 1997 Conference*, ed. Guy De Boe and Frans Verhaeghe (Zellik: Instituut voor het Archeologisch Patrimonium, 1997); Heinrich Härke, "The Circulation of Weapons in Anglo-Saxon Society," in *Rituals of Power*; Adelheid L.J. Thieme, "The Gift in Beowulf: Forging the Continuity of Past and Present," in *Michigan Germanic Studies* 22.2 (1996); John M. Hill, *The Cultural World in "Beowulf"* (Toronto: University of Toronto Press, 1995), and "Beowulf and the Danish Succession: Gift Giving as an Occasion for Complex Gesture," in *Medievalia et Humanistica* 11 (1982), which mostly reproduces a chapter from *The Cultural World*; Bjork, "Speech as Gift in *Beowulf*"; and Charles Donahue, "Potlatch and Charity: Notes on the Heroic in *Beowulf*," in *Anglo-Saxon Poetry: Essays in Appreciation for John C. McGalliard*, ed. Lewis E. Nicholson and Dolores Warwick Frese (Notre Dame: University of Notre Dame Press, 1975). Many other works mention gift giving in *Beowulf* without explicitly using gift theory. For example, Hugh Magennis discusses gift giving as part of hall life in *Beowulf* in *Images of Community in Old English Poetry* (Cambridge: Cambridge University Press, 1996), 62–8. Much of the scholarship on gift exchange reflects the preoccupation with reconstructing a secular Germanic Anglo-Saxon culture that occupied a great deal of scholarly attention from the nineteenth century on. See, for instance, Vilhelm Grønbech, *The Culture of the Teutons*, 2 vols., trans. W.J. Alexander Worster (1909–1912, London: Oxford University Press, 1932).

76 But for a take on the queen's role within the *comitatus* see Michael J. Enright, "Lady with a Mead-Cup: Ritual, Group Cohesion and Hierarchy in the Germanic Warband," in *Frühmittelalterliche Studien* 22 (1988). Also, focusing on *Judith*, Erin Mullally, "The Cross-Gendered Gift: Weaponry in the Old English Judith," in *Exemplaria* 17 (2005). Additionally, the following works focus on the economics of exchange in Anglo-Saxon England: Emilia Jamroziak, "Making and Breaking the Bonds: Yorkshire Cistercians

the religious context, but they also focus on the insight that Old English poetry often represents God along the model of the Anglo-Saxon lord[77] and that this model involves exchange of gifts and services.[78] Recognizing this parallel is crucial, and it is an insight the present study builds on; but (as we will see) the Anglo-Saxon authors considered in this book all take the reciprocity embedded within God's lordship beyond the mead hall by spiritualizing or abstracting the principles of reciprocity. Thus, "the gift" is usually studied in a very literal way (the exchange of objects between people) that shows how the circulation of objects creates particular types of self and community formation.[79] But in exchange language found in religious texts, the "thing" exchanged is very rarely an actual object, and exchange language is often used in metaphorical ways as various writers attempt to explain relationships that are abstract and imaginative without running into problematic doctrinal implications (the doctrine of grace is the one to watch out for and is central to Bede's teaching, as discussed in chapter 2). Thus, in this context, the work gifts perform is all the more obviously imaginative as the sources and expressions of human identity are imagined through exchange. Gifts participate in human identities, and are exchanged – between humans, between humans and God – forming those identities in complex (and symbolic) ways.

---

and Their Neighbours," in *Perspectives for an Architecture of Solitude: Essays on Cistercians, Art and Architecture in Honour of Peter Fergusson*, ed. Terry N. Kinder (Turnhout: Brepols, 2004); Nida-Louise Surber-Meyer, *Gift and Exchange in the Anglo-Saxon Poetic Corpus: A Contribution towards the Representation of Wealth* (Geneva: Slatkine, 1994); Roy Workman, "Ælfwine's Gifts," in *Suffolk Review* 4 (1979).

77 Alvin A. Lee, *The Guest-Hall of Eden: Four Essays on the Design of Old English Poetry* (New Haven: Yale University Press, 1972), 11, discusses God as lord and gift giver in Old English poetry. Magennis, *Images of Community*, considers the hall as an ideal community.

78 Examples of this are Thieme, "Gift Giving as a Vital Element of Salvation in *The Dream of the Rood*," in *South Atlantic Review* 63.2 (1998); and Ruth Louise Coy, "The Gift in Old English Literature: *Genesis A*, *Christ II*, and *Beowulf*" (PhD diss., University of Illinois, 1977).

79 Good examples can be found in Bazelmans, "Beyond Power"; Baker, *Honour, Exchange and Violence*, and, studying Icelandic literature, William Ian Miller, *Bloodtaking and Peacemaking: Feud, Law, and Society in Saga Iceland* (Chicago: University of Chicago Press, 1990). Chapter 3 from this book was previously published as "Gift, Sale, Payment, Raid: Case Studies in the Negotiation and Classification of Exchange in Medieval Iceland," in *Speculum* 61.1 (1986).

The central characteristic of the gift, the characteristic from which all else follows, is reciprocity – a gift expects a response.[80] Gifts create and maintain social ties. But reciprocity is used in different ways by different people. It is often used to mean fairly explicit systems of gift exchange, such as *do ut des* ("I give that you may give"), in which the giver gives to get back something he or she desires.[81] Yet reciprocity need mean nothing more than that some acknowledgment or response (such as gratitude) is an expected reaction to a gift,[82] or just that the parties involved in a gift are in some position of mutual interdependence.[83] When theorists maintain that there are no free gifts, this does not mean that gifts are always calculated and self-interested or never sacrificial. Rather, all gifts exist in a social context and do social work.[84] Even when people talk about gifts as though

80 In addition to Mauss's *The Gift*, Claude Lévi-Strauss's *The Elementary Structures of Kinship*, rev. ed., ed. and trans. Robert Needham, trans. James Harle Bell and John Richard von Sturmer (Boston: Beacon Press, 1969), and Marshall Sahlins's *Stone Age Economics* (Hawthorne: Aldine de Gruyter, 1974), focus especially on principles of reciprocity. Harry Liebersohn, *The Return of the Gift: The European History of a Global Idea* (Cambridge: Cambridge University Press, 2011), contextualizes Mauss's essay in broader eighteenth and nineteenth-century intellectual discussion of gift giving, noticing that while reciprocal gift giving was a feature of traditional European societies, it had become increasingly incomprehensible to Europeans until Mauss "rediscovered" it (Mauss built on the work of Bronisław Malinowski, *Argonauts of the Western Pacific*, published in 1922, working in Melanesia, and Grønbech described strikingly similar principles in his *Culture of the Teutons*, originally published [in Danish] in 1909–12).

81 The term comes from the Roman idea of contractual obligation, in which something is given in order to oblige the recipient to give something back in return. The concept featured in contract law, where it governed one-time exchanges. It also commonly governed relations between humans and gods. Rüpke explains that in such a case, the gift giving was a cycle: "I give the deity something, so that he or she may give me something in return … [A] sacrifice resembles a contract, it acquires a judicial component – my gift commits the god, morally at any rate, to give me in return something I value. The commitment is mutual: of course I will give thanks to the deity who has given me something by sacrificing in my turn again. There is thus a ceaseless cycle of obligation and gratitude … There is a chain of actions, a reciprocity of gifts," *Religion of the Romans*, 149.

82 Georg Simmel, "Faithfulness and Gratitude," in *The Sociology of Georg Simmel*, ed. and trans. Kurt H. Wolff (Toronto: The Free Press, 1950); Derrida, *Given Time*.

83 See Maurice Godelier, *The Enigma of the Gift*, trans. Nora Scott (Cambridge: Polity, 1999). The book's central argument is summarized in "Some Things You Give," in *The Enigma of Gift and Sacrifice*, ed. Edith Wyschogrod et al. (New York: Fordham University Press, 2002).

84 See James Laidlaw, "A Free Gift Makes No Friends," in *The Journal of the Royal Anthropological Institute of Great Britain and Ireland* 6.4 (2000), for the exception that proves the point.

they are unconstrained and unconstraining, there is still social pressure towards generosity and gratitude. Indeed, if the central function of gifts is to create social ties, the free gift would be useless.

Yet as Marcel Mauss notes in his seminal essay from 1925, *The Gift*, societies do not talk about gift giving in the same way they practice gift giving – there is a gap between discourse and praxis.[85] That is, the discourse of the gift, in which gifts are voluntary, free, and disinterested does not describe the way that gift giving is actually practised, in which gifts are constrained and self-interested.[86] That societies would practise such collective "misrecognition" (as Pierre Bourdieu terms it[87]), and what function it serves, has also proved tremendously productive for later scholarship. A gap between discourse and practice can easily leave the impression that gift giving is insincere: pretending to be other oriented, gift giving is *really* egoistic. From this perspective, it is far better that obligations and expectations must be clearly articulated; debts that masquerade as gifts are devious and suspect. Yet the gap is an essential feature of the gift, allowing it to mediate between the social beings that humans are in a way that reveals the actors' fundamental orientation towards social behaviour. The expectation

85 Often overlooked in applications of Mauss to modern-day gift practices is the fact that Mauss was not interested in gifts between intimates. However well his theory of reciprocity seems to explain Christmas gifts and dinner parties (Jacques Godbout, *The World of the Gift* [Montreal: McGill-Queen's University Press, 1998], 42–5, discusses Christmas practices in Maussian terms), his central interest was in the "primitive" precursors to trade agreements, credit, and contracts in societies and situations where there is no legal or executive power to enforce a contract. His focus therefore contributes to the sense that reciprocal gift giving is "about" power and economy, with people often downplaying the extent to which they are also "about" personal admiration, good will, and even love. Gifts therefore reveal the social attitudes and trustworthiness of potential trading partners, allies, and relatives, and bring into personal relationship people who were previously strangers. In such circumstances, the gift is risky, and the gift can easily turn back into violence if trust is breached. Lévi-Strauss, *Elementary Structures of Kinship*, and Marshall Sahlins, "The Spirit of the Gift," in *The Logic of the Gift: Toward an Ethic of Generosity*, ed. Alan D. Schrift (New York: Routledge), 1997, both discuss the ways that the gift is a substitute for violence. One of Lévi-Strauss's arguments is that gift giving (culminating especially in the "supreme" gift of a woman) allows potentially hostile tribes to make peace and to eventually merge together, creating larger forms of social organization. Sahlins considers the twentieth-century political dimensions of Mauss's conclusions.

86 Mauss, *The Gift*, 3.

87 Pierre Bourdieu, "Selections from *The Logic of Practice*," in Schrift, *The Logic of the Gift*, 198.

of some sort of return without clearly articulating what that return must be or when it must be given, or having any legal or executive mechanism to enforce a return, allows for the particular power of the gift for good or ill as it creates bonds between people. The gift promises to reveal character: it shows the giver's generosity and calls into question the recipient's character, allowing him to show that he understands the fundamental "rules" and obligations of social living and that he is himself generous and trustworthy. To spell out the exact obligations in gift giving destroys the gift, because doing so destroys the possibility of generosity and it also destroys the thing that makes the gift a powerful means of communication. But this gap is also a source of anxiety: Who decides what is generous? How does one judge selflessness? Because the gift is already insincere – talked about one way, but practised another – and because self-interest and selflessness often lie along the same course of behaviour, how can we tell whether the intention of the giver is pure or whether the gift is counterfeit? While intention, centrally important in prayer as in the gift, is a continuing theme that each of the Anglo-Saxon authors deals with, the issue of counterfeit is especially important in chapter 4.

There are five other contrasts embedded in reciprocity: 1) gift versus commodity, 2) reciprocity versus transactionality, 3) agonistic versus non-agonistic exchange, 4) egoistic versus altruistic giving, and 5) obligation versus freedom. In the first and second of these, something is exchanged. An object that is a gift in one context could be a commodity in another, and objects can be exchanged either reciprocally or transactionality. What distinguishes the type of exchange is the focus and attitudes of those exchanging, whether the primary focus is on maintaining the relationship or whether it is on the benefits themselves. As C.A. Gregory argues, the essential difference is that "commodity exchange establishes objective quantitative relationships between the objects transacted, while gift exchange establishes personal qualitative relationships between the subjects transacting."[88] In a commodity exchange, the relationship between the objects is established by price or some other commensurability in some sort of unitary value. In gift exchange, the relationship is established between the parties to the exchange, revealing the qualities of those exchanging. The objects exchanged are personified. They share in the identities of their givers and become the visible expression of the social identity of their recipients,

88 C.A. Gregory, *Gifts and Commodities* (London: Academic Press, 1982), 41.

connecting the bearer of gifts to a matrix of relationships embedded in the gift object. To be truly valuable, gift objects are non-alienable – a high-status gift object carries the identity of its past owners and gains value from that identity (thus the sword of Charlemagne has more value than a comparable sword of no lineage).[89] Chapter 2 will develop the idea of gifts and identity further in a context in which there is no gift object.

Reciprocity thus indicates a relationship established between people by means of objects or services exchanged. These relationships are materially beneficial to those involved (as a Roman patron/client relationship or a successful Germanic lord/thegn relationship) but are formed on the basis of the personal qualities of the two parties as an expression of friendship and trust, and as a matter of mutual loyalty.[90] Such relationships can also be more or less affective, depending on cultural values; Old English poetry presents the lord/thegn relationship as intimate and strongly affective. Transactional relationships, on the other hand, are formed with the intent of exchanging objects or services (wage labour, for instance); the focus of these relationships is the thing, not the persons.[91] The ties created, the "mutual debt," lasts only until both parties have fulfilled their agreed-upon obligations. However, reciprocity/transactionality is not binary. Relationships can be more or less transactional or reciprocal.[92] In fact, there are often things to be gained by blurring the boundaries.

Third, agonistic exchange refers to exchanges that are competitive, in which honour is at stake and one party loses honour while the other

89 Bazelmans, *By Weapons Made Worthy* and "Beyond Power," and Baker, *Honour, Exchange and Violence*, trace the way this works in the world of *Beowulf*.

90 But personal qualities could be strongly tied to material objects; wealth (and the ability to share it) could be seen as a concrete sign of a war-lord's "luck" (or *mana*), as Aaron Gurevich argues in "Wealth and Gift Bestowal among the Ancient Scandinavians," in *Historical Anthropology of the Middle Ages*, ed. Jana Howlett (Chicago: University of Chicago Press, 1992).

91 I am using these terms much more precisely than some other writers do. For instance, because Greco-Roman patron/client relationships materially benefit (and, on some level are formed in order to benefit) the parties involved they are sometimes called transactional. However, the thing that distinguishes them from a transactional relationship is the way they are conceptualized as being personal and based on the personal qualities of those involved.

92 For instance, one sign of the Bluth family's dysfunction in the American TV comedy *Arrested Development* is the highly transactional nature of their dealings with each other.

gains.[93] Mauss describes agonistic exchanges in the North American potlatch ceremony; this is also how William Ian Miller describes Icelandic gift exchange in *Bloodtaking and Peacemaking*.[94] In modern discussions of the gift, it is often assumed that all gift giving is, on some level, agonistic, as though the final desire is to be free of gift debts and the relationships attached.[95] But as noted by Maurice Godelier, an anthropologist whose fieldwork was done in Papua New Guinea, most exchanges in a society are actually non-agonistic, whether they are friendly reciprocities that knit families together or exchanges of women as wives between families or tribes.[96] In these cases, while honour might be at stake, it is not a zero-sum game. All parties can gain.

Fourth, gifts can be egoistic (benefiting the giver) or altruistic (benefiting the recipient at the expense of the giver). However, as Jacques Derrida points out, no gift can ever be purely altruistic: there is always a trace of the *ego* in the gift.[97] In Derrida's definition, the *ego* contaminates the purity of the gift, partially because of the way the giver imbues the gift with intention, meaning, and identity, which is then imposed on the recipient. Yet focusing on the experience of the giver at the expense of the experience of the recipient misses the way that gift exchange is a form of symbolic communication that involves the cooperation of both parties (and often, of those witnessing the gift) to make meaning.[98] The meaning of a gift cannot be unilaterally imposed. If we do not imagine that every exchange is a zero-sum game that has profit (of one sort or another) as its goal, and if we do not imagine that the one party gains *at the expense* of the other, we can then think about the way that gift exchange necessarily involves a giving subject and a receiving *subject* – both parties' active participation is necessary to make meaning. In fact, because generosity is socially arbitrated (one cannot declare oneself generous; one must be recognized as such by others), the giver cedes control over the meaning of the gift to the recipient

93 Such exchanges need not be hostile, but they are often a substitute for violence.

94 Miller, *Bloodtaking and Peacemaking*.

95 Lévi-Strauss, "To this very day, mankind has always dreamed of seizing and fixing that fleeting moment when it was permissible to believe that the law of exchange could be evaded … of a world in which one might keep to oneself," *Elementary Structures of Kinship*, 496–7.

96 Godelier, *The Enigma of the Gift*.

97 Derrida, *Given Time*, 14, 23.

98 Chris Wickham discusses the desire to control the meaning of the gift, "Conclusion," in Davies and Fouracre, *The Languages of Gift*, 240.

and those witnessing the gift (medieval gifts were not private). Nor can the recipient decide on his own whether a gift is generous; he must interpret the giver's intentions, and he must also do so within the interpretive community witnessing the gift.

Fifth, all gifts place some sort of obligation upon the recipient, however insignificant that response may be.[99] At the same time, to be a gift, the gift must involve an element of freedom. Exactly how much freedom is involved varies according to time and place and type of exchange.[100] The giver must have some choice in at least one of these areas: what is given, when, and to whom, and the recipient must have some choice as to exactly what will be returned and when. Usually, gifts are not legally enforceable. Thus, even in cases in which there may be a great deal of social sanction for failure to reciprocate, there is usually no legal or official sanction. (Obviously, these can become very muddy waters indeed when one of the parties is, say, a king.) This also means that, while it might be a person's duty to give or give back, that act could still be conceptualized as a gift if the exact terms are not clearly spelled out or if the return is merely token.[101] The freedom of the gift is what allows gift giving to perform

99 One might object that small gifts within family relationships and close friendships do not create obligation, especially when the giver is giving something that he no longer wants or needs – a very low-value gift. However, in these cases there is a preexisting and ongoing relationship. No one act of unreciprocated gift giving will damage the relationship; however, if one party always gives and the other always takes without any acknowledgment of the generosity of the first (indeed, perhaps she does not feel it is generosity!), the relationship is likely to suffer over the long term; thus, these also are not free gifts.

100 Sometimes there is very little freedom indeed, especially as certain forms of gift giving move closer to contract, tax, or sale. See Chris Wickham for gifts that "closely resembled sales" in the explicit nature of their return and their lack of uncertainty, "Compulsory Gift Exchange in Lombard Italy, 650–1150," in Davies and Fouracre, *The Languages of Gift*, 195. Wickham concludes that the practice of *launegeld* "used gift imagery for what were normally not very 'gifty' transactions, precisely because those social relationships remained so important to invoke," 215. The gift giving practice he examines exists in the "grey area" between gift and sale, and fell out of use once legal guarantors and central powers strong enough to force contract compliance were developed.

101 Indeed, over the course of the early Middle Ages, offerings to kings that were once conceptualized as voluntary gifts became formalized into taxes. In so doing, some amount of honour and affectivity is lost, but the king has a more predictable stream of revenue.

one of its main tasks: revealing character and establishing trust.[102] In the first place, it reveals the giver's generosity and communicates his friendly disposition towards the recipient. It also often reveals his ability to read social situations and gauge what gift would be proper. From the recipient's perspective, a person who pays a debt under threat of imprisonment shows merely that he does not want to go to prison; a person who repays a gift when there is no (ostensible) penalty for not doing so, shows himself to be a trustworthy, socially oriented person.

However, there is tension between the freedom, or openness, necessary for a gift to be a gift and the desire for a guaranteed outcome. Because openness entails risk and reveals generosity and trustworthiness of character (when it works), it is the higher-status form of exchange. We can call the result – the excess created by this form of exchange – honour. However, there are times when people would prefer a guaranteed outcome to the inefficiency and unpredictability of gift exchange. There is thus often a tendency to try to present things as gifts that are really commodities – to pretend to reciprocity while actually being entirely uninterested in the person giving and only interested in the benefits given. Chapter 4 addresses this idea further.

In real life, gift giving sometimes does not work. Acts of giving are misjudged and bungled; intention is misinterpreted by the recipient. Astute practitioners of the gift can use it to their own advantage, to consolidate power over people who do not want to be subservient,[103] or to gain things by gift that would not willingly be given any other way. The difficulty of reading intention, or of avoiding obligation without damaging social relationships or reputation, can make the gift dangerous.[104] In the idealized world of the gift, every gift is generous, interpreted correctly, received with gratitude, and returned with further generosity.

The Free Gift

What we know as the "free" gift – a gift given of the giver's own free will and which the recipient has no obligation to return – cannot do the same sort of social work as the reciprocal gift does. However, it presents an

102 Chapter 4 will discuss further the importance of choice, *agen cyre*, for Ælfric.

103 Cowell, *Medieval Warrior Aristocracy*.

104 Marcel Mauss, "Gift, Gift," in Schrift, *The Logic of the Gift*.

interesting problem in gift theory, namely because even the purest of free gifts[105] can be shown to create bonds between people. However, what is often not clearly recognized is that the ideology of the free gift (or the pure gift) developed in contradistinction to the commodity and came into its own with the rise of market capitalism.[106] In this case, the essential feature of the gift is that it exists outside of commerce, contradicting the economic model of the individual acting in his own self-interest, and creating space for non-transactional, non-self-interested interactions. Furthermore, for people whose ideal is the independence of the type of *homo economicus* descended from Adam Smith's work, the idea that gifts create obligations – create *debts*, as the terminology usually is – profoundly challenges ideals of personal autonomy. The free gift is valued because it preserves the essential independence of both parties involved in the transaction. That is, modern society has developed two opposed modes of exchange, both of which (in their ideal form) preserve independence: the mutually beneficial commodity exchange, made in the interest of both parties, in which the two parties exchanging are independent and owe nothing to the other once they complete the exchange; and the gift, valuable precisely because it denies the self-interest of the giver in seeking solely the good of the recipient without attempting either to profit from the gift or to indebt the recipient to the giver. Therefore, the free gift is set apart from the market, contaminated neither by profit nor interest.

That the free gift can never (one might suspect) be perfectly realized does not diminish its power. Anthropologists and others who study systems of exchange maintain that there is no such thing as a free gift. If we accept this (however provisionally at the moment), then we can see ways that the impossible ideal of the free gift attempts to contain certain anxieties inherent in modern ideals of individual autonomy and the totalizing nature of modern commerce. However, in attempting to maintain these ideals, the gift, taken to its conclusion, ends up idealizing a peculiar sort of masochistic nihilism: if a truly free gift, a pure gift, is one by which the giver gains nothing (thus, is non-commercial), then an even purer gift is one by which the giver actually loses, and the purest gift of all is one by

105 "Free" gift and "pure" gift have similar meanings. Generally, the *free* gift is free of obligation, while the *pure* gift is free of egoism.

106 Godbout, *World of the Gift*, 162. See also James Carrier, *Gifts and Commodities: Exchange and Western Capitalism since 1700* (New York: Routledge, 1995), especially chapter 7, "The Ideology of the Gift."

which the giver loses everything. The need for purity in the gift pushes the gift away from gratitude, generosity, and joy, and further into the territory of sacrifice, suffering, and loss, because the fact that the giver cannot possibly gain from the gift but actually loses proves her other-oriented intentions. Ironically, however, the more a gift denies the interests of the giver – the more sacrificial it is (and the more necessary it is to the recipient) – the greater the bond of obligation that it creates. That is, in seeking to escape economy, gifts that claim to be aneconomic end up creating a more powerful and more symbolic economy of gift and debt (called "gratitude")[107] that also has the tendency to affirm a hierarchy between giver and recipient. This problem creates a fascinating play of the gift, as both givers and theorists of the gift attempt to circumvent economy, to perform the calculus of no calculation, to give or imagine a gift that is truly free.[108]

This is exactly the sort of problem that would attract Jacques Derrida. In *Given Time I: Counterfeit Money*, Derrida begins with the usual modern understanding of the gift: "there must be no reciprocity, return, exchange, counter-gift, or debt. If the other *gives* me *back* or *owes* me or has to give me back what I give him or her, there will not have been a gift."[109] And yet, he says, the gift always, in fact, brings a return, even if only a symbolic equivalent in a word or gesture of thanks: "If [the recipient] recognizes it *as* gift, if the gift *appears to him as such*, if the present is present to him *as present*, this simple recognition suffices to annul the gift. Why? Because it gives back, in the place, let us say, of the thing itself, a symbolic equivalent."[110] If the donor gives anonymously, Derrida says, such anonymity still does not solve the problem: the giver, "as soon as he intends to give, [begins] to pay himself with a symbolic recognition, to praise himself, to approve of himself, to gratify himself, to congratulate himself, to give back to himself symbolically the value of what he thinks he has given."[111] The only way the gift can be saved from its contamination of self-interest, the only way the gift can be pure, is if there is no interest at all behind it, if it is unintentional. But a gift without intentionality is not a gift at all: it is an

107 See Simmel, "Faithfulness and Gratitude": "[T]he condition of gratitude easily has a taste of bondage," 47.

108 See, for instance, Jacques Derrida's meditations on the Akedah in *The Gift of Death*, trans. David Wills (Chicago: University of Chicago Press, 1996), 96–7.

109 Derrida, *Given Time*, 12. Italics original.

110 Derrida, *Given Time*, 13. Italics original.

111 Derrida, *Given Time*, 14.

accident. Thus, in denying reciprocity the pure gift degenerates to meaninglessness. It is intention and meaning itself that both create and destroy the gift: the very conditions of its existence render it impossible.

One might criticize Derrida's argument as mere linguistic display with little connection to how people actually live the gift. That is, we can all surely think of gifts generously given that have not reduced the recipient to lifelong servitude (as Alain Caillé notes in his critique of Derrida[112]). But here two strands of gift theory speak at cross purposes: theorists who have their homes in anthropology, sociology, or economics have trouble identifying a purely altruistic gift because of the nature of their disciplines, which would render anything truly non-social invisible. Furthermore, people do not follow abstract systems of rules perfectly. They behave in a "good enough" way, practising gift giving without the precision and introspective rigour demanded by theorists and philosophers. That a truly altruistic gift is impossible does not mean that people give up giving gifts, that gifts are not perceived as generous, or that people are not grateful for gifts received, any more than the fact that speakers can never perfectly control the meaning their audiences receive means people give up speaking or can never be understood.

The pure gift therefore has its home in the fields of ethics, philosophy, and theology, disciplines that think more abstractly about the nature of human obligation and freedom, of intention and will, about the nature of knowing and being known than do the empirical sciences. Thus, Derrida's point is that the gift is a phenomenon of language, and that gift exchange replicates certain problems inherent to meaning and communication in general, since both the gift act and the language act require two parties. While Derrida troubles the self/other dichotomy in speech, the link between gift and communication that he makes shows a way that prayer is doubly a gift: it *is* a gift (from humans to God, from God to humans), and it is also intended to communicate: to speak to God, who hears precators' intentions, and responds. However, Derrida's theory reveals an important feature of the pure gift: it is fundamentally non-social. Any time we try to imbue it with intention, to give it meaning or use, we weave it back into social relationships, which are, by nature, reciprocal. The pure gift demands an absolute freedom that is at odds with social bonds. The dream that lies at its heart is the complete independence of atomized individuals,

112 Alain Caillé, "The Double Inconceivability of the Pure Gift," in *Angelaki* 6.2 (2001), 37.

where no one owes anything to anyone. Such an ideal is not altruism; it is egoism of the purest kind. Thus, when Derrida addresses the gift, he not only addresses problems of language, he also addresses a problem embedded in relationships between *ego* and *alter*. That is, the gift is supposed to be a self-denying, other-oriented, altruistic act. However, as Derrida's formulation above shows, the "purest" gift that is still within the realm of the possible – the gift anonymously given, in which the recipient not only does not know *who* gave to him but also that he has received at all – is actually the most egocentric of gifts, since in that case it denies all agency on the part of the recipient, and the giver himself repays himself the symbolic equivalent of his gift. The very action that is supposed to be the highest representation of altruism is purely egocentric.[113]

The ideal of the free gift contains a modern economic understanding of the self; such an ideal disposes us to understand reciprocity as transactionality and to import attributes of the commodity to our understanding of concepts such as honour. Thus, even when we find aspects such as interiority that we associate with the modern individual (as we do in prayer practices) and find people conceptualizing themselves as distinct persons (individuals) before God, this does not mean that we find "the individual" in the modern sense, which also carries an economic charge. The modern economic self is formed *against* the other.[114] In the early medieval religious context (as in much gift giving, as chapter 2 discusses further) the self is formed *through* the other. Therefore, a mistake we often make in dealing with medieval forms of religion is in assuming a modern self-interested individual. This is perhaps especially apparent in the context of almsgiving (developed further in chapter 4), because almost all early medieval teachings on almsgiving address the responsibilities of and benefits to the almsgiver, treating the recipient of alms as instrumental to a dyadic relationship between the almsgiver and God. In Ælfric's teaching, everyone in the Christian community is both a giver of alms and a recipient of charity,

113 Or, as Derrida calls it, narcissistic, *Given Time*, 23–4. The whole chain of reasoning regarding the pure gift leads to a fascinating theological catch-22 explored by John Caputo in his article "The Time of Giving, the Time of Forgiving," in *The Enigma of Gift and Sacrifice*, in which he argues that for forgiveness to be truly unconditional, it can be given only to the utterly unworthy: unrepentant sinners.

114 In *Given Time* Derrida wrestles with the problem of self/other, but he does not seem to acknowledge the modern nature of the self embedded in his conception of the pure gift.

whether from other humans or from God. Thus, as Mauss recognized, gift giving is key to constructing social order; as such, it has its roots in religious ways of being and older notions of piety. The first gifts, life itself and all that sustains life, are given by God to humans and passed down from generation to generation, creating a moral imperative to give.[115] Most gifts are not given between equals but within hierarchical relationships (God/human, parent/child, lord/retainer); as such, they perform the function of maintaining not just social, but cosmological order. This order is enacted through prayer.

Prayer and the Gift

Situating the gift and prayer in conversation with each other allows this study to examine the way exchange forms personal identity[116] and involves negotiations of meaning on a more subjective level, but it also shows ways that people in a market economy are likely to mistake medieval prayer as transactional because it is reciprocal and expects benefits in return. Bede and Ælfric's teachings on prayer, and the practice represented in the works related to Alfred, conceptualize the exchange embedded within prayer as personal. Such prayer is not spoken of in numbers and amounts but rather as enacting a particular relationship with God. Thus, studying this body of texts allows us to see how they thought about relationships formed by exchange on a personal and subjective level. The gift is a form of symbolic communication in which intention matters. The gift in prayer is sometimes imagined as a perfect act of communication in which no meaning or value is lost before a God who sees all, and yet God's responses are frequently baffling. But human intention is a slippery thing, as often disguised as displayed, and a God who sees all can be as frightening as he is reassuring. Thus, teachings on prayer work out some of the more subjective aspects of gift exchange, especially as the gift relates to personal identity and promises to reveal character.

Yet the authors in this study clearly also envision prayer as essentially petitionary. Bede calls it "uerba obsecrationis"[117] ("words of supplication"),

115 As Godelier argues in his discussion of sacred objects among the Baruya people, "Some Things You Give."

116 Bazelmans, *By Weapons Made Worthy*, and Cowell, *Medieval Warrior Aristocracy*, both address this topic in the context of warrior aristocracy.

117 Homily 2.10, CCSL 122, 247, l. 50, translations mine.

and *oratio*, "in quibus desideria cordis nostri domino commendamus"[118] (prayer, "in which we confide the desires of our heart to the Lord"). Alfred prays for healing and, through prayer, earns reward, and the prayer Ælfric represents is often prophylactic. All of them use set prayers. All of them expect a response. None of these are "genuine" prayer, to use Heiler's term. For them, prayer is inextricably embedded in reciprocity, in a divine economy. Thus, their understanding does not represent either the type of prayer or the type of gift that has come to be thought of as "pure" or genuine.

As I mentioned earlier, prayer also had value in the material economy of the early Middle Ages. At certain times it is even possible to calculate the monetary value of prayer.[119] Among modern readers of medieval literature, the enmeshment of spheres that modernity separates – spiritual and material, intimate and economic, gift and profit – often leads to a sense that prayer is contaminated by its involvement in an exchange economy. This can be expressed in subtle ways. At the end of Arnold Angenendt's article on the way the "purchase"[120] of prayer enriched monasteries (he focuses on Cluny), and after a brief summary of the twelfth-century reform movements addressing monastic wealth, he takes care to note that "we should not consider the monasteries' accumulation of properties merely as stemming from greed and a love of the good life."[121] He continues by defending the work of the monasteries in terms now recognized as contributing to the social good: acts of charity, the disappearance of slavery. That is, he recognizes that modern readers are prone to adopt the criticisms of the later medieval reformers and see the whole series of exchanges involving prayer as corrupt from the beginning. However, there are really two perspectives layered here: that of the later medieval reformers who came to see *donationes pro anima*[122] as simony, and that of modern readers who see monasteries such as Cluny as parasites upon the social order in the way they trade a spiritual good for material goods.

---

118 Homily 2.10, CCSL 122, 247, ll. 25–6.

119 See Angenendt, "*Donationes pro anima*."

120 Angenendt, "*Donationes pro anima*," 133. However, according to Angenendt, what is bought is not prayer (even though it most literally is in the transactions he describes); it is "spiritual gifts."

121 Angenendt, "*Donationes pro anima*," 153.

122 *Donatio pro anima* is a gift given to a monastery in exchange for monastic prayer for the souls of the dead.

Such a perspective distantly echoes the position of Georges Duby. In an illuminating passage in his book on the early medieval economy, Duby notes that donations were given to the Church upon a person's death, as tithes, or as part of petitions for divine favour. These items

> were handed over to men entrusted with a special office – prayer. Thus, the penetration of Christianity led to the establishment within the community of a large group of specialists, who took part neither in working the land nor in warlike pillaging expeditions and who formed one of the most important sectors of the economic system. They produced nothing. They lived off subventions on the toil of others. In exchange for these payments, they would offer prayers and other sacred gestures for the well-being of the community.[123]

While he recognizes *donationes pro anima* as an economic improvement over the practice of burying grave goods,[124] Duby's attitude towards monks and churchmen as men who "produced nothing" is a typical modern-day attitude: those devoted to the work of prayer produced nothing *that we value* in a modern economy. Contrariwise (depending on one's view of religion), they *did* produce something of value, but only so long as it remains outside of systems of material exchange and real-world power. (One might note the way those who work in the humanities are increasingly seen as analogous to Duby's monks.) The passage is part of a larger section on what has been termed the "gift economy" of early medieval Europe. Duby, like Angenendt, shows that prayer was an element of exchange in this economy: when Lupus, the abbot of Ferrières needed lead for a building project, he asked the Anglo-Saxon king of Mercia for it, "promising him prayers in exchange."[125] Thus, it is not surprising to see Duby use the same economic language for gifts from humans to God:

---

123 Georges Duby, *The Early Growth of the European Economy: Warriors and Peasants from the Seventh to the Twelfth Century*, trans. Howard B. Clarke (Ithaca: Cornell University Press, 1974), 55. Duby sees religious power as an extension of political power and sets secular and church lords as the ruling class against labour. In his autobiography, *History Continues*, trans. Arthur Goldhammer (Chicago: University of Chicago Press, 1994), 96, the tension between classes is particularly clear as he recounts his work on the three estates.

124 Duby: "The conversion of Europe to Christianity did not suppress treasure-hoarding for funerary purposes, but it did radically alter its character. From being final and therefore sterile, it became temporary and potentially fruitful," *Early Growth*, 55.

125 Duby, *Early Growth*, 56.

"God's pardon could be purchased with offerings just as the king's peace could be bought for a fine."[126] The divine economy is imagined through the structures of the material economy.

A healthy body of scholarly literature more recent than Duby addresses the economic aspects of medieval spiritual practices and shows how the language of spiritual exchange and of purchase was used by medieval people themselves.[127] However, people who are thinking in terms of the gift do not necessarily understand or value the interpenetration of divine and material economies in the same way people in a capitalist market economy do.[128] I quote Duby because of the way his language overtly reflects a particular value judgment of this economic system. Duby writes from a Marxist perspective[129] that sees no essential difference between the interests of the secular rulers and the rulers of the Church, who unite together to protect the interests of the ruling class. The Church is corrupted by a bad-faith obfuscation, as men who "produce nothing" exploit the credulity of the populace to live as "*rentiers*" or "occup[y] a truly seigneurial position as idle consumers,"[130] trading the "nothing" of prayers for material comfort.

Similarly, that the divine economy would be embedded in the human economy of material things is often seen as corruption or contamination. The trade of material wealth for divine benefits contaminates what should be separate from all commerce. It should be obvious that this attitude is most immediately a product of Protestant critiques of the Catholic church (which then become secular critiques of institutional religion). However, the issue is much more complex than this, for, after all, the medieval church

126 Duby, *Early Growth*, 55.

127 See not only Angenendt's "*Donationes pro anima*," but also his "Sacrifice, Gifts, and Prayers in Latin Christianity." Ganz examines the model of exchange enacted in the Mass: "Giving to God in the Mass," and de Jong in "Carolingian Monasticism" argues that the spiritual authority gained through endowments for prayer was indispensable to those wielding secular power.

128 I am not claiming that Anglo-Saxon England was a gift economy; only that gift was a more prestigious mode of exchange than purchase. On the Anglo-Saxon economy, see Peter Sawyer, *The Wealth of Anglo-Saxon England* (Oxford: Oxford University Press, 2013).

129 See Duby, *History Continues*, 62–5.

130 Duby, *Early Growth*, 56.

condemned simony,[131] medieval people themselves were aware of the two-edged nature of gift giving,[132] and medieval monasticism underwent a series of reforms to address its accumulation of wealth.[133]

Whether prayer is an element of trade between humans or the means by which one petitions God, in neither case is prayer that involves exchange judged as truly *genuine*. To be pure, prayer must be *an*economic, removed from giving and getting, from the world of profit and interest. But then, within the world of the gift, the aneconomic gift – the gift by which the giver gains nothing – is also held to have the most value. Thus, prayer and the gift are both, in their highest forms, supposed to be purely other-oriented, a giving of the self to the other without expectation of return. And because purity can mean many different things depending on context, it is important to recognize that, in this case, it is the pure other-orientedness of intention that guarantees the genuineness of prayer or of the gift. Therefore, if prayer asks for benefits or favours, it is not pure prayer. If the return-on-investment is spiritualized so that the reward is heavenly rather than earthly, this still is not pure prayer. Within this understanding of other-oriented purity, the sense is that Christians like Bede, Alfred, and Ælfric do not do anything they do without hope of reward. It follows, then, that they do not see the good they do as intrinsically good, worth doing for its own sake, but only worth doing within a system in which they are rewarded – paid, really – for doing good. But this is an anachronistic evaluation stemming from a fundamental misunderstanding of the gift, which tends to conflate reciprocity, oriented towards the persons involved in the exchange and the relationships therefore established, with transactionality, oriented towards the things exchanged.[134]

This brings us back to the problem of the pure gift, which generates insight for the study of prayer: if true prayer must be aneconomic then it must go beyond petition, beyond language, beyond self-interest; it must

131 Simony is the sale of spiritual benefits; it mixes the human and divine economies in transgressive ways that allow people to bypass a system that should authenticate them, for instance, by buying ecclesiastical office or spiritual benefits. See Timothy Reuter, "Gifts and Simony," in *Medieval Transformations: Texts, Power, and Gifts in Context*, ed. Esther Cohen and Mayke B. de Jong (Leiden: Brill, 2001).

132 See, for instance, the anecdote with which Cowell begins *Medieval Warrior Aristocracy*, 15.

133 For a brief summary, see Angenendt, "*Donationes pro anima*," 150–3.

134 Chapters 3 and 4 will further address Alfred and Ælfric's use of the language of earning and of buying.

be purely other-oriented, but not in any way that rebounds upon the precator, allowing him to store up treasures either here on earth or in heaven. In addition, if the ideal of prayer is that it is spontaneous and sincere, representing the precator's own experience and her own inner heart, what we end up with is only the self endlessly re-representing itself and remaking itself further and further in its own image. That is, the ideal of aneconomic prayer – just like the pure gift – is purely egocentric, and at no time more so than when it denies that it is asking for anything at all. But this conclusion should not come as a surprise: the ideal of aneconomy is a product of the same culture that also overvalues the independent individual.

Modern readers of medieval literature tend to confuse reciprocity with transactionality, not only because obligation is at odds with ideals of the free gift, but also because the medieval gift is inextricably bound up with power and hierarchy, and because it invests heavily in commensurability between persons and things that seems to us crassly materialistic.[135] That is, returning to C.A. Gregory's distinction between gifts and commodities, transactions focus on the things exchanged and the material benefit to those exchanging, whereas the reciprocity of gift exchange seeks to create

135 Both Grønbech, *Culture of the Teutons*, 234–5, and Ernest Leisi, "Gold und Manneswert im *Beowulf*," in *Anglia* 71 (1952–3), 271, note how materialistic early Germanic culture seems while also correcting this perception by arguing that treasure is personalized by participating in the symbolic value of a person (an idea developed further by Gurevich, "Wealth and Gift Bestowal," Baker, *Honour, Exchange and Violence,* and Bazelmans, "Beyond Power"). We might also consider the way breaking the bond between persons and things, as modern culture tends to do, actually allows consumerism to flourish. When things are depersonalized they become more interchangeable, and they can then also function as an expression of individual taste rather than one's place in a matrix of social relationships. The difference is exemplified in the attitude one might have towards inheriting one's mother's dishes (in my case, cheap Corelle dishes in the blue and white pattern of the 1970s). If the dishes are imbued with her personality, they are irreplaceable, even if they are not something one would have chosen for oneself. But one might also see them as "just" dishes, unfashionable and lacking value, and discard them in order to buy new dishes that perfectly reflect one's own taste (i.e., one might suspect, current fashion). So strongly do we resist the conflation between persons and things that we tend to pathologize the feeling that things should be kept from a sense of obligation towards the persons who previously owned them (perhaps for good reason; we are drowning in things). However, it should also be noted that consumer items are almost all factory made (as in the example above), and therefore contain no "essence" of the original owner as *maker*, only as an expression of her choice as consumer. See Carrier, "Christmas and the Ceremony of the Gift," in *Gifts and Commodities* for an account of how factory-manufactured items are transformed from commodities into gifts.

relationships between persons.[136] Thus, transactionality commodifies persons, whereas reciprocity personifies things.[137] Things take on the characteristics or identity of their owners, both as a means of passing on the giver's "luck" and also of identifying certain qualities in the recipient.[138]

A particularly subtle example of the easy slippage between the two types of exchange can be found in scholarly treatments of honour. An example can be found in William Ian Miller's discussion of "units" of honour in "Gift, Sale, Payment, Raid: Case Studies in the Negotiation and Classification of Exchange in Medieval Iceland." When Miller speaks of "units of prestige" transferred instead of money, he treats honour as a standardizable thing, the "thing" traded for in agonistic exchanges.[139] Pierre Bourdieu follows a similar logic when he calls reputation a part of a person's "symbolic capital" and points out that it can be converted back into wealth.[140] In so doing, Bourdieu subsumes the gift back into the structures of commodity exchange by reducing symbolic capital's functionality to material gain. While Bourdieu's (and Miller's) insights are a helpful starting point to understanding honour, his theory treats economic reality as though it is *the* reality and reveals the Western materialist tendency to think in terms of *things* exchanged and gained. Bourdieu's point about different forms of capital is workable (generosity and trustworthiness are, after all, desirable qualities in a trading partner) as long as we understand that capital is the metaphor through which *we* think, not the terms in which Anglo-Saxons understood generosity or reputation.

---

136 Gregory, *Gifts and Commodities*, 19.

137 In the field of Anglo-Saxon studies, see especially *By Weapons Made Worthy* (Bazelmans's work on gift exchange and identity in *Beowulf*), and "Beyond Power," the article adapted from that larger project.

138 A point made by both Gurevich, "Wealth and Gift Bestowal," and Grønbech, *Culture of the Teutons*, vol. 2, chapter 1.

139 Miller, "Gift, Sale, Payment, Raid," 32. Pierre Bourdieu follows a similar logic when he calls reputation a part of a person's "symbolic capital" and points out it can be converted back into wealth, *The Logic of Practice*, trans. Richard Nice (Stanford: Stanford University Press, 1990), 119. Bourdieu subsumes the gift back into the structures of commodity exchange by reducing symbolic capital's functionality to material gain. While Bourdieu is not wrong, his theory treats economic reality as though it is *the* reality and reveals the Western materialist tendency to think in terms of *things* exchanged and gained. His point about different forms of capital is workable (generosity and trustworthiness are, after all, desirable qualities in a trading partner) as long as we understand that capital is the metaphor through which *we* think, not the terms in which Anglo-Saxons understood generosity or reputation.

140 Bourdieu, *The Logic of Practice*, 119.

If we assume that people exchange gifts to gain something wanted or needed for something less wanted or needed, we end up, *contra* Gregory, putting *things* back at the centre of the gift. It is thus easy to imagine that generous people in honour-based societies like that of the Anglo-Saxons trade wealth for honour when they gain a reputation for generosity by giving gifts. Yet when we imagine reputation to be a "thing," converting wealth into reputation still establishes a relationship between things, commodifying reputation. To establish a fair relationship between things, the properties of those things must be known – this is Gregory's point about commodities. Gift giving, on the other hand, establishes a relationship between people, revealing the "properties" of the people involved. Because of the gift's "openness" – the exact terms of the return are not spelled out – gift exchange shows the generosity of the giver and the trustworthiness of the recipient when she recognizes her "debt" and in turn becomes a giver. Thus, gift exchange reveals the character of the parties to the exchange, which is to say, it reveals their awareness of and orientation towards social ties and obligations. Such a revelation is the central point. Yet to insist that gift exchange establishes a relationship between people is not to posit that gift exchange is always altruistic or positive; gifts can be used to dominate and manipulate, and not all relationships are welcome. Furthermore, because gift exchange *can* be economically useful and *can* have benefits in the accumulation of things, the forms and structures of gift exchange can be used to mask, to varying degrees, an avaricious nature. In other words, the gift implies the desire for a relationship, but it does not necessarily manifest why the relationship is desired.

The gift medieval people idealized was not pure. In rare cases, it was so splendidly generous that it made those witnessing it gasp.[141] The only possible responses to such a gift were either life-long devotion and friendship or implacable hatred.[142] The recipient's response would be determined by

141 In gift theory circles such a gift is exemplified by the concept of potlatch (see Mauss, *The Gift*, 33–46). "Potlatch" can be used so loosely it comes to mean nothing more than reciprocal obligation (see, for instance, Donahue, "Potlatch and Charity"); however, its essential elements are that it is an agonistic, competitive gift exchange with honour at stake. In extreme cases it can lead to the destruction (rather than circulation) of gift items. The point I wish to emphasize here, however, is that spectacular generosity is not always benignly motivated or welcome.

142 For an example, see Cowell, *Medieval Warrior Aristocracy*, 15–16.

his attitude towards the bond created and his judgment of the intention and meaning behind the gift. More usually, the ideal gift was appropriately generous (think, for instance, of Hrothgar's gifts to Beowulf). Both ideals calculate in order to exceed calculation. That such gifts should be given secretly renders them meaningless – the gift's *point* is to have effect, on audience and recipient alike.[143] It finely calibrates its performance, tunes its meaning, tries to ensure it will be received in the spirit given. The best gifts of this kind are an expression of trust and a revelation of character as freedom and obligation are balanced against each other. Of course they bring honour to the giver.[144] Received and reciprocated rightly, they bring honour to the recipient, too. Egoism is not at odds with altruism.

Gift exchange is therefore the higher-status, more meaningful type of exchange. The reciprocal gift gives community, communication, and identity – all ideas that will be fleshed out in the later chapters of this book. There is stronger ideological contrast in Anglo-Saxon sources between gift and theft than there is between gift and purchase.[145] The most splendid gifts were necessarily interested – generously, but not quite freely, given. Because giving something as a gift invested it with symbolic meaning, the mode of exchange increased the value of the thing given: it was valuable precisely because of who gave it, because of the intention conveyed for

---

143 In fact, secrecy in gift giving could be interpreted more malignantly. According to Jürgen Hannig, *Ars donandi*, 154–5, in Gregory of Tours, bribes involve an element of secrecy, cited in Florin Curta, "Merovingian and Carolingian Gift Giving," in *Speculum* 81.3 (2006), 691.

144 Miller's study of Icelandic sagas treats honour specifically as a commodity economy and therefore argues that honour is a zero-sum game, *Bloodtaking and Peacemaking*, 29–34. A number of Anglo-Saxonists also show interest in the economy of honour: John Hill, *The Cultural World in "Beowulf"*; Baker, *Honour, Exchange and Violence*, expands Hill's discussion, citing both Ernst Leisi, "Gold und Manneswert"; and Michael Cherniss, *Ingeld and Christ: Heroic Concepts and Values in Old English Christian Poetry* (The Hague: Mouton, 1972).

145 That theft is so harshly punished reveals fissures in the medieval ideology much as the free gift does for the modern. Theft breaks the relationship between things and persons, presenting the possibility that objects are merely material and lifeless; things and persons are not, after all, commensurable, and therefore things cannot be embedded in an honour economy. This possibility destabilizes an entire social system that depends upon the spiritual life of things for its meaning and replication. Baker's chapter "Loot and the Economy of Honor" in *Honour, Exchange and Violence* makes some helpful distinctions between theft and loot and the way objects become invested with meaning; Leisi also addresses the topic.

ongoing relations, and because of the quality it recognized in the recipient.[146] As Ernst Leisi points out, a stolen sword (say) is therefore a type of "plagiarism," a false witness to the holder's character.[147] A purchased sword is little better; while having use value, it has no symbolic value. A sword received as a gift, however, has added value, the value of the giver.

While studies of the early Middle Ages have been quick to integrate anthropological insights on the gift to our understanding of the era, they still have not been brought to bear on the way medieval religious practice is devalued by modern assumptions surrounding the issue of reciprocity, and this, in part, explains the dearth of scholarship on Anglo-Saxon devotion that Allen Frantzen laments. As I have argued, medieval practice is devalued from two directions: prayer is not "genuine" according to a post-Romantic, anti-empiricist definition, and it is also not "pure." Anglo-Saxon prayer is firmly embedded in an economy both material and spiritual, whereas we insist that prayer, like the gift, must be aneconomic to be true.

I have spent this time invoking the spectre of the free gift, partially in order to exorcise it and partially because its wan glow throws into relief important characteristics of reciprocity that the rest of the book will develop. Examining prayer and the gift in works by Bede, the Alfredian circle, and Ælfric allows us to consider the way authors writing to different audiences at different periods in Anglo-Saxon England think about exchange between humans and God, and see that exchange to constitute human identity, personal and communal. As we will see, each of these authors imagines the exchange relationship between humans and God in different ways. In the following chapters, the study of each author's prayer is driven by these questions: If prayer is a gift, what does that mean? What is given or received? For each author, what does prayer ask for, and what do they expect in return? To what extent are prayer's effects assumed to be subjective or objective? What implications does reciprocity in prayer have for how humans imagine their relationship with God, and imagine themselves through that relationship? How does prayer build identity and

146 Grønbech, citing evidence from the Norse sagas, says, "A prudent man would not accept a gift until he had mingled mind with the giver, and knew his plans. Once a man had persuaded another to accept the gage of friendship, then he could be sure of his powerful support." *Culture of the Teutons*, 2:7.

147 Leisi, "Gold und Manneswert," 271. Thomas D. Hill discusses weapons as identifying markers of rank in "Beowulf as Seldguma: *Beowulf*, lines 247–51," in *Neophilologus* 74 (1990), 236–9.

accrue honour or worth? If reciprocity enmeshes both parties in webs of obligation, what does this mean in light of orthodox teachings on grace and God's sovereignty? To what extent can humans compel God to act through gifts, and what obligations do God's gifts place on humans?

Furthermore, in each chapter I consider what expectation each author has for the practice of prayer. That is, in prayer, what manner of thing is given or received? I argue that all of these authors understand the normal and foundational practice of prayer as set prayers. In so doing, each reifies prayer (although to different extents), treating it as a thing (or service) that can be given. In so doing, authors sometimes place more emphasis on the *words* of prayer, and sometimes on prayer as an *action*. For Bede and the Alfredian texts, the words of prayer have subjective effect upon the precator, but for Ælfric words are more like speech acts that perform allegiance and are expected to have real effect.

To give context for the Anglo-Saxon authors within early Christian teachings on and practices of prayer, chapter 1 gives an overview of the prayer tradition inherited by the Anglo-Saxons. I introduce the basic body of texts, and show different ways that reciprocity was imagined in the early teachings, and I introduce the key questions (determined by biblical passages) that teaching on prayer addresses and the way these establish the parameters for developing a theory of prayer. Chapter 1 also considers the expected practice of prayer, showing that, by the Anglo-Saxon period, at any rate, text-based, formal prayers were the ideal prayer practice, not spontaneous, formless prayer. Chapter 1 also addresses the fascinating economic implications of Neoplatonism reflected in the works of influential authors like John Cassian (d. 435) and St Augustine (d. 430). Both idealize wordless prayer and an eventual union with the Divine that escapes economy. In neither case, however, do these authors idealize aneconomy. In fact, while Cassian's practice is often understood by modern scholars to represent exactly an idealized aneconomic, pure prayer that extends beyond words, his prayer is actually a radically text-based destruction and remaking of the self that manages, by its very lack of spontaneity and individually oriented sincerity, to avoid the egoism inherent to aneconomic prayer. I conclude this chapter by looking at Anglo-Saxon contributions to the practice of prayer, most especially prayerbooks, and developments in personal prayer through the era.

Of all the authors here studied, the "spirituality" of Bede's work has received the most scholarly attention. Yet, as chapter 2 shows, the usual concerns of spirituality studies render parts of his presentation of prayer invisible or problematic. For Bede, prayer is intensely word based, ritualized, and reciprocal. Precators internalize the words of prayer into thoughts and externalize them into deeds, none of which are the produce of the precator's own self. And yet, Bede understands the human relationship with God enacted through prayer as a reciprocal gift exchange characterized by *gratia* that forms the precator's identity, transforming him from a state of not belonging to one of belonging. Thus, prayer is a gift from God that precators return as they enact it. While Mary is the central figure he uses to develop this idea, Bede's understanding of prayer follows the same logic as that of the Anglo-Saxon warrior returning his lord's gift of weapons by using those weapons to defend him. The weapons are a marker of who the warrior is, of his worth. Worth forms an identity that is socially mediated, not interior, but consists of the person's sense of how others see him. For Bede, the *gratia* performed through prayer creates a social relationship of exchange with God that is non-agonistic, leading to the honour of each. Thus, for Bede, gift exchange is not merely *symbolic* of intention and person; it actually *constitutes* the person.

In contrast, King Alfred has a less subjective understanding of prayer's efficacy than does Bede: Asser presents Alfred at prayer for healing in a way that shows Alfred expects prayer to *work* – to have real effect in this world. To contextualize Asser's depiction of prayer, chapter 3 examines the practice and representation of prayer within some of the texts associated with King Alfred. Because Asser's Alfred clearly expects prayer to be materially efficacious when he prays for healing, and because exchange communicates intention, unanswered prayer is meaningful and presents an interpretive problem: how does one understand the breakdown of reciprocity in unanswered prayer? When Asser's account is compared with the introductions to the prose Psalms and the translation of the prayer that begins the *Soliloquies*, we can see the way that the question of efficacy is subjectivized: the efficacy of prayer is "guaranteed" by the way it draws the precator into a Christological and Davidic narrative that in turn guarantees the precator before God as someone worthy to be heard. As the precator adopts the discipline of prayer, he reinterprets the events of his own life in light of the narrative of the Psalms and other prayers. Prayer is thus characterized as work that merits a response, but the unanswered prayer also becomes an avenue to ratify or guarantee Alfred's own character.

The laypeople who constitute Ælfric's audience present very different expectations for prayer than those represented by Bede and even Alfred: in a world animated by devils, prayer focuses largely on the need for protection and physical healing. As chapter 4 shows, Ælfric's teachings situate prayer much more strongly within a vision of communal wholeness and salvation constructed around a gift network binding together all members of society as brothers with mutual ties of prayer and alms that similarly bind humans to God. By creating a multiparty cycle of exchange, Ælfric disrupts overt transactionality. Yet in Ælfric's homilies lay prayer is also utilitarian and often prophylactic. Chapter 4 examines five of Ælfric's *Catholic Homilies* that establish the contours of the cosmological world in which precators pray and give Ælfric's most explicit teachings on prayer. One of the effects of the way Ælfric presents God and the devil as rival lords is that Ælfric presents a theory of prayer more heavily invested in material efficacy than Bede's or Alfred's. Prayer becomes, at its most essential, an action, a performance of allegiance; answered prayer communicates God's protection and power. Because of this, it runs the risk of privileging the precator's will rather than God's, closing down the openness characteristic of the gift and thereby trading generosity and trust for material and future security. In addition, Ælfric faces the same issue that Alfred does: what does it mean when prayers go unanswered? Ælfric ends *CH* I.31 with a coda meditating on this problem that further disrupts any sense of *do ut des* reciprocity. By teaching that Christians should not expect healing from God and arguing that there is no simple way to interpret unanswered prayer, he weakens the link between healing and meaning and clarifies the way that the gift is symbolically oriented towards the recognition and reward of honour.

Anglo-Saxon theories of prayer thus replicate and expose tensions within early medieval practices of gift exchange. The Anglo-Saxon gift is inherently interested, assumed to benefit both parties; it contains no ideal of disinterestedness or altruism. However, because benefits are necessarily a part of gift relationships, the lines between reciprocity and transactionality can become blurred. While this potentially creates problems in human gift relations, the religious context, with its careful examination of human motive and intention, amplifies the problem: do humans serve God because they get benefits or because they recognize who he is?[148] The danger is not that gift becomes commodity, a balanced exchange in which both parties get what they want and go their separate ways, but that reciprocity hides transactional intentions in which the focus is on the benefits rather than the relationship, creating a counterfeit of generosity or of gratitude that *seems* to give while really only taking.

148 A question first posed in the book of Job.

Chapter One

The Anglo-Saxon Inheritance

For what greater gift can be presented to God by a rational creature than a sweet-smelling word of prayer?

– Origen of Alexandria, *On Prayer*[1]

Sola est oratio quae deum vincit. (Prayer alone it is that conquers God.)

– Tertullian, *On Prayer*[2]

Prayer and Reciprocity

What do people think they do when they pray? The epigraphs above, from the two earliest Christian treatises on prayer, both imagine prayer as given to God, or as exacting a return from God. However, they exemplify different attitudes with which people can approach reciprocity in prayer. In the first (written in Greek ca. 232), Origen of Alexandria contextualizes the statement within a section on how people ought to pray. The "gift" is that offered at God's altar (Matthew 5:23–4); the precator's harmony with all Christians causes the "sweet smell." Although Origen certainly imagines prayer reciprocally, he emphasizes what humans give and how they give it, not the way that prayer obligates God's response. Tertullian's

1 Origen, *Origen's Treatise on Prayer*, trans. Eric George Jay (London: S.P.C.K., 1954; Eugene, OR: Wipf and Stock, 2010), 2.2, p. 83. Citations refer to the Wipf and Stock reprint.

2 Tertullian, *De oratione liber. Tertullian's Tract on the Prayer*; ed. and trans. Ernest Evans (London: S.P.C.K., 1953), cap. 29, l. 15.

statement comes at the end of his treatise (written around the turn of the third century) in a final encomium on the power of prayer to bring about God's miraculous intervention in the world. Although Tertullian is similarly concerned with human disposition before God, he stresses the efficacy of prayer: that God's response to prayer, properly made, is so sure that it "conquers." Though each statement represents but a small part of each author's full understanding of prayer, Origen's reflects a greater emphasis on the ethics of interpersonal behaviour and the interior work that prayer does, while Tertullian details correct ritual performance while emphasizing what humans owe God and what God, in turn, owes humans.

In late antiquity and the early Middle Ages, prayer was a given, and for many precators the reasons for praying were self-evident. As a result, early medieval authors do not spend a great deal of time explaining prayer, and when they do they often leave many of their foundational assumptions unsaid. We do not have many treatises like Origen's and Tertullian's. Most training in prayer must surely have been person-to-person, and much of it seems to have focused on bodily performance and what words to say. People learned prayer by doing. Any theorizing they did was *post hoc*, following practices in which they were already engaged (Origen, for instance, was raised in a Christian family, although Tertullian converted). Thus when we turn to the sources on prayer, we find prayers preserved in manuscript collections and in treatises, representations of prayer in narratives,[3] explications of biblical passages on prayer in commentaries and homilies, and monastic *regulae* on when and what to pray, but only a handful of texts that speak explicitly to a theory of prayer.

Within Anglo-Saxon studies, the scholarship that most specifically focuses on prayer has usually approached its study from two directions. The first is as a textual problem: on the sources of Anglo-Saxon prayers or on the prayers' manuscript contexts.[4] The source studies are most interested

3 See chapter 5 of E.G. Stanley, *In the Foreground: "Beowulf"* (Woodbridge: D.S. Brewer, 1994); A. Bravo, "Prayer as a Literary Device in *The Battle of Maldon* and in *The Poem of the Cid*," *SELIM* 2 (1992); and especially Donald G. Byzdl, "Prayer in Old English Narratives," *Medium Ævum* 51.2 (1982), in which he compares narrative prayers to Old English devotional prayers.

4 A helpful place to begin finding prayers themselves is Phillip Pulsiano's article, "Prayers, Glosses and Glossaries," in *A Companion to Anglo-Saxon Literature* (Oxford: Blackwell, 2001), and also his entry "Psalters," in *The Liturgical Books of Anglo-Saxon England*, ed. Richard Pfaff (Kalamazoo, MI: MIP), which gives the contents of manuscripts containing psalters, a great many of which also contain prayers.

in lines of cultural transmission, noting where prayers come from (Rome, Ireland, etc.), or studying the various Old English poems based on prayers, the liturgy, or devotional practice.[5] From this approach, the question "what is prayer" is (largely) obvious: prayers are texts that present themselves as prayers by virtue of their presence in prayerbooks, their transmission history, and the way they address God or the saints. However, complications arise insofar as the line between prayers and charms can be blurry. Perfectly respectable prayers – the Paternoster – could be used as charms or for contemplation. In this case, the difference is caused, to some extent, by the precator's own intentions. The manuscript contexts for prayer can here help us determine intention in a limited way insofar as manuscripts are created with particular uses in mind (for instance, the Galba/Nero prayerbook, a miscellany, was bound blank). The prayerbooks show us that Anglo-Saxons do not seem to have drawn the lines between types of prayers in the same places that we would; some prayerbooks include things we might call charms (see my critique of Sims-Williams's analysis of Royal in the introduction). But manuscript studies also show thematic groupings of prayers or overall thematic focus.[6] One way to answer some questions about prayers' actual use, then, is to look at their manuscript contexts. The limitation to these sorts of studies is that neither prayers themselves nor the manuscript contexts usually say anything explicitly about a theory or practice of prayer.[7]

---

5 These poems are the versifications of the liturgical prayers: three separate poems based on the Paternoster (now called *The Lord's Prayer I, II*, and *III*), two on the Gloria (*Gloria I* and *II*), one on the Creed, and *Christ I*, a versification of the "O Antiphons" of Advent. In addition, the poems called *A Prayer* and *Resignation*, as well as the *Dream of the Rood*, are often classed as devotional poetry. All of these poems are printed in ASPR VI, ed. Elliott Van Kirk Dobbie, except for *The Lord's Prayer I*, *Christ I*, and *Resignation* (sometimes called *The Penitent's Prayer*), which are in the Exeter Book (ASPR III, ed. George Philip Krapp and Elliott Van Kirk Dobbie), and the *Dream of the Rood*, which is in the Vercelli Book (ASPR II, ed. George Philip Krapp).

6 Barbara Raw, "Alfredian Piety: The Book of Nunnaminster," in *Alfred the Wise: Studies in Honour of Janet Bately on the Occasion of Her Sixty-Fifth Birthday*, ed. Jane Roberts et al. (Rochester, NY: D.S. Brewer, 1997), reads groupings of prayers in Nunnaminster against similar groupings in Royal. Michelle P. Brown argues that its overall focus is the *communio sanctorum*, *The Book of Cerne* (London: British Library, 1996), 147–8.

7 Cerne, the exception, begins with fragmentary devotional instruction; Ælfwine's Prayerbook, a miscellany, also includes brief order of personal morning prayer and some miscellaneous statements about the value of such prayers.

The second approach is scholars who study aspects of Anglo-Saxon prayer and piety that persist in later forms of devotion, such as penitential practice, devotion to the cross or the Virgin Mary, or early traces of affective piety.[8] Such studies often include information on some aspects of prayer (or the liturgy) without that being their main focus. For instance, Mary Clayton's book on the cult of the Virgin Mary contains two chapters charting the growth of her cult through her representation in liturgies and private prayers,[9] and charting the growth of penitential practice is important for our understanding of lay piety.[10] The few studies that focus more broadly on Anglo-Saxon "spirituality" or devotion (as an attitude, not a practice) often do not query carefully enough the assumptions and values embedded in the concepts, and the way these concepts direct our attention to certain forms of piety and not others.[11]

However, scant attention has been given to the ways Anglo-Saxons theorized prayer in those places where they teach more explicitly about it, or to the way they adapt the earlier teaching tradition. The current chapter, then, contextualizes the Anglo-Saxon teachings on prayer within the early Christian tradition that they inherited by presenting the major approaches to teaching prayer as well as the major English developments in the practice of prayer. In part, doing so will clarify what the expectations were for basic prayer practice and show where early medieval assumptions about ideal practice might differ from those of current readers. However, by examining the early Christian tradition, we also see that the traditional

8 Karen Louise Jolly et al., *Cross and Culture in Anglo-Saxon England: Studies in Honor of George Hardin Brown* (Morgantown, WV: West Virginia University Press, 2007); Mary Clayton, *The Cult of the Virgin Mary in Anglo-Saxon England* (Cambridge: Cambridge University Press, 1990).

9 Clayton, *The Cult of the Virgin Mary*, chapters 2 and 3.

10 Allen J. Frantzen, *The Literature of Penance in Anglo-Saxon England* (New Brunswick, NJ: Rutgers University Press, 1983); Catherine Cubitt, "Bishops, Priests and Penance in Late Anglo-Saxon England," *EME* 14.1 (2006).

11 Allen J. Frantzen's "Spirituality and Devotion in the Anglo-Saxon Penitentials," *EMS* 22 (2005), is one example. Milton McC. Gatch, "The Anglo-Saxon Tradition," in *The Study of Spirituality*, ed. Cheslyn Jones et al. (New York: Oxford University Press, 1986), uses "spirituality" in a somewhat loose way that seems to encompass personal devotional practice as driven by belief. Benedicta Ward begins by defining spirituality, which is the subject of her book; however, she specifically invokes the nineteenth-century sense of the term, describing "ascetic theology, and/or mystical prayer," *High King of Heaven: Aspects of Early English Spirituality* (Kalamazoo, MI: Cistercian Publications, 1999), xi.

body of teaching on prayer interacts with a central problem of will: does prayer "conquer God," as Tertullian says, bending him to the human will, or is it an act of submission? To conceptualize prayer as a gift (as Origen does above) does not solve the problem: is a gift a response in gratitude, an act of submission, or is it an attempt to produce a response, a return gift? Clearly, both prayer and the gift can be all of these things. At what points do writers on prayer emphasize submission, and at what points human desire and will? At what points do we see aneconomic ideas of prayer (and what produces them), and how do writers use economic ideas to link devotee to divinity?

The Greek and Roman prayer of the pagan religions that formed most Christian converts' understanding manifests a reciprocal pattern of "converse" between gods and humans. Evidence is sparser for early Germanic religion, but there is no reason to doubt that they had essentially the same understanding.[12] Thus, the central thesis of Simon Pulleyn's book, *Prayer in Greek Religion*

> is the importance of χάρις [*charis*] in Greek prayer. That word is often translated "grace" or "favour." In fact, it refers to a whole nexus of related ideas that we would call reciprocity. When one gives something to a god, one is giving χάρις in the sense that the offering is pleasing; but equally one is storing up for oneself a feeling of gratitude on the part of the god, which is also χάρις. The whole two-way relationship can be called one of χάρις.[13]

Similarly, Jörg Rüpke notes the "system of exchange" between gods and humans in Roman religion, in which prayer is central: "nothing works without a prayer, but ... [prayers] are usually accompanied by a gift."[14] Gifts from humans to gods and favours from gods to humans bind gods and humans together in "a ceaseless cycle of obligation and gratitude, which the usual concentration on individual exchanges expressed by the phrase *do ut des* tends to obscure. There is a chain of actions, a reciprocity

12 Little evidence exists for native Anglo-Saxon religion; however, it is likely that it shared points in common with most "primitive" and non-salvation religions, such that prayer asks the gods for favours and that early Anglo-Saxons saw sacrifice/gift as an important part of the relationship between gods and humans.

13 Simon Pulleyn, *Prayer in Greek Religion* (Oxford: Clarendon, 1997), 4.

14 Jörg Rüpke, *Religion of the Romans*, trans. Richard Gordon (Cambridge: Polity Press, 2007), 140.

of gifts."[15] Both prayer and gifts are thus tightly bound together in a way that is certainly "converse with [a] god," but that also so imbricates the material and the spiritual that it looks quite different from a devotional and purifying communion with the divine that denies the material and economic in prayer, and that influences the assumed definition in many current studies of prayer.

Early Greco-Roman Christianity thus spoke into the pagan experience of prayer and adapted these sorts of expectations.[16] For instance, according to Tertullian, Christian prayer replaces sacrifice: "Haec [oratio] est enim hostia spiritalis quae pristina sacrificia delevit"[17] (For this [prayer] is the spiritual oblation which has wiped out the ancient sacrifices). In the immediate context in which Tertullian quotes from the New Testament, the "ancient sacrifices" are those prescribed in the Old Testament.[18] The goals of Old Testament sacrifice are ritual purity and atonement for sin. Yet as an African Roman (and Christian convert), Tertullian's understanding of prayer as sacrifice is clearly informed by the *do ut des* reciprocity manifested in the sacrificial system of his own culture. In fact, he appeals to the principle of reciprocity some fifteen lines later: "Quid enim orationi de spiritu et veritate venienti negabit deus ... ?"[19] (For what will God deny to a prayer which proceeds from the Spirit and the Truth ...?) In both Judaism and the pagan religions, sacrifice seeks to maintain a relationship with the divinity, whether to gain benefits by performing services and giving gifts, as in the Greco-Roman system, or to purify the one sacrificing or the whole society of sin, as in Judaism, although the Jewish system denied that sacrifices were of any necessary benefit to God. For both, sacrifice was a central ritual action that maintained the social order and kept human and divine realms in right relationship to one another.

Gift theory features prominently in academic analyses of sacrifice.[20] Insofar as sacrifice is conceptualized as exchange between humans and

15 Rüpke, *Religion of the Romans*, 149.

16 The very earliest strata of Christian prayer is Jewish, but by the time of Tertullian and Origen, most converts were gentiles.

17 Tertullian, *De oratione*, cap. 28, l. 1; trans. Evans.

18 According to Evans "an odd phrase or two show" that the prayer he refers to seems most immediately to be the consecration prayer for the Eucharist, *De oratione liber*, xiii, although Tertullian moves straight into a chapter on the efficacy of prayer in general with which he ends the treatise.

19 Tertullian, *De oratione*, cap. 29, ll. 1–2; trans. Evans.

20 Jeffrey Carter, ed., *Understanding Religious Sacrifice* (London: Continuum, 2003), 3.

gods, it operates under much the same logic as human gift giving. Marcel Mauss, who co-authored one of the classic works on sacrifice, notes some of the distinctive elements: "It is [the spirits of both the dead and the gods] who are the true owners of the things and possessions of this world ... The purpose of destruction by sacrifice is precisely that it is an act of giving that is necessarily reciprocated." Because the gods come first they own all things, which means that humans can never have the upper hand in gift giving. Thus, gift theory usefully address the relationship between the divine realm and the gift giving impulse, chiefly in considering what creates the obligation to give. Maurice Godelier argues that the obligation to give (either give back to the gods/ancestors or give on to other people) is created by the sense that the gods or ancestors give all humans have, including life. This first gift can never be repaid in full, which obligates humans to give gifts back to the gods in sacrifice and also to share what they have received with each other in the giving of gifts. Sacrifice and gift giving never cancel out the "debt" of the first gifts; rather, they create webs of relationships in which humans can continue to expect good things from the gods and can develop relationships of trust with each other – human gift giving symbolically reenacts gifts between humans and gods. Gifts stand at the very centre of a social order ratified by the divine origin of all things.

If we take Tertullian seriously, then, Christian prayer replaces gifts to God – it is a gift to God – performing the same function as sacrifice by putting humans and God in right relationship to one another and acknowledging human dependence upon God's gifts. In early Christianity the sacrament of the Eucharist performed by priests, the *opus Dei* performed by monks, and the prayers performed privately or corporately by all believers participate in the gift economy between God and humans. The Mass, conceived of as a thanksgiving to God that reenacts his own sacrifice, composed of both prayer and offerings of bread and wine, brings to humans further *gratia* from God (conceptualized more or less spiritually or materially depending on the time and place). The Daily Office of prayers performed by monks was an offering to God both on their own behalf and on the behalf of the whole world.

Old English poetry invokes God's creation of all things in order to clarify human duty in return. Thus, *Cædmon's Hymn*, in some ways the originating moment of the written poetic tradition in Old English, invokes the human obligation to praise and honour God as a response to his creative work. *Genesis A* opens with a similar declaration of the very great human *riht* (duty, privilege) to praise God, the uncreated creator of all things.[21] *Maxims I* states that God must be praised in return for the things he has given:

God sceal mon ærest hergan
fægre, fæder userne, forþon þe he us æt frymþe geteode
lif ond lænne willan; he usic wile þara leana gemonian.[22]

(People must first beautifully praise God because from the beginning he granted us life and fleeting joy; he wishes to remind us of those gifts.)

Lean, often translated gift or loan, is difficult to translate succinctly. It always includes the idea of some sort of return (whether reward or retribution); in this case, the *lean* given are life and joy, which obligate humans to respond in praise. God's position springs from his eternality and from his role as creator; humans enter into a reciprocal relationship with God through praising him. The praise constitutes the return gift. In the most absolute Christian formulations (Augustine, much later Calvin), God's gifts so completely define the conditions of human existence that humans can never obligate God to respond to their requests. God responds only and continually out of his own grace, generally poured out upon humanity, which therefore does not return any particular act of human gift.[23] Yet each of the authors studied in this book resists, each in his own way, the idea of complete human abjection before God and insists that humans have something to give back, that fulfilling the duty (*riht*) to return God's benefits gives them further rights (also *riht*). As God is humanized, inevitably he is personified, and as he is humanized he becomes subject to human structures and obligations, even as some teachers (such as Augustine) resist this same pressure.

It can be difficult to access a particular community's understanding of prayer through the textual evidence preserved. The Anglo-Saxons inherited conventional language for prayer and adopted conventional explications of prayer passages in their own sermons. Words for prayer make interesting semantic shifts as they are translated from language to

21 Chapter 4 will further analyse the way Ælfric's *CH* I.1 uses this same appeal to the human duty to praise God.

22 Krapp and Dobbie, eds., ASPR III, ll. 4b–6.

23 Chapter 2 will further consider medieval formulations of the doctrine of grace and the way that early medieval teaching resists God's unilateral grace.

language: some are more or less situated in fields that invoke exchange. Yet even when the words remain the same, they cannot always have meant the same thing.[24] Furthermore, the semantic range of words for prayer in different languages presents suggestively different frames of reference. While the root of the Modern English "to pray" (from Latin *precari* via Old French) lies in formal petition to gods or men, in modern-day usage it has almost wholly lost any non-religious meaning.[25] In scholarly and religious usage "prayer" can refer to a variety of interior devotional acts (worship, contemplation, meditation, etc.), not all of which have to do with petition. Thus, current-day scholarly and devotional writing on prayer frequently refers to the Creed as a prayer, although it makes no petitions.[26] The most common words for prayer in Old English, the verb *biddan* (to ask), and the nouns *ben* (a request) and *gebed* (a prayer) are more firmly situated in the semantic field of petitioning and exchange than Latin *oratio*.

The meanings of prayer words in different languages can also influence each other. John Cassian, whose *Conlationes* (ca. 420) were influenced by Greek teaching, exemplifies this in his commentary on I Timothy 2:1. In this passage the apostle Paul urges, originally in Greek, that "supplications, prayers, intercessions, and thanksgivings be made for all men."[27] Commentators took this verse as a schema to define the types of Christian prayer. Cassian draws on this tradition, defining "prayers" in this way: "Orationes sunt quibus aliquid offerimus seu uouemus deo, quod Graece dicitur εὐχή, id est uotum"[28] (Prayers are those acts by which we offer or vow something to God, which is called *euche* in Greek – that is, a vow).

24 See Scott DeGregorio, "The Venerable Bede on Prayer and Contemplation," *Traditio* 54 (1999), for a comparison of Bede's "puritas oratio" with Cassian's use of the same phrase.

25 *OED Online*, s.v. "pray, v."

26 Anglo-Saxon texts do not call the Creed a prayer. Ælfric makes a clear distinction between them: "Ælc cristen man sceal æfter rihte cunnan ægþer ge his pater noster ge his credan; Mid þam pater nostre he sceal hine gebiddan. mid þam credan he sceal his geleafan getrymman" (Every Christian should rightly know both his Paternoster and his Creed. With the Paternoster he should pray; with the Creed he should confirm his faith), *CH* I.20, 335, ll. 1–3. All Old English translations are mine unless otherwise noted.

27 Biblical translations are from the Douay-Rheims 1899 American Edition unless otherwise noted.

28 John Cassian, *Conlatio* 9, 12, ll. 7–8, ed. Michael Petschenig, CSEL 13 (Vienna: Verlag der Österreichischen Akademie der Wissenschaften, 2004), 261; trans. Boniface Ramsey, *The Conferences* (New York: Newman, 1997).

Cassian shows awareness that *oratio* does not have the same semantic range as *euche* while adopting *euche*'s meaning. In both cases, prayer as vow harmonizes with pre-Christian practices of prayer, in which petitioners promised the gods something (*votum*, in Latin) in exchange for an answered prayer.

However, in Latin the most common verbs for prayer (out of a rather large vocabulary) are *oro* (from *os*, mouth, thus speak, pray), *rogo* (ask, request), *precor* (ask, beg), *obsecro* (beseech, entreat), *supplico* (pray humbly, supplicate), *deprecor* (plead against, intercede), and *clamo* (call, cry out). All of these represent various shades of petitioning. *Oro* is in some ways the most interesting, in that its semantic range includes both religious petition and legal/political arguments.[29] It emphasizes the formal, public nature of the speech. *Oratio*, the noun, and the most common word for prayer, means speech, language, and, in particular, formal language, speeches,[30] before ecclesiastical Latin adopts it as the common word for prayer. Thus, Latin emphasizes the formality of the language. Indeed, Roman pagan prayers were quite formal and set, with greater emphasis on ritual words and gestures than on prayer as an expression of the petitioner's personality or feeling.[31]

Insofar as *oratio* replaces sacrifice, as Tertullian stated, it could be that the formal nature of the utterance – either taken as its rhetorical beauty, or the way it correctly follows ritual procedure – allows prayer to function as a gift (*votum*, in this case) to God. Certainly, Tertullian believes that prayer should be "de toto corde devotam"[32] (devoted from the whole heart). Yet Tertullian embeds devotion (*devoveo*, to vow, offer) within a discussion on correct ritual form: the preceding chapters consider things like washing the hands before prayer, postures for prayer, whether virgins should wear veils, and when to respond to prayer with "alleluia." Thus, Tertullian does not clearly specify what exactly it is that makes prayer function as a gift or sacrifice, and, in fact, a variety of authors could quote Tertullian's point verbatim yet all mean different things.

29 See Lewis and Short, s.v. *oro*, sense II.A: "to argue, to treat, to plead." Alois Walde and J.B. Hofmann, *Lateinisches etymologisches Wörterbuch*, vol. 2 (Heidelberg: Carl Winter, 1954), give the earliest written use of *oro* in the *Duodecim Tabulae*.

30 As opposed to *sermo*, which is ordinary speech, see sense II.

31 Rüpke, *Religion of the Romans*, 68. The same understanding is clearly reflected in Tertullian.

32 Tertullian, *De oratione*, cap. 28, l. 11; trans. Evans.

While Old English does not have a specific verb that means only "to pray," the most common verb for prayer is *biddan*, to petition or ask, a word used in both secular and religious contexts. Thus, while in all three languages prayer asks for good things from God, in Greek prayers are promises; in Latin, speeches; in Old English, requests. *Biddan* is narrower than Modern English "prayer" in that it means petition alone (rather than including any wider idea of discourse with God), and broader in that it covers both secular and religious petitions. Furthermore, while *halsian* is sometimes used for prayer (in collocation with *biddan*), Ælfric never uses it for speech directed towards God, probably because *halsian* has a stronger binding force (e.g., "Ic halsige ðe þurh ðone lifiendan God" [I adjure you through the living God])[33] associated with exorcism and conjuration. Old English has further verbs used for address to God; *clipian* (to cry out) is the most common of these. People cry out to God for help or for favour; thus it still operates within the petitionary context. The Old English vocabulary for prayer places it squarely within practices and expectations of petition and the reciprocal economy petition invokes.

Traditional Teaching on Prayer

Three Traditions

Early Christian praxis and teaching on prayer give context to the Anglo-Saxon texts that adopt and adapt this same tradition. Yet these earlier works often presuppose different practices of prayer than that of Anglo-Saxon England, as well as different understandings of how prayer works and what its goals are. This section looks at the different milieux that produced teaching on prayer by first situating the tradition of Christian teaching within its social and institutional context, and then examining teachings on the central prayer for both public and private worship, the Paternoster, and in commentary on additional key biblical passages that present a basic theory of prayer. Teaching on prayer differs according to whether that

33 This is an example BT gives of the way it is used in conjuring/exorcism situations (trans. of Mt. 26:63). That is, *halsian* appeals to some power outside the speaker for its binding force.

prayer is private (i.e., at home),[34] monastic, or congregational. Early prayer practices inform study of the early liturgy, which was multifaceted, complex, and poorly documented,[35] as well as studies of "spirituality" more generally. As this project is not intended as a liturgical study, what follows is a necessarily brief summary, focusing only on those considerations that bear immediately on the early Christian understanding of prayer.

Through the late antique and early medieval period, prayer at set hours became increasingly professionalized. In the early church all Christians were expected to pray the Paternoster (also known in English as the Our Father or Lord's Prayer) three to seven times a day, depending on time and place,[36] and to assemble together for morning prayer. Regular attendance at church and weekly participation in the Eucharist was also expected of

34 "Private" prayer can mean different things depending on time and place. Michael S. Driscoll notes that the distinction between texts intended for liturgical versus private prayer is anachronistic, "The *Precum libelli* and Carolingian Spirituality," in *Proceedings of the North American Academy of Liturgy Annual Meeting* (Valparaiso, IN, 1990), 70. Kate Heulwen Thomas also notes the difficulty of identifying texts intended for private prayer, as the relationship between prayers intended for public or private use tends to be cyclic, "The Meaning, Practice and Context of Private Prayer in Late Anglo-Saxon England" (PhD diss., University of York, 2011), 16. Thomas uses "'private prayer' to refer to prayer that is undertaken without the involvement of another human being. This may or may not take place in solitude," 22. Indeed, Thomas observes that even prayer that does take place in solitude might be imagined as a part of communal prayer, as when a travelling monk observes the hours away from his monastery, while the *Regularis Concordia* makes explicit space for prayer for personal benefit within communal practice, 84. Many early authors do not make a clear distinction between prayers prayed alone and prayers prayed communally. In one respect, the question is a matter of the location of the body (at home, or alone, or in church); in another respect, the question is a matter of the precator's intention and imagination.

35 For an overview of the state of the study of early Christian worship, see Paul F. Bradshaw, *The Search for the Origins of Christian Worship: Sources and Methods for the Study of Early Liturgy*, 2nd ed. (Oxford: Oxford University Press, 2002).

36 See Eric George Jay's introduction to *Origen's Treatise on Prayer* for a helpful introduction to early Christian prayer. All of the sources he examines are Greek with the exception of Tertullian. An Appendix, pp. 36–44, summarizes information about the practice of prayer from the Didache through Origen. Bradshaw comes to the conclusion that private prayer three times a day, as the Didache represents, was the oldest practice. Tertullian teaches six hours of prayer, although Origen has only three, *Search for the Origins*, 175. Praying at particular times of the day was probably adopted from Jewish practice.

all Christians.[37] Private prayer – prayer within the home – might take place with the whole household assembled, although the devout also prayed by themselves.[38] This private prayer was apparently based fundamentally on the Paternoster with potential room for additional personal intercessions.[39] With the growth of cathedral and monastic prayer in the fourth century, it becomes increasingly difficult to see what practice of prayer lay Christians were expected to observe; the written record increasingly reflects clerical and monastic rather than lay prayer.[40] Thus, there are three basic contexts for the practice of prayer: household prayer (as a household or alone); monastic prayer, based especially on the practice of the Egyptian ascetics and later based on the Benedictine and other rules (which also involved corporate and single-person prayer); and cathedral prayer, performed by priests at which laypeople might be present. As Paul F. Bradshaw points out, "The differences between the [cathedral and monastic] types of worship, however, relate not merely to the people who participated in them but to their external forms and ultimately to their spirit and purpose."[41] The early teachings on prayer reflect these different contexts and expectations. As Bradshaw differentiates,

37 Benedicta Ward, citing John Chrysostom, "Bede and the Psalter" (Jarrow Lecture, 1991), 1–2. Cyprian mentions daily participation, *De dominica oratione*, in *Opera, pars II*, ed. C. Moreschini, CCSL 3A, 101, ll. 331–3.

38 Bradshaw, *Search for the Origins*, 172. Augustine's primary teaching on prayer was in the form of a letter to a Christian noblewoman, Proba, a widow who (if she followed Augustine's advice) spent much of her time in prayer on her own and with her family, *Epistola 130, Ad Probam*, ed. Klaus Daur, CCSL 31B (Turnhout: Brepols, 2009), 212–37.

39 In the earliest Latin treatise on prayer, Tertullian says: "et sunt quae petantur pro circumstantia cuiusque, praemissa legitima et ordinaria oratione quasi fundamento, accedentium ius est desideriorum superstruendi extrinsecus petitiones, cum memoria tamen praeceptorum, ne quantum a praeceptis, tantum ab auribus dei longe simus" (and as there are things to be asked for according to each man's circumstances, we have the right, after rehearsing the prescribed and regular prayer as a foundation, to make from other sources a superstructure of petitions for additional desires: yet with mindfulness of the precepts, lest we be as far from the ears of God as we are from the precepts). *De oratione*, cap. 10, ll. 3–8; trans. Evans.

40 Throughout this book I use "lay" to mean ordinary Christians, those who were neither priests nor monastics.

41 Bradshaw, *Search for the Origins*, 173.

> The cathedral office had a strong ecclesial dimension: here was the Church gathered for prayer, exercising its royal priesthood by offering a sacrifice of praise and thanksgiving on behalf of all creation and interceding for the salvation of the world. The monastic office, on the other hand, was centred around silent meditation on the word of God and supplication for spiritual growth and personal salvation. Its ultimate aim was spiritual formation.[42]

In the main, the cathedral type of prayer, eventually focused on the Eucharist and its model of reciprocal gift giving between humans and God,[43] is especially infused with the structure of gift giving, whereas monastic prayer, reflecting a more abstract conception of God, emphasized knowledge, an idea of purity related to the Greek concept of *apatheia*, and contemplative practice.

As an example, we can see the different emphases reflected in both Origen's and Cassian's commentary on I Timothy 2:1 (briefly mentioned above). Origen explains the four types of prayer:

> Now I consider that "supplication" [*deësis*] is the prayer of a man who lacks something, sent up with entreaty for the obtaining of it; "prayer" [*proseuche*] is that sent up with greater magnanimity by a man for greater gifts and accompanied by words of praise; "intercession" [*enteuxis*] is a request to God on behalf of certain persons made by one who has a greater boldness; and "giving thanks" [*eucharistia*] is an acknowledgement with prayer upon receiving good things from God, when the acknowledgement of the greatness, or what seems greatness in the eyes of him who has received it, of the kindness conferred upon him is received by God in exchange.[44]

Origen, whose treatise also contains a chapter explaining the Septuagint's use of *euche* to mean "vow" (the vow one makes to God in exchange for some favour), explicates the four types of prayer in such a way that prayer centres on petition and reciprocity. As a teacher rather than a contemplative, Origen addresses his work to two laypeople: Ambrosius, a wealthy

42 Bradshaw, *Search for the Origins*, 174.

43 See Arnold Angenendt, "*Donationes pro anima:* Gift and Countergift in the Early Medieval Liturgy," in *The Long Morning of Medieval Europe: New Directions in Early Medieval Studies*, ed. Jennifer R. Davis and Michael McCormick (Aldershot: Ashgate, 2008).

44 Origen, *Origen's Treatise*, 14.2, p. 122.

man, and Tatiana, his wife or his sister. They were devout but not eremitic (although Tatiana had apparently taken a vow of chastity), and had asked for instruction in prayer.[45] In imagining prayer as embedded in reciprocity and including ethical behaviour, Origen concretizes the relationship between humans and God in a way suitable for laypeople who are devout, not mystical.

Cassian, for his part, defines the four types of prayer as follows (following the passage from I Timothy, quoted above):

> [O]bsecratio inploratio est seu petitio pro peccatis, qua uel pro praesentibus uel praeteritis admissis suis unusquisque conpunctus ueniam deprecatur[46] ... Orationes sunt quibus aliquid offerimus seu uouemus deo, quod Graece dicitur εὐχή, id est uotum[47] ... Tertio loco ponuntur postulationes, quas pro aliis quoque, dum sumus in feruore spiritus constituti, solemus emittere, uel pro caris scilicet nostris uel pro totius mundi pace poscentes ...[48] Quarto deinde loco gratiarum actiones ponuntur, quas mens, uel cum praeterita dei recolit beneficia uel cum praesentia contemplatur, seu cum in futurum quae et quanta praeparauerit deus his qui diligunt eum prospicit, per ineffabiles excessus domino refert.[49]

> (A supplication is an imploring or a petition concerning sins, by which a person who has been struck by compunction begs for pardon for his present or past misdeeds ... Prayers are those acts by which we offer or vow something to God, which is called *euche* in Greek – that is, a vow ... In the third place there are intercessions, which we are also accustomed to make for others when our spirits are fervent, beseeching on behalf of our dear ones and for the peace of the whole world ... Finally, in the fourth place there are thanksgivings, which the mind, whether recalling God's past benefits, contemplating his present ones, or foreseeing what great things God has prepared for those who love him, offers to the Lord in unspeakable ecstasies.)

45 Origen, *Origen's Treatise*, p. 81, nn. 1 and 2.
46 Cassian, *Conlatio* 9, CSEL 13, 261, 11, ll. 4–6; trans. Ramsey.
47 Cassian, *Conlatio* 9, CSEL 13, 261, 12, ll. 7–8; trans. Ramsey.
48 Cassian, *Conlatio* 9, CSEL 13, 262, 13, ll. 6–9; trans. Ramsey.
49 Cassian, *Conlatio* 9, CSEL 13, 262, 14, ll. 12–16; trans. Ramsey.

Although the Greek tradition informs Cassian's explication, his work reflects the eremitic milieu of Egypt and Syria, where he travelled to learn from the hermits. This passage shows both how stable the teachings on prayer can be (some two hundred years separate him from Origen, who seems unlikely to be a direct source) and how writers can shift the focus of their commentary while staying within the same basic structure. Thus, while all the terminology still has to do with petition, Cassian narrows the definition of "supplication" to begging pardon for sin, and the final definition, although it makes return ("refert") to God, also looks forward to the great things that await, especially after death. His commentary clearly reflects the more narrowly monastic concerns of cleansing from sin and experience of the presence of God.

Just as it becomes difficult to say much about lay private prayer, the cathedral and monastic offices begin to influence each other as monks begin to be ordained and become involved in administering the cathedral sacraments, especially the Mass.[50] As a result, the two orientations of gift giving and purity influence each other. In addition, the development of penitential practices adds another way of thinking about and enacting the person's relationship with God and the spiritual community. Penance and prayers *pro anima* (for the souls of the dead) increasingly take on the social forms of gift giving when penitents give land, money, or other donations to monasteries in exchange for prayers and masses on their behalf. Penitential practice as developed by the Irish and then taken to the Continent encourages the counting of prayers through the practice of tariffed penances and commutations.[51] These developments continue throughout the Anglo-Saxon period, although most of the historical documentation comes from Carolingian France. While some of the occasions for Anglo-Saxon teaching on prayer are penitential, occurring during Lent, none of them address performing penance specifically.

---

50 Bradshaw, *Search for the Origins*, 173–4. In the late Anglo-Saxon Benedictine reform the cathedrals were monasticized, blending monastic and cathedral prayer yet further. Monks also began taking on the duty of saying masses for the dead. See Angenendt, "*Donationes pro anima*," for developments in Francia.

51 Arnold Angenendt et al., "Counting Piety in the Early and High Middle Ages," in *Ordering Medieval Society: Perspectives on Intellectual and Practical Modes of Shaping Social Relations*, ed. Bernhard Jussen, trans. Pamela Selwyn (Philadelphia: University of Pennsylvania Press, 2001).

The Paternoster

Four major treatises on prayer exist from the period preceding the Anglo-Saxon era.[52] Literal line-by-line explication of the Paternoster constitutes a fundamental part of teaching on prayer. The Paternoster itself makes for somewhat laconic instruction on prayer. It appears twice in the Gospels, Matthew 6:9–13 (the longer version of the prayer) and Luke 11:2–4, where it responds to Jesus's disciples' request that he teach them how to pray.[53] In both cases, the central instruction consists of what words to say. To this, Luke adds two parables, one on persistence in asking and the other assuring that God gives good gifts to those who ask him. The context in Matthew 6, where the prayer is part of the Sermon on the Mount, precedes it with two instructions: pray secretly and pray in few words. After the prayer, Jesus gives further instruction on forgiving others' offences and on fasting.

In each treatise the core of traditional exegesis is remarkably stable; however, it can be contextualized within each particular author's concerns and interests and audience. The earliest in any language is Tertullian's *De oratione*, written around the turn of the third century. It was probably originally a homily addressed to catechumens and then expanded. Tertullian particularly focuses on explicating the "novam orationis formam"[54] (new plan of prayer) established by Jesus. Particularly distinctive to Tertullian's work is his emphasis on the ritual performance of prayer, such as the washing of hands, correct posture, and appropriate clothing. Origen's *On Prayer* (*Peri euches*), ca. 232–5, is the earliest treatise in Greek. Origen's treatise considers prayer more broadly; the explication of the Paternoster

---

52 For a summary list of early Western writings on the Paternoster, see Karlfried Froehlich, "The Lord's Prayer in Patristic Literature," in *A History of Prayer*, ed. Roy Hammerling (Leiden: Brill, 2008). For a more complete treatment, see K.B. Schnurr, *Hören und Handeln* (Freiburg: Herder, 1985). Also in *A History of Prayer*, see Roy Hammerling, "The Lord's Prayer: A Cornerstone of Early Baptismal Education"; and "The Lord's Prayer in Early Christian Polemics in the Eighth Century."

53 The prayer from Matthew: "Pater *noster qui in caelis es* sanctificetur nomen tuum veniat regnum tuum *fiat voluntas tua sicut in caelo et in terra* panem nostrum supersubstantialem (Lk.: cotidianum) da nobis hodie et dimitte nobis debita (Lk.: peccata) nostra sicut et nos dimisimus debitoribus nostris et ne inducas nos in temptationem *sed libera nos a malo.*" Italicized phrases are not found in the version in Luke, which also has other minor differences in wording.

54 Tertullian, *De oratione*, cap. 1, l. 3; trans. Evans.

takes up about a third of his treatise.[55] His methodology tends towards the philological (as we would call it); he often defines keywords in order to explicate the meaning of passages and he usually gives examples from the Old Testament to support his claims, all of which make his treatise more obviously scholarly and much longer than the rest. While Origen does not neglect ritual performance, he spends much more space considering the nature of God and humans in strongly philosophical terms that clearly speak to the intellectual milieu of Alexandria, where he wrote it.[56]

Tertullian and Origen's treatises are independent of each other; however, in his own *De dominica oratione* (ca. 250), Cyprian freely adapts Tertullian,[57] and John Cassian's *Conlationes* 9 and 10 (ca. 420) has elements in common with Origen because of the eastern milieu. Like Tertullian, Cyprian directed his treatise towards the training of catechumens; however, as a bishop, Cyprian is more carefully pastoral than Tertullian. His adaptation pays more balanced attention to the disposition of the body, the mind, and the words one says. As the only one directed towards a monastic audience, Cassian's is unusual among the four treatises. Like Origen, Cassian addresses the topic of prayer more generally; however, he also describes the interior discipline of prayer in a way none of the other authors does. Cassian also discusses the use of the Psalms, which formed the core of monastic prayer and increasingly became central to lay piety through the Carolingian reforms.

While Augustine's *oeuvre* abounds with discussion of prayer, he never wrote a treatise on the subject.[58] The closest to one is his *Epistula 130*

55 The Didache, Hippolytus's *Apostolic Tradition*, and passages from Clement of Alexandria's *Stromata* all contain teaching about prayer, but Origen's is the first systematic treatment of the topic in Greek. Greek teaching has little influence in Anglo-Saxon England, and so I do not fully account for it here. Origen's treatise is interesting by way of contrast and also because it represents the Greek tradition that influences Cassian. Bede's teaching also contains some vague echoes of Origen. Some of Origen's homilies were known in Anglo-Saxon England, but there is no evidence that they knew the treatise on prayer. See "Origen" in the index to Helmut Gneuss and Michael Lapidge, *Anglo-Saxon Manuscripts* (Toronto: University of Toronto Press, 2014).

56 Because Neoplatonism strongly informs Origen's thinking, his work is often situated in the "grand narrative" of mysticism.

57 *De dominica oratione*, CCSL 3A, 87–113.

58 In the 1960s Thomas A. Hand took it upon himself to remedy Augustine's failure in never writing a full treatise on prayer: "Strange as it may seem, [Augustine] never wrote what could be called a Treatise on Prayer … During the past few years I have culled more than five hundred texts relevant to Prayer from the writings of Augustine and

addressed to a widowed noblewoman named Proba, in which he explains the basics of Christian prayer, including the briefest of the discussions of the Paternoster. His *Enarrationes in psalmos* also contains much that might be called a "theory" of prayer,[59] and his homilies on the prayer become the standard that later homilists such as Caesarius of Arles and Hrabanus Maurus adapt. Perhaps partially because of Augustine's influence and partially because of the constraints of the genre, homiletic teaching on the Paternoster shows much less variation in its focus and explication. Almost wholly concerned with line-by-line explication, it gives very little additional information. Commentaries, such as those by Ambrose (a commentary on the sacraments), Jerome, and Bede (commentaries on Matthew and Luke respectively),[60] include brief line-by-line explications of the prayer in the same tradition as the homilies but usually with even less detail.[61] Monastic *regulae* represent the other major source for instruction on

---

have endeavoured to fit them into his own doctrinal background … I have made him speak for himself and, consequently, feel justified in calling the work 'Saint Augustine on Prayer,'" *St. Augustine on Prayer* (Westminster, MD: Newman, 1963), x. Hand's book is essentially a mash-up of everything Augustine ever said on prayer, although Hand does not consider historical differences in the understanding of prayer as he chooses what to include.

59 *Enarrationes in psalmos, LI–C*, ed. D.E. Dekkers and J. Fraipont, CCSL 39 (Turnhout: Brepols, 1956). Augustine has four explications of the Paternoster extant (counting all the sermons as one): in his commentary on *De sermone Domini in monte*, ed. Almut Mutzenbecher, CCSL 35 (Turnhout: Brepols, 1967), 106–30; four catechetical sermons on the prayer, numbers 56–9, *Sermones in Matthaeum*, ed. P.-P. Verbraken et al., CCSL 41Aa (Turnhout: Brepols, 2008); in his anti-Pelagian text *De dono perseverantiae*, PL 45, cols. 993–1034; and in his *Epistola 130, Ad Probam*, CCSL 31B, 212–37. Augustine's explication in *De dono perseverantiae* uses Cyprian's treatise to argue that the Catholic Church's historical understanding is that perseverance is a gift from God; thus, he interprets every petition except the fifth as a petition for perseverance.

60 Jerome, *Commentariorum in Matheum*, ed. D. Hurst and M. Adriaen, CCSL 77 (Turnhout: Brepols, 1967), 36–7, ll. 753–89. Bede, *In Lucae evangelium expositio*, ed. D. Hurst, CCSL 120 (Turnhout: Brepols, 2001), 227–8; the commentary on Matthew that goes by his name (and includes a line-by-line explication) is pseudonymous. See George Brown, *A Companion to Bede* (Woodbridge: Boydell, 2009) for a list and discussion of Bede's works.

61 Although Froehlich mentions that "it is hard to find any author who does not remark upon, or at least allude to, these few biblical verses [of the Paternoster]," "The Lord's Prayer," 59, most of this commentary is not systematic, and very little of it includes details about actually praying, either from a practical or theoretical standpoint. The more fruitful place to look for early literature that theorizes prayer is in the Greek tradition. The Greek texts on prayer – from people like Clement, Evagrius, and Origen – were not tremendously influential in the west, except through Cassian.

prayer. The most famous is Benedict's, written in the mid-500s. However, these give practical information on performing prayer, which includes organization of the Psalms for the Divine Office, while taking for granted the reasons for performing prayer.

Thus, most explicit teaching on prayer takes the form of literal explication of the central prayer text, the Paternoster. Most of it addresses laypeople or catechumens more specifically, although the early teachings on prayer assume more frequent and consistent lay performance of prayer and church attendance than was standard in the Anglo-Saxon era.[62] Explications of the Paternoster explain right doctrine, show concern that precators not fall into error by diminishing God's power or agency, and they often guide towards right moral orientation. They are not usually concerned with a psychology of prayer, nor do they explain it as interior mental discipline. However, the treatises regularly bookend the explication of the prayer with further instruction, some of which the homiletic genre also reflects.

The Paternoster begins with an invocation followed by seven petitions. The first three petitions all address God: that his name be hallowed, his kingdom come, and his will be done. The overall thrust of the explication of these petitions clarifies that humans are not praying for God's benefit, as though God needs human hallowing to make him holy, or as though God's will cannot be carried out without human prayer. Precators pray that these things will be brought about in themselves and in all people. The petitions thus turn back on precators (in some authors more strongly than others), reminding them to keep God's name holy and to act according to God's will. The last four petitions all ask for benefits for the precator: that God would give bread, forgive sins, not lead into temptation, and deliver from evil. Explicators interpret the request for "daily bread"[63] in two

62 Bede states the ideal that the faithful should hear Mass and receive communion on Sundays and major feast days; however, the requirements for participation in communion were strict enough that frequent communication seems unlikely to have been attained. See Alan Thacker, "Monks, Preaching, and Pastoral Care in Early Anglo-Saxon England," in *Pastoral Care before the Parish*, ed., John Blair and Richard Sharpe (Leicester: Leicester University Press, 1992), 154–5. The Fourth Lateran Council of 1215 mandates that laypeople should confess (and thus, presumably, participate in communion) yearly, a much lower standard than Bede advocates.

63 Matthew uses a *hapax legomenon*, *epiousion*, which translates to Latin as "supersubstantialem" and to English as "daily." Origen and Cassian both remark on the strangeness of the word and interpret it to indicate that the prayer asks for Christ as bread. Neither of them interprets the clause to mean that Christians should ask for temporal goods.

ways. The first interpretation instructs Christians to pray for their temporal needs, but just a sufficiency and just for today – that is, Christians should not pray to get rich or for excessive physical comfort but only to have their basic needs met.[64] The second interpretation gets more emphasis: Christ is understood to be the bread of life, and by requesting daily bread, precators request to be continually found in Christ. In addition, Augustine and Cyprian make explicit connection between Christ as bread and the Eucharist.[65]

For "Forgive us our debts as we forgive our debtors," Augustine states the basic principle most concisely: "nos admonemus, et quid petamus, et quid faciamus, ut accipere mereamur"[66] (we remind ourselves of both what we should ask for, and what we should do in order that we may merit to receive it). However, the commentators develop this basic idea in a variety of ways. Tertullian distinctively contextualizes the petition within legal concepts of judgment and restitution: wrongdoing "iudicio debeatur et ab eo exigatur ... nisi donetur exactio"[67] (owes a debt to judgment and is avenged by it ... unless restitution be remitted). As the author of *De paenitentia* (*On Penitence*), Tertullian influenced the development of early penitential doctrine.[68] Cyprian says that we cannot receive forgiveness without giving it.[69] Cassian, who places more emphasis on human ability, says that forgiving our debtors gives Christians power, in a way, to moderate their own sentence because God will be more merciful to those who have showed mercy.[70] In all cases, the authors show a strong sense of reciprocal justice or morality, although they sometimes emphasize the necessity to give to others what we seek from God[71] and sometimes the necessity of paying back what we owe to God.[72]

---

64 Augustine gives more latitude than the others, saying that people can desire health, honour, and power if they desire them in order to care for their dependents, *Ad Probam*, CCSL 31B, 220–1, 12. However, he also states that everything prayed for should be done to the end that "contemplemur domini delectationem in aeternum" (we may contemplate the joy of the Lord forever), *Ad Probam*, CCSL 31B, 233, 27.

65 *Ad Probam*, CCSL 31B, 227–8, 21; *De dominica oratione*, CCSL 3A, 101, 18.

66 *Ad Probam*, CCSL 31B, 228, 21; trans. Roland Teske, WSA II/2, 194.

67 Tertullian, *De oratione*, cap. 7, ll. 8–9; trans. Evans.

68 *De paenitentia*, ed. J.G. Ph. Borleffs, CCSL 1 (Turnhout: Brepols, 1954), 319-40.

69 Cyprian, *De dominica oratione*, CCSL 3A, 104–5, 23.

70 Cassian, *Conlatio* 9, CSEL 13, 270, 22, ll. 4–15.

71 Augustine, *Ad Probam*, CCSL 31B, 228, 21, ll. 393–5.

72 For Tertullian the debt is caused by trespass, as quoted above. For Origen, to live is to incur debts to God and humans, and those debts must be paid. See *Origen's Treatise*, 28.1–5.

In the penultimate petition Tertullian sees it necessary to clarify that God does not tempt humans.[73] The other Fathers interpret the phrase to mean that God sometimes allows the adversary to tempt humans. When this happens, temptation either punishes or proves character; they often invoke the example of Job.[74] Cassian adds that this petition is made so that God does not allow the precators to be overwhelmed when they fall into temptation.[75] The final petition, deliverance from evil, is sometimes taken as a petition to be delivered from the evil *one*, the devil.[76] They always treat it only briefly, as it is seen either as a restatement of the previous clause or as a summary of the rest of the prayer.

In sum: explications of the Paternoster do not treat it as a means for precators to bend God to their will, but as a reminder of their obligation – what they pray for should have effect in them and should make a real difference in their own actions and disposition. God does not need human prayer to carry out his own will. Rather, praying the Paternoster trains Christians in what it means to call God "father." Like a father, God will provide; however, most of the teachings deemphasize the material benefits implied by "daily bread," and promise only that God will protect the petitioner from ultimate destruction by the devil. Thus, humans cannot obligate God to act by praying the prayer; the teaching preserves God's agency by reminding precators of their obligation.[77]

Other Biblical Passages

Teaching on prayer centres on the Paternoster; however, other biblical passages also present issues often addressed in teaching. When added to explications of the Paternoster, these flesh out the basic theory of prayer presented in teaching contexts. One can find (usually brief) comments on

73 Tertullian, *De oratione*, cap. 8, ll. 4–6; trans. Evans.

74 As Cyprian says, *De dominica oratione*, CCSL 3A, 106, 25, as well as Cassian, *Conlatio* 9, CSEL 13, 271, 23, l. 24.

75 Cassian, *Conlatio* 9, CSEL 13, 271, 23, ll. 22–3.

76 Cassian, for example, *Conlatio* 9, CSEL 13, 272, 23, ll. 1–4.

77 As the Paternoster's use in charms attests, early teaching on the prayer does not give the full story as to its use. This issue will be considered further when we examine Ælfric's teaching on the Paternoster in chapter 4.

key New Testament passages in commentaries or sermons.[78] The biblical passages lead to certain theoretical issues regarding prayer that many early teachers comment on at one point or another. These are:

1. Prayer should be "secret" and brief. None of the commentators takes secrecy to mean that people should prefer prayer while alone, as they all assume corporate prayer is the central expression of Christian prayer. In fact, none of them makes much differentiation between prayer alone or within community.[79] Rather, they interpret the passage, Matthew 6:6–7, to mean that prayer takes place in the "heart." By this Tertullian and Cyprian mean that God sees everything and is everywhere present, even in the most private of places, and that prayer should be offered in a modest and restrained way, even in silence.[80] For Origen, the mind is the place where God dwells.[81] Cassian does not fully follow him in this; for him, praying from the heart means drawing the heart away from "omnium cogitationum siue sollicitudinum strepitu"[82] (the clatter of every thought and concern) and praying silently, so as not to disturb one's brethren and to avoid revealing our intentions to "inimicos nostros, qui orantibus nobis maxime

78 There are repeated assurances, both explicit and through parables, that those who ask will be heard and will receive (Matthew 7, 21:22; Mark 11:24–5; Luke 11:9; John 11:22, 14:13–14, 15:7, 15:16, 16:23–4; Philippians 4:6; James 1:5–6, specifically in asking for wisdom, 4:2–3; I John 3:22, 5:14–15). Some of these passages (e.g., Mark 11:24–5) emphasize belief as a condition of being heard; the passages in John add the additional detail of asking in Jesus's name. And some tie answered prayer to obedience (I John 3:22) or forgiveness of enemies (Mark 11:24–5). There are additional parables or examples given to model desirable behaviours in prayer (such as the exemplary figures of the Pharisee and the publican in Luke 18:10ff). Furthermore, Christians are to "pray without ceasing" (I Thessalonians 5:17), pray everywhere (I Timothy 2:8), pray for their enemies (Matthew 5:44, Luke 6:28), and, when they do not know how to pray, the Holy Spirit will intercede for them (Romans 8:26). Finally, the list of "supplications, prayers, intercessions, and giving of thanks" that are to be "made for all men" (I Timothy 2:1) are often used to classify different types of prayers (e.g., Cassian, *Conlatio* 9, CSEL 13, 259–64, 915).

79 Cyprian uses the plural pronoun of the Paternoster, *our* Father, to teach: "Publica est nobis et communis oratio, et quando oramus, non pro uno sed pro populo toto rogamus," (Our prayer is public and common; and when we pray, we pray not for one, but for the whole people"), *De dominica oratione*, CCSL 3A, 93, ll. 106-8; trans. Ernest Wallis, "On the Lord's Prayer," ANF 5, 119, 8.

80 Tertullian, *De oratione*, 1, ll. 22–7; Cyprian, *De dominica oratione*, CCSL 3A, 91–2, 4–5.

81 Origen, *Origen's Treatise*, 22.2.

82 Cassian, *Conlatio* 9, CSEL 13, 282, 35, l. 26; trans. Ramsey.

insidiantur"[83] (our enemies, who plot against us greatly as we pray). By "enemies" Cassian means the devils who feature prominently in the accounts of the Egyptian ascetics. "Brief" prayer means, as Augustine says, without a superfluity of words.[84] In no case does this mean that Christians should avoid prolonged prayer when the spirit so leads them. For both Origen and Cassian brevity also means care that the mind does not wander to "corrupt thoughts,"[85] which, for Cassian, devils implant.[86]

2. Brevity in prayer is in some tension with the command to pray without ceasing.[87] How to do this inspires the greatest diversity in answers. For instance, some understood the command to mean praying *continually*; the development of the Divine Office responded to this understanding, as did the earlier lay practice of praying the Paternoster at set times during the day.[88] The Egyptian ascetics Cassian studied often understood the command to mean praying *continuously*. The expectation was that the ascetics literally prayed, usually by reciting the Psalms, every waking moment, while reducing the hours of sleep to the bare minimum.[89] However, Cassian also says that precators reach the state of ceaseless prayer when the mind has been "ab omnium carnalium passionum nexibus absoluta, et illi uni summoque bono tenacissima adhaeserit cordis intentio"[90] (freed from the bonds of every fleshly passion, and the heart's attention is unwaveringly fastened upon the one and highest good). As a result, for the thoughts of the pure mind, "quidquid in se receperit, quidquid tractauerit, quidquid egerit, purissima ac sincerissima erit oratio"[91] (whatever they

83 Cassian, *Conlatio* 9, CSEL 13, 283, 35, ll. 8–9; trans. Ramsey.

84 *Ad Probam*, CCSL 31B, 227, 20, ll. 367–71.

85 Origen, *Origen's Treatise*, 21.1.

86 Cassian, *Conlatio* 9, CSEL 13, 283, 36, ll. 12–14.

87 I Thessalonians 5:17.

88 Cyprian, *De dominica oratione*, CCSL 3A, 111–13, 34–6.

89 "Omnis monachi finis cordisque perfectio ad iugem atque indisruptam orationis perseuerantiam tendit" (The whole purpose of the monk and perfection of his heart tends toward continual and uninterrupted perseverance in prayer), Cassian, *Conlatio* 9, CSEL 13, 250, 2, ll. 19–20; trans. Ramsey. Note that perseverance in prayer is not the same thing as prayer, however. The goal is toward "perfection": "ut eo usque extenuata mens ab omni situ carnali ad spiritalia cotidie sublimetur, donec omnis eius conuersatio, omnis uolutatio cordis una et iugis efficiatur oratio" (so that every day the mind, purged from all carnal desires, may be lifted towards spiritual things, until its whole life and the heart's every thought are made one continuous prayer), Cassian, *Conlatio* 10, CSEL 13, 294–5, 7, ll. 28–30; trans. Ramsey.

90 Cassian, *Conlatio* 9, CSEL 13, 257, 4, ll. 18–20; trans. Ramsey.

91 Cassian, *Conlatio* 9, CSEL 13, 257, 4, ll. 25–6; trans. Ramsey.

take in, whatever they reflect upon, and whatever they do will be most pure and sincere prayer). Augustine's solution follows in this same vein: ceaseless desire for the heavenly kingdom constitutes ceaseless prayer.[92] But he also gestures in the direction of action: "Et cuius lingua durat meditari tota die laudem Dei? … Quidquid egeris, bene age, et laudasti Deum"[93] (But whose tongue could bear to practice the praise of God all day long? … Whatever you do, do it well and you have praised God). Bede finds a similar solution: all the actions of a just man constitute ceaseless prayer.[94]

3. Similarly, why does God command people to persevere in prayer?[95] A related question: if God knows what we need before we ask it and is well-disposed towards us, why pray? The latter question tends to come up within the works of more philosophically oriented teachers. Thus, Origen first addresses the question as a response to the more esoteric philosophical Greek ideas concerning prayer.[96] Augustine also addresses the question both in his Sermon 80.2[97] and in his commentary on the Sermon on the Mount. In the commentary, the reason he gives is that "ipsa orationis intentio cor nostrum serenat et purgat capaciusque efficit ad excipienda

---

92 "Numquid sine intermissione genu flectimus, corpus prosternimus, aut manus leuamus, ut dicat: *Sine intermissione orate*? Aut si sic dicimus nos orare, hoc puto sine intermissione non possumus facere. Est alia interior sine intermissione oratio, quae est desiderium. Quidquid aliud agas, si desideras illud sabbatum, non intermittis orare. Si non uis intermittere orare, noli intermittere desiderare" (But can we bend the knee without ceasing, prostrate the body, or raise the hands, as he says, Pray without ceasing? If we say these are prayer, I think we are unable to do it without ceasing. But there is another kind of interior prayer without ceasing, which is desire. Whatever else you do, if you desire that sabbath, you will not cease to pray. If you do not wish your prayer to cease, do not let your desire cease). Enarratio in psalmum 37.14, *Enarrationes in psalmos I–L*, ed. D.E. Dekkers and J. Fraipont, CCSL 38, ll. 8–14; translation is my own.

93 In psalmum 37, sermo 2.16, ll. 5–6, 9.

94 "… omnia quae iustus secundum Deum gerit et dicit ad orationem esse reputanda" (everything that the just man does and says according to the will of God ought to be counted as prayer), *In Lucae* 5, CCSL 120, 322, ll. 1056–8.

95 In passages such as Luke 11:8–9, "Dico vobis et si non dabit illi surgens eo quod amicus eius sit propter inprobitatem tamen eius surget et dabit illi quotquot habet necessarios et ego vobis dico petite et dabitur vobis quaerite et invenietis pulsate et aperietur vobis" (Yet if he shall continue knocking, I say to you, although he will not rise and give him, because he is his friend; yet, because of his importunity, he will rise, and give him as many as he needeth. And I say to you, Ask, and it shall be given you: seek, and you shall find: knock, and it shall be opened to you).

96 Origen, *Origen's Treatise*, 5.2.

97 PL 38, col. 493–8.

diuina munera … Fit ergo in oratione conuersio cordis ad eum"[98] (the effort itself of prayer calms and cleanses our heart and makes room for receiving the divine gifts … Thus, prayer causes a turning of the heart to him). Indeed, one of Augustine's central concerns in his explication of the Paternoster is that precators not think that it is prayer "quibus dominum seu docendum seu flectendum esse credamus"[99] (by which we believe that we should either instruct or persuade the Lord), as though prayer can compel God to act, or that he needs to be informed of human need. Thus, the usual answer to the question is Augustine's: that precators pray to increase their own desire for that which they pray.

4. But what should Christians pray for? While all commentators prefer asking for spiritual above material benefits, they differ in the relative asceticism of their answers. For Augustine, prayer increases desire for the eternal good of heaven; however, he also concedes that people may pray for things like social position if the thing prayed for helps precators provide for their dependents.[100] On the other end of the spectrum, Cassian never once considers that the fourth petition in the Paternoster (for daily bread) could refer to literal bread,[101] while Tertullian allows people to add their own specific additional requests at the end of the Paternoster.[102]

5. When Jesus said, "Si quid petieritis me in nomine meo hoc faciam"[103] (If you ask anything in my name I will do it), what are the practical limits on this? The many, many promises in the New Testament of God's generous response to prayer seem to open up the dangerously naive possibility that prayer might work like a magic genie, an idea that puts human will at the centre of prayer and a promise that would not be born out in real-life experience and thus could both lead to presumption and damage faith. Gregory sets the standard response: "Sed quia nomen Filii Iesus est, Iesus autem Saluator uel etiam salutaris dicitur, ille ergo in nomine Saluatoris petit, qui illud petit quod ad ueram salutem pertinet"[104] (But because … the name of the Son is Jesus, and Jesus means saviour or saving, he asks

98 Augustine, *De sermone Domini in monte*, ed. Almut Muntzenbecher, CCSL 35 (Turnhout, Brepols, 1967), 104, ll. 283–5.

99 *Ad Probam*, CCSL 31B, 226, 21, ll. 377–8; trans. Teske, WSA II/2, 193.

100 *Ad Probam*, CCSL 31B, 12.

101 Cassian, *Conlatio* 9, CSEL 13, 267, 21.

102 Tertullian, *De oratione*, cap. 10, ll. 4–7.

103 John 14:14.

104 Homilia 27, in *Homiliae in evangelia*, ed. Raymond Étaix, CCSL 141 (Turnhout: Brepols, 1999), 234, ll. 140–2; translation is my own.

in the name of the Saviour who asks for that which pertains to true salvation). Both Bede and Ælfric have passages following Gregory's teaching.[105]

The answers to these questions have implications for the way prayer works as a total system, encompassing thoughts, words, and deeds, and having the power to transform the one praying. The answers theorize prayer in such a way as to decentre human will; in presenting prayer as a response to God, rather than God responding to prayer, they make human will follow God's. Proper prayer (what they might have called, in contrast to Heiler, "genuine" prayer) involves discipline of the mind and body and forms part of a moral framework of Christian behaviour as well as enacting a position of dependence upon God. Such an idea of prayer is just as true for the teaching addressed to laypeople as for monastics, although monastic discipline is much more stringent.

Set Prayers versus Spontaneous Prayer

But the absence of teaching on prayer is often just as striking as the teaching on prayer. For instance, while the *Regula Benedicti* establishes the hours of prayer and which psalms, prayers, and scripture readings should fill those hours, it pays only minimal attention to the theoretical issues of prayer – what it supposes prayer to accomplish or how prayer accomplishes it.[106] In Gregory's series of forty sermons not one teaches either wholly or largely on prayer; the only teaching on prayer is a short passage on praying in Jesus's name, cited above. In Augustine's hundreds of sermons, only four primarily address prayer;[107] all of these are on the Paternoster, and all of these focus on a line-by-line explication of the literal meaning

105 Bede, Homily 2.12, in *Opera homiletica*, ed. David Hurst, CCSL 122 (Turnhout: Brepols, 1955); Ælfric, Homily 35, in *Catholic Homilies: The Second Series*, ed. Malcolm Godden (London: Oxford University Press, 1979).

106 In cap. 20 Benedict speaks to reverence in prayer, likening prayer to God to prayer to a powerful man, and admonishing that it be done humbly, respectfully, with purity of heart ("puritate cordis"): "Et ideo brebis [*sic*] debet esse et pura oratio, nisi forte ex affectu inspirationis diuinae gratiae protendatur" (Prayer should therefore be short and pure, unless perhaps it is prolonged under the inspiration of divine grace), *Benedicti Regula*, ed. R. Hanslik, CSEL 75 (Vienna: Hölder-Pichler-Tempsky, 1977), 20.4; trans. Timothy Fry et al., *RB1980* (Collegeville, MN: Liturgical Press, 1981).

107 *Sermones* 56–9; some of his other sermons, such as the several on the Psalms already quoted, also have significant things to say about prayer.

rather than presenting a fuller theology of prayer. He frequently weaves the fifth petition of Paternoster (forgive us our debts as we forgive our debtors) into sermons, but his congregation must have been a vengeful lot, because he invariably uses it to preach against revenge rather than about prayer. Like Gregory, most of his sermons do not address questions of prayer at all except in passing.

Teaching on prayer often gives little indication whether people are assumed to be praying alone or in community, whether their devotions include spontaneous prayer, whether wordless prayer is a goal, or what the mind should do while praying. All of these elements have important consequences for an economic (or aneconomic) understanding of prayer – the way the give and take of the practice of prayer relates entities to each other, what exactly is given in prayer, and the interior work prayer is supposed to do. Evidence from one place and era is sometimes used to explicate evidence from another place and era, or else students of prayer fill in the gaps with intuitions shaped by their own understanding of prayer. Because Cassian gives one of the few descriptions of the interior discipline of prayer, his text is especially pressed into service. As we have seen, teaching on prayer *is* quite traditional, but we cannot assume without further consideration that a text from one place will be understood the same way when used in a new place.

For many who study prayer, prayer by oneself represents a different type of piety than communal prayer. They represent two stages of religious (and thus social) development: an earlier stage of communal and ritualistic religious practice, and a later stage that emphasizes individual interiority and moral responsibility. The two are understood to contain different ways of understanding the self: as essentially communal or as an individual.[108] However, it is often difficult or even impossible to tell whether teachers assume that their congregants will pray by themselves or communally. Even while noting how difficult it is to distinguish between "liturgical prayer" and "private devotion" (to use Geoffrey Shepherd's terms),[109] most scholars

108 Thus the growth of personal prayers, like Anselm's or the later mystics have been used to trace the roots of European individualism. See, for example, Colin Morris, *The Discovery of the Individual, 1050–1200* (New York: Harper and Row, 1972), 10–13, or Aaron Yakovlevich Gurevich, *The Origins of European Individualism* (Oxford: Blackwell, 1995), 5.

109 Geoffrey Shepherd, "English Versions of the Scriptures before Wyclif," in *Cambridge History of the Bible*, ed. Peter R. Ackroyd et al. (Cambridge: Cambridge University Press, 1969), 2:370.

preserve the basic distinction, as though the two types of prayer do different kinds of work.[110] While it is true that narrative sources, such as hagiographies, sometimes make note of where a person's body is when praying, teaching on prayer makes no such distinction – even when explicating the Gospel injunction that prayers be secret, as noted above. Within the early medieval monastic milieu, with its emphasis on interiority, all prayer is in some sense individual – that is, offered up by a person alone before God – whether that person prays with a congregation or in his own room. At the same time, single precators in any given act of prayer are imagined as joining in a community of all praying Christians, living and dead; the prayers deemphasize individual expression, and the work they perform is both universal and personal.

In addition, the sources are extremely laconic as to whether they expect unstructured or spontaneous prayer either in the communal liturgy or in private devotion. The scholarship on prayer tends to assume a central place both for private piety and for individual spontaneous[111] prayer, locating "true" prayer in the silences between the canonical hours or within the liturgical service rather than in the actual set prayers themselves and privileging wordless forms of prayer. For instance, John E. Skoglund says, "Free prayer has had a place in Christian worship from the beginning ..." but he also notes, "Following the Fourth Century in both the East and West prayers became increasingly fixed."[112] Bradshaw states the common

110 The scholarly insistence on the distinction can seem misplaced. For instance, M.J. Toswell writes of Bede's report that Augustine of Canterbury, upon landing in Kent, "immediately found a church building in which he could confirm his own personal and private Christian faith," *The Anglo-Saxon Psalter* (Turnhout: Brepols, 2014), 40, even though the passage she quotes from the *Historia* speaks of corporate worship: "In hac ergo et ipsi primo conuenire psallere orare missas facere predicare et baptizare coeperunt" (In this church they first began to meet to chant the psalms, to pray, to say mass, to preach, and to baptize), 39 (Toswell uses Colgrave and Mynors's translation of the *Historia*, 1. 25, p. 77).

111 I use this term advisedly, because every reference to spontaneous prayer that I have run across seems to rely heavily on verbal formula that can be modified as the precator wishes.

112 "Free Prayer," in *Studia Liturgica* 10 (1974): 151, 153. Theodore Klauser also supports this, documenting the "decline of the 'Prayer of the Faithful,'" as he puts it, within the liturgy. Originally a part of the Mass allowing for silent intercessory prayer prayed by the congregation, this prayer fell victim to attempts to rein in the length of the service, first by substituting in a litany (keeping the element of intercession, but losing the period of silent prayer), and eventually, under Gregory the Great, drastically curtailing this as well, *A Short History of the Western Liturgy: An Account and Some Reflections*, trans. John Halliburton (London: Oxford University Press, 1969), 47–54.

position succinctly: "It should be noted that the psalms here [recited alternating with silent prayer] were not understood as being prayer themselves – the sources often speak of prayer *and* psalmody – but as readings, as the fount of inspiration for the fount of prayer which followed each psalm."[113] The issue is more complicated than Bradshaw makes it seem. In fact, patristic authors on prayer treat the recitation of set prayers as central to the practice of prayer and make no mention of spontaneous prayer.

This is not to say people never prayed spontaneously, of course, or even to claim that they never used their own words (indeed, patristic texts contain many composed prayers). However, spontaneous, wordless prayer was not the normal practice of prayer taught, and there was no particular value for spontaneity. Furthermore, in the cases in which early authors do specifically mention wordless prayer (Augustine's ceaseless desire, mentioned above, or Cassian's "fiery prayers," discussed in more detail below), they clearly do not imagine the same thing usually meant by spontaneous or free prayer today, which is much more highly verbal and is informed by the rejection of form and liturgy brought about by Reformation-era tendencies.[114] Thus, what is given in set prayer (or what is received) is not spontaneous words as the expression of the precator's own self. The early authors do not usually imagine ritual, set prayer as a lower form leading to a higher goal of spontaneous prayer – prayer was not imagined to "work" in that way.

The Paternoster and the Psalms formed the foundations of Christian prayer. In addition, many of the commentators certainly assume the usual forms of prayer will be set prayers. Tertullian admits that "praemissa legitima et ordinaria oratione quasi fundamento, accendentium ius est desideriorum superstruendi extrinsecus petitiones ..."[115] (we have the right, after rehearsing the prescribed and regular prayer as a foundation, to make from other sources a superstructure of petitions for additional desires).

113 Bradshaw, *Search for the Origins*, 174 (italics original).

114 Spontaneous prayer gained ideological value in the Protestant Reformation when there was a very lively debate about whether set prayers or spontaneous prayer was superior. See Lori Branch, "Rejection of the Liturgy, the Rise of Free Prayer, and Modern Religious Subjectivity," in *Restoration* 29.1 (2005). In noting the importance of set prayer texts to early Christian prayer I do not mean to imply that the ideal was a mechanical reproduction of formal prayers word for word, especially as prayers diverge from biblical text. While this sort of recitation is likely in communal contexts (the Psalms), the oral experience of texts is rarely as stable as is allowed by widespread literacy and printing technologies.

115 Tertullian, *De oratione*, cap. 10, ll. 4–6; trans. Evans.

Yet he assumes that the desires will be communicated by adding petitions from other prayers. He does not seem to imagine that the "other sources" merely give the correct content for desire, since he goes on to warn: "cum memoria tamen praeceptorum, ne quantum a praeceptis tantum ab auribus dei longe simus"[116] (yet with mindfulness of the precepts, lest we be as far from the ears of God as we are from the precepts).

Cyprian is clearer:

> Amica et familiaris oratio est Deum de suo rogare, ad aures eius ascendere Christi orationem. Agnoscat pater filii sui uerba, cum precem facimus: qui habitat intus in pectore ipse sit et in uoce, et cum ipsum habeamus apud patrem aduocatum pro peccatis nostris, quando peccatores pro delictis nostris petimus, aduocati nostri uerba promamus. Nam cum dicat: Quia quodcumque petierimus a patre in nomine eius dabit nobis, quanto efficacius impetramus quod petimus Christi nomine, si petamus ipsius oratione?[117]
>
> (It is a loving and friendly prayer to beseech God with His own word, to come up to His ears in the prayer of Christ. Let the Father acknowledge the words of His Son when we make our prayer, and let Him also who dwells within in our breast Himself dwell in our voice. And since we have Him as an Advocate with the Father for our sins, let us, when as sinners we petition on behalf of our sins, put forward the words of our Advocate. For since He says, that "whatsoever we shall ask of the Father in His name, He will give us," how much more effectually do we obtain what we ask in Christ's name, if we ask for it in His own prayer!)

For Cyprian, the Paternoster has greater value as a prayer than the precator's own words (indeed, he, like Tertullian, affirms that the Paternoster contains all that a person needs to ask for),[118] because it comes from God himself. Although the Paternoster is the most valuable prayer, in this sense, Cyprian's attitude indicates a general preference for established and authoritative prayers over spontaneous prayer.

Augustine, however, repeats in multiple places that desire for God is itself prayer, even most essentially prayer. He says this in his exposition of

---

116 Tertullian, *De oratione*, cap. 10, ll. 6–7; trans. Evans.

117 Cyprian, *De dominica oratione*, CCSL 3A, 91, 3, ll. 30–8; trans. Wallis, 448, 3.

118 Cyprian, *De dominica oratione*, CCSL 3A, 107, 27.

the Psalms, quoted above, and repeats it in his letter to Proba.[119] However, in the letter he assumes a central place for verbal practice of prayer by continuing: "In ipsa ergo fide et spe et charitate continuato desiderio semper oramus"[120] (When we cherish uninterrupted desire along with the exercise of faith and hope and charity, we pray always. But at certain stated hours and seasons we also use words in prayer to God). Further on he states that prayers should be brief, noting that God does not need human words to see human need;[121] however, he then affirms: "Nobis ergo verba necessaria sunt"[122] (To us, therefore, words are necessary …), and he moves from that statement into his explication of the Paternoster. Thus, although words express the desire for God only inadequately, the practice of prayer still necessarily uses words. However, words are *not* central for Augustine because they are needed to communicate with God but because they train the desires and actions of those who pray.

However, of all the early Latin writers on prayer, Cassian garners most attention because of the way his teaching on "preces ignates" (fiery prayers) seems to fall in line with ideals of pure or genuine prayer, an aneconomic spirituality centred on individual experience.[123] In fact, although the end result might be something William James or Friedrich Heiler would be pleased to call "genuine prayer," the underlying commitments are quite different. In religious scholarship on prayer, these ideals are informed by notions of economic purity formed against market capitalism. In secular scholarship, the same ideals have been reaffirmed by the academic interest in the formation of the individual and in the preference for creativity and innovation over tradition.

In the early teaching on prayer, those teachers whose training and theology was shaped by the abstractions of Neoplatonism – to some extent Augustine and, even more strongly, Cassian and Origen – value wordlessness in prayer.[124] However, their preference is not caused by any sense

119 *Ad Probam*, CCSL 31B, 225–6, 17–18.

120 *Ad Probam*, CCSL 31B, 225, 18, ll. 327–9; trans. Teske, WSA II/2, 192.

121 *Ad Probam*, CCSL 31B, 226, 18, ll. 341–6.

122 *Ad Probam*, CCSL 31B, 227, 21, l. 376; trans. Teske, WSA II/2, 193.

123 Both DeGregorio, "Venerable Bede on Prayer," and Rachel Fulton, "Praying with Anselm at Admont," in *Speculum* 81 (2006), use Cassian to establish a sort of early medieval spirituality.

124 Origen's Alexandria was one of the centres of Neoplatonic thought in his day. In the Greek tradition the value of wordlessness and interiority is much more strongly present than in the Latin (which, like Tertullian, tends to emphasize ritual correctness). Augustine spent ten years as a Manichean.

that economic exchange specifically contaminates the spiritual. Augustine quite happily talks about purchasing divine favour with almsgiving and the like; anything material can symbolize the spiritual. Rather, it results from the desire for unmediated experience of the Divine Being that draws all things into unity. Wordlessness in prayer reflects spirit communing with Spirit in the still depths within, as the heart or mind is made stable through spiritual discipline and the cultivation of a state of *apatheia*. For them purity is detachment from worldly mutability, cultivating the stability of calm peacefulness through which the human mind can participate in the changeless eternal. The end result mirrors the desire for aneconomy in fascinating ways. However, this likeness can lead to overlooking or downplaying important aspects of their conception of prayer.

All prayer is, at some level, embedded in economy, whether a transactional economy in which people "buy" salvation with prayer and good deeds, or a reciprocal economy in which God gives salvation as a gift in return for gifts, or merely an economy of communication, in which words are given and (imagined as) received. Because prayer communicates, the requirement, so often seen in twentieth- and twenty-first-century writing on prayer, that prayer be aneconomic to be pure (or rather, to not be corrupt) sets up an irresolvable conflict. Prayer must involve exchange insofar as it imagines something passing between *ego* and *alter*. William James, in spite of his understanding that true prayer is beyond forms, noticed this:

> [I]f [prayer] be not a give and take relation; if nothing be really transacted while it lasts; if the world is in no whit different for its having taken place; then prayer, taken in this wide meaning of a sense that *something* is *transacting*, is of course a feeling of what is illusory, and religion must on the whole be classed, not simply as containing elements of delusion – these undoubtedly everywhere exist – but as being rooted in delusion altogether, just as materialists and atheists have always said it was.[125]

According to James, prayer has to have some effect to be other than delusion. And yet, for prayer *not* to involve exchange there must be either no effect or else there must be no *ego* or no *alter*, no giving self or no receiving Other. In fact, prayer is transaction *even if* the Other is wholly imagined

125 William James, *Varieties of Religious Experience: A Study in Human Nature* (1902; rprnt. New York: Mentor, 1958), 353, italics original.

– if those praying imagine they pray to another who is not in fact there – because that prayer is given within a system that attributes meaning to anything that follows it. The requirement that prayer be aneconomic sets up the absurdity that the purest prayer is that which is unanswered, and where meaning cannot be attributed even to lack of an answer. In this case, pure prayer is that performed by the *ego* who does not imagine there is anyone there to receive it, or that there is benefit of any kind to the act of praying. Only an atheist could pray purely.[126]

And yet Cassian shows us that the ideal of aneconomic prayer might be reached another way. Such prayer affirms the existence of both parties, but combines them together in such a perfect unity that there is no longer *me* or *you*, erasing meaning, erasing intent, leaving nothing in the memory except a trace, although the trace is a sense of something lost, not gained. Cassian called the purest prayer "preces ignates" (fiery prayers), prayer "quae ore hominum nec conprehendi nec exprimi potest"[127] (which can be neither seized nor expressed by the mouth of man) and which come when a mind rooted in a

> uerum puritatis proficit adfectum … ad deum preces purissimi uigoris effundere, quas ipse spiritus interpellans gemitibus inenarrabilibus ignorantibus nobis emittit ad deum, tanta scilicet in illius horae momento concipiens et ineffabiliter in supplicatione profundens, quanta non dicam ore percurrere, sed ne ipsa quidem mente ualeat alio tempore recordari.[128]
>
> (true disposition of purity … pours out to God wordless prayers of the purest vigor. These the Spirit itself makes to God as it intervenes with unutterable groans, unbeknownst to us, conceiving at that moment and pouring forth in wordless prayer such great things that they not only – I would say – cannot pass through the mouth but are unable even to be remembered by the mind later on.)

Cassian idealizes aneconomic prayer in mystical rapture, in which the *ego* gives nothing/everything and receives nothing/everything in one fiery

126 John Caputo explores the atheistic/religious strain in Derrida's works in *The Prayers and Tears of Jacques Derrida: Religion without Religion* (Bloomington: Indiana University Press, 1997).
127 Cassian, *Conlatio* 9, CSEL 13, 263, 15, ll. 15–16; trans. Ramsey.
128 Cassian, *Conlatio* 9, CSEL 13, 263, 15, ll. 17, 21–6; trans. Ramsey.

moment of complete unity of *ego* and *alter* beyond time, beyond meaning, beyond, even, memory – beyond everything that could draw such a state back into any form of usefulness. Further, Cassian imagines such a state as pure gift – that is, something that cannot be earned or asked for but only desired. While it more usually comes to more seasoned practitioners, it can come indiscriminately upon beginners or those advanced in eremitic discipline.[129] These prayers are then experienced afterward as something taken, not given – while the precator seems to remember that the experience happened, as the final sentence above indicates, he cannot hold its content in his memory afterward. Yet this is not the only kind of prayer for Cassian; rather, it is a rare and occasional result of the discipline of prayer,[130] which comes after step-by-step advancement in the different kinds of prayer: supplication, prayer, intercession, and thanksgiving.[131]

Rachel Fulton's use of Cassian in her study of Anselm's prayers replicates Bradshaw's claim; for her written prayers serve as tools to teach the craft of praying.[132] Fulton's goal is to consider the question of how repetition of set prayers can be "considered 'real prayer,' when it would seem at least by some modern definitions rather closer to a political or social performance."[133] She musters Cassian's description of the use of short prayer texts in order to reconstruct an interior discipline of prayer for Anselm, a figure often identified in the Christian prayer tradition as innovative. Fulton describes the use of prayer texts as tools to reach a state of "genuine" prayer, beyond words (she quotes James and Heiler).[134] However, she assumes "genuine prayer" inhabits the spaces between set prayer in a way that may be true for Anselm, but is not true for Cassian. Like Cassian, Anselm was concerned with the experience of God,[135] and

129 Cassian, *Conlatio* 9, CSEL 13, 263–4, 15, ll. 26–9, 1-6.

130 The Paternoster "prouehit tamen domesticos suos ad illum praecelsiorem quem superius commemorauimus statum eosque ad illam igneam ac perpaucis cognitam uel expertam, immo ut proprius dixerim ineffabilem orationem gradu eminentiore perducit" (nonetheless raises his familiars to that condition which we characterized previously as more sublime. It leads them by a higher state to that fiery and, indeed, more properly speaking, wordless prayer which is known and experienced by very few), Cassian, *Conlatio* 9, CSEL 13, 25, ll. 18–22; trans. Ramsey.

131 Cassian, *Conlatio* 9, CSEL 13, 260, 9, ll. 8–16.

132 Fulton, "Praying with Anselm," 707.

133 Fulton, "Praying with Anselm," 701.

134 Fulton, "Praying with Anselm," 703.

135 She quotes Anselm: "The purpose of the prayers and meditations that follow is to stir up the mind of the reader to love or fear of God ...," "Praying with Anselm," 709.

he used what she takes as the same text-based techniques to get there. The kind of prayer Fulton describes uses written prayers as a starting point for catena-like meditational practices, where ideas, texts, and images are mentally linked together in a chain (*catena*) to form the means by which a practitioner's mind can be moved to prayer.[136] She describes a reconstructed pattern that the mind of the precator might follow:

> from text (Anselm's second prayer) to commentary (Honorius's *Sigillum*) to liturgical chant (Song of Songs 3.6) to image (Admont MS 18, fol. 163r) to psalm (Psalm 109) to text (Anselm's third prayer) to image (Admont MS 289, fol. 21v) to liturgical chant (the hymn and other neumed texts of the banderoles) and back ... There is a restlessness to the experience ... [137]

Such meditation is supposed to result, eventually, in "real" prayer: "here, at last, ... our nun ... will find herself in the presence of the Lady for whose attention she has longed and so will be able to turn to her and her Son,"[138] thus arriving at a sense of the presence of and communion with the divine.[139] As Fulton shows, these meditational practices leave ample room for individual creativity in the practice of, or surrounding, prayer. And while her reading of Anselm is compelling and reaffirms the sense that a theory of prayer is undergoing a shift with Anselm, Cassian does not teach this type of catena-like prayer. Although he also finds creativity in the process he describes,[140] that creativity does not come from making something unique and original, but rather from conforming oneself to and internalizing a standard outside oneself.

In *Conference* 9 Cassian and his travel companion and fellow monk, Germanus, learn about prayer from Abba Isaac, an Egyptian monk: he discusses preparation of the heart for prayer, explains the four types of

136 As Fulton notes, "Praying with Anselm," 731n125, this type of process is described in Mary Carruthers, *The Craft of Thought: Meditation, Rhetoric, and the Making of Images, 400–1200* (Cambridge: Cambridge University Press, 1998).

137 Fulton, "Praying with Anselm," 730.

138 Fulton, "Praying with Anselm," 730.

139 To clarify, Mary is mediator; Christ is divine.

140 For Germanus, prayer is, in fact, a creative act: failure in prayer leads the soul to become "palpator tantummodo spiritalium sensuum ac degustator, non generator nec possessor effectus" (a mere toucher and taster of spiritual meanings and not a begetter and possessor of them), Cassian, *Conlatio* 10, 307, 13, ll. 1–3; trans. Ramsey. But the idea of creativity put forth is quite different from something sourced in the individual.

prayer, explicates the Paternoster, and describes fiery prayer. Later, in *Conference* 10, they return to Isaac, and Germanus confesses that the previous teachings were too advanced for him. He has no idea how to pray as Isaac taught. Furthermore, his problem is just exactly a catena-like wandering of the mind, restlessness of experience, as the mind flits from passage to passage instead of staying rooted in the text prayed at the present moment:[141]

> Cum enim capitulum cuiuslibet psalmi mens nostra conceperit, insensibiliter eo subtracto ad alterius scripturae textum nesciens stupensque deuoluitur. cumque illud in semet ipsa coeperit uolutare, necdum illo ad integrum uentilatio oborta alterius testimonii memoria meditationem materiae prioris excludit. de hac quoque ad alteram subintrante alia meditatione transfertur, et ita animus semper de psalmo rotatus ad psalmum, de euangelii textu ad apostoli transiliens lectionem, de hac quoque ad prophetica deuolutus eloquia et exinde ad quasdam spiritales delatus historias per omne scripturarum corpus instabilis uagusque iactatur.[142]

> (For when our mind has understood a passage from any psalm, imperceptibly it slips away, and thoughtlessly and stupidly it wanders off to another text of Scripture. And when it has begun to reflect on this passage within itself, the recollection of another text shuts out reflection on the previous material, although it had not yet been completely aired. From here, with the introduction of another reflection, it moves elsewhere, and thus the mind is constantly whirling from psalm to psalm, leaping from a gospel text to a reading from the Apostle, wandering from this to the prophesies and thence being carried away to certain spiritual histories, tossed about fickle and aimless through the whole body of Scripture.)

141 This is a different process from the conflation of *lectio*, *meditatio*, and *oratio* outlined by Jean Leclercq in *The Love of Learning and the Desire for God: A Study of Monastic Culture*, trans. Catharine Misrahi (New York: Fordham University Press, 1982), 73, especially. Leclercq illustrates the extent to which every activity became subsumed into prayer. However, one of the big differences between Cassian and Benedict is that Cassian's Conferences 9 and 10 address prayer within a more loosely structured eremitic tradition wherein many of its practitioners could not read, rather than the cenobitic focus found in Benedict's *Regula* (and other similar rules).

142 Cassian, *Conlatio* 10, CSEL 13, 306, 13, ll. 16–26; trans. Ramsey.

In response to the problem Germanus presents, Isaac takes them back to the rudimentary beginnings of the discipline of prayer. He instructs that the novice should choose a short phrase from the Psalms as a "formula," something like Psalm 69:2: "Deus in adiutorium meum intende: domine ad adiuuandum mihi festina"[143] (O God, come to my assistance; O Lord, make haste to help me), which he recommends because it is appropriate for all situations (to prove his point he gives an exhaustive list of appropriate situations). The novice is then to pray this phrase without ceasing – that is, as the Egyptians understood it, continuously – in and around the daily regimen of private and communal prayers largely derived from the Psalms: "hunc in opere quolibet seu ministerio uel itinere constitutus decantare non desinas"[144] (You should not stop repeating it when you are doing any kind of work or performing some service or are on a journey) until "incessabili eius exercitatione formatus etiam per soporem eum decantare consuescas"[145] (you are formed by having used it ceaselessly and are in the habit of repeating it even while asleep). Isaac continues:

> Istam, istam mens indesinenter formulam teneat, donec usu eius incessabili et iugi meditatione firmata cunctarum cogitationum diuitias amplasque substantias abiciat ac refutet, atque ita uersiculi huius paupertate constricta ad illam euangelicam beatitudinem, quae inter ceteras beatitudines primatum tenet ["beati pauperes spiritu"].[146]
>
> (Let the mind hold ceaselessly to this formula above all until it has been strengthened by constantly using and continually meditating upon it, and until it renounces and rejects the whole wealth and abundance of thoughts. Thus straightened by the poverty of this verse, it will very easily attain to that gospel beatitude which holds the first place among the other beatitudes ["blessed are the poor in spirit"].)

143 The Latin is that used in *Conlatio* 10, CSEL 13, 297, 10, ll. 23–5; the translation is Douay-Rheims.
144 Cassian, *Conlatio* 10, CSEL 13, 302, 10, ll. 7–8; trans. Ramsey.
145 Cassian, *Conlatio* 10, CSEL 13, 302, 10, ll. 15–17; trans. Ramsey.
146 Cassian, *Conlatio* 10, CSEL 13, 303, 11, ll. 1–6; trans. Ramsey.

The end result of this discipline is that the one praying would begin to experience the words of the Psalms as his own words:

> ita incipiet decantare, ut eos non tamquam a propheta conpositos, sed uelut a se editos quasi orationem propriam profunda cordis conpunctione depromat uel certe ad suam personam aestimet eos fuisse directos, eorumque sententias non tunc tantummodo per prophetam aut in propheta fuisse conpletas, sed in se cotidie geri inplerique cognoscat. tunc enim scripturae diuinae nobis clarius perpatescunt et quodammodo earum uenae medullaeque panduntur, quando experientia nostra earum non tantum percipit, sed etiam praeuenit notionem, sensusque uerborum non per expositionem nobis, sed per documenta reserantur. eundem namque recipientes cordis affectum, quo quisque decantatus uel conscriptus est psalmus, uelut auctores euis facti praecedemus magis intellectum ipsius quam sequemur.[147]

> (he will begin to repeat them and to treat them in his profound compunction of heart not as if they were composed by the prophet but as if they were his own utterances and his own prayer. Certainly he will consider that they are directed to his own person, and he will recognize that their words were not only achieved by and in the prophet in times past but that they are daily borne out and fulfilled in him. For divine Scripture is clearer and its inmost organs, so to speak, are revealed to us when our experience not only perceives but even anticipates its thought, and the meanings of the words are disclosed to us not by exegesis but by proof. When we have the same disposition in our heart with which each psalm was sung or written down, then we shall become like its authors, grasping its significance beforehand rather than afterward.)

The way the monk reproduces the Psalms is not quite the exact opposite of what Fulton describes for Anselm, but it is very different. The main difference here is that no personal creativity (in the sense of creating prayers) is in fact at work; the precator never prays his own words – nor does Isaac present that as desirable. The continued repetition of the prayer formula should blot out "the rich and full resources of all thoughts," erase that distracting interior monologue, lead to a radical unmaking of the psyche, and remould it according to the form of the Psalms.[148] In fact, if the novice

147 Cassian, *Conlatio* 10, CSEL 13, 304–5, 11, ll. 17–23, 7; trans. Ramsey.

148 As Isaac says, the monk should use his prayer formula "donec incessabili eius exercitatione formatus" (until [he is] formed by having used it ceaselessly), Cassian, *Conlatio* 10, CSEL 13, 302, 10, ll. 15–16; trans. Ramsey.

were to pray his own words, or even his own personal psalm mash-up, that would destroy the very thing this discipline of prayer reaches for: that personal experience be subsumed beneath the experience of the Psalmist, leading to a very personal (but not individual, and not creative as we tend to think of it) identification with Christ.[149] This idea *is*, in fact, the exact opposite of the modern ideals of genuineness and sincerity in prayer put forward by James, Heiler, and all those following in the post-Reformation ideal of spontaneous prayer. Ideally, the Egyptian ascetic does not pray from his own experience and does not pray his own words but begins to adopt the words and experience of someone else, the Psalmist.[150] Spontaneous prayer, in its endless iteration and re-representation of the self to the self (or, if you will, the self to God) would be powerless to effect the kind of transformation the ascetics sought.

Hence, the emphasis on the silences between the Psalms as the location of "real" (or "personal") prayer we find in authors such as Columba Stewart and Bradshaw[151] is not something Cassian exactly supports. Yes, a type of formless, fiery experience of the presence of God is a desired state, but this (as he says repeatedly) practitioners rarely experience. That fiery prayer is prayer does not make not-prayer the word-dependent discipline that leads up to the personal appropriation of the Psalms. Otherwise, how would people be able to pray without ceasing?

We cannot, however, assume that later Western writers adopted Cassian's ideals in prayer. As DeGregorio argues, although Bede seems to know Cassian, his own ideal of "pure" prayer is to focus the heart

149 See Bradshaw on the Christological interpretation of the Psalter, "apparently derived by the desert tradition from the exegetical method adopted by Origen from classical literature," *Search for the Origins*, 174n15. He cites Marie-Josèphe Rondeau, *Les Commentaires patristiques du Psautier*; Paul F. Bradshaw, "From Word to Action: The Changing Role of Psalmody in Early Christianity"; and Graham W. Woolfenden, "The Use of the Psalter by Early Monastic Communities."

150 Fulton, on considering prayers as tools, says, "we must first trust both their makers (typically other human beings, but also, if we are the makers, ourselves) …," "Praying with Anselm," 731. But for Cassian, what could be trusted more than the words of inspired Scripture?

151 Stewart, *Cassian the Monk* (New York: Oxford University Press, 1998), 100–4. Bradshaw says, "It should be noted that the psalms here [recited alternating with silent prayer] were not understood as being prayer themselves – the sources often speak of prayer *and* psalmody – but as readings, as the fount of inspiration for the fount of prayer which followed each psalm," *Search for the Origins*, 174.

"through righteous action."[152] Furthermore, Cassian's ideas of prayer, and sometimes his phrasing, bear the unmistakable stamp of Eastern practice and patterns of thought that never really caught on in the Latin church in the period under consideration, even though Cassian's work was known and, in many ways, influential.[153] Even so, Cassian's example – the most complete presentation of the interior practice of the discipline of prayer we have – should give scholars pause when they come to silent points in the liturgy or in private prayer. We should not rush to fill these in with spontaneous prayer or even catena-like meditation. The ideal Cassian presents is important in another way: it shows how early monastic prayer consciously resists the individual as the precator seeks to be subsumed within the identity of Christ.

None of the later authors says anything about the methods Cassian presents, although Psalm 69:2 is commonly used in the Office and recommended for personal prayer. In fact, the type of prayer Cassian presents would be possible only within a highly committed, disciplined, eremitic structure. It would even be difficult to carry out in a post-Benedict monastic community, and would have been totally out of reach of laypeople or clerics. To find that Cassianic ideals would be absent from Ælfric's teaching to laypeople is therefore no surprise. As a layperson, Alfred also was not in a position to pray like a monk, and yet the discipline of prayer he presents and the way he seems to envision the central place of the Psalms in prayer reaches for a similar identification between precator and Christ as that presented by Cassian, although without (as far as can be determined) the same methodology.

As a monk writing to monks,[154] Bede's writing situation is the closest to Cassian's. Bede usually assumes the prayers his audience prays are formal

152 DeGregorio, "Venerable Bede on Prayer," 24.

153 Stephen Lake, "Knowledge of the Writings of John Cassian in Early Anglo-Saxon England," in *ASE* 32 (2003), argues that beyond Bede and perhaps Aldhelm, Cassian was not widely known in Anglo-Saxon England.

154 Bede's sermons are in Latin, indicating a religiously trained, Latinate audience. However, monks in Bede's day took on the pastoral care of the community around them, and it is not unlikely that laypeople could have been present at church preaching, especially at particular times of the year, or that monks could have adapted Bede's sermons for vernacular preaching; see Thacker "Monks, Preaching, and Pastoral Care." To this it must be added that most instances of address in Bede's homilies do presume a monastic audience. See Lawrence T. Martin's "Introduction," in *Bede the Venerable: Homilies on the Gospels* (Kalamazoo: Cistercian Publications, 1991), xi.

set prayers, whether recited communally as part of the liturgy or else alone. There are several reasons for this. As monks, Bede's audience would have been praying the hours daily, with the result that their formational experience with prayer would have been the set prayers chanted communally at the hours. Bede also repeatedly emphasizes the necessity of congruence between thoughts and words in a way that implies practitioners pray words familiar from long habit, words that they could easily say without attention. My point, however, is not that people never prayed spontaneously or composed their own prayers (the next chapter begins with a composed prayer by Bede),[155] but rather that what is now called "free" prayer (spontaneous verbal devotion) was not particularly valued as an end in itself, nor could prayer function in the way that Cassian, Augustine, Bede, or Alfred imagine it does – to retrain desire, transform the precator, or allow him to take on the persona of Christ in prayer – if it were spontaneous.

However, two things indicate that something has changed between Cassian's Egypt and Bede's England. The first is the development of private penance.[156] The monastic context represented by Cassian shows a

155 Hagiographical narratives represent saints praying "spontaneously" as well. Hugh A.G. Houghton, "The Discourse of Prayer in the Major Apocryphal Acts of the Apostles," in *Apocrypha* 15 (2004), argues that narrative accounts of prayer in the Apocryphal Acts of the Apostles reflect the features of "the improvised liturgical prayers of the early Church," 175. The tendency over time was for prayer to become more set and less spontaneous. Byzdl, "Prayer in Old English Narratives," examines the formulaic ways narrative prayers reflect the structure of private prayers found in prayerbooks and considers how narrative prayers contribute to the construction of distinct saintly characters rather than standing as particular examples of "spontaneous" prayer, which practice (as opposed to the attitudes and maybe even the prayers themselves) hearers might be expected to adopt.

156 In the early church, penance was imposed for serious sins. The penitent performed it publicly, and it could only be performed once in a lifetime (Tertullian's *De paenitentia*, which mostly addresses penitence for catechumens, lays out the logic for one-time penance, called exomologesis). Praying the Paternoster daily was understood to cleanse precators from the small daily sins that one cannot avoid by the nature of this life (for instance, Cyprian, *De dominica oratione*, CCSL 3A, 96, 12, ll. 199–202). The Irish developed a system of private confession to a priest, who would then impose a penance for the penitent to perform. See Frantzen, *Literature of Penance*, 22–6, on the originality of Irish penitentials in a Continental context. Early penitentials record this practice, listing "tariffs," the penances assigned for specific sins. In addition, the Irish developed the practice of commuting penances, in which a shorter and more severe penance could be substituted for a longer one. People who were unable to perform their penance (say, because they did not know the Psalms or were too weak to fast) could pay someone else to take on their penance (see Angenendt et al., "Counting Piety," 28–30), although

strong awareness of human sinfulness. The point of monastic ascesis – ascetic practice – is to train the mind to stability[157] so that the weight of the flesh does not weigh down the soul as it seeks to rise to participate in the divine nature.[158] Compunction – sorrow that incites the mind to prayer – plays a central role.[159] Prayer (and the other ascetic practices that accompany it) reaches for purity. At the most basic level Cassian certainly understands purity as sinlessness. But the sins ascesis cleanses are not only personal sins; Cassian also conceptualizes cleansing as a loosening of the hold that earthly and material things have over the precator (one example of this pervasive theme can be found in 10.6). That is, monks move from a state of awareness of their own personal sins to awareness of a generalized human state of sin (separation from God) that they participate in by virtue of their humanity.[160] The stability resulting from detachment from the transitory material world enables the monk to participate in the changeless stability of the divine nature.

In contrast, in the practice of penance as it developed later, the penitent confesses his or her own specific sins and repays or makes amends to God for them through performing series of prayers, fasting, and other good deeds.[161] Penitential practice thus individualizes sin in a way that monastic ascesis did not. Furthermore, although both practices use the

---

Frantzen's comments on the practicality of penances, 16, and the rigours of early commutation, *Literature of Penance*, 54–5, are a necessary counterbalance to Angenendt's emphasis on their extreme nature. Angenendt argues that early medieval piety became much more focused on the "counting and accumulation of acts of piety" leading towards a "bookkeeping" attitude towards sin and good deeds, rather than a focus on interior moral development, 15. That is, from Angenendt's perspective, the point of acts of piety became to gain a certain sort of freedom from God's claims by paying one's debts rather than to cultivate dependence on God through gifts.

157 Cassian, *Conlatio* 9, CSEL 13, 256–7, 6.

158 Cassian, *Conlatio* 9, CSEL 13, 253–4, 4.

159 Cassian, *Conlatio* 9, CSEL 13, 274–6, 29.

160 In discussing the Irish origins of penance, Frantzen, calls these the two levels of mortification. The first, penance performed for correction of wrongdoing, he calls disciplinary. The second is devotional; it sought forgiveness for the general moral failings rather than particular, *Literature of Penance*, 29–30.

161 See Frantzen, *Literature of Penance*. The early Irish were influenced by Egyptian practices as mediated through Cassian's works (among others), 25–6. The Irish, however, extend penitential practice to laypeople, who confessed and performed disciplinary penance for their own sins; see 30–60 on the extension of penance to the laity.

language of purity (or cleansing) and both involve the practice of prayer, fasting, and almsgiving, the point of the first is *apatheia*, detachment that enables one to participate in the divine nature, while the goal of the second is, as Tertullian says, to make restitution for the debt caused by sin.[162] The penitential understanding did not, of course, replace the ascetic, but it did gain prominence over the course of the Anglo-Saxon period and beyond.

The second indication that something has changed is the new prayer "technology" apparently invented by Bede: the breviate psalter.[163] As Fulton notes, composed prayers are tools for lifting the mind to God, and new ones tend to be made when the old ones no longer seem to work.[164] Therefore, a new form of prayer, in this case the breviate psalter, would seem to indicate a shift in underlying use or theory. But we will pick up the Anglo-Saxon innovations in the next section.

Prayer in Anglo-Saxon England

This section presents developments in the practice and textual presentation of Anglo-Saxon prayer as context for the chapters that follow. Anglo-Saxon England inherited some elements of the teachings on prayer and prayer practice detailed above; however, the written evidence is thinner and largely of a different type, and it becomes harder to say what constituted the typical lay practice of prayer. Although they were innovators in the prayerbook tradition, Anglo-Saxon England produced no treatises on prayer along the lines of Tertullian's or Origen's productions. Furthermore, not all of the early treatises made their way north. Of the number, the most commonly circulating in England were Cassian's *Conlationes*, represented in four manuscripts of Anglo-Saxon provenance and cited by various Anglo-Saxon authors,[165] and Augustine's letter to Proba, also extant in four copies. Cyprian's *De dominica oratione* is attested in two late manuscripts. Tertullian and Origen were not unknown as authors, but no evidence survives that the Anglo-Saxons knew their

162 Tertullian, *De oratione*, cap. 7, ll. 5–9.

163 Ward, *Bede and the Psalter*.

164 Fulton, "Praying with Anselm," 716.

165 Excerpts in Gneuss and Lapidge, no. 173; chapters 1–10 in no. 627; chapters 1–10, 14–15, 24, and 11 in no. 700; complete in no. 834.5. See Lake, "Knowledge of the Writings" for uses by Anglo-Saxon authors.

treatises on prayer.[166] Thus, the material adapted by the Anglo-Saxons is somewhat narrower in scope, consisting rather of commentaries on the Paternoster (and other biblical passages) and homilies. The commentaries and homilies draw from the same storehouse of traditional teachings as the treatises, but the information they give is almost wholly exegetical information, and the exegesis is quite brief. For instance, Bede's explication of the Paternoster is found in his commentary on Luke.[167] Rather than the more usual line-by-line explication, he condenses his commentary by dividing the prayer into two parts, those requests that pertain to eternal things and those that pertain to temporal. He also spends a significant amount of space addressing the differences found between the versions of the prayer in Matthew and Luke.

By the beginning of the Anglo-Saxon era the major performative contexts for prayer are the liturgy of the Mass, celebrated in churches and cathedrals, and the Daily Office and private prayers observed in monasteries.[168] It becomes much more difficult to say what normal expectations for lay prayer were and even more difficult to say anything about actual practice. Certainly, Bede thought church attendance on Sundays reasonable.[169] He expected that all Christians should be able to say the Paternoster and the Creed in their own language, a standard that Ælfric and Wulfstan repeat near the end of the era.[170] How they expected these texts to be used

166 Michael Lapidge, "Catalogue of Classical and Patristic Authors and Works Composed before AD 700 and Known in Anglo-Saxon England," in *The Anglo-Saxon Library* (Oxford: Oxford University Press, 2005). Of the nearly two dozen Augustinian letters attested, the one to Proba is the most commonly represented. It is found in Gneuss and Lapidge, nos. 167, 266.5, 583, and 750.5. Cyprian's treatise is in nos. 595.5 and 699.

167 *In Lucae*, CCSL 120, 227–8. Ward translates the Paternoster section in *High King of Heaven*, 82–4.

168 See Jesse D. Billett, *The Divine Office in Anglo-Saxon England, 597–c. 1000* (Woodbridge, 2014), for the development of the Office over time. He argues that the Office was not regularized to the Benedictine Rule until the tenth-century reforms; before that point, monasteries followed their own customaries.

169 Bede, "Epistola ad Ecgbertum," in *Opera Historica*, ed. Charles Plummer (Oxford: Clarendon, 1896), 419.

170 "In qua uidelicet praedicatione populis exhibenda, hoc prae ceteris omni instantia procurandum arbitror, ut fidem catholicam, quae apostolorum symbolo continetur, et dominicam orationem … omnium, qui ad tuum regimen pertinent, memoriae radicitus infigere cures. Et quidem omnes, qui Latinam linguam lectionis usu didicerunt, etiam haec optime didicisse certissimum est; sed idiotas, hoc est, eos qui propriae tantum linguae notitiam habent, haec ipsa sua lingua discere, ac sedulo decantare facito. Quod non solum de laicis, id est, in populari adhuc uita constitutes, uerum etiam de clericis

is less certain. None of the teaching on prayer addressed to laypeople (or the conciliar records) says anything about the laity praying at fixed hours, although Bede recommends they say the Creed in the morning and pray the Paternoster often.[171] It seems extremely unlikely that laypeople would have been expected to pray three, six, or seven times a day, as the earlier treatises teach (although there is also nothing stopping them from doing this and monastic practice would have modelled it). In fact, penitential practice, introduced by the Irish church, provides the most frequently attested context for lay prayer, where the Paternoster or the Psalms might be assigned as part of penance in addition to fasting and almsgiving.[172]

Accounts of the extent of actual lay piety in Bede's day vary. Henry Mayr-Harting, for instance, assumes a high level of piety for those who converted to Christianity (there was still substantial pagan presence).[173] As monasteries were instrumental in evangelizing the countryside, at least in Northumbria,[174] laypeople were exposed to monastic ideals, especially

---

siue monachis, qui Latine sunt linguae experts, fieri oportet" (In this preaching to the populace, I consider it most important that you attempt to fix ineradicably in the memory of all those under your rule the beliefs of the Church, as set out in the Apostles' Creed, and also the Lord's Prayer ... It is most certain that all those who have learned to read Latin will know these well, but the unlearned, that is to say those who only know their own language, must learn to say them in their own tongue and to chant them carefully. This ought to be done not only by the laity, that is to say those living the ordinary life of the populace, but also by the clergy and the monks, who are experts in Latin): Bede, "Epistola ad Ecgbertum," in *Opera Historica*, ed., Plummer, 408–9; trans. Judith McClure and Roger Collins, *Ecclesiastical History of the English People* (Oxford: Oxford University Press, 1994), 345–6. Ælfric repeats this ideal in the opening lines of *CH* I.20, and Wulfstan refers to the Paternoster and the Creed as that which "ælc cristen man mid rihte cunnon sceal" (every Christian must rightly know): Homily 7a in *The Homilies of Wulfstan*, ed. Dorothy Bethurum (Oxford: Clarendon, 1957), ll. 5–6.

171 "Epistola ad Ecgbertum," 409. He also idealizes daily communion for all Christians, while at the same time noting how far from that ideal current English practice was, 419.

172 John T. McNeill and Helena M. Gamer, *Medieval Handbooks of Penance: A Translation of the Principal* Libri Poenitentiales (New York: Columbia University Press, 1938), translate a number of documents related to penance, including early penitentials.

173 Henry Mayr-Harting, *The Coming of Christianity to Anglo-Saxon England*, 3rd ed. (London: Batsford, 1991), 259–60.

174 See Sarah Foot, "Parochial Ministry in Early Anglo-Saxon England: The Role of Monastic Communities," in *Studies in Church History* 27 (1989). For emendments to Foot's argument, see Catherine Cubitt, "Pastoral Care and Conciliar Canons: The Provisions of the 747 Council at Clovesho," in *Pastoral Care before the Parish*, ed. John Blair and Richard Sharpe (Leicester: Leicester University Press, 1992).

in penitential practice.[175] Still, there were not enough priests to staff local churches, and many of these priests themselves lacked adequate Latin.[176] It is improbable that most laypeople would have been able to pray the Psalms, even as a penitential requirement, when all those in orders had not even attained such a skill. Mayr-Harting mentions the little oratories that sprang up across the countryside as "little more than places of private prayer, except when they were visited by the bishop or the clergy of a monastery or minster which served them with mass and the sacraments."[177] And yet we need not assume the oratories were in regular use for private prayer; we need assume no more than that itinerant priests used them when they came through to administer the sacraments, as Thacker does.[178] Thacker states that the monastic emphasis on ascetic practice and penitence for laypeople reflects ideals that likely turned away as many laypeople as they attracted. Still, it is quite likely that prayer replaced (or joined) the types of native healing and prophylactic practices that the Church forbade. If laypeople were to follow Ælfric's advice in *De auguriis*, to pray while travelling, and at the end of *CH* I.31, to pray while picking herbs, they might be praying the Paternoster all the time. Saints' cults were also a focus of piety and prayer.[179] Therefore, the most normal expression of lay prayer was likely in response to perceived need for healing and for protection. Physical needs then present the model for eternal salvation.[180] The central aspects of

---

175 Thacker, "Monks, Preaching, and Pastoral Care." Thacker sees the monastic ideals as so dominant within teaching to laypeople that they had little practical applicability to married people: "Taking such a somber view of sexuality, the monastic elite of the early English church effectively turned their backs upon the married," 156. However, the English penitentials reflect spiritual direction for laypeople. See Frantzen on the extension of penance to laypeople, *Literature of Penance*, 30–60. Sarah Hamilton, concludes that penitential practice reached even the lower orders, although she is looking at Continental sources, *The Practice of Penance, 900–1050* (Woodbridge: Boydell, 2001), 206.

176 Bede's statement above makes this clear, but the English clergy's lack of Latin is noted and lamented in various eras: in the 747 Council of Clovesho, no. 27, in Arthur West Haddan et al., eds., *Councils and Ecclesiastical Documents Relating to Great Britain and Ireland*, vol. 3, (Oxford: Clarendon, 1964), and by Alfred in his own day, in the preface to the translation of Gregory's *Pastoral Care*, in *King Alfred's West-Saxon Version of Gregory's Pastoral Care*, ed. Henry Sweet (London: N. Trübner, 1871), 1–2.

177 Mayr-Harting, *The Coming of Christianity*, 247.

178 Thacker, "Monks, Preaching, and Pastoral Care," 147.

179 Thacker argues that most lay piety would have been formed by and directed towards the cults of the saints, 166–9.

180 Chapter 4 on Ælfric considers this further.

lay piety were probably the sacraments of baptism and the Eucharist, and, in addition, the Church desired to bring as many people into the practice of penance as they could.[181] The most pious laypeople were likely to join monasteries themselves.

For monks, the Psalms would still have been central to the experience of prayer. Their recitation forms the bulk of the Daily Office and was also central to prayer in the cell. Benedict's *Regula* organizes the Psalms such that monks pray the entire number through each week in the Office (although Benedict's was one rule among many that early English monasteries used). In Ireland, the monks of Columbanus's monastery at Bangor recited them over the course of two days.[182] Influenced by such examples, Ceolfrith, abbot of Jarrow (d. 716), in his own personal prayer is said to have prayed the psalter two and even three times daily.[183] In her thorough and multifaceted study of the psalter, *The Anglo-Saxon Psalter*, M.J. Toswell charts psalter use throughout the Anglo-Saxon period. However, because her focus is not on prayer per se, she largely overlooks the shifting theoretical distinctions for prayer indicated by changes in the use of the psalms as we move from Bede to Alcuin, to Alfred, to the later Anglo-Saxon period.[184]

Bede's breviate psalter represents the first Anglo-Saxon innovation in prayer; it perhaps marks the first separation between liturgical service books and a text designed for private prayer. Benedicta Ward describes it:

> [H]e selected verses from each psalm which could be used as direct prayer or praise, as food for meditation, pleas for mercy, protest, contrition, or adoration and exultation. Sometimes one verse alone was used, sometimes several. The verses were also selected so that a sense of the meaning of the psalm as a whole was retained; it would be possible to recall the whole psalm from these clues.[185]

Thus, Bede represents the whole of the Psalms using select verses. Such a change points to a different experience of prayer than that represented by Cassian, although it is difficult to say exactly in what way the goals of

181 Thacker notes the way secular power could be used to enforce ecclesiastical sanctions, "Monks, Preaching, and Pastoral Care," 160–1.

182 Frantzen, "Spirituality and Devotion," 27.

183 Ward, "Bede and the Psalter," 3.

184 Toswell, *Anglo-Saxon Psalter*, chapter 1, looks at Bede, Alfred, and Ælfric's use of the psalms in their written works.

185 Ward, "Bede and the Psalter," 10.

praying the Psalms might have shifted. Ward calls it a memory device that enables people to pray to God.[186] While we do not know how Bede intended this work to be used, one possible use – although this is speculation – is that the breviate psalter aids in penitential practice, allowing those unable to pray the Psalms in their entirety to pray them symbolically in shortened form. However, Bestul notes that in all three of the early manuscripts that preserve it (all from the early ninth century, and all Continental), it is part of a devotional anthology, and the incipit of one of the manuscripts explains that it is convenient for daily prayer.[187] Although this evidence comes a century after Bede, it supports Ward's statement that the shortened psalter was a tool for private prayer.[188]

Alcuin's preface on the use of the Psalms, *De laude psalmorum*, might further help to shed light on the use of the breviate psalter.[189] Alcuin's training in prayer took place in York, a similar Northumbrian context to Bede's, and he brought Anglo-Saxon practices with him to the Frankish court, where Charlemagne invited him to help with a program of liturgical reform. Alcuin knew Bede's breviate psalter: he gave a copy to his friend Arno, archbishop of Salzburg.[190] *De laude psalmorum* indicates a way of using the Psalms directed by personal need rather than following a set program. While Cassian gives a specific phrase taken from one of the psalms as remedy to any situation so that reliance on it will bring the mind to "poverty," Alcuin lists various psalms as remedies for specific situations. For instance, "Si diversis tribulationibus afflictus sis ... decanta illos psalmos quorum caput est: *Deus, Deus meus, respice in me*" (and two more)[191] (If you are afflicted by various troubles ... recite those psalms which begin: "God, my God look on me" ...). This change is important:

186 Ward, "Bede and the Psalter," 13.

187 Thomas H. Bestul, "Continental Sources of Anglo-Saxon Devotional Writing," in *Sources of Anglo-Saxon Culture*, ed. Paul Szarmach and Virginia Darrow Oggins (Kalamazoo, MI: MIP, 1986), 106.

188 Ward, "Bede and the Psalter," 10.

189 Edited by Jonathan Black, "Psalm Uses in Carolingian Prayerbooks: Alcuin and the Preface to *De psalmorum usu*" in *Medieval Studies* 64 (2002). Donald A. Bullough calls the same text <*Quia*> *Prophetia spiritus*, in *Alcuin: Achievement and Reputation* (Leiden: Brill, 2004), 7. The text is also printed in PL 101, cols. 465b–68a, as a preface to *De psalmorum usu*, now known to be pseudonymous. *De laude psalmorum* was attached to *De psalmorum usu* at an early date: see Bullough, 7.

190 Bullough, *Alcuin: Achievement and Reputation*, 181.

191 Black, "Psalm Uses: Preface to *De psalmorum usu*," ll. 187–8 and 195–6.

the psalms now respond to the precator's specific situations and inward states. According to Alcuin, the Psalms also have special value to connect the precator to God: "Vox enim psalmodiae cum per intentionem cordis agitur, per hanc omnipotenti Domino ad cor iter paratur"[192] (Through the voice of psalmody, when brought forth through the effort of the heart, a way is prepared to the heart by Almighty God). As a "sacrificium ... divinae laudis"[193] (sacrifice of divine praise), the Psalms work to purify or cleanse the mind,[194] so that God can pour into it the grace of compunction.[195] Thus, Alcuin also places the Psalms in a strongly penitential context, reflecting developments in penitential practice.[196]

However, we are still not at a point where precators produce prayer from their own hearts; rather, the psalms produce the disposition of the heart. Alcuin privileges the forms of prayer found in the Psalms as especially valuable for communicating with God: "Nullus itaque mortalium potest nec verbis nec mente virtutem psalmorum ... explicare"[197] (For no mortal can set forth in words or in thought the power of the psalms). "In psalmis invenies tam intimam orationem, si intenta mente perscruteris, sicut non potes ullatenus per te ipsum excogitare"[198] (In the psalms you will find such profound prayer, if you study with attentive mind, that you could not at all invent such for yourself). Alcuin's promise is not quite that the Psalms reveal the inmost heart of precators to God but rather that they cleanse the heart as precators pray in response to their perceived need. The Psalms as prayer gain intimacy of the Psalms in the way they allow precators to enter into the intimacy of God's words and God's works, which are still beyond them even as they pray those words. The Psalms communicate the Christological narrative: "In Psalmis itaque invenies, si intenta mente perscruteris et ad spiritalem intellectum perveneris, dominici Verbi incarnationem passionemque et resurrectionem atque ascensionem"[199] (In the Psalms, if you study with attentive mind and reach their spiritual

192 Black, "Psalm Uses: Preface to *De psalmorum usu*," ll. 93–6.
193 Black, "Psalm Uses: Preface to *De psalmorum usu*," l. 100.
194 Black, "Psalm Uses: Preface to *De psalmorum usu*," l. 108.
195 Black, "Psalm Uses: Preface to *De psalmorum usu*," l. 98.
196 This trajectory continues. Ward quotes a post-Alcuinian breviate psalter that selects only those verses from the psalms appropriate for "someone who wants to call upon God and beg mercy for his sins," qtd. in "Bede and the Psalter," 12.
197 Black, "Psalm Uses: Preface to *De psalmorum usu*," ll. 115–16.
198 Black, "Psalm Uses: Preface to *De psalmorum usu*," ll. 125–8.
199 Black, "Psalm Uses: Preface to *De psalmorum usu*," ll. 120–4.

understanding, you will find the incarnation, passion, resurrection, and ascension of the Word of the Lord). Yet they also provide a key to the events of the precator's own life: "invenies omnium rerum quae tibi accedunt intimam gratiam actionum"[200] (you will find the inmost grace of events and all things that happen to you). Thus, they present a double narrative that precators enter into as they pray: the meta-narrative of Christ, plus a key to mapping that story onto the events and situations of the precators' own lives.

The structure of the psalms and the liturgy formed Alcuin's training in prayer, but he also knew the earliest prayerbook tradition. Somewhere around the time of Bede's death (735) the English seem to have started compiling books of prayers as aids to personal devotion.[201] With one minor exception, these books did not include instruction on how to pray or why;[202] rather, they begin with Gospel extracts and continue on to a compendium of prayers taken from the liturgy, the psalms, patristic authors, and other sources, named and anonymous. They aided in private devotional prayer, yet they do not lay out a devotional program to perform from beginning to end, as their organization makes clear.[203] Rather, they seem to present collections of useful prayers for reference (although the way people used these books is still not clearly known). Four of these books still exist (one in fragmentary form): the Royal Prayerbook, the

200 Black, "Psalm Uses: Preface to *De psalmorum usu*," ll. 132–4.

201 The earliest extant prayerbooks are from England. All of them contain Irish elements, indicating possible Irish influence; however, there are no earlier Irish prayerbooks extant. The English books are preserved in manuscripts roughly contemporaneous with the earliest Continental prayerbooks; however, the English books seem to be copies of older exemplars, and Alcuin seems to be a key figure in bringing the English tradition to Francia.

202 Cerne begins with fragmentary instruction on how to gain the intercession of the saints and "alle soðfeste … in caelo et in terra" (all the righteous … in heaven and on earth): see Arthur Benedict Kuypers, ed., *The Prayer Book of Aedeluald the Bishop* (Cambridge: Cambridge University Press, 1902), 3.

203 In Royal, for instance, numbers 3 and 23 are creeds, 29 and 33 are confessions, 15 and 19 are titled morning prayers; prayers attributed to Augustine are scattered throughout, and numbers 11, 35, and 40 have been called charms. Some sections do cohere, for instance, a collection of abecedarian prayers, number 25. While Brown argues that Cerne's central theme is the *communio sanctorum*, *Book of Cerne*, 147–8, the prayers in the book are clearly copied from a number of other sources, and it contains a number of repeated prayers. Thus, Cerne is hardly coherent enough, in full, to use as a devotional program, either.

Book of Cerne, the Book of Nunnaminster, and the Harley Fragment.[204] All four manuscripts are of Mercian provenance,[205] and all of them contain older material potentially connecting them to an earlier Northumbrian provenance.[206] Royal is the oldest manuscript, dating from the last half of the eighth century.[207] Cerne, from the early ninth century, is more clearly a copy of older exemplars, possibly dating back to Bishop Æthelwold of Lindisfarne (721–40).[208] Nunnaminster (late eighth or early ninth century)

---

204 Royal: BL, Royal 2.A.xx, edited as an appendix to Kuypers, *Prayer Book of Aedeluald*, 200–25. Kuypers's edition is little more than a transcription of the MS. The manuscript is also described with a descriptive list of its contents (and some of the prayers printed out) as an appendix to Walter de Gray Birch, ed., *An Ancient Manuscript of the Eighth or Ninth Century* (1889; Rprnt. from the Collections of the University of California Libraries), 101–13. Patrick Sims-Williams, *Religion and Literature in Western England* (Cambridge: Cambridge University Press, 1990), spends chapter 10, "Prayer and Magic," analysing its contents, as well as the Harley Fragment. Cerne: Cambridge UL, L1.1.10, edited by Kuypers, *Prayer Book of Aedeluald*. Brown, *Book of Cerne*, is a detailed study of the manuscript but not an edition. Nunnaminster: BL, Harley 2965, edited as Birch, *An Ancient Manuscript*. The Harley Fragment consists of a partial litany followed by seven prayers, the last of which is also partial: BL, Harley 7653, edited as an appendix to vol. 2 of F.E. Warren, *The Antiphonary of Bangor: An Early Irish Manuscript in the Ambrosian Library at Milan* (Woodbridge: Boydell & Brewer, 1895). Birch gives a descriptive list of its contents similar to the one he gives of Royal, *An Ancient Manuscript*, 114–19. Sims-Williams proposes that the fragment is closely related to Royal, *Religion and Literature*, 281, and discusses it along with Royal. Bestul, "Continental Sources," would also add as evidence of an early prayerbook the single-leaf fragment, Oxford Bodl., Seldon Supra 30 (8th c.), which contains two prayers.

205 Brown, *Book of Cerne*, 172.

206 The books' mixture of prayers from Irish sources with Roman material and inclusion of prayers by Northumbrians like Bede and the anchorite Alchfrith seem to point towards Northumbria.

207 See Bestul on its Northumbrian ancestry, "Continental Sources," 110.

208 An "Aedeluald episcopus" is named in an acrostic poem on fol. 21a, and a breviate psalter on fols. 87b–98 is attributed to an Oeðelpald, leading scholars to conclude that the manuscript was either prepared for someone so named or copied from an exemplar prepared for an Æthelwald. The two candidates are Æthelwald who was bishop of Lichfield from 818–30 (the right date and provenance for the manuscript) or Æthelwald, bishop of Lindisfarne from 721–40. The presence of a strong Irish element in Cerne makes Æthelwald of Lindisfarne an attractive candidate. David N. Dumville, "Liturgical Drama and Panegyric Responsory from the 8th Century," *Journal of Theological Studies*, ns. 23.2 (1972), argues for the earlier Æthelwald of Lindisfarne and that the core body of texts in Cerne is therefore a copy of an older collection. See also Kuypers, *Prayer Book of Aedeluald*, xi–xiv, and Brown, *Book of Cerne*, 181–3.

contains items related to Royal and Cerne[209] and two items derived from the prayerbook Alcuin compiled for Archbishop Arno of Salzburg.[210] It also contains evidence that suggests it may have been owned at one point by Ealhswith, King Alfred's wife.[211]

While the three complete books show a similar form and share some prayers in common, each has its own characteristics. Royal begins with the incipits of the four Gospels, and Sims-Williams argues that the collection as a whole emphasizes God's healing and protective power (and that, in fact, the book itself might have been prophylactic).[212] It includes three prayers against bleeding and an exorcism[213] that have been characterized as charms. On the basis of the prayers against bleeding, Sims-Williams speculates a female user.[214] Cerne and Nunnaminster's Gospel extracts are from the Passion. Michelle P. Brown argues that Cerne focuses on the communion of the saints as a theme.[215] No similarly detailed work has been done on Nunnaminster, although Barbara Raw briefly outlines differences in emphasis between it and Royal.[216] Thus, although these books innovate in the way they gather together prayers from various sources for non-liturgical use and in the way they begin to build a corpus of prayers from sources other than the liturgy and the Psalms, they do not present the personalized emphasis on emotive devotion characteristic of a more fully interiorized and individualized spirituality.

209 Raw, "Alfredian Piety," 146.

210 Bestul, "Continental Sources," 112 and 117.

211 The boundaries of her property in Winchester, which she gave to the abbey she founded there, were added to fol. 40b at the end of the manuscript.

212 Sims-Williams, *Religion and Literature*, 286.

213 The prayers against bleeding are numbers 11 and 40 (which gives two versions of the same prayer). The exorcism, addressed to "satanae diabulus aelfae," is Number 35, Kuypers, *Prayer Book of Aedeluald*, 221, fol. 45b.

214 Sims-Williams, *Religion and Literature*, 282. In fact, all the books show some evidence of female use or copying from feminine-gendered exemplars (in most, masculine or feminine gendering of the prayers is inconsistent). Birch argues Nunnaminster was written for an abbess of the head of a nunnery, *An Ancient Manuscript*, 15. Harley contains some prayers gendered for a feminine speaker, and Cerne has one prayer gendered feminine, probably as a result of copying from an exemplar. According to Brown, Cerne has little evidence of feminine ownership compared to the other prayerbooks, *Book of Cerne*, 181.

215 Brown, *Book of Cerne*, 147–8.

216 Raw, "Alfredian Piety."

Alcuin represents the next stage of prayerbook development. Probably inspired by English prayerbooks, he compiled a florilegium, *De laude Dei*, which Donald A. Bullough compares to the English prayerbooks. *De laude Dei* consists of four books.[217] The collection begins with short extracts from the Old and New Testaments rather than the Gospels and the occasional addition of a short invocation or prayer, followed by a breviate psalter intended as a continuous prayer, then short patristic excerpts and prayers. The final book contains a lengthy sequence of liturgical texts, concluding with verses from Christian poems.[218] Bullough contrasts *De laude Dei* with Cerne in particular in order to highlight its difference in structure and scope. He says, "The overall impression given by its contents is … that we have here a personal reflection of the public worship and private study of Alcuin's York years."[219] He later reiterates that the book seems intended for private use, probably to read from rather than as items to be memorized.[220]

Alcuin also sent a devotional compilation to Arno, archbishop of Salzburg. The *manualis libellus* exists today only in imperfect copies, but a letter sent with it lists its contents.[221] By this we know that the central texts were a copy of Bede's breviate psalter, verse-by-verse commentary on the seven penitential and fifteen gradual psalms and Psalm 118, and a copy of an earlier letter on confession addressed to the youths of St Martin's. In Alcuin's *Vita* he is said to have compiled a prayerbook for Charlemagne

217 *De laude Dei* is extant in two manuscript copies, Bamberg, Stadtbibl. Msc.Patr. 17 (B.II.10), fols. 133–161v, from Mainz in the early eleventh century, which is digitized online, and El Escorial MS B-IV-17, fols. 93–108, doubtfully attributed to the south of France, in the third quarter of the ninth century. Radu Constantinescu, "Alcuin et les 'libelli precum,'" in *Revue d'histoire de la spiritualité* 50 (1974), summarizes and edits some parts of the contents of the Bamberg MS. See also David Ganz, "Le *De laude Dei* d'Alcuin," in *Annales de Bretagne et Des Pays de l'Ouest* 111 (2004), and Bullough, *Alcuin: Achievement and Reputation*, 178n140, for further details on the manuscripts and printing history. Donald A. Bullough discusses the contents in further detail, with particular attention to the liturgical materials, in "Alcuin and the Kingdom of Heaven: Liturgy, Theology, and the Carolingian Age," in *Carolingian Essays* (Washington, DC: Catholic University of America Press, 1983).

218 Bullough, *Alcuin: Achievement and Reputation*, 180–1.

219 Bullough, *Alcuin: Achievement and Reputation*, 177.

220 Bullough, *Alcuin: Achievement and Reputation*, 224.

221 Bullough, *Alcuin: Achievement and Reputation*, 181–2. A number of copies exist but none of them is complete: see Bullough, "Alcuin and the Kingdom of Heaven," 20n42 and 67–8. The texts are printed in PL 100, cols. 575–96 and 598–638.

himself. The book no longer exists, although Stephan Waldhoff has reconstructed its contents using the list of contents in Alcuin's *Vita* as well as texts found in various early manuscripts.[222] Regardless of whether Alcuin actually compiled such a book (Jonathan Black, for one, doubts that this is the case),[223] he did outline a plan of private devotion for the emperor, a letter beginning "Beatus igitur David."[224] In this letter, Alcuin gives instruction for prayer at seven hours during the day and night, then gives a short series of prayers for the hours appropriate for a busy layman. The prayers include the Paternoster and then largely consist of phrases taken from the Psalms, concluding with as many psalms as the precator wishes. Alcuin himself also wrote prayers that became part of the contents of prayerbooks.

Alcuin's work has several distinctive characteristics: its emphasis on personal confession reflects his own interest in the topic and responds to the growing need for confessional prayers caused by developments in penitential practice.[225] According to Michael S. Driscoll, he is the first to treat the seven penitential psalms as a distinct group.[226] *Deus inaestimabilis*, his most famous prayer, an adaptation of the prophylactic lorica tradition to the needs of confession, is often included in manuscripts as an opening prayer to this group.[227] In addition, works like *De laude psalmorum* and *Deus inaestimabilis* show increased emphasis on the personal situation of the precator. As discussed above, *De laude* prescribes certain psalms for certain situations. *Deus inaestimabilis* gives a template for persons to confess their specific sins. The prayer lists some two dozen body parts that could possibly be involved in (and thus need forgiveness for) sin – a tool for "an extremely thorough examination of the conscience," as Driscoll

222 Stephan Waldhoff, *Alcuins Gebetbuch für Karl den Grossen* (Münster: Aschendorff, 2003).

223 Black, Review of *Alcuins Gebetbuch für Karl den Grossen* by Stephan Waldhoff, in *Speculum* 83.3 (2008).

224 Waldhoff prints the most recent edition of the text as item 1a in the appendix of *Alcuins Gebetbuch*. It is also in PL 101, cols. 509–10a, where it is wrongly attached to the *Officia per ferias*.

225 Driscoll, "*Precum libelli*," 73.

226 Michael S. Driscoll, "The Seven Penitential Psalms: Their Designation and Usages from the Middle Ages Onwards," in *Ecclesia Orans* 17 (2000), 157.

227 Jonathan Black, "Psalm Uses in Carolingian Prayerbooks: Alcuin's *Confessio peccatorum pura*," in *Mediaeval Studies* 65 (2003), 2. Black gives background to and an edition of this prayer in this article.

says.[228] Yet the prayer could be used, like the loricae, in a prophylactic way, with recitation intended to protect precators from judgment by cleansing them of sins committed knowingly and unknowingly, by themselves or by their participation in the human condition in general. Alcuin also, significantly, reintroduces prayer *ad horas* as a feature of lay devotion by establishing a devotional program, largely based on the Psalms but focused towards confession of sins, suitable for people such as Charlemagne, with substantial secular duties. The Carolingian reforms thus set a new standard for lay piety, centred on the Psalms, especially among the aristocratic ranks, as the later copies of *Beatus igitur David* as a guide for private devotion attest,[229] as well as the inclusion of *De laude psalmorum* in places like the Frankish noblewoman Dhuoda's handbook of instruction written for her son.[230]

The ecclesial and monastic reforms in which Alcuin played a central role had far-reaching impact. Through him, English forms of piety were exported to the Continent, where they were modified, and, in turn, brought back to England. In England, the Carolingian developments seem to have had greater effect on monastic rather than lay devotion; they inspired people like King Alfred but were especially influential towards the end of the Anglo-Saxon period. Although Continental prayerbooks show evidence of lay piety, late Anglo-Saxon prayerbooks continue to be mostly owned by churchmen.[231] However, they have a different character than the early books. Notably, the Psalms are given a central place, replacing the Gospel extracts. In fact, at the end of the period, the most common manuscript context for prayers apparently intended for private use is appended to the end of psalters.[232] The later books also include a great number of

---

228 Driscoll, "*Precum libelli*," 73.

229 Thomas, "Meaning, Practice and Context," 36.

230 *Dhuoda, Handbook for Her Warrior Son*, ed. and trans. Marcelle Thiébaux (Cambridge: Cambridge University Press, 1998), 232–6.

231 As Bestul points out, there is no evidence that late Anglo-Saxon England adopted Carolingian standards of lay piety. Aside from Alfred's enchiridion, the only prayerbook possibly owned by a layperson was that donated by Alfred's grandson Athelstan to Old Minster, Winchester (BL, Cotton Galba A.xviii), "Continental Sources," 117–18. This book is a psalter with Latin prayers added, and it was written on the Continent.

232 See Bestul for a preliminary checklist of English manuscripts containing private prayers, "Continental Sources," Appendix, 124–6. Twenty of the thirty-nine manuscripts listed are identified as psalters; the majority of these are from the eleventh century or have prayers that were added to them in the eleventh century.

prayers taken from liturgical sources but modified to reflect a single user by switching plural pronouns to singular and changing endings to reflect the gender of the user.[233]

In addition, people like King Alfred, Ælfwine, the dean of New Minster, Winchester (d. 1057), and Bishop Wulfstan (also called Wulstan), of Worcester (d. 1095), compiled personal enchiridions for their own use.[234] These were not prayerbooks; they contained a great deal of edifying and useful information beyond prayers. However, they also contain coherent series of prayers – the precursors of little private offices – for use in private devotions.[235] Alfred's book no longer exists; we know of it from Asser.[236] Ælfwine's and Wulfstan's do survive. Both of these books seem designed to meet the needs of busy churchmen who travel. They contain items such as calendars, prognostications, and collectars. Ælfwine's also contains computistical elements and various prayers: some organized into offices, and some private prayers. Wulfstan's contains a psalter as well as hymns, blessings, and a sequence of private prayers. An additional manuscript, the Galba/Nero prayerbook (named after the library shelfmarks of its manuscripts), written in many different hands, has the same miscellaneous characteristic, although in this case Bernard J. Muir postulates that Galba/Nero reflects the needs and interests of a community.[237] Ælfwine's book has evidence of use by people after him.[238] This was not uncommon. In fact, the early English prayerbooks remained in use in the later period,

233 Thomas, "Meaning, Practice and Context," 84–9.

234 Ælfwine's: BL, Titus D. xxvii + xxvi, dated between 1023 and 1032, edited as Beate Günzel, *Ælfwine's Prayerbook* (London: Boydell, 1993). Wulfstan's: Corpus Christi College, Cambridge, MS. 391, written 1065–6, edited as Anselm Hughes, *The Portiforium of Saint Wulstan*, 2 vols. (London: Henry Bradshaw Society, 1958). Thomas discusses all of these in "Meaning, Practice and Context."

235 Thomas proposes that late Anglo-Saxon prayerbooks include devotional series of prayers that show private offices in an early stage of development: "Meaning, Practice and Context," 115–25, 180–208.

236 Asser, *Asser's Life of King Alfred*, ed. William Henry Stevenson (1904; rprnt. Oxford: Clarendon, 1959), cap. 24.

237 Bernard J. Muir, ed., *A Pre-Conquest English Prayer-Book* (Woodbridge: Boydell, 1988), xvi–xvii. Muir notes that the manuscript was first prepared as a blank book, and the items were written in over time. The manuscript was split up and is now preserved as BL, MS Cotton Galba A.xiv and BL, MS Nero A.ii (ff. 3–13), from the eleventh century.

238 Some of the prayers were modified in the twelfth century to reflect a female precator, Günzel, *Ælfwine's Prayerbook*, 3.

as evidenced by prayers added to Royal in the tenth or eleventh century and glosses added to Cerne in a tenth-century hand.[239]

Thus, innovations in prayer are often laid on top of an older stratum of practices, the two then existing side-by-side, rather than the new completely replacing the old. Over the course of the Anglo-Saxon period, there was increasing use of devotional prayers in addition to the Psalms, which always remained central to prayer and become more central to prayer-books. In Alfred's day, high-status laypeople (at least) showed increasing interest in performing devotional prayer privately. (Chapter 3 discusses this development further in the Alfredian context.) While the prayer texts widen to include non-biblical and non-liturgical prayer for private use, and while there is a slowly increasing place for the individual's experience at the centre of the practice of prayer, the same preference for set and formal prayer over spontaneous prayer is evident from the beginning of the period to the end. Prayer is a ritualized performance that precators inhabit rather than create; as they inhabit it, it recreates them.

By the end of the Anglo-Saxon period, monastic prayer begins to reflect the personal situation and feelings of the one praying to a greater extent, although formal, set prayer continues to be the ideal. Although the confessional and penitential context for prayer increases over the period, teachings on prayer do not reflect the sort of counting of prayer characteristic of commuted penance,[240] nor do they reflect the legal concept of reparation to God as judge present in a writer like Tertullian. The abstract Neoplatonic understanding of the Divine Being reflected in writers such as Cassian and, in some contexts, Augustine lends itself to an aneconomic understanding of prayer because God is not fully personified (or rather, anthropomorphized); however, the Anglo-Saxons tend to remove such an abstract conception of God as they adapt earlier texts for their teachings on prayer and thus they more fully personify God.

The present study examines how Anglo-Saxons teach and understand prayer in those relatively few places where they explicitly teach it or where, like the Alfredian texts, evidence is given as to how precators might have understood and practised this teaching. However, because students of prayer

239 See Brown for an account of all the later corrections, additions, and glosses, *Book of Cerne*, 45–51.

240 Penitentials list penances, which would have included fasting and alms, in time (weeks, months, or years) rather than in numbers of prayers. Counting prayers is therefore more strongly characteristic of commutations and prayers *pro anima*.

bring their own assumptions about prayer practice, what prayer is, what it means, and how it works to the study of prayer, I have first presented in summary fashion the basic context for prayer that the Anglo-Saxons inherited and then developed. In the early monastic ideal, prayer was a discipline that formed precators according to a standard outside themselves, purifying them from fleshly desire (in the Egyptian context), cleansing them from sin, and transforming them as they inwardly integrated the words of the prayers into their thoughts and actions and learned to interpret their own life events through a Christological narrative. Bede's teaching reflects the monastic ideal, and, for him, prayer's most important effects are subjective upon those praying. The works associated with Alfred attest that this ideal also made some inroads into lay practice, although without the full structure of the Office, and with greater emphasis on specific requests. Ælfric directs his teaching, for the most part, towards lay practitioners, for whom he does not seem to expect a great deal of regular practice. In his teaching, prayer is an expression of allegiance, but it is seen as largely prophylactic. Ælfric correspondingly pays more attention to the objective efficacy of prayer and the problem of unanswered prayer: God protects those who pray to him, but precators also earn honour through praying rightly. Each author expects that prayer, as a gift and as a request for gifts, participates in the personhood of the one offering it, although each understands this participation in different ways. As we will see, this is so even though the prayers are not conceptualized as a production of the precator's own heart. The ensuing chapters will tease out those differences.

Chapter Two

Gratiam pro gratia: Bede on Prayer

Teque deprecor, bone Iesu, ut cui propitius donasti uerba tuae scientiae dulciter haurire, dones etiam benignus aliquando ad te, fontem omnis sapientiae, peruenire, et parere semper ante faciem tuam.

(And I beg you, good Jesus, that, as you favourably gave him sweetly to drink the words of your wisdom, you would also kindly grant hereafter to arrive at you, the fount of all wisdom, and to appear ever before your face.)

– The Venerable Bede, *Historia Ecclesiastica*[1]

With this prayer, which functions as a sort of colophon,[2] the Venerable Bede (c. 673–735) ends his most famous work, the *Historia Ecclesiastica Gentis Anglorum*. The prayer exemplifies the reciprocal and intimate way that Bede views prayer and the way reciprocity creates a particular form of subjectivity through the relationship enacted between humans and God in prayer. Several features in the above passage characterize Bede's teaching on prayer, as evidenced in his homilies. The reciprocity Bede imagines is that God might grant future favours on the basis of favours already received and used ("cui propitius donasti uerba tuae scientiae dulciter haurire"). He modestly elides the fact that the favour he received is the

1 Bede, *Historia ecclesiastica gentis Anglorum*, ed. Michael Lapidge et al. (Paris: Les Éditions du Cerf, 2005), 3:194, book 5, ch. 24; my translation.

2 Colophons often contain prayers. Richard Gameson, *The Scribe Speaks? Colophons in Early English Manuscripts* (Cambridge: Cambridge University Department of Anglo-Saxon, Norse, and Celtic, 2002), reproduces a great many.

book just finished, the *Historia*, a major undertaking situating the English people in their place within the community of God's own people. On this basis, of a gift received and used in the service of God, Bede asks to be allowed into Jesus's presence in eternity. Bede imagines God as a lord, and yet he also addresses Jesus intimately by his personal name rather than as *Dominus*, mixing the respect and affective loyalty characteristic of Anglo-Saxon depictions of lordship.

The prayer moves from mediation to presence. Bede acknowledges he has already received the words of Jesus's wisdom and he desires to move to the source of that wisdom. And yet Bede does not picture a mystical union with Christ, in which self and other collapse into one; rather he desires the favour of appearing in Jesus's presence ("parere semper ante faciem tuam"). This is key: he does not ask that *he* might see Jesus's face, but that *Jesus* might see and acknowledge him. For Bede, prayer forms personal identity as precators imagine themselves in relation to God, as seen by God. Bede does not imagine the praying self as formed *against* an other, within an economy of individuals. Rather, the self is constituted as it sees itself through the eyes of another, God, and as it receives and returns God's gifts. Furthermore, the precator prays within a community that is always already praying and which the precator joins in any particular instance of prayer. Therefore, even when a text focuses on personal prayer (as is largely the case in the texts examined in this chapter), the precator is not conceptualized as an individual at prayer.

Exactly what constitutes an "individual" bears consideration. The concept comes up repeatedly in studies of prayer, which often see a distinction between prayer alone and prayer in community.[3] Furthermore, many studies of prayer seek to chart the course of devotional prayer, which is seen as an individual (or at least solitary) endeavour. However, scholars often draw a sharper line between "individual" and corporate prayer than the sources themselves do. While "individual" might be used in the sense I just used it, to denote a single person out of a collective, the term is fraught because it is at the centre of a long-running scholarly debate concerning when the individual was invented or discovered. The birth of the individual was first located in Renaissance Italy, but scholars of earlier eras

3 For instance, M.J. Toswell deals with this problem in her study of the psalter, *The Anglo-Saxon Psalter* (Turnhout: Brepols, 2014), 23–32. As she states, it can be difficult to tell whether psalters were created for corporate liturgical use or individual personal use.

and places have sought to insert their own field of study into the trajectory of this conversation (usefully troubling linear narratives of development in the process). Subjective forms of devotion have often been marshalled as evidence for the existence of individuality at various times and places.[4] As scholars such as Bruce Holsinger and Rachel Fulton make clear, the debate will not be put to rest any time soon, and scholarship has largely moved away from the broad claims of linear progress towards the individual.[5] Indeed, Bede's sense of personal formation, highly dependent as it is on monastic discipline, could not have been the type of subjectivity experienced by "medieval people" in aggregate. Neither am I attempting to define an all-encompassing modern self (although this is easier to do, insofar as it reflects a familiar culture). Rather, I am specifically focused on the type of individual as created by particularly modern forms of exchange and as idealized in Western democratic forms of government.

This individual is someone with an autonomous, privatized identity. The identity of the individual is distinct from the other, unique; thus, the self is defined against the other. The individual, defined as the basic unit of value, shifts the centre of authority away from the king, the clan, or

4 The two most relevant examples are Colin Morris's *The Discovery of the Individual, 1050–1200* (New York: Harper and Row, 1972), in which he resists the idea that the individual was discovered during the Renaissance, locating it instead between the eleventh and twelfth centuries and paying particular attention to forms of religious expression; and David Brakke et al., eds, *Religion and the Self in Antiquity* (Bloomington, Indiana University Press, 2005), which speaks into the same conversation, although this collection of essays seeks to historicize the "self" rather than the individual. Allen J. Frantzen, in seeking to include the Anglo-Saxon period in the historical development of the individual, defines it as a person with self-awareness, interiority, and self-consciousness, *Anglo-Saxon Keywords* (Malden: Wiley-Blackwell, 2012), 148. This is not, however, the type of individual that is generally understood as being "invented." Gavin Flood's study of "interiority" in Christianity, Hinduism, and Buddhism, *The Truth Within: A History of Inwardness in Christianity, Hinduism, and Buddhism* (Oxford: Oxford University Press, 2013), warns us that interiority and individuality should not be too readily equated. In his examination of these three religious traditions he argues that "subjectivity" is shared, not individual and privatized, 8. Carolyn Walker Bynum also cautions against the study of the medieval "individual" without contextualizing him or her within the community; see *Jesus as Mother: Studies in the Spirituality of the High Middle Ages* (Berkeley: University of California Press, 1984), 82–109. Thus, Frantzen's definition is too broad to be really helpful in tracing a history of the "individual."

5 Their introduction to *Medieval Communities and the Matter of Person* (New York: Columbia University Press, 2007) gives a very nice overview of the debate, 1–11.

the state.[6] The individual is also conceptualized as a subject acting independently in his[7] own self-interest. We might call this the modern economic individual: in any transaction between individuals, each one wants to maximize his own profit while minimizing losses, although this is not to say that such transactions cannot be mutually beneficial.

Maurice Godelier situates the concept of the individual within theories of exchange. He argues that in a market society, the "individual" stands outside of exchange, beyond the market. His body is his own property, and even though he may sell (i.e., alienate) parts of himself (his blood, his labour, his skills), it cannot be turned into a commodity by being bought and sold as a whole.[8] The ideal of the pure gift, which I have described in the introduction, posits that something exists outside of the market; the individual, as Godelier describes it, represents the ideal that people are the agents of the market, not its objects. Thus, individual identity is not constituted through exchange. Yet like the pure gift, the individual has an ideological function, mystifying the way modern societies try to unitize or standardize individuals through the educational system and for the convenience of employers. The ideology of individual identity also weakens the ties between individuals and communities, making individuals easier to extract from their communities so that they can move around according to the labour needs of the market. Individual mobility can be mutually beneficial, of course: employers have a deeper pool of skilled employees, and individuals have a bigger market for their skills.

Even though the modern economic individual is not constituted through exchange, clearly those of us in a modern commodity economy construct our identities in part through what we buy. Purchase, however, is seen as

6 Morris certainly understands the individual defined *against* the other, *Discovery of the Individual*, 31; therefore when Christianity became the dominant religion, it no longer contained the sort of pressure towards individualism found in pre-Constantinian Christianity, which required individual conversion and commitment, 24. Characteristic of the modern Western individual are the sense of the individual *against* society and as the source of value. This definition is largely taken from Morris, 3 (the basic unit of value), 7 (as the centre of authority). Morris is especially interested in religious practice and development, noting that Christianity has a greater place for personal belief and individual salvation than other forms of religion.

7 As in the introduction, p. 21 n. 64, I use the masculine pronoun intentionally.

8 Maurice Godelier, *The Enigma of the Gift*, trans. Nora Scott (Cambridge: Polity Press, 1999), 205.

the choice of an agent. The items we buy reflect an identity imagined as innate and interiorly constituted. That identity is assumed to be a unique combination of convictions and tastes arrived at by the self-reflexive individual. In contrast, the identity formed through gifts is an identity received.[9] That is, people do not, for instance, choose their weapons from the local sword mart; rather, they receive weapons (or armour, or jewels) as gifts that confer social identity. People are defined by birth, marked by family heirlooms, and receive identity through the things others give them – none of these markers of identity are individually chosen. Gift objects enmesh them in a web of social identity in which the human parts constitute a whole.

Jos Bazelmans's study of *Beowulf* through the analytic frame of structuralist anthropology describes how received identity works in a reciprocal society that conceptualizes identity as "worth" constituted through exchanges between lords and their retainers:

> The visualization and enlargement of "worth" is realized for the warrior-follower on the one hand by the efforts of the lord who provides him with famous weapons and later with valuables and land, and by the efforts of the warrior-follower himself who achieves fame in his warlike enterprises, and on the other hand for the king by the efforts of the warrior-follower who offers him the booty of his glorious enterprises.[10]

---

9 Or taken. See Peter Baker's chapter "Loot and the Economy of Honour," in *Honour, Exchange and Violence in "Beowulf"* (Cambridge: D.S. Brewer, 2013), on the role of looting in masculine warrior identity. But even the identity formed through looted objects is not internalized until given and given back: "the killer's honour is further augmented when he presents the loot to his king," 62.

10 Jos Bazelmans, "Beyond Power: Ceremonial Exchange in *Beowulf*," in *Rituals of Power: From Late Antiquity to the Early Middle Ages*, ed. Frans Theuws and Janet L. Nelson (Leiden: Brill, 2000), 152. By "worth" Bazelmans means a socially mediated sense of personal identity. One could just as easily say "honour" (in fact, Bazelmans occasionally does use this term), but Bazelmans prefers the word cognate with Old English. I like Bazelmans's use of "worth" because of the way the word blends the concepts of reputation and value. Baker also discusses the concept of honour as related to a warrior's identity; he defines it as "the esteem in which one is held by others, measured by what they say," *Honour, Exchange and Violence*, 13. The central idea for my purposes is that individual self-assessment can produce neither worth nor honour. No one can be honourable merely in his own eyes, and persons do not determine their own value.

The gift of weapons and rings to a retainer shows that the lord recognizes his personal qualities (his "worth"); they "are the visible signs of the inherent or proven worth of those that own them."[11] Others' recognition of personal worth is intrinsic to the value of the items; a purchased sword is therefore worthless, and a stolen sword is worse than worthless; as an antisocial action, it damages worth.[12] The gift objects participate in the identity of those who give them and of those who receive;[13] as they circulate, they become invested with the personality of everyone who has held them, creating personal identity out of the constituent parts of others, embodied in the objects the warrior wears. This system, then, does not amass wealth, but amasses worth,[14] done through the "circulation of beings and things,"[15] which are commensurate with each other.

The exchange dynamics of modern individual identity, therefore, contrast sharply with those of reciprocal identity in the social world of Bede's day. Even though the modern individual is embedded in market dynamics and is, in some sense, commodified for the labour market, personal identity is not conceptualized as a product of exchange. Furthermore, even though the precator that appears in Bede's sermons is not conceptualized as an individual and the words he prays are not his own, Bede still presents prayer as a personal act and as forming personal identity. That identity is constituted through exchange: the sense of participating in a reciprocal gift relationship with God.

While the martial world Bazelmans describes, with its investments in violence and in material things, obviously differs from life in Bede's monastery, Bede nonetheless imagines God as similar to an Anglo-Saxon

11 Bazelmans, "Beyond Power," 351, citing Michael D. Cherniss, *Ingeld and Christ: Heroic Concepts and Values in Old English Christian Poetry* (The Hague: Mouton, 1972).

12 Theft is rather a form of plagiarism, according to Ernst Leisi, "Gold und Manneswert im *Beowulf*," in *Anglia* 71 (1952–3), 271.

13 This is what Bazelmans means by "commensurability," "Beyond Power," 313. Baker also considers the identity invested in objects as they are looted, showing that violence is an intrinsic part of the warrior identity: "Because a warrior and his treasure are commensurable, sharing the property of honour, when that warrior meets a violent end, his killer carries off his honour with his belongings," *Honour, Exchange and Violence*, 62.

14 At the same time, we must avoid the tendency to commodify worth. See above, pp. 42–4.

15 Bazelmans, "Beyond Power," 345.

lord.[16] For Bede, God's gifts work analogously to the weapons and land that an Anglo-Saxon warrior would receive from his king and that he would be expected to use in that king's service. In the process of receiving and enacting those favours, the person receives and performs his own identity. The higher-status economy of honour characterized by gift and favour underlies this model, rather than purchase and payment. Furthermore, because precators are imagined as participating in a reciprocal gift relationship with God rather than a transactional commodity relationship, the gifts God gives are commensurate with himself, and the gifts precators return are likewise commensurate with themselves. Unlike commodities, which balance and break relationships, gifts create and maintain them. In prayer, this happens in an even more "literal" way, since God's gifts constitute the precators' own selves, which are shaped and transformed as they enact those gifts, thereby returning them to God and continuing the gift cycle, characterized by *gratia* (meaning both favour and gratitude), between them. Even though this model of gift giving is masculine, for Bede such reciprocity is as open to women as to men. In fact, the central figures in all Bede's major homilies on reciprocity and on prayer are women whose behaviour is exemplary for men and women alike.

To tease out the implications of reciprocity for self-formation in Bede, in the remainder of this chapter I examine Bede's teachings on prayer in his homilies in four parts. First, I briefly describe Bede's homiletic corpus and its thematic concerns. Second, I build on the idea of reciprocal identity to examine the reciprocal relationship established in the opening homilies of the cycle, in which Bede concentrates on the *gratia* relationship between humans and God exemplified in the figure of Mary and establishes the reciprocal context for prayer in his later homilies. In this part I will bring together discussion of the doctrine of grace and implications of the reciprocity embedded in the social relationship that *gratia* denoted before Christian theologians borrowed it. Third, I will discuss the several distinctive features of Bede's conception of prayer as they appear in the homilies. These features, such as his statements that the only legitimate request is for salvation and that prayer is action, are important to understand the way

16 God is also imagined as father. The Anglo-Saxon lord is patterned on the patriarchal father, and gifts (as I mention in the introduction) attempt to recreate family-like bonds between non-related persons. Socially speaking, the lord becomes a type of surrogate or foster father.

prayer works as gift and also constitutes (and transforms) personal identity. Fourth, I conclude by using the context established by *gratia* and by Bede's conception of prayer to read two of his homilies in more detail. Homily 2.10 explicitly pictures prayer as a gift humans give to God and shows the way the *devotio* (devotion) performed in prayers is exteriorized and interiorized, creating a coherent self formed relationally through God's gifts. Homily 1.22 represents both communal and personal prayer as transforming precators from "Gentile dogs" to "Israelite sheep" as they participate in the *gratia* relationship with God performed through prayer.

Together, these four sections advance the argument that Bede imagines human identity constituted through prayer as a gift, given by God and returned by humans as they internalize and enact the prayers they pray. For Bede, the self is constituted through gifts in a way similar to Bazelmans's construction of "worth" through the social recognition of gifts, but in an even more intrinsic way. Bede does not imagine God's gifts as material markers of identity (for the most part), but rather that God recognizes humans by giving good words, good thoughts, and good works; humans receive identity by enacting these gifts, using them in the service of their lord. Prayer is the means by which this exchange takes place. Bede understands prayer as intrinsically *logos* oriented; the praying self integrates the words of prayer into its thoughts and deeds, thus patterning itself after the word it prays.

Bede's Homilies

While Bede is still most famously known for his *Historia*, the central task of his life was biblical commentary and creating the educational tools necessary for understanding Christian doctrine and practice.[17] Recent scholarship has addressed itself to rectifying the neglect of Bede's exegetical works and to reassessing Bede's authority and innovation as a Christian Latin writer in the process. The essays in the collection *Innovation and Tradition in the Writings of the Venerable Bede* argue against the older view of Bede as a derivative compiler and for a much more central and active role of Bede as "a creator of Christian Latin culture," an *auctor*, and a

17 The most recent introductory overview to Bede's literary output is George Hardin Brown, *A Companion to Bede* (Woodbridge: Boydell, 2009). This is a heavily rewritten version of his earlier *Bede the Venerable* (Boston: Twayne, 1987). For a historical introduction, see Peter Hunter Blair's classic *The World of Bede* (1970; rprnt. Cambridge: Cambridge University Press, 1990), with a new foreword by Michael Lapidge.

"patristic figure."[18] As Joyce Hill shows, Bede influenced medieval exegesis down through the Carolingian era and beyond immensely.[19] Bede's corpus is, as one might expect, filled with prayer, prayers, and people praying. However, he most explicitly details a theory of prayer in his fifty-homily series. The homilies themselves still suffer from a relative lack of attention, with most scholars focusing on source issues, preaching situations and technique, or dissemination, and relatively few focusing on development of specific thematic or theological ideas.[20]

As Bede has, in the past, been considered a derivative writer, it is worth taking a moment to sketch out the differences between his homily cycle and that written by Gregory the Great. The scope of Bede's cycle is most

---

18 Roger Ray, "Who Did Bede Think He Was?" 11; Scott DeGregorio, "Footsteps of His Own: Bede's Commentary on Ezra-Nehemiah," 167; Joyce Hill, "Carolingian Perspectives on the Authority of Bede," 235. All in Scott DeGregorio, ed., *Innovation and Tradition in the Writings of the Venerable Bede* (Morgantown: West Virginia University Press, 2006).

19 See Hill, "Carolingian Perspectives." Bede becomes a central figure for the transmission of Latin Christianity, both in the way he becomes a mediator of the older Latin tradition and through his own innovations, 249. The earliest line of transmission out of Anglo-Saxon England was through St Boniface's missionary activities in Germania, 230.

20 On Bede's sources: Rosalind Love, "Bede and John Chrysostom," in *Journal of Medieval Latin* 17 (2007); Lawrence T. Martin, "Bede's Originality in His Use of the Book of Wisdom in His *Homilies on the Gospels*," in DeGregorio, *Innovation and Tradition*; Frederick M. Biggs, "Bede's Use of Augustine: Echoes from Some Sermons?"," in *Revue Bénédictine* 108.3–4 (1998); A.G.P. van der Walt, "Reflections of the Benedictine Rule in Bede's Homiliary," in *Journal of Ecclesiastical History* 37.3 (1986). On Bede and preaching: Lawrence T. Martin, "Bede and Preaching," in *The Cambridge Companion to Bede*, ed. Scott DeGregorio (Cambridge: Cambridge University Press, 2010) (which replicates information in the introduction to his translation, *Homilies on the Gospels*); John Bequette, "Bede's Advent Homily on the Gospel of Mark: An Exercise in Rhetorical Theology," in *American Benedictine Review* 57 (2006); Eric Jay Del Giacco, "Exegesis and Sermon: A Comparison of Bede's Commentary and Homilies on Luke," *Medieval Sermon Studies Newsletter* 50 (2006); Lawrence T. Martin, "The Two Worlds in Bede's Homilies: The Biblical Event and the Listeners' Experience," in *De Ore Domini*, ed. Thomas L. Amos et al. (Kalamazoo: MIP, 1989). Cyril Smetana, "Paul the Deacon's Patristic Anthology," in *The Old English Homily and Its Backgrounds*, ed. Paul E. Szarmach and Bernard F. Huppé (Albany: State University of New York Press, 1978), established that Paul made frequent use of Bede's homilies in his widely disseminated homiliary, through which Bede's homilies became known to subsequent generations on the Continent and in England. Works specifically focused on Bede's spirituality are discussed in detail below: Scott DeGregorio, "Affective Spirituality: Theory and Practice in Bede and Alfred the Great," in *EMS* 22 (2005), and "The Venerable Bede on Prayer and Contemplation,"

closely akin to Gregory's forty Gospel homilies.[21] Lawrence T. Martin argues that Bede composed his homilies to supplement Gregory's collection.[22] Both cycles use the biblical readings established in the Neapolitan liturgy,[23] but they share only one overlapping pericope between them, for

in *Traditio* 54 (1999); Benedicta Ward, *High King of Heaven: Aspects of Early English Spirituality* (Kalamazoo: Cistercian Publications, 1999), and "Bede and the Psalter," Jarrow Lecture (Newcastle upon Tyne: Saint Paul's Parish Church Council, 1991); and M.T.A. Carroll, *The Venerable Bede: His Spiritual Teachings* (Washington, DC: Catholic University of America Press, 1946). On the audience's identification with Mary: Daniel J. Heisey, "Mary and Mysticism in Bede's Homilies," in *American Benedictine Review* 64.1 (2013).

21 Gregory's homilies were probably split into two books, the second of which begins with Christ's resurrection. The first is randomly ordered in the PL. *Homiliae in evangelia*, ed. Raymond Étaix, CCSL 141, (Turnhout: Brepols, 1999), follows the order given in PL 76 but devotes a section of the introduction to untangling the proposed dates for which the sermons were written, lvix–lxx. Although none of the extant manuscript copies has homilies 1–20 in a stable order, David Hurst, in his translation, *Gregory the Great: Forty Gospel Homilies* (Kalamazoo: Cistercian Publications, 1990), rearranges them in accordance with the liturgical year, beginning just before Advent with the feast day of St Felicity on November 23. Even if this was not the order in which they were written, it is the order in which they would be preached. Because of the variant ordering between editions, I will refer to the homilies by the numbers given in the translation with the pericopes, cross-referenced to the numbers in the CCSL with the rubrications from the PL. Quotations come from the CCSL. For an account of the manuscript copies of Gregory's homilies in England, see Thomas N. Hall, "The Early English Manuscripts of Gregory the Great's *Homilies on the Gospel* and *Homilies on Ezechiel*," in *Rome and the North: The Early Reception of Gregory the Great in Germanic Europe*, ed. Rolf H. Bremmer, Jr, et al. (Paris: Peeters, 2001).

22 Lawrence T. Martin, "Introduction," in *Bede the Venerable: Homilies on the Gospels*, trans. Lawrence T. Martin and David Hurst (Kalamazoo: Cistercian Publications, 1991), 1:xvi. Aaron J Kleist delivers the important warning that Bede's homiletic collection is not quite as coherent as the neat fifty-homily CCSL edition by David Hurst or Martin and Hurst's two-volume translation make it look. See Kleist, *Striving with Grace: Views of Free Will in Anglo-Saxon England* (Toronto: University of Toronto Press, 2008), 59–60, for an outline of the problems, and the table untangling the various editions and authorship questions, 249–66. The chief issue is not the homilies that Hurst includes (all of which are thought to be genuine, although he divides up the homilies differently than the PL does), but the homilies printed by Migne in the PL as uncertain. According to Kleist many of these are actually Bedan. As is the case with Gregory's homilies, a congregation hearing Bede's homilies read would have heard them in the order of the liturgical year, starting at Advent. However, many of Bede's homilies became most widely circulated in the collection of Paul the Deacon, where they would have been mixed in with others' homilies rather than read as a set.

23 *Opera homiletica*, ed. David Hurst, CCSL 122 (Turnhout: Brepols, 1955), viii.

Christmas, for which Bede could have seen the need to amplify Gregory's rather short sermon.[24] The two authors approach Advent through different sets of pericopes. Both authors design their Advent homilies to prepare the hearts of their hearers for Christ to come into them as he came into the world at Christmas. Bede's pericopes focus on Mary, strongly emphasizing *gratia* between Mary and God, while Gregory's pericopes focus on the figure of John the Baptist, whom he presents as exemplary in humility. John functions as a forerunner of this double advent. As John prepared the way for the coming of Christ, with an emphasis on good works, preaching the Gospel and repentance of sins, so too does he become both a preacher whose words Gregory's own audience must hear[25] and a model to emulate in his humility as a forerunner of Christ.[26] Insofar as Gregory conceives of either of these comings in the context of exchange, he imagines a sort of violent "seizing" of the kingdom through contrition. Although "[u]ult a

24 Martin, "Introduction," in *Bede the Venerable*, 2:xvi.

25 In Homily 6 (Homily 20, CCSL 141, 153–69, rubricated *Sabbato Quatuor temporum ante Natalem Christi*, on Lk. 3.1–11, John's preaching in the wilderness) Gregory puts his hearers in the same position as John's hearers: "Sed quia iam peccauimus, quia usu malae consuetudinis inuoluti sumus, dicat quid nobis faciendum sit, ut fugere a uentura ira ualeamus" (But since we have sinned, since we have become accustomed to an evil way of life, let John tell us what we must do to escape the wrath to come), 159, ll. 144–6; trans. Hurst, 40. John's sermon ends with exhortations to righteous living that Gregory applies to his audience as well.

26 Gregory uses John's example to describe a humility that his hearers can emulate in Homily 4 (Homily 7, CCSL 141, 45–52, rubricated *Dominica quarta in Adventu Domini*, on Jn. 1.19–27): "Restat ergo ut in omne quod scit sese mens deprimat, ne quod uirtus scientiae congregat, uentus elationis tollat. Cum bona, fratres, agitis, semper ad memoriam mala acta reuocate" (It remains, then, that the mind should abase itself in regard to everything it knows, lest the wind of exaltation blow away what the virtue of knowledge is vigorously gathering in. When you do something good, my friends, always call to mind the evils you have done), 51, ll. 131–4; trans. Hurst, 25. And he concludes, "In cunctis ergo quae agitis, fratres mei, radicem boni operis humilitatem tenete, nec quibus iam superiores, sed quibus adhuc inferiores estis aspicite" (My friends, in everything you do hold on to humility as the root of good works. Do not look at the things which make you better now, but at those which make you still bad), 52, ll. 164–6; trans. Hurst, 27. Homily 5 (Homily 6, CCSL 141, 38–44, rubricated *Dominica tertia Adventus Domini*) continues using John as an example. Gregory's application is that all Christians should be messengers of God, able to give counsel and encourage others, 42–3, and avoid idle talk, 44. Finally, "ut in quantum uires suppetunt, si annuntiare eum non negligitis, uocari ab eo angeli cum Iohanne ualeatis" (Then as far as your strength allows it, if you do not neglect to make him known, you may be worthy to have him call you an angel along with John), 44, ll. 152–3; trans. Hurst, 33.

nobis omnipotens Deus talem uiolentiam perpeti"[27] (Almighty God desires to suffer this kind of violence from us), Gregory focuses firmly on stressing his audience's need to repent[28] as well as human agency and responsibility within repentance,[29] rather than building a picture of a particular kind of relationship between God and humanity. Bede's concerns reflect a different sensibility as well as different pericopes: Bede emphasizes the relationship between humans and God as expressed through the gift of Jesus's coming into the world at Advent.

The pericopes Bede uses make both John the Baptist[30] and Mary central characters, establishing a relationship with God defined by his munificence

27 Homily 20, CCSL 141, 169, ll. 383–4; trans. Hurst, 48.

28 For instance, he ends Homily 3 (Homily 1, CCSL 141, 5–11, rubricated *Dominica secunda Adventus Domini*, on Lk. 21.25–33, on the signs of Christ's second coming) with a call to repentance in light of the second coming: "Illum ergo diem, fratres carissimi, tota intentione cogitate, uitam corrigite, mores mutate, mala tentantia resistendo uincite, perpetrata autem fletibus punite. Aduentum namque aeterni iudicis tanto securiores quandoque uidebitis, quanto nunc districtionem illius timendo praeuenitis" (Give hard thought to that day, dearly beloved; amend your lives, change your habits, resist and overcome your evil temptations, requite your evil deeds by your tears. The more you now anticipate his severity by fear, the more securely will you behold the coming of your eternal Judge), 11, ll. 151–5; trans. Hurst, 20.

29 Again, Homily 6 (Homily 20, CCSL 141) portrays repentance as an active seizing of the kingdom of heaven: "Recogitemus ergo, fratres carissimi, mala quae fecimus et nosmetipsos assiduis lamentis atteramus. Hereditatem iustorum, quam non tenuimus per uitam, rapiamus per paenitentiam. Vult a nobis omnipotens Deus talem uiolentiam perpeti. Nam regnum caelorum rapi uult nostris fletibus, quod nostris meritis non debetur" (Dearly beloved, let us think over the evils we have committed; let us give ourselves to continual sorrow. Let us seize by our repentance the inheritance of the righteous which we have not kept by our way of life. Almighty God desires to suffer this kind of violence from us. He desires us to seize by our tears the kingdom of heaven which is not owed us on our merits), 169, ll. 381–6; trans. Hurst, 48. Humanity's greater responsibility in salvation is consistent with Gregory's position on the doctrine of grace, according to Kleist: "Prevenient grace does not make humans irresistibly choose good, Gregory suggests, but enables them either to cooperate with or reject God," *Striving with Grace*, 43.

30 Bede's first Advent homily (Mark 1:4–8, on the baptism John gave) begins with the figure of John the Baptist, the precursor to Christ's coming. He begins by focusing on John's baptism as an anticipation of the baptism Christ brings, as the necessary confession and correction of sins that could then be fulfilled in Christ's baptism of forgiveness. It is then Christ's baptism that gives "dationem carismatum in spiritu" (the charismatic gifts of the Spirit), Homily 1.1, CCSL 122, 6, l. 160; trans. Lawrence T. Martin and David Hurst, *Bede the Venerable: Homilies on the Gospels* (Kalamazoo: Cistercian Publications, 1991), 1:7. Bede moves on from there to a typological

and the proper human response to his gifts.[31] These opening homilies set the relational context for the later homilies on prayer, creating a narrative that Bede's hearers can recreate in their own lives as they also meditate on the significance of God's gift of his Son to and in them. Bede uses John to emphasize baptism, the first act that brings a person from death to life, introducing him to God's family. Yet he focuses more on Mary, presenting her as a loyal servant, receiving God's gift of his Son in her own body and then giving thanks for the great gift she has been given. In her obedience, she serves as a model for Christians, who must also receive Christ within themselves, and in whom Christ must grow to fullness in order to come forth into the world. Like Mary, Christians should show grateful awareness for this greatest of gifts which they have received. As they do this, their humility and gratitude move them into an intimate and dependent relationship with God. Bede builds this theme through the first four homilies.

While Bede explicates a twofold scheme of grace in Homily 1.2, which he then illustrates through Mary, many of Bede's homilies show a pattern

---

explication of the figure of John in which John becomes an exemplary saint by separating himself from the allurements of the world. He thus designates the lives of the saints, who "tota semper intentione animi praesentis saeculi desideria spernunt" (always reject the desires of the present world with the whole intention of their minds), Homily 1.1, CCSL 122, 2, ll. 40–1; trans. Martin and Hurst, 1:2. Bede begins laying the foundation for his understanding of humility, to which he returns in Homily 1.4. He says here in Homily 1.1 that what the elect have that others do not is a heightened sense of their sins: "[Q]uia minus perfectos se esse deprehendunt sordes suae fragilitatis undis paenitentiae diluunt" (because they apprehend themselves to be less perfect, they wash away the stains of their weakness with the waves of repentance), CCSL 122, 3, ll. 77–8; trans. Martin and Hurst, 1:4. Bede ends the sermon with an exhortation to prepare for the celebration of Christ's nativity by examining consciences, wiping away negligences, and acquiring virtues, CCSL 122, 6, ll. 177–9; trans. Martin and Hurst, 1:7–8. So far, this is much like Gregory. This is not surprising. Bede borrows slightly from Gregory's homilies at this point, and like Gregory, he is discussing John the Baptist. Bede begins to develop his own context for understanding the relationship between God and man in his next homily, on grace.

31 Although none of the extant MS collections preserves Bede's homilies in any particular order, Hurst arranges them according to the Neapolitan pericopes in his introduction to Bede, *Opera homiletica*, vii. The numbering followed in this chapter is Hurst's (Migne uses a different order; the two numbering systems are helpfully collated by Kleist, *Striving with Grace*, Appendix II, 249–66) because they would have been used in the order of the liturgical year, making the development of the themes outlined above loosely cohere.

of gift giving in which he associates various gifts with various members of the Godhead: the foundational gifts come from God's creative act;[32] further gifts, from Christ's incarnation and sacrifice; and "charismatic" gifts, through the Holy Spirit.[33] God the Father gives the final gift: the eternal reward in the heavenly kingdom. Continual gift giving, with its attendant concepts of grace and humility, establishes a relationship between humans and God that Bede continually invokes in the subsequent homilies. The first homily on prayer, 1.22, falls in Lent, a typical time in any sermon series for teachings on prayer in its collocation with fasting, almsgiving, and vigils. As he approaches Easter, the theme of Christ's sacrifice begins to dominate over gift giving. After Easter, in short order, three more homilies on prayer follow, 2.10, 12, and 14. As the liturgical year moves towards Pentecost, Bede begins to ruminate on the meaning and effect of the Holy Spirit. The Holy Spirit enables Christians to perform good works. Several sermons on apostles exemplify this theme; this naturally leads Bede back to considering gift giving as he emphasizes that everything Christians have, including their good works, are gifts from God that they must use appropriately. The cycle concludes with two homilies outside of the liturgical calendar on the dedications of a church. In these homilies, Bede considers the heavenly and eternal congregation that the earthly church pictures, which ties back to gift giving: God gives a place in the eternal kingdom as the final gift that humans receive for using the gifts they have been given on earth.

Gratia and Principles of Reciprocity

Gratia is a major theme in Bede's opening homilies, and it is also central to Bede's conception of prayer. The doctrine of grace is one of the core (and contested) doctrines of Christian theology. The doctrinal debates can become highly philosophical and abstract, dealing as they do with the nature

32 "[D]e plenitudine conditoris nostri … omnes quicquid boni habemus accepimus" (all of us have received whatever good we have from the fullness of our Maker), Homily 1.2, CCSL 122, 8, ll. 52–3; trans. Martin and Hurst, 1:11.

33 For example, "Baptizat quippe spiritu sancto qui munere spiritus sancti peccata dimittit et accepta remissione peccatorum etiam spiritus eiusdem gratiam tribuit" (He indeed baptized with the Holy Spirit who pardoned sins by the favor of the Holy Spirit; and when they had received forgiveness of sins he also bestowed the grace of the same Spirit), Homily 1.1, CCSL 122, 6, ll. 157–60; trans. Martin and Hurst, 1:7.

of human freedom and will, the effects of the Fall, the redemptive nature of Christ's sacrifice, and God's will and foreknowledge. Yet the Latin term for grace, *gratia*, widely used in both secular and religious contexts, refers in its basic meaning to the favourable disposition one person has for another, although it can also mean "gift" and "gratitude."[34] The participants show *gratia*, in concrete ways: through giving gifts and benefits, and, given in return, gratitude, which they display, not merely feel. Therefore, central to *gratia* are questions of obligation and freedom: the type of obligation humans have towards God and God has towards humans, as well as how much freedom each has to act within a reciprocal economy.

In spite of the sometimes contentious nature of disputes surrounding the doctrine of grace, Bede's teaching does not focus on the doctrinal debate. Rather, his homilies show a social understanding of *gratia* as a disposition of favour, expressed in the gifts that weave together the relationship between God and man. In these homilies, the figure of Mary exemplifies the ideal form of this relationship; as she receives God's gifts to her, she brings Christ forth into the world, thus meriting further gifts. One of the major theoretical (and philosophical) problems at the centre of the doctrine of grace is the question of human agency, or will. Bede bases a major portion of his longest explication of grace, Homily 1.2, on an Augustinian sermon; however, he shifts the exchange paradigms in a way that allows for greater human agency. God and man cooperate together in gift giving in a way that brings honour to both parties.

To more clearly highlight the issues at stake in Bede's discussion of grace, this section begins by using gift theory to consider what is at stake in different models of exchange: different forms of selfhood are embedded in different types of exchange. I then apply these insights to the social concept of *gratia* as found in the reciprocal Greco-Roman patron/client relationship, which early Christian writers adapted to explain God's grace. However, they resisted reciprocal aspects of the social relationship as undermining God's agency (usually referred to in theological discussions as "sovereignty"). I therefore next show that both Paul and Augustine modify *gratia* in ways that clarify that humans can never obligate God to save them: God is always the giving subject; humans always receive. Yet Augustine, who certainly does not believe that humans can "purchase" salvation, uses purchase and wage-earning metaphors to

34 Lewis and Short, sense 2.b.

explain obligation to his audience. After examining those metaphors, I finally look at the way that Bede, explicating the same biblical passage as Augustine and using Augustine as his primary source, shifts the exchange metaphors, giving correspondingly more agency to humans as giving subjects within the relationship with God.

Gratia illustrates nicely the central tenet of gift theory: that gifts are spoken of as though they are voluntary, but "in reality they are given and reciprocated obligatorily."[35] Mauss also states that gift giving is "apparently free and disinterested but nevertheless constrained and self-interested."[36] In a telling mistake, those who follow Mauss often understand him as saying that under the surface, *all* gifts are coercive,[37] and that the goal of a counter-gift is to cancel the "debt" of the first gift, freeing the recipient from dependence on the giver or enabling the recipient to come out ahead in a contest of honour.[38] According to this way of thinking, the goal of gift exchange is to become free of it; to keep, as Lévi-Strauss says, to oneself.[39] However, Mauss's study was driven by his interest in gift giving as a means of exchange in pre-market economies and an early form of contract.[40] In most of his examples, gift exchange takes place, not between people acting as individuals, but acting as the heads of families or clans. Thus, as Maurice Godelier points out, Mauss attends mainly to agonistic – competitive – gift giving like the North American Indian potlatch, in which

35 Marcel Mauss, *The Gift: The Form and Reason for Exchange in Archaic Societies*, trans. W.D. Halls (New York: W.W. Norton, 1990), 3.

36 Mauss, *The Gift*, 3.

37 In fact, Pierre Bourdieu refers to the "symbolic violence" of the gift, maintained and made "misrecognizable" by moral obligations and emotional attachments, *The Logic of Practice*, trans. Richard Nice (Stanford: Stanford University Press, 1990), 126. Bourdieu approaches his theories of the gift from his field work focusing on contests of honour among the Kabyle, a North African honour-based society.

38 This is essentially William Ian Miller's approach in *Bloodtaking and Peacemaking: Feud, Law, and Society in Saga Iceland* (Chicago: University of Chicago Press, 1990). As Baker notes, not all honour-based systems are agonistic, *Honour, Exchange and Violence*, 37n7.

39 Claude Levi-Strauss, *The Elementary Structures of Kinship*, ed. and trans. Robert Needham, trans. James Harle Bell and John Richard von Sturmer (rev. ed. Boston: Beacon, 1969), 497.

40 Mauss: "We shall describe the phenomenon of exchange and contract in those societies that are not, as has been claimed, devoid of economic markets … In these societies we shall see the market as it existed before the institution of traders … We shall see how it functioned … before the discovery of forms of contract and sale," *The Gift*, 4.

the participants compete, through spectacular generosity in gift giving, for power and prestige.[41]

We can clear up some confusion by following Godelier to note that many theorists fail to make a clear distinction between agonistic (competitive) and non-agonistic (cooperative) gift giving. Mauss studies agonistic gift giving; the potlatch, as a substitute for battle (the prize is usually honour, not wealth), is an extreme example. But Mauss's insights are frequently applied to gift giving of all forms – public, political, and corporate, or personal, private, and intimate. Because Mauss writes of gift giving as, in reality, "self-interested," many assume that such gift giving is also individualistic and therefore assume that all exchanges take place between the type of self-interested individuals embedded in modern economic theory. All gifts are then assumed to be calculating, egoistic, self-interested. If this is what is meant by the position that there are no free or pure gifts, it is indeed a cynical position to adopt! But people can mean two things when they say that there is no free or pure gift: either the claim just discussed – that no gifts are purely altruistic, of the sort idealized in contrast to the market economy, and that some advantage always accrues to the giver; or the second claim – that most gifts happen within already-established relationships, in a state of "generalized reciprocity," in which reciprocal dependence already features. In this case, even though giving generally benefits the giver, no one keeps account of who has given what and whose turn is up next; rather, a brother (for instance) gives in response to his sister's need, and a sister gives out of her excess, and each will eventually get back more or less what they have given in.

The agonistic gift is usually public and communal. Marshall Sahlins picks up this thread when he puts the political aspects in Mauss's conclusion to *The Gift* in conversation with Hobbes's *Leviathan*.[42] Hobbes argues that the state of nature is the "warre" of every man with every man – the self-interested individual, who has a right (eventually ceded to the state) of using violence to protect his own interests. Sahlins argues that Mauss presents the gift as a substitute for violence, an alternative action that quells violence. But here Sahlins specifically speaks of gifts between

41 Maurice Godelier, "Some Things You Give, Some Things You Sell, but Some Things You Must Keep for Yourselves," in *The Enigma of Gift and Sacrifice*, ed. Edith Wyschogrod et al. (New York: Fordham University Press, 2002), 25.

42 Marshall Sahlins, "The Spirit of the Gift," in *The Logic of the Gift: Toward an Ethic of Generosity*, ed. Alan D. Schrift (New York: Routledge, 1997), 85–95.

warring peoples that establish peaceful relations and the ability to trade with each other. Claude Lévi-Strauss also notes the close relationship between the gift and violence: "Exchanges are peacefully resolved wars, and wars are the result of unsuccessful transactions."[43] Lévi-Strauss primarily studies the "gift" of women in exogamous marriage arrangements, the kinship ties that result, and the process of making enemies (and everyone unknown is an enemy) into friends and kin.

Once the gift has done its work, creating kin groups and peace, gifts become non-agonistic. This gift usually circulates within communities and families, not between them. As Godelier points out, most gift giving is actually non-agonistic.[44] One of the key markers of non-agonistic gift giving is, according to him, that "[t]he giving of gifts and counter-gifts creates a state of mutual indebtedness and dependence which presents advantages for all parties."[45] The Roman patron/client or the lord/thegn relationships are (ideally) non-agonistic. Participants enter voluntarily and attempt to create family-like relationships of mutual benefit and trust. Thus, one could imagine that elements of quelling "warre" might pertain to establishing the initial relationship; each party needs to demonstrate that he is well-intentioned towards the other. However, each person generally desires to win the admiration, affection, and trust of the other, not to gain honour at the expense of the other. The relationship is fundamentally cooperative, and each party gives and receives as needed without the one-to-one return of transactionality. That is, as Godelier helps us see, these types of gift exchanges never create balance in which giving cancels the "debt" between the two parties. Rather, "[t]hey create new debts that counterbalance the earlier ones. According to this logic, gifts constantly feed obligations."[46] The term for the obligation caused by gifts is "gratitude." Because gratitude, as Georg Simmel argues, strengthens social order, it is a matter of morals, not manners.[47] Failures in gratitude reflect on people's moral character, not

43 Levi-Strauss, *Elementary Structures of Kinship*, 67.

44 Godelier, "Some Things You Give," 25–6.

45 Godelier, *Enigma of the Gift*, 48.

46 Godelier, "Some Things You Give," 26.

47 Georg Simmel: "Gratitude, in the first place, supplements the legal order. All contacts among men rest on the schema of giving and returning the equivalence. The equivalence of innumerable gifts and performances can be enforced. In all economic exchanges in legal form, in all fixed agreements concerning a given service, in all obligations of legalized relations, the legal constitution enforces and guarantees the reciprocity of service and return service – social equilibrium and cohesion do not exist without it. But there

their social polish, and we must be careful not to sentimentalize it: gratitude can be felt as a burden or as a joy.[48] In a non-agonistic relationship, both parties are indebted to each other, and the interests of one party are not seen to be at odds with the interests of the other. In an economy of honour, non-agonistic giving contributes to the honour of both. When Bede imagines the relationship with God as reciprocal, he imagines it as non-agonistic, cooperative, contributing to the honour of both. Furthermore, the relationship is one the precator wishes to continue, not to leave.

Gratia's social aspect becomes obscured as theologians parse the doctrine of grace in ever more abstruse and specialized language; however, the reciprocity and mutual obligation embedded in *gratia* create some problems for Christian theologians when they adopt the term for doctrinal use. Even though a *gratia* relationship is hierarchical, once the patron has graciously shown his favour and the client has shown his gratitude, the patron is as enchained in the obligations as the client. However, while obligation – the nature of the social relations between people – is a concept central to gift theory, the core of the debates over the doctrine of grace is usually the question of human volition, the ability to choose between good and evil. Eugene TeSelle summarizes the controversy surrounding the doctrine of grace in two central questions: "the effect of the sin of Adam and Eve upon their descendants," and "the ability of sinners to return to God" whether by grace or by free will.[49] Jaroslav Pelikan, however, puts the early, pre-Augustinian debates on grace in the context of the then-dominant pagan understanding of fate. Part of what was at stake at this point was concern to clarify that God was not subject to fate but free to

---

also are innumerable other relations, to which the legal form does not apply, and in which the enforcement of the equivalence is out of the question. Here gratitude appears as a supplement. It establishes the bond of interaction, of the reciprocity of service and return service, even where they are not guaranteed by external coercion": "Faithfulness and Gratitude," in *The Sociology of Georg Simmel*, ed. and trans. Kurt H. Wolff (Toronto: The Free Press, 1950), 44.

48 Simmel: "[T]he condition of gratitude easily has a taste of bondage, that it is a moral *character indelibilis* (inextinguishable element). A service, a sacrifice, a benefit, once accepted, may engender an inner relation which can never be eliminated completely, because gratitude is perhaps the only feeling which, under all circumstances, can be morally demanded and rendered": "Faithfulness and Gratitude," 47.

49 Eugene TeSelle, "The Background: Augustine and the Pelagian Controversy," in *Grace for Grace: The Debates after Augustine and Pelagius*, ed. Alexander Y. Hwang et al. (Washington, DC: Catholic University of America Press, 2014), 1.

act as he saw fit, showing favour on whom he would show favour.[50] The goal of early formulations of the doctrines surrounding the nature of sin and the human freedom to choose the good, then, was to preserve God's freedom as well as human freedom. As Pelikan reveals (although this is not his main point), the elements of the doctrine of grace that tend to be emphasized at any given time and place respond to the intellectual pressures of that specific time and place. Thus, if one imagines God as embedded in social relationships (Neoplatonism did not), one could reword the central issue to replace human volition with social obligation: humans are obligated to God. The question then becomes whether a human being can choose to do good such that God would be obligated to show his favour.

Bede puts much greater emphasis on human obligation than on volition. By treating grace as though it were a social relationship between humans and God, he also enmeshes God within the reciprocal obligations of *gratia*. Aaron J Kleist gives a helpful account of the relationship between Bede's teaching on grace and those of Augustine and Gregory. He concludes that Bede's understanding is more indebted to Gregory, who gives a greater role to the human ability to cooperate with or reject God than does Augustine, while adding further emphasis on human merit.[51] Kleist's interest lies in tracing the development of the doctrine in Anglo-Saxon England, not in the more specific issue that interests me here, the type of personhood or reciprocal social structures embedded in the concept. It is therefore instructive to remember *gratia*'s place within the field of petition and giving from which Augustine borrowed it and to consider the ways it could still carry the more concrete semantic charge of social models of reciprocity and obligation. In fact, the primary meaning of the Old English word used to translate *gratia*, *gifu*, is "gift," and there are places in Bede's sermons where the more concrete semantic range of *gifu*, as well as social practices of reciprocity, seems to underlie his understanding of grace.

Here let me apply the theoretical discussion of the gift to the concept of *gratia* in summary form: even though *gratia* is often spoken of as *gratuitus* (free, although "free" merely means it goes beyond obligation; it is received as generous), socially speaking, the sort of favour *gratia* implies is reciprocal. *Gratia* follows the distinction Mauss makes for the gift, being

---

50 Jaroslav Pelikan, *The Christian Tradition*, vol. 1 (Chicago: University of Chicago Press, 1975), 283–4.

51 See Kleist, *Striving with Grace*, for an explication of Bede's understanding of the doctrine of grace.

in theory voluntary but in reality obligatory. The gift creates moral obligation (gratitude), not legal. As Simmel says, a general lack of gratitude is a moral failing. Thus, while *gratia* has the characteristic of non-agonistic relationships – voluntarily given, desired, and non-agonistic – as Godelier helps us see, it is not a free gift.[52] *Gratia* creates and maintains relationships, freely entered into, between social unequals. Like the sort of gift giving Bazelmans charts between Germanic warriors, *gratia* signals esteem, a recognition of the personal qualities of the parties involved; thus Latin authors show preference for the language of friendship (*amicus*) rather than dependence (*cliens*).[53] Richard P. Saller clarifies the type of reciprocity found in *gratia* in patronage relationships: it was "often provoked by a *beneficium* or *officium* for which it constituted a kind of repayment ... [T]he relationship was thought of as something like that of a debtor and creditor."[54]

The terminology here easily misleads, because we associate payments and debt with impersonal institutions like banks, but the *gratia* relationship was not impersonal. Furthermore, the "kind of repayment" *gratia* obligates is not *in fact* a repayment: the return is open, not specified, thus leaving an element of freedom. The relationship also had an affective component, inextricably linking the public and private.[55] As illustration, Saller quotes Pliny's idealistic description of a patronage relationship in which he was client: "I came to love him through admiration, and, contrary to the general rule, when I knew him intimately, I admired him even more ... I was only a young man at the time, and yet he showed me the regard and, I venture to say, the respect he would have shown an equal."[56] In many ways, the idealized relationship between an Anglo-Saxon lord and his retainers was similar, although the affective aspect was even more pronounced, and the relationship, through the mutual recognition of "worth," even more central to a retainer's sense of his own identity. To

52 As defined in, for instance, Jonathan Parry, "The Gift, the Indian Gift and the 'Indian Gift,'" in *Man* 21.3 (1986); and Jacques Derrida, *Given Time I: Counterfeit Money*, trans. Peggy Kamuf (Chicago: University of Chicago Press, 1994).

53 Richard P. Saller, *Personal Patronage under the Early Empire* (Cambridge: Cambridge University Press, 1982), 9–10.

54 Saller, *Personal Patronage*, 21.

55 Saller, *Personal Patronage*, 26. A key point to his argument is that there was no distinction between the personal and the bureaucratic in the early Empire (the focus of Saller's study).

56 Ep. 4.17.4f, qtd. in Saller, *Personal Patronage*, 26–7.

cite only the most obvious example, the speaker of the Old English poem *The Wanderer* places a higher value on the bond and the bind of the gift (to borrow Derrida's phrase[57]) than he does on independence. He experiences his wide freedom in the world as loneliness as he

sohte sele dreorig   sinces bryttan,
hwær ic feor oþþe neah   findan meahte
þone þe in meoduhealle   min mine wisse,
oþþe mec freondleasne   frefran wolde,
weman mid wynnum.[58]

(sadly sought a hall of a giver of treasures, where, far or near, I could find one who would know my mind [or intention, love] in the mead-hall, or comfort me in my friendless condition, attract me with joys.)

The Wanderer values exactly the social bonds the gift creates, a space where friends welcome and know him, where he has particular rights and duties within a particular group of people.

In the pre-Christian Greek and Roman religions, relationships between gods and men followed the same exchange dynamic as relationships between patrons and clients.[59] According to Claude Moussy, the earliest form of the word (*grates*) developed from the Indo-European root meaning "to talk to a god," specifically in the context of praise, sacrifice, asking for favours and giving thanks for them – a reciprocal relationship between gods and men that benefitted both.[60] In this respect, *gratia* and the Greek *charis* (χάρις) both follow similar trajectories. Simon Pulleyn argues that the fundamental relationship between Greeks and their gods was governed by *charis*, the

57 Derrida, *Given Time*, 27.
58 George Phillip Krapp and Elliott Van Kirk Dobbie, *The Exeter Book*, ASPR III (New York: Columbia University Press, 1936), 134, ll. 25–9.
59 Jörg Rüpke, *Religion of the Romans*, trans. Richard Gordon (Cambridge: Polity), 100–2. "If one concentrates only on the isolated act, it is easy to fall into mistaken generalizations (such as the over-familiar 'principle' *do ut des*, I give so that you may give, and so on). Rather, gift giving constitutes a system of exchange, in which the (human) participants operate with a notion of generalized, or non-specific, reciprocity, just as they do in 'horizontal' transactions with one another. What they expect is a long-term gift-equilibrium, not an immediate one-to-one return," 102.
60 Claude Moussy, *Gratia et sa famille* (Paris: Presses Universitaires Blaise Pascal, Clermont-Ferrand, 1966), 35–40.

Greek word that also came to mean the doctrinal concept of "grace." In both of these relationships, humans had a claim on the gods' help when they sacrificed to the gods. As Pulleyn describes, "The worshipper establishes with the god a relationship not of strict indebtedness but rather one where the god remembers the gift and feels well disposed in future."[61]

It fell to the apostle Paul to redefine *charis* for the purposes of Christian doctrine. Paul's use of the term has naturally generated a great deal of discussion, central as it is to key Christian doctrines. One of the important passages is Romans 5:15–17 (I have inserted the Greek terms in parentheses):

> But the free gift (*charisma*) is not like the trespass. For if the many died through the one man's trespass, much more surely have the grace (*charis*) of God and the free gift (*dōrea*) in the grace (*chariti*) of the one man, Jesus Christ, abounded for the many. And the free gift (*dōrema*) is not like the effect of the one man's sin. For the judgment following one trespass brought condemnation, but the free gift (*charisma*) following many trespasses brings justification. If, because of the one man's trespass, death exercised dominion through that one, much more surely will those who receive the abundance of grace (*charitos*) and the free gift (*dōreas*) of righteousness exercise dominion in life through the one man, Jesus Christ.

The Greek words for gift, *charisma* and *dōrea*, are often translated simply as "gift," but I quote from the New Revised Standard Version from 1989, which translates *charisma* and *dōrea* in the passage as "free gift" to drive home the theological point that salvation is gratuitous. Michael L. Satlow articulates the interpretive issue in the passage:

> In this brief passage, Paul emphasizes no fewer than four times that Christ was a "gift" (*dōrea*). ... There is certainly an unresolved tension here: on the one hand, Paul asserts that God gave Christ freely *and expects nothing in return*. On the other hand, Paul certainly thinks that we owe God for this gift and that God too expects our appreciation and piety in return. Paul is struggling with the nature of this gift.[62]

61 Simon Pulleyn, *Prayer in Greek Religion* (Oxford: Clarendon, 1997), 13. James R. Harrison cites the same attitude in the Roman sources, *Paul's Language of Grace in Its Graeco-Roman Context* (Tübingen: Paul Mohr Verlag, 2003), 210.

62 Michael Satlow, *The Gift in Antiquity* (Hoboken: Wiley-Blackwell), 3–4, italics mine.

In the Romans passage, Paul certainly says that God gave Christ freely, but it actually says nothing at all about whether he expects a return. Because I approach this passage through theories of exchange, what strikes me is the way modern commentators (Satlow is here exemplary; he explicates according to common Protestant doctrine) locate Paul's putative struggle at exactly the point where the modern world diverges from the ancient: the free gift.[63] That is, the struggle he attributes to Paul might be our own. In fact, Paul's point is cleared up if we understand that by free gift *we* mean one that is unconstraining and unconstrained, where the giver gives gratuitously while the recipient is not obligated to any sort of return. Following this chain of logic, in which the gift does not reflect or create social ties, John Caputo (using Derrida's definition of the pure gift) argues that the radical nature of Jesus's message was, in fact, that God gives salvation to those who did not and would never accept it, on the grounds that grace that expects a return is not a free gift.[64] Paul's emphasis could be, however, not on *human* freedom to act but on *God's* freedom to act. If so, his point is that God's gift cannot be predisposed by any human action. God is not a Greco-Roman patron; people do not need to approach him with gifts or be already in his household to receive his *charis*, his *gratia*. Indeed, there are no gifts that created beings, fallen out of favour through sin, can give to the source of life. Rather, God offers his *gratia* freely, to enemies as well as friends, and people receive it, in turn, with *gratia*. God's free gift *does* obligate humans, but through the moral weight of gratitude, not through force.[65]

---

63 Harry Liebersohn argues that as new forms of social organization came about in the late eighteenth and early nineteenth centuries, the norms of reciprocal gift giving became increasingly incomprehensible to Europeans, *The Return of the Gift: The European History of a Global Idea* (Cambridge: Cambridge University Press, 2011), 166–7.

64 John D. Caputo, "The Time of Giving, the Time of Forgiving," in *The Enigma of Gift and Sacrifice*. One implication, which was found in Gnosticism (see Pelikan, *Christian Tradition*, 282–3) but which was not common in the Middle Ages, as far as I know, is that since humans can do nothing to merit God's favour, they can do nothing and need do nothing for salvation, opening up a sense of distance between *gratia*-endowed humans and God. The idea that humans can do nothing to merit salvation is stated in a hardened form in the Calvinism of the Reformation, and one can see the anxiety it causes in various literary works as authors such as John Donne and James Hogg, in *Confessions of a Justified Sinner*, struggle with the implications.

65 Harrison, *Paul's Language*, examines the Greco-Roman ideologies of benefaction, especially in the cult of the emperor Augustus, to contextualize Paul's teaching on grace. His overarching argument is that Paul contrasts the fullness of God's beneficence with human beneficence, especially as it formed part of the cult of the emperor Augustus.

Whether or not my amateur reading of Paul passes muster with trained theologians and biblical scholars, it is certainly the way Augustine understood *gratia* in the source that Bede used in his Homily 1.2 to explicate John 1:16.[66] In Augustine's reading of the verse in his lectures on the Gospel of John,[67] Augustine argues that all freedom is on God's side, while all obligation is on the human side. John 1:16 states, "et de plenitudine eius nos omnes accepimus gratiam pro gratia"[68] (And of his fullness we all have received, and grace for grace). The verse presents a translation problem: is "gratiam *pro* gratia" to be understood as excess ("grace upon grace") or as exchange ("grace in exchange for grace")? The Greek clarifies the superlative nature of God's grace (*charin anti charitos*, "grace *upon* grace"), but the Latin (like the English) hovers ambiguously between the meanings of excess or exchange: is this grace *in exchange* for grace? Grace *in proportion to* grace? Grace *by virtue of* grace? And whose *gratia* are we talking about when the word can mean either favour or gratitude?[69] Is John saying that human gifts predispose God's favour, or that humans return thanks to God for his favour?

The Latin translations circulating at the time translated the passage two ways. The version above is the Vulgate, but the Vetus Latina versions often lacked the *et*, which is how Bede quotes the verse.[70] Augustine makes

---

Beneficence traditionally involved some amount of worth in the recipient. In contrast, God's gifts respond only to human need, not to human worth, and he extends his grace to enemies (not friends) before they have even asked for it. Humans can do nothing, before or after God's gift, to obligate God.

66 As the major interpreter of the concept of grace, Augustine's conception of grace has generated as much discussion as Paul's. For a recent reassessment of the afterlife of the Pelagian controversy see Hwang et al., *Grace for Grace*. For a treatment of Augustine's teaching on grace in his sermons, see Anthony Dupont, Gratia *in Augustine's Sermones ad populum during the Pelagian Controversy: Do Different Contexts Furnish Different Insights?* (Leiden: Brill, 2013). For a summary of the orthodox Augustinian position, as well as its knowledge and reception in Anglo-Saxon England, see Kleist, *Striving with Grace*.

67 Augustine, Tractatus 3, *In Ioannis evangelium tractatus*, ed. R. Willems, CCSL 36 (Turnhout: Brepols, 1954), on John 1:15–18.

68 Homily 1.2, CCSL 122, 8, ll. 34–5. This is the version Bede uses. The Vulgate reads: "… accepimus et gratiam pro gratia." Biblical translations are taken from the Douay-Rheims unless otherwise noted.

69 Interestingly, as we shall see in Augustine's commentary on the verse, Tract. 3.8, CCSL 36, he uses a version reflecting the Vulgate.

70 For transcripts of the Vetus Latina manuscripts see P.H. Burton et al., eds., *Vetus Latina Iohannes*, The Verbum Project, April 2015, http://www.iohannes.com/vetuslatina/.

a point of using a version that matches the Vulgate in order to argue for a reading that prefers an excess of grace, in which all *gratia* comes from God:

> *Et de plenitudine eius nos omnes accepimus.* Quid accepistis? *Et gratiam pro gratia.* Sic enim habent uerba euangelica, collata cum exemplaribus graecis. Non ait: Et de plenitudine eius nos omnes accepimus, gratiam pro gratia; sed sic ait: *Et de plenitudine eius nos omnes accepimus, et gratiam pro gratia,* id est, accepimus, ut nescio quid nos uoluerit intellegere de plenitudine eius accepisse, et insuper gratiam pro gratia. Accepimus enim de plenitudine eius, primo gratiam; et rursum accepimus gratiam, gratiam pro gratia.[71]

> ("And of His fullness have all we received." What have you received? "And grace for grace." For so run the words of the Gospel, as we find by a comparison of the Greek copies. He does not say, And of His fullness have all we received grace for grace; but thus He says: "And of His fullness have all we received, and grace for grace" – that is, have we received; so that He would wish us to understand that we have received from His fullness something unexpressed, and something besides, grace for grace.)

The *et* allows Augustine to emphasize the superlative, inexpressible nature of God's grace towards abject humanity who do nothing but receive.

However, in arguing for God's grace, the primary paradigm Augustine uses is not a patron/client relationship but rather one characterized by purchasing or wage earning. That Augustine does so draws attention because the types of exchange assume different kinds of relationships. In contrast to the patron/client relationship, wages/purchase posit an impersonal relationship between two agents who are morally independent, in which the worker has the right to sell his own labour to the employer, and where their obligation towards each other does not extend beyond the terms of the work and the payment.[72] Both relationships are freely entered into and hierarchical, but *gratia* is personal, and the client might gain the patron's favour by performing some service or giving a gift. Conversely,

71 Tract. 3.8, CCSL 36, ll. 1–10. Augustinian translations not otherwise attributed are mine, although based on NPNF, First Series, vol. 7.

72 The gospels contain a parable, Matt. 20:1–16, of the labourers in the vineyard, making use of this understanding of employment.

the patron might win the client's gratitude by showing him favour. In either case, they continue in a relationship of good will, each "owing" the other services within a relationship idealized as a warm one between *amici* (friends) who mutually admire one another.[73]

But Augustine begins first by arguing against thinking of grace as something that can be bought, correcting the error that humans can in any way buy God's favour with good works. He emphasizes this repeatedly: "gratia tibi data est, non merces reddita ... Non enim praecedentibus meritis emisti quod accepisti"[74] (grace is given to you, not wages paid ... Indeed, you did not by previous merits purchase what you received). He hammers on this point: "Quid est gratis data? Donata, non reddita. Si debebatur, merces reddita est, non gratia donata"[75] (What is "freely given"? "Given," not paid. If it was owed, wages were rendered, not grace given). Augustine displaces any human ability to control the transaction, to imagine that what they receive is a "return" (*reddita*) on labour. Rather, he emphasizes the completeness of human helplessness and the gratuity of God's *gratia*: "Non se quisque compalpet, redeat in conscientiam suam ... inueniet non se dignum fuisse nisi supplicio. Si ergo supplicio dignus fuisti, et uenit ille qui non peccata puniret, sed peccata donaret; gratia tibi data est, non merces reddita"[76] (Let not each one flatter himself, but let him return into his own conscience ... he will find that he was not worthy of anything except punishment. If, therefore, you were worthy of punishment, and he came who would not punish sins, but forgive sins, grace was given to you, not wages rendered). God gives, *dat*, first; he does not *reddat*, as though he has taken or received something from a human first-giver, as though God is the recipient and not the giving subject. Humans cannot give the first gift.[77]

And yet, Augustine continues on to use the language of wage and debt as a metaphor for the exchange between humans and God. After receiving

73 Saller, *Personal Patronage*, 8–15.

74 Tract. 3.8, CCSL 36, ll. 19–21.

75 Tract. 3.9, CCSL 36, ll. 54–6.

76 Tract. 3.8, CCSL 36, ll. 13–14, 16–19.

77 Simmel: "I am caused to return a gift, for instance, by the mere fact that I received it. Only when we give first are we free, and this is the reason why, in the first gift, which is not occasioned by any gratitude, there lies a beauty, a spontaneous devotion to the other ... which cannot be matched by any subsequent gift, no matter how superior its content": "Faithfulness and Gratitude," 47.

the "first grace" of faith, Augustine, addressing his audience, says, "promereberis Deum uiuendo ex fide"[78] (you will win over God in living by faith). He shortly continues:

> Si enim fides gratia est, et uita aeterna quasi merces est fidei: uidetur quidem Deus uitam aeternam tanquam debitam reddere (cui debitam? Fideli, quia promeruit illam per fidem); sed quia ipsa fides gratia est, et uita aeterna gratia est pro gratia.[79]
>
> (Indeed, if faith is grace, eternal life is like the wages of faith: it seems indeed God renders eternal life as if owed (owed to whom? To the faithful, because they merited it through faith), but because faith itself is grace, eternal life is also grace for grace.)

After arguing earlier for "gratiam pro gratia" as excess of grace, Augustine shifts to emphasize the exchange latent in the phrase; grace becomes the coin, as it were, which the faithful trade for further grace. Augustine next uses the language of debt, borrowing an example from Paul[80] who, although unworthy (*indignum*), having received unmerited grace, "[i]am debitum flagitat, iam debitum exigit"[81] (now demands the debt, he requires what is owed). Only, in a surprise twist in the end, the debtor is not Paul but God himself: "Quod ergo praemium immortalitatis postea tribuit, dona sua coronat, non merita tua"[82] (Therefore, in later granting the reward [although the idea is perhaps of giving from surplus] of immortality, he crowns his own gifts, not your merits). Through these two metaphors, wage and debt, Augustine conveys the key idea that God is always the giving subject, humans always receive. The faithful act as an *alter* to God's *ego*, a sort of shell company allowing God to trade with himself. This trade puts God's limitless immortality into circulation, allowing the faithful a share in it (*praemium*). Through the metaphors of wage and debt, Augustine creates room for human agency, although that agency is always as the recipient, never the giving subject.

78 Tract. 3.9, CCSL 36, ll. 11–12.
79 Tract. 3.9, CCSL 36, ll. 15–19.
80 II Tim. 4:6–8.
81 Tract. 3.10, CCSL 36, ll. 10–11.
82 Tract. 3.10, CCSL 36, ll. 17–18.

Augustine's idea of *gratia* therefore preserves God's moral independence,[83] while clarifying human obligation to respond to God's grace. For instance, he says, "Expellite ergo de cordibus uestris carnales cogitationes, ut uere sitis sub gratia"[84] (Therefore, expel from your hearts carnal thoughts that you might be truly under grace), and "Coronat autem in nobis Deus dona misericordiae suae: sed si in ea gratia, quam primam accepimus, perseueranter ambulemus"[85] (Yet, God crowns in us the gifts of his own mercy, if we walk with perseverance in that grace which we first received). All obligation is on humans' side; all freedom is on God's. To clarify, I am not here speaking to the doctrinal question of human free will; rather, to the extent of obligation embedded in reciprocity. Even in a voluntary and hierarchical relationship, such as the patron/client, receiving the client's gifts obligates the patron to respond. The obligation is not juridical and legally enforceable, but moral. A patron who accepts gifts but refuses favour will eventually damage his reputation – he lessens his "social capital," to borrow the term from Bourdieu. For Augustine, the value of preferring the language of purchase and debt, rather than the language of patron/client, is that it frees God from the claims of true reciprocity. While using the language of exchange, Augustine resists actual reciprocity.

As Bede adapts Augustine in his own homily on the same passage, Bede also wants to emphasize the superlative nature of God's grace; however, he does not use metaphors of wage, purchase, or debt but rather more clearly the language of benefaction. Because of this, he emphasizes the magnanimous nature of God's gifts and the responsibility of humans to use those gifts. Bede's homily therefore creates a role for humans as givers back. He creates a sense of the superlative nature of grace while situating grace within an exchange paradigm of the gift.

According to Kleist, Homily 1.2 is one of Bede's longest explications of grace, in which grace receives more emphasis than merit.[86] Even so, when compared to the Augustinian source, Bede clearly shifts the exchange paradigm in a way that gives more agency to humans as giving subjects. But first, throughout the homily Bede emphasizes that whatever humans

83 "Moral independence" means that no moral tie binds the two parties created through the exchange of gifts. See Louis Dumont, *Essays on Individualism: Modern Ideology in Anthropological Perspective* (Chicago: Chicago University Press, 1986), 25.

84 Tract. 3.19, CCSL 36, ll. 1–2.

85 Tract. 3.10, CCSL 36, ll. 25–7.

86 Kleist, *Striving with Grace*, 79.

have comes from God, clarifying that no human action precedes or predisposes God's action: "omnes quicquid boni habemus accepimus curandum summopere"[87] (all of us have received whatever good we have from the fullness of our maker). Adapting Augustine, he explains that *gratiam pro gratia* is twofold grace: "nos gratiam accepisse testatur [euangelista] unam uidelicet in praesenti alteram in futuro; in praesenti quidem *fidem quae per dilectionem operatur* in futuro autem uitam aeternam"[88] ([The evangelist] is testifying that we have received a twofold grace, namely one grace in the present and another for the future – in the present, *faith which works through love*, and for the future, life eternal). Although here it seems that God gives humans "good works" and then eventually gives eternal life as two separate, not-necessarily-related bestowals, the first *gratia* and the second *gratia* are not unconnected.

Like Augustine, Bede clarifies that no human action precedes or predisposes God's action. Bede points out that "de plenitudine conditoris nostri non quidam sed omnes quicquid boni habemus accepimus"[89] (not only some of us, but all of us have received whatever good we have from the fullness of our Maker). The fact of this indebtedness entails obligation for gratitude upon the recipient: "ne si ingratus largitori remanserit, perdat bonum quod accepit"[90] ([b]y remaining ungrateful towards his benefactor, he may lose the good which he has received). By refusing to enter fully into the relationship of *gratia* by not recognizing the obligation that God's gifts place upon a person, by refusing to give *gratia* in response to *gratia*, the recipient will lose that which God gave in the first place and risks bringing the relationship to an end.

Gratitude is not merely a feeling of gratitude, but a disposition enacted by returning favours to the giver. For Bede, humans enact gratitude through the continued use of God's gifts; gratitude for God's grace incurs obligation in humans but also a desire to use the gifts given them or else lose them. Bede quotes the words of Paul to affirm gratitude enacted: "Et gratia eius … in me uacua non fuit, sed plus illis omnibus laboraui"[91] (His grace has not been fruitless in me, but I have labored more than any of

87 Homily 1.2, CCSL 122, 8, ll. 53–4; trans. Martin and Hurst, 1:11.
88 Homily 1.2, CCSL 122, 9, ll. 71–3; trans. Martin and Hurst, 1:11.
89 Homily 1.2, CCSL 122, 8, ll. 52–3; trans. Martin and Hurst, 1:11.
90 Homily 1.2, CCSL 122, 8, ll. 55–6; trans. Martin and Hurst, 1:11.
91 Homily 1.2, CCSL 122, 9, l. 63; trans. Martin and Hurst, 1:11.

them). Humans do not receive God's favour towards them in exchange for serving him but they owe God gratitude because of his gifts.

In Augustine's discussion, faith is the first "grace" God gives humans. He defines faith passively, as something done to the sinner: "Hanc ergo accepit gratiam primam peccator, ut eius peccata dimitterentur"[92] (This first grace therefore the sinner receives, that his sins should have been forgiven). A little later he asks a question Bede picks up: "Quid est ergo: *gratiam pro gratia*? Fide promeremur Deum"[93] (What is *grace for grace*? By faith we render God favourable to us). Augustine does not define faith any further at this point. Although Bede adopts this explanation, he greatly restructures Augustine's discussion of faith, continuing on to define faith as the *works* of faith: believing, loving, and more good works more generally.[94] As Bede explains it, God gives the elect faith; the elect in gratitude return this faith to him in the form of good works; God rewards them with eternal life. The saints are those who respond to his gifts in gratitude, returning the grace given them for more grace, *gratiam pro gratia*.

Therefore, putting grace in the context of gift giving enables Bede to portray the relationship between God and man as exceptionally intimate; the superlative nature of God's grace comes from the intimacy of the reciprocal relationship, one in which man and God work together through their mutual exchange of gifts to bring mutual honour – man's salvation and God's glory: "In misericordia quippe et miseratione nos coronat quando propter bona opera quae nobis ipse misericorditer exercenda donauit supernae beatitudinis praemia retribuit"[95] (He crowns us indeed in mercy and compassion when he repays us with the reward of heavenly blessedness for the good works which he himself has mercifully granted us to carry out). This is one way that Bede sums up this relationship. Because

92 Tract. 3.8, CCSL 36, ll. 21–2.

93 Tract. 3.9, CCSL 36, ll. 1–2.

94 "Fides quippe quae per dilectionem operatur gratia Dei est; quia ut credamus ut diligamus ut operemur bona quae nouimus ..." (Faith which works through love is indeed a grace of God, because our believing, our loving, our doing works which we know to be good ...), Homily 1.2, CCSL 122, 9, l. 74–6; trans. Martin and Hurst, 1:11–12. In contrast, Augustine's discussion remains with the more abstract concept of faith.

95 Homily 1.2, CCSL 122, 9, ll. 92–4; trans. Martin and Hurst, 1:12. Compare this with Augustine's formulation, Tract. 3.10, CCSL 36, ll. 15, 17–18, quoted above: "[I]pse dedit fidem primo ... Quod ergo praemium immortalitatis postea tribuit, dona sua coronat, non merita tua" (It was God who first gave faith ... Therefore, in afterwards paying the rewards of immortality, he crowns his own gifts, not your merits).

of this intimacy the fitting final reward – the second grace in the twofold scheme of grace Bede borrows from Augustine – is that the saints should see God face to face in order to contemplate the mysteries of the Trinity directly. Bede defines immortality using John 17:3, "Haec est autem uita aeterna ut cognoscant te"[96] (Now this is eternal life, that they may recognize you). This final, greatest gift "quoniam in huius saeculi uita fieri non potest"[97] (cannot happen in the life of this world). By situating contemplation within the gift giving relationship Bede removes the concept from its possible Neoplatonic resonances, concretizing and socializing it. For Bede, the reward for a life lived in service of God is that one may finally see, face to face, him whom one has served.

Thus, Bede imagines the relationship between humans and God as reciprocal, adapting *gratia* in its full social meaning while emphasizing that first gifts, the most valuable gifts, come from God: humans give gratitude in response to God's grace. Humans do not give gifts to free themselves from obligation or to win in a zero-sum contest of honour. The relationship between the two is non-agonistic, mutually beneficial, and leads to the honour of each. As humans receive God's gifts and use them in his service, God continues giving.

Mary: Grace Enacted

Homily 1.2 establishes the central reciprocity of the relationship between God and humans that Bede refers to or takes for granted throughout the rest of his homilies. Both Homily 1.3 on the Annunciation and 1.4 explicating the Magnificat[98] present Mary as an example of one who enacts the reciprocity of twofold grace (although Bede does not use this specific term outside of Homily 1.2). In 1.3 God favours Mary by recognizing her service to him through virtue and purity, and giving her in return the gift of his son. In 1.4 Mary responds to God primarily as a generous gift giver. Mary's example shows how personal identity is constituted through gifts received and used, forming a sense of the self as recognized by God, through God's gifts. That is, in giving Mary the gift of bearing his son, God recognizes Mary's worth, conferring identity upon her. As

96 Homily 1.2, CCSL 122, 11, ll. 141–2; trans. Martin and Hurst, 1:14.
97 Homily 1.2, CCSL 122, 11, ll. 143–4; trans. Martin and Hurst, 1:14.
98 On Luke 1:26–38 and Luke 1:39–55, respectively.

she receives and enacts this identity, she gives back to God by using his gifts – God gives his son; Mary gives her womb. Honour accrues to both through this circulation.

While Bede presents Mary as singular in grace, he also presents her as a model for all Christians, but especially those devoted to chastity.[99] Mary's example has special resonance for people, many of whom, like Bede himself, would not have chosen for themselves the monastic life of chastity. Bede's homilies on Mary reorient thinking; chastity is not something imposed upon a person by the fate of the parental gift of a child to a monastery, but is rather a gift directly from God, given not in response to merit but by God's special grace. As Bede's audience receives and enacts this gift already received, they too can share in the gift of bringing Christ into the world.

Bede's account of the Annunciation negotiates the delicate doctrinal balance between grace and good works, making Mary a valued participant in the relationship with God through her humble use of the gifts given her, which then function as her return gift to God. After the angel's greeting, Bede affirms,

> Vere etenim gratia erat plena cui diuino munere conlatum est ut prima inter feminas gloriosissimum Deo uirginitatis munus offerret. Vnde iure angelico aspectu simul et affatu meruit perfrui quae angelicam studebat uitam imitari. Vere gratia era plena cui ipsum per quem gratia et ueritas facta est Iesum Christum generare donatum est. Et ideo uere dominus cum illa erat quam et prius nouo castitatis amore a terrenis ad caelestia desideranda sustulit.[100]

> (And indeed, truly full of grace was she, upon whom it was conferred by divine favor that, first among women, she should offer God the most glorious gift of her virginity. Hence she who strove to imitate the life of an angel was rightfully worthy to enjoy the experience of seeing and speaking with an angel. Truly full of grace was she to whom it was granted to give birth to Jesus

99 The tradition of viewing Mary this way goes back to Origen and reached the Middle Ages via Ambrose, Jerome, and Augustine. These authors especially develop Mary as a model for celibate Christians. See Mary Clayton, *The Cult of the Virgin Mary in Anglo-Saxon England* (Cambridge: Cambridge University Press, 1990), 5, 11–12. See also Heisey, "Mary and Mysticism," for a recent reading of the identification of Mary with the homilies' hearers (which is essentially how he defines "mysticism" in this article). Heisey lists all the homilies in which Mary has a role.

100 Homily 1.3, CCSL 122, 16, ll. 60–8; trans. Martin and Hurst, 1:21.

> Christ, the very one through whom grace and truth came. And so the Lord was truly with her whom he first raised up from earthly to heavenly desires, in an unheard of love of chastity.)

The cycle is this: God favours Mary in allowing her to offer back to him the "gift of her virginity." Because of this virginity, she is worthy of speaking with an angel. Offering her virginity, she is further "granted to give birth to Jesus Christ." At the end of the passage Bede comes back full circle: Mary's love of chastity was also one of God's gifts. She has responded to this gift by enacting it, giving her a "gift of virginity" to offer back to God, which draws her into a *gratia*-cycle so intimate she becomes the mother of God's own son.

In the Magnificat Mary states her gratitude in response to God's gifts. After Elizabeth, Mary's cousin and the mother of John the Baptist, enumerates the blessings Mary has received, Mary "non amplius tacere potuit dona quae perceperat"[101] (could no longer remain silent about the gifts which she had attained). Then, "[q]uibus primo dona sibi specialiter concessa confitetur deinde generalia Dei beneficia quibus generi humano in aeternum consulere non desistit enumerat"[102] (With [the Magnificat] she first confesses those gifts which had been specially conceded to her, and then she enumerates too those ordinary kindnesses of God with which he does not stop consoling the human race forever). As is appropriate to a *gratia* relationship, Mary responds to the obligation of the gift by expressing her gratitude, not only in the words of the Magnificat. Her thoughts and deeds also align with the words: she "omnes interioris hominis sui affectus diuinis laudibus ac seruitiis mancipat qui obseruantia praeceptorum

101 Homily 1.4, CCSL 122, 25, ll. 148–9; trans. Martin and Hurst, 1:35.

102 Homily 1.4, CCSL 122, 25, ll. 161–3; trans. Martin and Hurst, 1:36. In addition: She "expectabat reuerenter donec ipse donorum distributor quid sibi doni specialis tribuisset quid secreti reuelasset quandocumque uellet ostenderet. At postquam eadem quae sibi erant carismata praestita per alios spiritu reuelante esse patefacta cernebat mox etiam ipsa thesaurum caeli quod in corde seruabat aperuit" (reverently awaited what was hidden until the distributor of gifts himself might reveal, at whatever time he so willed, what sort of special gift he had bestowed upon her and what sort of secret he had revealed ... But now that she discerned that those same charismatic gifts with which she had been endowed had been disclosed to others by the revealing Spirit, she herself then also disclosed the heavenly treasure which she was keeping in her heart [through the Magnificat]), ll. 145–9; trans. 36.

Dei semper eius potentiam maiestatis se cogitare demonstrat"[103] (commits all the affection of her interior self to divine praises and subjection, and by her observance of God's commands she demonstrates that she thinks always of the might of his majesty). Mary's grateful response is not merely words of praise, nor merely affection, nor merely service: it draws all aspects of the person – her thoughts, words, and deeds[104] – together in a response focused on the worth of God. The obligation God's gifts lay upon her shapes her enaction of herself; everything received is returned in a service to God that encompasses all parts of herself. The cooperation between them, God's gifts and Mary's use of them, produces something new, bringing forth Christ into the world.

Mary's response of grateful humility fits her for further divine gifts: "nequaquam se donis caelestibus quasi a se haec essent extulit sed ut magis magisque donis esset apta diuinis in custodiam humilitatis gressum mentis fixit ... *Ecce ancilla domini*"[105] (she by no means extolled herself for these heavenly gifts as though they had been given for her sake. In order that she might be fit for more and more divine gifts, she placed her steps firmly in the custody of humility of mind ... "Behold, the handmaid of the Lord"). Mary positions herself as God's dependent, humbly expecting further gifts from her gracious master. Her humility is an expression of the extent of her gratitude. Her response to the angel, "Ecce ancilla domini," shows, according to Bede, her

> [m]agnam quippe humilitatis constantiam tenet quae se ancillam sui conditoris dum mater eligitur appellat ... nec se tamen de singularitate meriti

103 Homily 1.4, CCSL 122, 25, ll. 164–7; trans. Martin and Hurst, 1:36.

104 According to Patrick Sims-Williams, "Thought, Word, and Deed: An Irish Triad," in *Eriu* 29 (1978), this triad was popularized by the Irish and spread to the rest of the Continent via Anglo-Saxon influence. The idea does appear in some patristic sources (notably, Gregory's Homily 39, Sims-Williams, 82) but not with the frequency it does in Irish sources. Many of the appearances Sims-Williams lists are found in prayers recorded in English prayer books like Royal and Cerne, which post-date Bede. Although Bede does not use the triadic formula, the collocation of thoughts, words, and deeds makes frequent appearance in Bede's teachings on prayer. One of the most straightforward uses is in Homily 2.12: "ut non uerba tantum et opera nostra sed ipsa quoque cordium secreta diuinis aspectibus digna reddamus (that we may render not only our words and works, but also the very secrets of our hearts ...), CCSL 122, 265, ll. 192–4; trans. Martin and Hurst, 2:115, but the interplay between the three elements also pervasively structures Homily 2.14 on prayer and Homily 2.22, as discussed below.

105 Homily 1.4, CCSL 122, 21–2, ll. 19–23; trans. Martin and Hurst, 1:31.

excelsioris singulariter extollit sed potius suae conditionis ac diuinae dignationis in omnibus memor famularum se Christi consortio humiliter adiungit famulatum Christo deuota quod iubetur inpendit. *Fiat*, inquit, *mihi secundum uerbum tuum*; fiat ut spiritus sanctus adueniens me caelestibus dignam mysteriis reddat.[106]

(great constancy of humility, since she named herself the handmaid of her Maker at the time when she was chosen to be his mother. … Nevertheless she did not extol herself in a singular way on account of the singularity of her higher merit, but being mindful instead of her own condition and of God's dignity, she humbly joined herself to the company of Christ's servants and committed herself devotedly to Christ in what was ordered. "Let it be done to me," she said, "In accordance with your word" – "Let it be done that the Holy Spirit's coming to me may render me worthy of heavenly mysteries.")

The gratitude of Mary's response and her humility, an expression of the extent of her gratitude, are part of Mary's return gift of service to God. She acknowledges the generosity of God's gift by placing herself among God's servants rather than asserting any prerogatives as his mother. But while Mary acknowledges her lowliness, this is not the way God names her: he calls her mother of his Son and gives her the honour due that position, responding to her gratitude with further *gratia*. Both behave with perfect generosity towards each other. God proves himself to be one who rewards his servants, those who use and return his gifts. Thus, God honours Mary through his messenger: the angel salutes her with a greeting "humanae consuetudini inaudita … beatae Mariae dignitati congrua"[107] (unheard of … in human custom … fitting to the dignity of blessed Mary"). Furthermore, he privileges her in a special way: "Nec praetereundum quod beata Dei genetrix meritis praecipuis etiam nomine testimonium reddit. Interpretatur enim *stella maris*. Et ipsa quasi sidus eximium inter fluctus saeculi labentis gratia priuilegii specialis refulsit"[108] (Nor should we overlook the fact that the blessed mother of God rendered testimony of her preeminent merits even by her name, for it has the meaning "star of the sea," and like an extraordinary heavenly body among the storms of this tottering world she shone brightly with the grace of her special privilege).

106 Homily 1.3, CCSL 122, 20, ll. 219–20, 222–8; trans. Martin and Hurst, 1:27.
107 Homily 1.3, CCSL 122, 16, ll. 59–60; trans. Martin and Hurst, 1:21.
108 Homily 1.3, CCSL 122, 15, ll. 53–6; trans. Martin and Hurst, 1:21.

The passage just quoted exemplifies the dual way that Bede treats the issue of merit within the *gratia* relationship. In Homily 1.2 he carefully shows that all gifts humans have come from God and that everything humans do to merit the grace of God they do through his gift in the first place, but Bede's later treatment of the subject assumes both this and also that saints merit the favour of God.[109] Such a dual perspective speaks to the socially mediated nature of worth. It is not produced by the person but conferred through gift and recognized by others. God's gift makes Mary's merit socially apprehensible, giving her her identity, which she then enacts.

Thus Mary gains the grace of special privilege through her preeminent merits, signified by her name, "star of the sea." Mary subjectively values herself and her gifts with humility, showing the extent of her gratitude. But Bede, giving an observer's perspective, venerates her rather than speaking of her as God's lowly servant. In Bede's view, Mary is singular in her purity, obedience, and humility. God gives her virtues, but like the weapons of an Anglo-Saxon warrior, they are merits insofar as she makes use of them. That Mary has made use of them merits her further singularity: she is singular in being given the *literal* gift of bearing Christ in her body. The veneration Bede exemplifies also becomes a part of God's grace: as observer, he ratifies the objective view of Mary and attributes to Mary's merit that which God gave her in the first place. Mary "[n]il ergo meritis suis tribuit quae totam suam magnitudinem ad illius donum refert"[110] (therefore attributes nothing to her own merits, but she refers her whole greatness to [God]), but Bede does not question that Mary is indeed great – she "[eum] cororaliter generare meruit"[111] (was worthy to bring him forth physically). While Bede reports that everything she had came from God, he, unlike Mary, attributes this merit to her own preeminence since he continually refers to her merit and her worth without continually mentioning that it was also God's gift in the first place.

There is then some sense of the astounding nature of God's gifts as Bede continues, drawing parallels between Mary and ordinary humans. At the beginning of Homily 1.3 Bede established that the Annunciation is not just to Mary but to all the elect, especially, by implication, those committed to chastity: "Vt ergo ad promissae salutis mereamur dona pertingere

109 See Kleist, *Striving with Grace*, 70.
110 Homily 1.4, CCSL 122, 26, ll. 191–2: trans. Martin and Hurst, 1:37.
111 Homily 1.4, CCSL 122, 26, l. 209; trans. Martin and Hurst, 1:37.

primordium eius intenta curemus aure percipere"[112] (That therefore we may deserve to reach the gifts of promised salvation, we must take care to receive its beginning with an attentive ear). For a moment he leaves ambiguous whether he means Christ as the beginning or origin of salvation, or the story of the Annunciation and Nativity as the beginning of the salvation process offered to humans. Through this ambiguity, Bede implies an equivalence for his audience between receiving the story and receiving Christ; as the congregation hears the story of the Annunciation they can replicate Mary's conception of Christ[113] by hearing the story of his Nativity and internalizing it.

Much is made of the two medieval models for virtuous women embodied in Mary: virginity and motherhood. But Bede uses Mary as a model for all Christians, most immediately his monastic audience: men, some of whom were donated, who were devoted to a life of celibacy, an end of social reproduction, a sort of death. Yet Mary's virginity becomes productive through her acceptance and use of God's gifts; as ordinary humans show themselves receptive of God's commands they, like Mary, bring forth Christ into the world and through this merit a reward: "tamen in eadem uita perpetua beatitudinis locum et ipsi sint habituri qui eius fidem ac dilectionem casto in corde concipiunt qui sedula in mente praeceptorum eius memoriam portant qui hanc et in mente proximorum solerti exhortatione nutrire satagunt"[114] (those who conceive his faith and love in a chaste heart, who bear the recollection of his precepts in a sincere mind, and who busy themselves nourishing this recollection also in the mind of their neighbours by skillful exhortation, they too will have a place in the same everlasting life of blessedness [as Mary]).

At the end of Homily 1.3, Bede draws his hearers into a gift relationship with God as well by calling on them to imitate Mary's

112 Homily 1.3, CCSL 122, 14, ll. 6–7; my translation. Martin and Hurst's translation clarifies the ambiguity of the phrase, 19. On the implication towards those committed to chastity, see Clayton, *Cult of the Virgin*, 15.

113 According to tradition, Mary conceived Jesus through her ear. Clayton mentions this tradition, *Cult of the Virgin*, 6. Several passages throughout her book give evidence for Anglo-Saxon knowledge of the *conceptio per aurem* tradition. See, for example, 88. It is also referenced in the Old English Martyrology; see J.E. Cross, "The Influence of Irish Texts and Traditions on the 'Old English Martyrology,'" in *Proceedings of the Royal Irish Academy* 81C (1981), 182.

114 Homily 1.4, CCSL 122, 27, ll. 221–5; trans. Martin and Hurst, 1:38.

uocem mentemque nos … pro modulo nostro sequentes famulos esse nos Christi in cunctis actibus nostris motibusque recolamus … sicque perceptis eius muneribus gratias recte uiuendo reddamus ut ad maiora percipienda digni existere mereamur. Precemur seduli cum beata Dei genetrice ut fiat nobis secundum uerbum eius …[115]

(voice and mind … let us recall that we are Christ's servants in all of our acts and motions … [S]ince we have received his gifts, let us give thanks by living properly, so that we may show ourselves worthy of receiving greater gifts. Let us unremmittingly [*sic*] pray, along with the blessed mother of God, that it may be done to us in accordance with his word …)

As his audience accepts the gift of chastity they have been given, they are to realize that this gift puts them in special relationship to God. Because they have *already* received his gifts, they must show *gratia* in return, by serving him. Their response to God's gifts precipitates further gift giving, forging a relationship between them of a lord and his household. Finally, God's gift of his Son becomes assurance that God will listen to his dependents' requests: "Nec dubitandum quin nos de profundis ad se clamantes citius exaudire dignabitur propter quos necdum se cognoscentes ipse ad profundam hanc conuallem lacrimarum descendere …"[116] ([T]here is no doubt that he will very quickly deign to hearken to us who cry out to him from the depths, since for our sake, when we did not yet recognize him, he deigned to descend to this deep valley of tears …).

For Bede the Magnificat directly responds to God's gifts. It sets a model of a relationship that monks will enact on a small scale every day at Vespers[117] as they chant the Magnificat themselves as part of the liturgy. Key to this model is a conception of humility that centres on the human response to God's gifts. Chanting Mary's hymn daily gives monks a chance to reflect on Mary's example. It prompts prayers and tears by which the mind cleanses itself. It therefore gives a model for the intimacy of the relationship between human and God, an intimacy that can never be presumed upon because its primary condition is humility, the recognizing of gifts and favour unasked for and unearned.

115 Homily 1.3, CCSL 122, 20, ll. 231–3, 236–9; trans. Martin and Hurst, 1:27–8.
116 Homily 1.3, CCSL 122, 20, ll. 242–5; trans. Martin and Hurst, 1:28.
117 As Bede mentions at the end of the homily, CCSL 122, 30, l. 355; trans. Martin and Hurst, 1:43.

Bede's first four homilies introduce themes of *gratia* and gifts that he touches on and references repeatedly throughout the succeeding homilies. Homilies 5 and 6 continue to build on these themes as Advent transitions to Christmas. Homily 1.6, the first for Christmas, details the gift of Christ, but also presents other models available to Bede for conceptualizing the human relationship with God, namely taxation and servitude. These models, however, never attain the same importance as the gift giving model. Through the motif of the giving of gifts and the explication of grace and humility, Bede establishes a particular relationship between humans and God, one in which all good and all gifts proceed from God's favour; humans enter a reciprocal relationship by using these gifts in the service of their lord, thereby meriting further gifts. Thus, the reciprocity is not transactional or merely passive. As humans in humility recognize that all they have comes from God, *gratia* then obligates them to use these gifts in the service of their Lord. Once they recognize this, God endows them with even greater gifts, the ability to act in such a way as to deserve the future gifts of the heavenly kingdom. Bede characterizes God's gifts in three stages: the initial gift of God's Son, the continuing gifts of the Holy Spirit teaching humans to live well, and the future, promised gift of eternal life in the heavenly kingdom. Within this particular kind of relationship people pray to God.

Bede's Understanding of Prayer

"[S]piritalium orationum gratia refertos dominum quaerere"[118] (seek the Lord abundantly provided with the gift of spiritual prayers), Bede says in Homily 2.10. In this case, the gift is most immediately to God from those seeking the Lord, but Bede also understands prayer as a gift from God to humans. But what manner of thing is this prayer that is so exchanged? Studies that focus on Bede's spirituality tend to overlook the way that Bede most centrally portrays prayer as ritual performance. Bede understands prayer to be set prayer in which precators use words that are not their own to pray for salvation. For Bede, as this section will show, the words of prayer are primary, yet he also classifies prayer with action more than with speech. Through using God's gift of prayer to them, people

118 CCSL 122, 247, l. 22; trans. Martin and Hurst, 2:89.

internalize the words in thought and externalize them in deeds. In the end, prayer is in some sense subjectively efficacious; it transforms the one praying as it integrates thoughts, words, and deeds to one harmonious whole, performing an ideal of salvation as wholeness.

The small corpus of studies on Bede's spirituality[119] tends to borrow the preoccupations of spirituality outlined in the introduction, with spirituality studies' emphasis on private individual prayer, conceptualized as affective and intimate, its understanding of "true" prayer as spontaneous or formless and wordless, and its affinity with mysticism. Bede's piety does not fit neatly within the definitions of spirituality, something that each of the scholars who have written on his prayer mention even as they use the ideals of spirituality to define prayer.[120] We can, of course, use the preoccupations of later ages to examine earlier ones. Nothing human comes *ex nihilo*, and so continuities between Anglo-Saxon and later forms of devotion are certainly worth study. The article that does this most explicitly is DeGregorio's "Affective Spirituality: Theory and Practice in Bede and Alfred the Great," which follows Allen Frantzen's call for studies that place Anglo-Saxon England in the "grand narratives of devotion and mysticism" for the later Middle Ages.[121] DeGregorio is here interested in the development of affective spirituality and the "invention" of the individual, and so he situates himself in particular against R.W. Southern, who argues that medieval spiritual writing begins in the late eleventh century,

119 Only DeGregorio focuses specifically on Bede's spirituality, in "Venerable Bede on Prayer," and "Affective Spirituality." Ward considers Anglo-Saxon spirituality more generally in *High King of Heaven*, but Bede is one of her major sources; Gerald Bonner includes some discussion of prayer in "The Christian Life in the Thought of the Venerable Bede," in *Durham University Journal* 63.1 (1970); as does Carroll in *Venerable Bede: Spiritual Teachings*.

120 Ward, who recognizes the slippery nature of "spirituality" equates the term, in her usage, with "the desires and religious aspirations of men within their cultural context" combined with a "meaning given to it in the nineteenth century when it was coined ... to describe a field of study earlier called ascetic theology, and/or mystical prayer," *High King of Heaven*, x, xi. Carroll does not define what she means by spirituality; when she describes characteristics of Bede's spirituality she seems to describe some combination of his education and personality, *Venerable Bede: Spiritual Teachings*, 40ff.

121 Allen J. Frantzen, "Spirituality and Devotion in the Anglo-Saxon Penitentials," in *EMS* 22 (2005), 117. DeGregorio quite literally follows Frantzen; his article comes right after Franzten's in volume 22 of *EMS*.

especially with Anselm (d. 1109).[122] Two of its distinctive aspects are prioritizing the "inner life" (a characteristic of Anselm)[123] and a shift from fear-based to love-based devotion.[124] However, insofar as Anglo-Saxon spirituality has been left out of these grand narratives, it is largely because its forms and ideals lack the obvious markers that would make it easy to situate within the preoccupations of spirituality.

DeGregorio's earlier article, "The Venerable Bede on Prayer and Contemplation," points us in a helpful direction when he argues that Bede did not associate prayer with contemplation but with action.[125] According to DeGregorio, Bede's teaching on prayer reflects the least contemplative of the Latin writers, Gregory, and that even with Gregory's work Bede largely ignored the "subtle interior dynamics of the spiritual life" that interested Gregory,[126] showing "little interest in exploring the interior workings and slippery paradoxes of the spiritual life that so captured Gregory."[127] Yet DeGregorio writes this against the assumption that spirituality predisposes, that prayer's highest goal is contemplative practice. As a result, he sees the active orientation of Bede's prayer as something that needs explaining. He does so by contextualizing it within the pastoral concerns manifested in Bede's work, especially his desire to see reform in the Anglo-Saxon church, and through the active role monks had in providing pastoral care to laypeople in his day.[128] Thus, DeGregorio sets his essay against an assumed background of contemplative prayer and he at times seems to consider the active type of prayer he argues Bede presents as intended for a less sophisticated audience:

> sources had to be selected, adapted, digested, and reworked in order to make them accessible to his newly Christianized Anglo-Saxon audience. Such an audience, Bede may well have thought, would benefit less from thinking

122 R.W. Southern, *The Making of the Middle Ages* (New Haven: Yale University Press, 1953).
123 DeGregorio, "Affective Spirituality," 130.
124 DeGregorio, "Affective Spirituality," 131.
125 Bonner similarly notes Bede's emphasis on the active life, "Christian Life," 41.
126 DeGregorio, "Venerable Bede on Prayer," 13.
127 DeGregorio, "Venerable Bede on Prayer," 14.
128 DeGregorio, "Venerable Bede on Prayer," 5–7.

of unceasing prayer in terms of desire than in terms of the performance of just deeds.[129]

Perhaps. But DeGregorio at this moment ignores the similarity between Bede's definition of prayer and that of Origen, who writes fully within the eastern, "mystical" tradition and whose account of prayer no one would accuse of being unsophisticated.[130] That is, for Bede – as for Origen – prayer's natural affinity was with the active life.[131] As DeGregorio further points out, two different things are meant by contemplation: it can either mean the spiritual discipline, the goal of which is to "penetrate God's 'divine majesty and essence'"[132] – which is *not* the goal of Bedan prayer; or it can mean careful study of and rumination on the mysteries of the scriptures, leading to more virtuous living.[133] The latter concept is, in fact, more in line with the ancient Greek idea of the contemplative life. Bede's piety – and

---

129 DeGregorio, "Venerable Bede on Prayer," 21. Carroll, *Venerable Bede: Spiritual Teachings*, makes a similar move in her section on prayer specifically, also called "Prayer and Contemplation." She discusses the verbal, petitionary, and active character of prayer, 199–200, 200–1. When she turns to contemplation, she does so with a transition to "Prayer in its higher forms … " demoting the petitionary prayer just discussed, 211.

130 See Origen: "The man who links together his prayer with deeds of duty and fits seemly actions with his prayer is the man who prays without ceasing, for his virtuous deeds or the commandments he has fulfilled are taken up as part of his prayer. For only in this way can we take the saying 'Pray without ceasing' as being possible, if we can say that the whole life of the saint is one mighty integrated prayer," *Origen's Treatise on Prayer*, trans. Eric George Jay (Eugene, OR: Wipf and Stock, 2010), 12.2. I am *not* arguing that Bede was indebted to Origen for his understanding of prayer. Although some of Origen's homilies were known in Anglo-Saxon England in Latin translation, there is no evidence that Origen's treatise on prayer was known. See "Origen" in the index to Gneuss and Lapidge.

131 The concept of the active and contemplative lives has a very deep history during which the meanings associated with the terms have shifted. See Robert Neelly Bellah, "To Kill and Survive or Die and Become," in *The Robert Bellah Reader*, ed. Steven M. Tipton (Durham: Duke University Press, 2006); and Mary Elizabeth Mason, *The Active Life and Contemplative Life: A Study of the Concepts from Plato to the Present* (Milwaukee: Marquette University Press, 1961). As Mason shows, Gregory the Great associates the active with love of neighbour and the contemplative with love of God. Every Christian is, of course, to be engaged in both these loves; Gregory sees each as varying stages of the same person's life, not the life callings of different people (i.e., the later active and contemplative orders).

132 DeGregorio, "Venerable Bede on Prayer," 32; also discussed by Carroll, *Venerable Bede: Spiritual Teachings*, 211–13.

133 DeGregorio, "Venerable Bede on Prayer," 32.

piety is a better word for it than spirituality – while it hopes for experience of the presence of God in the future, glimpses of which might be experienced in this life, is oriented towards action in the present. The active, word-based, reciprocal nature of Bede's prayer needs further attention.

The particular interests of spirituality studies have obscured the distinctive characteristics of Bede's understanding of prayer. Bede assumes that set prayers form his audience's regular practice of prayer. The monastic audience of Bede's homilies[134] would have been praying the hours daily. As a result, their formational and usual experience with prayer would have been the set prayers chanted communally at the hours. We have already seen evidence of this with Bede's reference to the Magnificat, sung every evening. Furthermore, even their private prayer would have been structured around set prayers: as I show in chapter 1, most injunctions to pray concern praying the Paternoster and the Psalms;[135] and Bede's own most original work is the breviate psalter, a tool shortening the Psalms in a way that must have been intended for private use.[136] Bede repeatedly emphasizes the necessity of congruence between thoughts and words in a way that implies that precators pray words familiar from long habit, words that

134 Alan Thacker, "Monks, Preaching, and Pastoral Care in Early Anglo-Saxon England," in *Pastoral Care before the Parish*, ed. John Blair and Richard Sharpe (Leicester: Leicester University Press, 1992), argues that while Bede's direct audience was largely monastic, there is some evidence that several times a year his sermons were directed towards an "augmented" audience (Holy Saturday, for instance, 140–1) and that Bede's sermons would have served for monks to adapt for their own preaching. To this it must be added that most instances of address in Bede's homilies do presume a monastic audience. See Martin, "Introduction," in *Bede the Venerable*, 1:xi. Specifically, Bede's teachings on prayer assume people who would have been praying regularly. Furthermore, because the homilies are in Latin, it would be difficult for most laypeople hearing them to understand them if they were read in Latin.

135 And, in fact, explications of the Paternoster emphasize that it completely covers all a person would need to pray for. For laypeople most encouragements to pray concern praying the Paternoster. For monks, it is the Paternoster, the Psalms, and other biblical prayers. See Toswell's introduction to *The Anglo-Saxon Psalter*, 1–38, for information on training in the Psalms.

136 Toswell: "The breviate psalter stands perhaps as Bede's one entirely original contribution to the practice of the psalms in early Christianity," *Anglo-Saxon Psalter*, 42–3. However, Toswell goes on to write as though Bede himself came to the "realization that the psalter could be used for prayer," 56. As we have seen in chapter 1, the Psalms had long been used in personal prayer. As Ward sees it, *Bede and the Psalter*, these psalms are used more as hooks for personal meditation and prayer than as prayer itself, but she invokes Cassian at this point in a questionable way, as chapter 1 makes clear.

they could easily say without attention. In doing so, it is often difficult to tell when he imagines people praying alone or communally: corporate and private prayer fulfilled many of the same functions, since precators could apply the prayers to themselves while chanting with the congregation, or pray privately for corporate needs.[137] In any case, the fundamental situation of prayer, whether alone or in service, was that every specific instance of prayer joined the single voice with the Church as a whole, present and distant, living and dead. More importantly, the discipline of prayer integrates the *words* – given by God through the Psalms and the other prayers of the Church – into thoughts and deeds, thereby transforming those praying as they conform interiorly and exteriorly to the prayers. Thus, though prayer is personal, it is not particularly individual.

For Bede prayer is not "communication with God" more broadly. Prayer is petition and thanks for favours granted; the only legitimate petition is for salvation. By salvation, however, Bede does not merely mean eternal life at some point in the future; salvation also means the present transformation of the people at prayer, individually and communally. In Homily 2.23, Bede states clearly that prayer for salvation is the only petition that God promises to hear and to grant. He limits the problematic promise in John 16:23, that anything asked in Jesus's name will be given to the petitioner, to salvation alone. As I noted in chapter 1, this passage forms part of the standard early Christian teachings on prayer. Explicators usually clarify that Christian prayer does not centre on the will of the precator; prayer does not have an efficient or "tight" economy, where a particular input has a guaranteed outcome, which would potentially make prayer closer to magic and would certainly put human will and desire at its centre, rather than God's will.

Bede's explication shares the traditional concern, but he presents a more rigorous approach to what it means. He first uses the standard explication, which plays on the meaning of Jesus's name ("God saves"): "[I]llos solum in nomine saluatoris petere qui ea quae ad perpetuam salutem pertinent

137 In fact, in two places where he does make a distinction between private and communal prayer, the prayers fulfil the same function. In Homily 1.18 he speaks of the saints mourning in this life, both alone and communally, and explicates doves as signifying secret tears of prayer and pigeons as signifying the Church's public gatherings, CCSL 122, 130, ll. 71–80; in Homily 1.22 (below) he gives two allegoreses: the Church praying for an erring soul, and the person praying for his or her own soul.

petunt"[138] ([T]hose people alone ask in the name of the Savior who ask for those things which pertain to eternal salvation). Many of the Fathers allow that people can ask for material things as well, so long as their requests are not excessive or greedy. Bede also makes this allowance in 2.14, but he takes a harder line:

> Male petunt et illi qui terrena magis in oratione quam caelestia bona requirunt ... *Neque enim prohibentur* ciues patriae caelestis in terra peregrinantes pro pace temporum pro salute corporum pro ubertate frugum pro serenitate aurarum pro ceteris uitae huius necessariis dominum petere, si tamen haec non nimie petantur *et si ob id solummodo petantur ut abundante uiatico in praesenti liberius ad futura dona tendatur.*[139]
>
> (They also ask wrongly who in their prayers demand earthly rather than heavenly goods ... The citizens of the heavenly fatherland, while they are pilgrims on this earth, *are not forbidden* to ask the Lord for peaceful times, bodily health, abundant crops, good weather, and other necessities of this life, if these things are not asked for inordinately, *and if they are asked for only for this reason, that with abundant food for the journey in this present life, they may more freely reach out toward future gifts.*)

Comparing this to Gregory makes Bede's shift in emphasis obvious:

> In domo enim Iesu Iesum non quaeritis, si in aeternitatis templo importune pro temporalibus oratis. Ecce alius in oratione quaerit uxorem, alius petit uillam, alius postulat uestem, alius dari sibi deprecatur alimentum. *Et quidem* cum haec desunt, ab omnipotenti Deo *petenda sunt.* Sed meminisse continue debemus quod ex mandato eiusdem nostri Redemptoris accepimus: "Quaerite primum regnum Dei et iustitiam eius, et haec omnia adicientur uobis." *Et haec itaque ab Iesu petere non est errare, si tamen non nimie petantur.*[140]

138 Homily 2.12, CCSL 122, 260, ll. 9–10; trans. Martin and Hurst, 2:108. Compare this with Gregory: "[I]lle ergo in nomine Saluatoris petit, qui illud petit quod ad ueram salutem pertinet" (One who asks in the Savior's name asks what pertains to actual salvation), Homily 27, CCSL 141, 234, ll. 141–2; trans. Hurst, Homily 27, 217.

139 CCSL 122, 275, ll. 107–9, 112–17; trans. Martin and Hurst, 2:128. Italics mine.

140 CCSL 141, 235, ll. 153–62; trans. Hurst, 217. Italics mine. The passage quoted is Matt. 6:33.

(You are not seeking Jesus in the house of Jesus if you are praying unreasonably for temporal things in the temple of eternity. One seeks in his prayer for a wife, another a country estate, another for clothing, another prays earnestly for food. *We are indeed to ask* these things from almighty God when we lack them. But we must constantly remember what we have received from our Redeemer's precept: "Seek first the kingdom of God and his justice, and all these things will be given you as well." *To ask these things of Jesus, then, is not to go wrong, if our requests are not excessive.*)

While Gregory corrects his audience, he also assures them that they are free to pray for temporal things so long as their requests are not excessive, and he words his assurance positively: "et quidem … petenda sunt" (we are indeed to ask). Bede concedes in the negative, "Neque enim prohibentur" (are not forbidden) and ends by emphasizing once again that even these requests are to be made with an eye for eternal salvation, while Gregory again reminds that such requests can be made, just not excessively.

Bede takes a sterner tone, partly because he addresses a monastic audience, people held to a higher standard of renunciation, whereas Gregory preached to mixed congregations.[141] But more importantly, it reflects Bede's understanding that salvation does not happen at the end of one's life or at the end of time when one is saved from hell. Rather, it is a process of integrating all the parts of the person and the community into a coherent whole reflecting the lordship of Christ (an idea that he develops further in Homily 1.22, discussed below). That process of integration is the project of prayer, through which the precators become that for which they pray, faithful servants of God. Prayer can transform only if people pray for transformation. If people pray for material goods, good works can become a means to that end, a transactional bargain with God in which the precator's focus easily slips from persons to things. In Bede's relational context for prayer such calculation debases the *gratia* relationship, introducing the possibility that people would serve God to aggrandize themselves in this world rather than out of the desire to see God face to face in the eternal kingdom.

---

141 It is interesting to note, however, that authors writing to monastic audiences, such as Origen and Cassian, do not evidence any anxiety that this promise will be misused or misapplied. Origen mentions it in his treatise on prayer, *Origen's Treatise*, 15.3, 129, and 10.2, 110. Cassian discusses it in *Conlatio* 9, ed. Michael Petschenig, CSEL 13 (Vienna: C. Geroldi Filium Bibliopolam Academiae, 1886), 272, 24.

Bede conceptualizes prayer action, not merely a spoken request. Prayer becomes an enactment of the salvation for which one prays as the precator uses present gifts in the hope of future gifts. Bede does not merely align prayer with the active life, as DeGregorio and Bonner note, he equates prayer with *action* – something done, not merely something said. Bede's understanding of how people fulfil the command to pray without ceasing is instructive here: they do it by performing good works. Thus, in Homily 2.22 he explains:

> quia quicquid boni operantur aut dicunt qui simplici intentione Deo deseruiunt totum profecto hoc uicem pro eis orationis adimplet quando deuotionem mentis eorum diuinis commendat aspectibus. Neque aliter apostolicum illud praeceptum quo ait, *sine intermissione orate*, perficere ualemus nisi sic omnes actus sermones cogitatus ipsa etiam silentia nostra ita domino donante dirigamus ut singula haec cum timoris illius respectu temperentur ut cuncta perpetuae nostrae saluti proficua reddantur.[142]
>
> ([W]hatever good work those who are zealous in their service of God perform or speak about with unfeigned intention fills for them the place of prayer, when it directs the devotion of their minds to the divine presence. We are not otherwise capable of carrying out the command of the Apostle wherein he says, *Pray without ceasing*, unless we direct all our actions, utterances, thoughts, and even our silence, by God's gift, in such a way that each of these may be carried out with regard to fear of him, so that all of them may be rendered profitable for our eternal salvation.)

If, as noted in chapter 1, Augustine blurs the line between desire and prayer,[143] in contrast, as we see here, Bede blurs the line between prayer and good works. He does so in a way that integrates the interior state of "unfeigned (*simplici*) intention" and "thoughts" with the exterior "actions," so that the prayer of good works becomes a type of service to God, because it "deuotionem mentis eorum diuinis commendat aspectibus"

142 CCSL 122, 344–5, ll. 91–9; trans. Martin and Hurst, 2:223. This same idea is found more succinctly in the passage already mentioned from his commentary on Luke: "Aut certe omnia quae iustus secundum Deum gerit et dicit ad orationem esse reputanda" (yet surely everything that the just man does and says following the will of God ought to be counted as prayer), *In Lucae* 5, CCSL 120, 322, ll. 1056–8; trans. mine.

143 Enarratio in psalmum 37.14, CCSL 38, ll. 8–12, 14–15.

(directs the devotion of their minds to the divine presence). The wording here seems to resonate faintly with Augustine's "interior … oratio, quae est desiderium" (interior prayer, which is desire). Bede, however, emphasizes the way people perform their devotion to God through good works, in this way enacting what they pray for through interiorizing and exteriorizing their prayer. "Good work" brings about the "devotion of their minds." Bede imagines prayer as bringing one into the divine presence, carrying out actions, utterances, thoughts, and silence with regard to the fear of God, and so gaining *gratia* that will bring further *gratia*.

The interiorization and exteriorization of integrated prayer within the congruence between what one says, what one thinks, and what one does is a continual theme in Bede, appearing in each homily on prayer. This congruence makes petition effective through making the precators "worthy." In Homily 2.14, for one example, Bede says:

> regnum caelorum non otiosis et uacantibus sed petentibus quaerentibus pulsantibus dandum inueniendum et aperiendum esse testatur. Petenda est ergo ianua regni orando quaerenda recte uiuendo pulsanda perseuerando. Non enim sufficit uerbis tantummodo rogare, si non etiam quaesierimus diligentius qualiter nobis sit uiuendum ut digni simus impetrare quae poscimus.[144]

> ([T]he kingdom of heaven is not to be given to, found by, and opened to those who are idle and unoccupied, but to those who ask for it, seek after it and knock at its gates. The gate of the kingdom must be asked for by praying; it must be sought after by living properly; it must be knocked at by persevering. It is not sufficient to ask in words only if we do not also seek diligently how we ought to be living, so that we may be worthy to obtain that for which we plead.)

The congruence between words and deeds (in this instance) makes a petition obtainable, but the two operate as integral parts to the petition for salvation. However, Bede does not imagine that people trade the good deeds (of living properly and persevering) for entrance to the heavenly kingdom, as though good deeds are somehow separable from the person performing them or the two things are commensurate (i.e., good deeds are worth immortality). Rather, the good deeds constitute the worth of

144 CCSL 122, 272, ll. 6–13; trans. Martin and Hurst, 2:124.

those involved: the diligence of the precator, the generosity of the one petitioned, who recognizes the worthiness of the person, not the worth of the gifts. And yet, as Bede says in Homily 1.2 (discussed earlier) all good works come from God; those who receive them enact them.[145] Therefore, deeds do not *simply* reveal the personal characteristics of those performing them; rather, the gifts of God, as people receive and enact them, constitute the person. In the end, the gift given by God, and the gift returned to God is the precator's self. Bede thinks of salvation in terms of being-subject-to; petition and its attendant good works move a person from outside the kingdom to inside the kingdom through God's *gratia* and through the way enactment of this *gratia* transforms the one praying. As we will see, Bede conceptualizes this same movement from outside to inside in terms of purity and desire in 2.10 and purity and transformation in 1.22. Both homilies model the way Bede imagines set prayers, prayed for salvation, and integrated into the precators' thoughts and deeds to function as gifts from God and to God. In both cases, integrated prayer places one in a position in which one can be heard and can belong.

Spiritalium orationum gratia: Homily 2.10, Purity and Devotion

Homily 2.10 most clearly shows the way that purity in the petitioning relationship works to transform petitioners into that which they petition to be. The homily roots the concept of purity within the word-based nature of prayer that precators then enact exteriorly and interiorly as a gift to God. While the "pure" gift is purely altruistic, with no advantage to the giver and no place for egoism, "purity" for Bede has a different resonance, largely because he sees little tension between *ego* and *alter*. For Derrida, the subject and object created by the gift are problematic – "'one' … gives 'something' to 'someone other.'"[146] This creates by default an economy,[147] circulation, in which the one gets return in some form (even if it is only self-recognized) for having given, rendering the purity of the gift impossible.[148] Thus, purity for Derrida becomes incoherent and meaningless: *necessarily* meaningless, because to imbue it with meaning – which requires the intention of a subject and a receiving object – reinserts it into an economy.

145 CCSL 122, 9, ll. 92–4.
146 Derrida, *Given Time*, 11.
147 Derrida, *Given Time*, 23–4.
148 Derrida, *Given Time*, 13–14.

It should come as no surprise that such negation is *not* what Bede means by pure prayer. Not only does Bede not recognize the tension between *alter* and *ego* that troubles Derrida (largely, I think, because, for Derrida, the self must always be self-interested), the economy between human and divine does not posit either a Divine subject and human object, or a human subject and Divine object. Rather, the giving subject gives to a receiving subject.[149] One of the major features of the gift is that, even as gratitude obligates both parties to act in each other's interest, the gift preserves some element of agency for both: the giver chooses to give, and the recipient has some freedom in the return[150] – admittedly, not *perfect* freedom (but Bede neither idealizes perfect freedom nor sees it as possible, as 1.22 below shows). The two of them, giver and recipient, work together to make meaning out of the gift.

Furthermore, even though Bede considers interior states in prayer, purity is not a self-produced purity of intention. It is not "sincere," as we tend to define the term. As Adam B. Seligman puts it, sincerity emphasizes interiorly generated intention, "something within the social actor or actors. … Rather than becoming what we do in action through ritual, we do according to what we have become through self-examination. This form of thought emphasizes tropes of 'authenticity.'"[151] Even though it might be tempting to call the congruence between words and deeds by the name of sincerity, the "authenticity" Bede aims for is not internally produced. From the sincere perspective, the congruence of word and deed acts as guarantee for the sincere intention of the one praying, of his "simplex intentio."[152] But Bede more commonly calls the congruence between thought, word, and deed by the name of purity.[153] For Bede, as we will see at the end of Homily 1.22, "purity" means that the parts add up to a coherent whole.[154] Prayer is a *logos*-oriented integration of thoughts and

149 Derrida's interest is really more on the give-and-take of language than in gift giving practices. Thus, his argument on the narcissism of the giving subject, cited above, is based on grammar. The giving subject/receiving subject is grammatically impossible, but possibility is not constrained by grammar.

150 Derrida ignores this point, emphasizing obligation instead.

151 Adam B. Seligman et al., *Ritual and Its Consequences: An Essay on the Limits of Sincerity* (Oxford: Oxford University Press, 2008), 4.

152 CCSL 122, 344, l. 92. *Simplex*, "unmixed," also overlaps with notions of purity.

153 Most notably at the end of Homily 1.22, "pure orandi" and "orationis puritas," CCSL 122, 160, ll. 162, 164.

154 See CCSL 122, 160, ll. 142–5, quoted below.

deeds to the words of prayer, in which the word is primary and creates the praying self, which the precator receives and enacts.

Homily 2.10 is an after-Easter homily on the women who come to Jesus's tomb bearing spices on the morning of his resurrection.[155] For the purposes of prayer, Bede's explication of Luke 24:1 is the important part: "una autem sabbati valde diluculo venerunt ad monumentum portantes quae paraverant aromata"[156] (And on the first day of the week, very early in the morning, they came to the sepulchre, bringing the spices which they had prepared). It would be easy (if mistaken) to read the homily as though it presents a particular interior model of devoted love that motivates their actions and which Bede's audience should emulate: "Quod autem mulieres dominum quaesiturae ualde diluculo uenerunt ad monumentum magnam sui amoris erga illum deuotionem demonstrant"[157] (The fact that the women came to the tomb very early in the morning in order to seek the Lord proves the great devotedness of their love for him). But when Bede applies their example to his audience he transmutes this "desire to find the Lord"[158] not into a call to emulate the women's *devotio amoris*, but to perform good works and pray; he continually shifts devotion from an interior state to something enacted. Bede's audience should express their devotion to the Lord through the gift of their prayers as enacted through their deeds and internalized in their thoughts.

Bede's explication of this verse is outlined thus:

The women seek the Lord at dawn = We seek the Lord shining with good works.
They bring spices = We bring the gift of spiritual prayer.
Brought early in the morning = Accompanied by good works and inward compunction.
Prepared beforehand = Having purged our thoughts of pointless thoughts.

---

155 The pericope is Luke 24:1–9. Martin discusses this homily briefly in his article examining the way Bede applies scriptural exposition to his audience, "Two Worlds," 30–1.

156 Vulgate Luke 24:1; Douay-Rheims Luke 24:1.

157 Homily 2.10, CCSL 122, 246, ll. 13–15; trans. Martin and Hurst, 2:88.

158 "si dominum inuenire ... desideramus," Homily 2.10, CCSL 122, 246, ll. 18–19; trans. Martin and Hurst, 2:89.

In his typological interpretation, Bede shifts the focus from the women's supposed motive, devoted love, to what is "proper" for one seeking one's Lord. He thus shifts the emphasis from love as the source of action to the necessity for good works to accompany prayer. While the women's seeking of the tomb "sui amoris erga illum deuotionem demonstrant"[159] (proves the great devotedness of their love for [the Lord]), Bede never specifically asks his audience to feel the *amor* associated with *devotio*. Rather he asks them to perform *devotio* through the gift of their prayers: "Decet autem nos sicut operum bonorum luce fulgidos ita etiam spiritalium orationum gratia refertos dominum quaerere"[160] (Just as it is proper for us to seek the Lord shining with the light of good works, so also is it proper for us to seek him abundantly provided with the gift of spiritual prayers). Prayer functions in a double way as both the gift a dependent brings as acknowledgment of dependence and in hope of gaining a response to a request, as Bede makes clear in this negative example:

> Nam qui ad orandum ecclesiam ingressus inter uerba obsecrationis consuetudinem superfluae cogitationis ab animo repellere neglegit quasi dominum quaerens minus parata secum aromata detulit.[161]
>
> (One who enters a church to pray, and neglects to drive away from his mind its usual superfluous thoughts while he pours forth his words of entreaty, is like a person seeking the Lord without bringing with him the spices he has prepared.)

Relationally, this means that people confirm their place in the *gratia* relationship through bringing their petitions to their Lord. Petition expresses their sense of their dependence on the Lord, while at the same time reinforcing the sense of privilege inherent in the freedom to come before him. The gift of prayer that they bring binds together feeling and action as an expression of gratitude. Prayer is also the request itself. Bede describes these prayers in more detail: "Aromata etenim nostra uoces sunt orationum in quibus desideria cordis nostri domino commendamus"[162] (Our spices are our voices in prayer, in which we set forth before the Lord the

159 Homily 2.10, CCSL 122, 246, l. 15; trans. Martin and Hurst, 2:88.
160 Homily 2.10, CCSL 122, 247, ll. 21–2; trans. Martin and Hurst, 2:89.
161 Homily 2.10, CCSL 122, 247, ll. 49–52; trans. Martin and Hurst, 2:90.
162 Homily 2.10, CCSL 122, 247, ll. 24–6; trans. Martin and Hurst, 2:89.

desires of our hearts). Exactly whose desires these are will be addressed in a moment. For now, we notice that Bede once again shifts from desire to works. Two things accompany prayer, good actions first of all:

> Diluculo igitur aromata ad monumentum domini ferimus cum memores passionis ac mortis quam pro nobis suscepit et actionum bonarum proximis foris lucem monstramus et suauitate purae conpunctionis intus in corde feruemus quod et omnibus horis et tunc maxime fieri oportet cum ecclesiam oraturi ingredimur.[163]
>
> (We bear spices to the tomb of the Lord early in the morning when, mindful of the passion and death which he underwent for us, we show to our neighbor outwardly the light of our good actions, and are inwardly aflame in our heart with the delight of simple compunction. We must do this at all times, but especially when we go into church in order to pray.)

And, second, pure thoughts:

> aromata namque quae ad obsequium domini portemus prius parasse est adeo cor ante tempus orationis a superuacuis expurgare cogitationibus ut in ipso tempore orandi nil sordidum mente recipere nil rerum labentium cogitare nulla praeter ea quae precamur et ipsum cui supplicamus meminere nouerimus.[164]
>
> ([T]he earlier preparation of the spices we carry to perform our service to the Lord is the purging of our hearts from pointless thoughts before the time of prayer, so that at the time of prayer we are able to admit nothing unclean into our minds, and to think of nothing that concerns transitory matters beyond what we are making our entreaty for, and to remember who it is whom we are supplicating.)

Bede continually binds these three things together in his discussions of prayer: the words and actions of prayer itself, good works, and singleness of mind. Bede gives here not a formula for how to get what you want from God but the way that prayer transforms. Bede does not frame the issue at stake in prayer as one of incongruence between the primary inner self and

163 Homily 2.10, CCSL 122, 247, ll. 30–5; trans. Martin and Hurst, 2:89.
164 Homily 2.10, CCSL 122, 247, ll. 42–7; trans. Martin and Hurst, 2:89–90.

action as a reflection of the self (i.e., the true, inner self is not expressed in prayer), but rather as one of understanding one's position in relation to God and that what one owes God be enacted both through the actions of good deeds and of thought. As I said before, this is what Bede means by purity, and his idea of purity is *logos* oriented. Still, purity is not produced through *mere* words, but by receiving words as given, as a recognition of identity conferred. Such a conception of the self is fundamentally relational – the person is "true" or "pure" only as he or she enacts what she or he is expected to be, a devoted subject of the Lord.

It is thus significant that when those praying express the desires of their hearts, they do not actually express desires originating with themselves in their prayers. When Bede says, "Aromata etenim nostra uoces sunt orationum in quibus desideria cordis nostri domino commendamus"[165] (Our spices are our voices in prayer, in which we set forth before the Lord the desires of our hearts), he continues to identify these desires with the "mundissima sanctorum praecordia"[166] (the purest inmost longings of the saints). These desires are not primarily the desires of the person praying; rather, those praying adopt the desires of the saints captured and preserved within the prayers of the Church which those praying are then to enact.

People earn the final reward of the heavenly kingdom through the purity of their lives, but this must be understood in the context of integrated prayer. Through his understanding of *logos*-oriented purity, Bede reforms the Cassianic notion of purity as *apatheia* – the monk's disengagement from the material world and bodily desires – into a purity comparatively more engaged with the world, more integrated within community, and more concretely relational in its conception of God. His is not a watered-down version of monastic prayer aimed at unsophisticated new Christians,[167] but a coherent reorientation of the relationship between humanity and God expressed in prayer as Bede moves away from Neoplatonic abstraction and towards a more concretely realized gift-oriented relationship with God.

Bede links purity of thoughts and purity of works in such a way that true pure prayer means congruence between what one *says* (prayer), *does*

165 Homily 2.10, CCSL 122, 247, ll. 24–6; trans. Martin and Hurst, 2:89.

166 Homily 2.10, CCSL 122, 247, l. 27; trans. Martin and Hurst, 2:89. Although I might translate "mundissima" as "finest" to avoid terminological confusion.

167 As DeGregorio implies. See above, p. 150.

(works), and *thinks* (thoughts) – an integrated performance of precators' subjection to God. Consistently throughout Bede's work, works and thoughts originate in the words of prayer. Unlike the women, who seek Christ's tomb early in the morning out of devotion, many in Bede's congregation would have found themselves in church first, devoted to such a life by their parents. Furthermore, they would not be praying their own thoughts and feelings, but the prescribed prayers of the Divine Office.[168] The person's works and thoughts must conform to these prayers, and devotion ideally springs from this practice as precators internalize the words and the practice of prayer. Without this congruence prayer-as-gift is neither prayer nor a gift at all but rather a species of neglect: "quasi dominum quaerens minus parata secum aromata detulit"[169] (like a person seeking the Lord without bringing with him the spices he has prepared).

In this way prayer both expresses and creates devotion. Bede presents the women who seek Jesus's tomb as a model, but the way that he consistently displaces "devotio amoris" with the good works surrounding prayer suggests that he understands devotion much as he understands humility and the response of *gratia*. That is, devotion is not primarily a feeling, but the dutiful, moral response to gifts, expressed through good works and pure thoughts. Bede asks his audience to emulate the women's devotion by adopting the women's story as a model for how they should approach the Eucharist, and to seek their Lord with the same devotion. But for them to do this, the order of events is backward: the women come to seek the Lord because they are devoted. Bede's audience grows in devotion because, responding to God's gifts, they come.

Gratia inpetrandi: Homily 1.22, From Dogs to Sheep

In this Lenten homily Bede lays out the way that prayer is an essential expression of the dependent relationship of humans upon God, complemented by God's reciprocal responsibility to hear the prayers of those whom he has deigned to call his own. Bede situates prayer within what we might call the "psychology of repentance." Although focusing more explicitly on personal prayer than the other homilies, Homily 1.22 situates prayer

168 Although, as Jesse D. Billett shows, *The Divine Office in Anglo-Saxon England, 597–c. 1000* (London: Boydell, 2014), the Divine Office does not mean the Benedictine Office at this early point.

169 Homily 2.10, CCSL 122, 247, ll. 51–2; trans. Martin and Hurst, 2:90.

both within the community and within the person. Crucially, Homily 1.22 also indicates the way that prayer is the essential means towards transformation from not-belonging to belonging, from slavery to sins instigated by the devil to obedience to the commands of Christ wherein lies full humanity. Complicating this, the homily also apparently presents a complex "psychology" of sin and repentance that, for modern readers, is too easily read through an interiorization of the "true" self as the source of action.

The pericope for this homily is Matthew 15:21–8, in which a gentile woman asks Jesus to heal her demon-possessed daughter. Patristic authorities primarily represent the gentile woman as an example of humility.[170] For Bede, the gentile woman affords an opportunity to talk about prayer in a far more detailed way than other commentators do. It is a nicely balanced and deceptively simple homily. Bede first explicates the literal sense, then gives two allegorical readings: the mother stands first for the Church, who pleads for her "daughter": any soul in the Church who has fallen under the influence of malign spirits. Next, the mother stands for the person praying for the healing of his "daughter": his own demon-dominated conscience.

Bede's allegoresis presents an apparent challenge to my argument about the nature of prayer in Bede's homilies. My argument about prayer in Bede has been twofold. First, prayer is primarily situated within a reciprocal *gratia*-relationship with God in which prayer and good deeds are interior and exterior enactments of God's gifts. This means that in prayer he understands the self as constituted through its imagined relationship to God and through adopting the prayers of the community of saints and living Christians. As a result, second, the self is primarily performed through enacting prayer and good deeds that create and reinforce these relationships. Change in exterior action leads to interior change. This makes the interior attributes of the mind or heart (feeling, emotion) not the *causes* of exterior change but the products. We would expect, then, to see an emphasis on *doing* (performing devotion, as in Homily 2.10, or performing

170 There are several Augustinian sermons on the topic (77, 77a, 77b). Sermon 77 is about humility, 77a is about conversion, and 77b is about praying, although Augustine switches straight over to Matt. 7:7–8 ("Ask and you shall receive") to talk about prayer. However, he does mention the idea, found in Bede, of the woman being transformed through Christ's "training" her in persistence from a dog to a sheep. Jerome makes her an example of humility, patience, and faith in *Commentariorum in Matheum*, ed. D. Hurst and M. Adriaen, CCSL 77 (Turnhout: Brepols, 1967), 132, ll. 1536–1601.

repentance) rather than on *being* (being devoted, as the women in 2.10 are, or being penitent). An initial reading of the repentant sinner seems to place emphasis on interior states as the source of repentance and of the "true self" that the penitent must reform and enact.

As in Homily 2.10, Bede initially situates prayer in the reciprocal relationship of lordship and petitioning. This is evident from the beginning from the literal level, which presents the problem that the woman has no apparent right to bring her petitions before Jesus, being "gentilis a diuinorum eloquiorum funditus erat segregata doctrinis"[171] (as a gentile … completely separated from the teachings of the divine thoughts). Bede continues, explaining that, even so, "nec tamen illis quas eadem eloquia praedicant priuata uirtutibus"[172] (she was nevertheless not deprived of the virtues which those thoughts proclaim). The passive "nec … priuata" indicates that those virtues were something given her of which she could have been deprived. Yet the givenness is not overt – Bede elides the giving agent. The woman manifests these four virtues (faith, patience, constancy, and humility) in her subsequent petitioning of Jesus to heal her daughter. The virtues manifest in her petition serve to prove to those watching, the disciples and the Jews, that the woman deserved to have her request granted because, fundamentally, she recognized that Jesus was God and recognized her position in relationship to him.[173] That is, the woman's virtues, received and manifested, serve to gain for her the ability to have her petition heard. However, this is not something she presumes upon. When Jesus implies that she is a dog (that is, *not* one of his own), Bede takes this as a kind of test of her constancy and humility. She "domini quidem sententiam confirmat nec a suae tamen petitionis inprobitate quiescit"[174] (confirmed the Lord's statement, but nevertheless she did not rest from the audacity of her request). She responds as she does because she relied upon the largess of Jesus's grace: "quae indigna quidem sit integris dominicae doctrinae qua Iudaei utebantur epulis refici sed quantulacumque ei a

171 Homily 1.22, CCSL 122, 156, ll. 4–5; trans. Martin and Hurst, 1:215.

172 Homily 1.22, CCSL 122, 156, ll. 5–6; trans. Martin and Hurst, 1:215.

173 "Vnde recte a pio saluatore … audire meruit : *O mulier magna est fides tua ; fiat tibi sicut uis*. Magnam quippe satis habebat fidem …" (Hence from the benevolent Savior … she rightly deserved to hear: "O woman, your faith is great. Let it be done to you as you wish." Indeed, she had great enough faith …): Homily 1.22, CCSL 122, 157–8, ll. 60–4; trans. Martin and Hurst, 1:217.

174 Homily 1.22, CCSL 122, 157, ll. 48–50; trans. Martin and Hurst, 1:217.

domino foret inpertita gratia hanc sibi ad salutem sufficere posse putauerit"[175] (Being unworthy to be refreshed by the meal of the Lord's entire teaching, which the Jews had for their use, she nevertheless supposed that however small the grace imparted to her by the Lord might be, it could be sufficient for her salvation). Paradoxically, her humble recognition that she has nothing to offer him to make him hear her petition, that she is thrown fully upon his grace, which she nevertheless believes is enough for her, prompts Jesus to extend his healing to her daughter. In contrast to Mary, this woman seemingly comes from outside the *gratia* relationship, presuming to make her petition on the basis of her four virtues, but knowing that her virtue is not enough to oblige Jesus to respond to her request. Implicit is the idea that because of her belief, the woman is transformed from a dog to a sheep, from one with no right to ask favours, to one with a right to ask.[176]

Bede's allegorization first focuses on the role of the Church in bringing salvation for the souls entrusted to her care. The woman represents the Church, praying for "anima quaelibet est in ecclesia malignorum magis spirituum deceptionibus quam conditoris sui mancipata praeceptis"[177] (any soul in the Church that is delivered up to the deceptions of malign spirits rather than to her Maker's commands). The "soul's" central problem is that she has fallen under the influence of devils rather than obeying the commands of her "Maker," who has authority over her.[178] Here Bede understands that prayer works objectively; it cannot work without Christ's intervention:

> pro qua necesse est ecclesia mater dominum sollicita interpellet ut quam ipsa foris monendo obsecrando increpando non ualet ille interius inspirando corrigat atque ab errorum tenebris conuersam ad agnitionem uerae lucis excitet.[179]

175 Homily 1.22, CCSL 122, 157, ll. 57–60; trans. Martin and Hurst, 1:217.

176 Augustine also emphasizes the idea of her transformation in Sermon 77, in which her perseverance effects her transformation, and 77b, in which the instantaneous nature of her transformation is emphasized.

177 Homily 1.22, CCSL 122, 158, ll. 90–2; trans. Martin and Hurst, 1:218.

178 This reflects the ransom theory of atonement, which is explored in more detail in its relationship to Ælfric's teaching in chapter 4.

179 Homily 1.22, CCSL 122, 158, ll. 92–6; trans. Martin and Hurst, 1:218.

(The Church, as a solicitous mother, must intercede for this soul so that since the Church is not capable of converting such a one by warning, entreating and rebuking her outwardly, Christ may convert her by inspiring her interiorly, and, when she has been turned from the darkness of error, he may rouse her to the acknowledgement of the true light.)

To be transformed, the deceived person must come to an awareness of her situation through the inspiration of Christ. It looks as though the "interior" state of inspiration by Christ brings about the exterior transformation. We can see how interior inspiration works in the next allegory, in which Bede shifts the allegorical signification so that the mother represents "quis nostrum"[180] (any one of us) and the demon-possessed daughter represents that one's defiled conscience. Up to this point in the homily, Bede's presentation of the figure of the mother, who perseveres in[181] her "mentem" (mind) in entreaty, whose prayer springs from her inner constancy ("intus gerat pectoris constantiam"),[182] and whose requests (as the Church) will be heard "si mentem ab intentione proposita non mutauerit"[183] (if she does not turn aside her mind from its proposed intention), seem to challenge my contention that prayer in Bede works through exterior actions. Furthermore, Bede says that the Church *cannot* convert an errant soul outwardly, but that Christ must convert her inwardly, thereby seeming to indicate that the individual's action springs from interior disposition.

But what does this look like as Bede applies it to his audience? The second allegorization answers this question and shows that Bede subtly shifts his emphasis onto action. Bede does *not* picture a psychic split between consciousness and conscience, a body inhabited by duelling impulses, an id and a superego that the ego must choose between. Rather, Bede imagines the soul as a territory controlled either by devils or by God.[184] He imagines the sinner as one seduced away from the commands of his true Lord, "cogitationem de corde progenitam diabolica"[185] (by thoughts born of the devil's heart), putting himself into the false position of serving his Lord's enemy. The soul's primary problem is that he has responded to

180 Homily 1.22, CCSL 122, 159, l. 107; trans. Martin and Hurst, 1:219.

181 "[N]e sic quidem ab instantia precandi desistit uel a sperando pietatis munere mentem reuocat," Homily 1.22, CCSL 122, 157, ll. 44–6.

182 Homily 1.22, CCSL 122, 157, ll. 56–7.

183 Homily 1.22, CCSL 122, 159, l. 104; trans. Martin and Hurst, 1:219.

184 That is, a psychomachia rather than a psychology.

185 Homily 1.22, CCSL 122, 159, l. 111; trans. Martin and Hurst, 1:219.

the thought (*cogitatio*) of the devil as though he were subject to him. In this case, action does not follow interior disposition but instead follows a relationship; that is, the commands of one's lord, imagined as an external force. Action, both verbal and physical, does not express one's true interior self perceived as an independent subject; rather, action responds to and enacts one's position as a subject *to* – in this case, either God or the devil. From Bede's perspective, responding to the devil is a sort of madness because the person under discussion is "one of us," a subject of God. Christ's inspiration "converts" this person to recognize his crime. His conscience is polluted,[186] but Christ causes him to become aware of his sin and of his devilish tormentor. The soul's pollution seems to come as he recognizes the disjuncture between what is and what ought to be. His position is "in the church," but his condition is devil-dominated.

Bede describes the moment of conviction as a moment in which the person recognizes not his error, not his incoherence or insincerity, not his failure to live by his best impulses, not even his guilt, but his crime.[187] Naming sin "reatus" (guilt for a crime) situates it within a legalistic relationship typical within penitential discourse. The person has trespassed against his Lord, not against himself, by madly enduring the devil's harassment rather than obeying the commands of his Lord.[188] The penitential relationship conceptualized God as Judge, changing what the human has to offer from a gift to restitution, the payment for a crime. Bede accordingly acknowledges the disruption of the *gratia*-relationship as the petitioner seeks to be reinstated into it:

> Ideoque necesse est talis ut reatum suum cognouerit mox ad preces lacrimasque confugiat sanctorum crebras intercessiones et auxilia quaerat qui pro animae eius salute rogantes domino dicant, precamur domine *miserator et misericors patiens et multae miserationis* dimitte eam quia clamat post nos dimitte reatum et dona gratiam.[189]

186 "Pollutam," Homily 1.22, CCSL 122, 159, l. 109.

187 "Reatus," Homily 1.22, CCSL 122, 159, l. 119, primarily judicial guilt for the offence of which he stands charged rather than the subjective feeling of guilt. See Lewis and Short. Bede uses the word to denote judicial or assessed guilt. This invokes penitential paradigms of imagining God as judge and sin as a crime against God.

188 Note the earlier formulation of this same idea: "malignorum magis spirituum deceptionibus quam conditoris sui mancipata praeceptis," Homily 1.22, CCSL 122, 158, ll. 91–2. The devil has no authority to give commands; his influence is spurious.

189 Homily 1.22, CCSL 122, 159, ll. 118–24; trans. Martin and Hurst, 1:219.

(as soon as such a one has recognized his crime, he must flee to petitions and tears; he must seek the frequent intercessions and help of the saints, so that asking for the salvation of his soul, they may say to the Lord, "We entreat you, Lord who are compassionate and merciful, patient and full of compassion, pardon her because she is crying after us. Pardon her crimes and give her grace.")

But Bede quickly moves back into a *gratia*-framed relationship with God as Benefactor, for this is where transformation is to be found:

indubia mente de largitoris summi bonitate confidat quia qui de latrone confessorem de persecutore apostolum de publicano euangelistam de lapidibus potuit facere filios Abrahae ipse etiam canem inpudentissimum conuertere Israheliticam possit in ouem; cui merito donatae castitatis etiam uitae aeternae pascua largiatur, id est peccatorem conuersum a uia sua mala iustum facere dignetur quem merito bonae actionis ad regnum caeleste perducat.[190]

(with his mind free of doubt let him trust in the goodness of the supreme Benefactor, for the one who could make a confessor from a robber, an apostle from a persecutor, an evangelist from a publican, and who could make sons for Abraham from stones, could turn even the most shameless dog into an Israelite sheep. He may even bestow upon him, as a reward for chastity attained, the pasture of eternal life – that is, he may deign to make righteous a sinner who has turned from his evil way, and as a reward for his good action he may lead him to the heavenly kingdom.)

The things that distinguish a confessor from a robber, or a dog from a sheep, are the things they do in response to God's *gratia*. In *gratia*, God "deign[s] to make righteous," and the sinner responds in *gratia* by turning from his evil way. And it is what they *do* – attaining chastity, turning from evil ways, or petitioning humbly and persistently – that causes God to give the further *gratia* of the heavenly kingdom.

Central to this transformation is repeated, persistent prayer and the enactment of the posture and affect that go with it. Sorrow (inner affect) does not accompany this prayer, but tears (an outward performance). The one

190 Homily 1.22, CCSL 122, 159, ll. 129–37; trans. Martin and Hurst, 1:219–20.

praying for the intercession of the saints prostrates[191] himself because that is the position in which a person begs. His prostration results from his begging, from his realization of his crime, not from his *intimus affectus*, which then, rather than causing his action, accompanies it. To be sure, feelings and thoughts are important for Bede, but as his ensuing discussion of the mechanics of prayer indicates, these things follow the fact, the gift, of prayer. He situates prayer within a relational context – the sinner responds to Christ, understands his crime, and begs to be cleared of his crime and have the relationship restored through the repeated action of prayer. This is how prayer transforms.

Bede ends the sermon by emphasizing the necessity of one's thoughts matching what one prays. For prayer to be transformational, it must be integrated into both actions and thoughts. The repeated action of prayer transforms the sinner in and of itself (as a response to God's grace). Bede shows this by ending the sermon with a couple of practical points on the act of praying itself. First, he emphasizes the necessary congruence between words and thoughts: "Notandum interea quod haec orandi pertinacia ita solum meretur esse fructifera, si quod ore precamur hoc etiam mente meditemur neque alio clamor labiorum quam cogitationum scindatur intuitus"[192] ([T]his tenacity in praying can only deserve to bear fruit if what we ask for with our mouth we also meditate on in our mind, and if the crying of our lips is not cut apart in another direction from the focus of our thoughts). Bede demands purity in prayer, that one's thoughts match one's actions. But it is worth noting again that, for Bede, the *act* of praying (the words) comes before interior thoughts. He assumes, with his monastic audience in mind, that they already enact prayer, and that these actions of prayer must then be interiorized so that thoughts match the action. The one praying must discipline his mind to do what his mouth already says. This congruence between words and thoughts then allows prayer to become transformative. All of a person's good works form the basis of that person's prayer for salvation and entry into the heavenly kingdom, but they also help to realize that salvation in the present life. As the precator interiorizes these just actions, they are God's means to effect the prayed-for transformation, to expel the "tumults of depraved thoughts" and loosen the bonds of sin. All the actions of one's life must be a preparation for prayer in order to attain this congruence between thoughts and

191 "pronus," Homily 1.22, CCSL 122, 159, l. 125.

192 Homily 1.22, CCSL 122, 160, ll. 142–5; trans. Martin and Hurst, 1:220.

words: "Quaecumque enim saepius agere loqui uel audire solemus eadem necesse est saepius ad animum quasi solitam propriamque recurrant ad sedem"[193] (Whatever things we are accustomed to do, speak, or hear most often, these same things will necessarily return to our mind most often as though to their accustomed and proper place). In a petitionary model, preparation for petition easily slides into petition itself.

Bede recognizes that the battle to control one's thoughts is brought about "antiqui hostis instinctu"[194] (at the instigation of the ancient enemy), and that the ability to pray is itself, like any other good deed, a gift: "Sciens enim utilitatem orandi et inuidens hominibus gratiam inpetrandi"[195] (He [the enemy] is aware of the benefit of praying, and he envies human beings the gift of having their requests granted). So Bede returns to the idea of the gift: all that humans have, even the transformational ability to pray itself, comes from the grace of the supreme Benefactor. This gift is one that transforms humans as they use it. When, in humility, they recognize that central fact of their relationship – that they can make no demands of God based on their own merits or anything they could offer to God – they enter into what is to Bede an astounding relationship with God, marked by a notable freedom to persist in prayer, to demand that he hear their requests.

Conclusion

In this chapter, I have argued that, for Bede, the ritual actions and words of formal prayer come first, as a gift from God, and are the elements out of which a person constructs coherent self-identity. There is no particular primary interior "self" who loves or is devoted to God before being transformed by God's *gratia*, which is received and enacted through the "good deeds" of prayer, almsgiving, etc. that people are given to perform. God's way of transforming people is through good works for them to carry out. Bede assumes that the words and actions of prayer come first. Because of Bede's emphasis on *simplex intentio*, on *devotio*, on the internalization of prayer, it is easy to read him as sharing an essentially modern conception of sincerity or a sense of the affective individual. But Bede conceptualizes congruence between thoughts, words, and deeds, which I have also called "integrated prayer," as "purity" rather than "sincerity." The iterative

193 Homily 1.22, CCSL 122, 160, ll. 167–70; trans. Martin and Hurst, 1:221.
194 Homily 1.22, CCSL 122, 160, l. 150; trans. Martin and Hurst, 1:220.
195 Homily 1.22, CCSL 122, 160, l. 151–2; trans. Martin and Hurst, 1:220.

recitation and actions of prayer – adopting words which are *not* one's own – is what gives prayer its purifying potential. In fact, to pray "sincerely," to produce words reflective of one's own inner self (whatever that might mean), would defeat the purpose. Such prayer could never be transformational because, in so doing, the precator would merely re-represent the self to the self rather than using the words given by God to transform a dog to a sheep, a sinner to a saint. For Bede, precators achieve purity as they become more integrated into the believing community, and as their thoughts and deeds become more coherently integrated to the words of prayer. For Bede, God's *gratia* makes people fully human because God's *gratia* gives them the means to become human. In the end, prayer is secondarily a gift of the self *to* God; it is primarily a gift of the self *from* God, through prayer. God's gifts confer identity that precators enact and return.

Bede wrote as a monk to monks and, as we will see, his idea of prayer is the least embedded in a material economy of the authors in this study. Bede believes that all prayer should be for salvation, that people work salvation out throughout their whole lives as they integrate prayer more fully into all their words and actions, and that prayer enacts an exceptionally close *gratia* relationship between the Lord and his retainers. The following chapters include greater focus on lay prayer. Indeed, the central figure for the next chapter, King Alfred, is a layman himself. As represented by Asser, Alfred clearly does not believe that the only legitimate thing to pray for is salvation, and he has a much more concrete expectation of prayer's material efficacy than Bede does. Yet the Psalms feature largely in Alfred's piety, which is heavily influenced by the monastic tradition (shaped, at this point, by developments in the Carolingian empire). Bede emphasizes enacting an identity given by God; Alfred's vision is that prayer authorizes the precator by inserting him in the Davidic and Christological narrative. And if prayer, for Bede, is gift, for Alfred, prayer is work.

Chapter Three

Does Prayer Work? The Prayers of King Alfred

[T]æc me þinne willan to wyrcenne, þæt ic mæge þe inweardlice lufian toforon eallum þingum mid clænum geþance 7 mid clænum lichaman; forþon þe þu eart min sceoppend ...

(Teach me to work your will, that I may inwardly love you above all things with pure thought and with pure body, because you are my creator ...)

– concluding prayer, *Consolation of Philosophy*[1]

According to his biographer, King Alfred (849–99) spent much of his adult life struggling with a mysterious illness. In the *Life of King Alfred*, Asser recounts the history of this illness in a chronologically reversed passage that seems to many readers unnecessarily convoluted: Asser relates the events backward, starting with an account of the illness that plagued Alfred his entire adult life and moving in reverse order from there to a youthful request for illness that God granted.[2] The events, in chronological order, are that Alfred, in "primaevo iuventutis suae flore"[3] (the first flowering of his youth), prayed for an illness to control his sexual urges. God answered

1 *King Alfred's Old English Version of Boethius*, ed. Walter John Sedgefield (Oxford: Clarendon, 1899), 149, ll. 21–4. Crossed thorn has been expanded to *þæt*, and nasal bars have been silently expanded.

2 Asser, *Alfred the Great*, trans. Simon Keynes and Michael Lapidge (London: Penguin, 1983), 255n143.

3 Asser, *Asser's Life of King Alfred*, ed. William Henry Stevenson (1904; rprnt. Oxford: Clarendon, 1959), 56, l. 42; trans. Keynes and Lapidge, 89.

this prayer through the *munus* (gift or reward) of the disease of *ficus*.[4] After a time, Alfred prayed for a lesser illness that would be easier to bear. God also answered that prayer by, shortly thereafter, entirely healing him. Finally, he was stricken with a second, more severe illness at his wedding. This illness, which "quasi inutilem eum, ut ei videtur, in divinis et humanis rebus propemodum effecit"[5] (rendered him virtually useless – as it seemed to him – for heavenly and worldly affairs) stayed with him at least to the point of Asser's writing.[6]

In the words of Asser's editor, William Stevenson, the chapter "is an instructive specimen of his confused arrangement and puzzling phraseology."[7] Indeed, to many the portrayal of Alfred as one who spends a great deal of time worrying and praying about his health seems so strikingly unattractive that the passage has been used as evidence that the *Life* is a later forgery.[8] Plummer and Stevenson have labelled his piety "morbidly religious,"[9] and Alfred Smyth has called him neurotic.[10] In response, more recent scholarship has placed this passage in the context of Carolingian developments in lay aristocratic piety. Paul Kershaw argues that Asser's treatment of Alfred's piety and illness is conventionally Carolingian in the claims it makes to the ruler's piety,[11] while Pratt argues that the Carolingian cast to Alfred's piety is unusual in a West Saxon context.[12] Both Kershaw

---

4 *Asser's Life*, 56, l. 57–8: "fici dolorem Dei munere incurrit" (he contracted the affliction of *ficus* as a reward from God). My translation. Keynes and Lapidge translate *ficus* (lit. "fig") as "piles." It is often understood as hemorrhoids; David Pratt follows Craig's suggestion that it was actually Crohn's disease, "The Illnesses of King Alfred the Great," in *ASE* 30 (2001), 73. I leave the term untranslated.

5 *Asser's Life*, 57, ll. 68–70; trans. Keynes and Lapidge, 90.

6 *Asser's Life*, chapter 91.

7 *Asser's Life*, 294, n. to chapter 74.

8 See, most recently, Alfred P. Smyth, *King Alfred the Great* (New York: Oxford University Press, 1995), in the chapter "Neurotic Saint and Invalid King." Smyth's argument that Asser's *Life* is a forgery is not widely accepted. Paul Kershaw, "Illness, Power, and Prayer in Asser's Life of King Alfred," in *EME* 10 (2001); Pratt, "Illnesses of King Alfred"; and Scott DeGregorio, "Texts, *Topoi* and the Self: A Reading of Alfredian Spirituality," in *EME* 13.1 (2005), respond to Smyth's characterization of Alfred's piety by contextualizing it within practices and developments in Alfred's own day.

9 Charles Plummer, *The Life and Times of Alfred the Great* (Oxford: Clarendon, 1902), 28; *Asser's Life*, 294.

10 Smyth, *King Alfred the Great*, chapter 8.

11 Kershaw, "Illness, Power, and Prayer," 201–24, 219.

12 Pratt, "Illnesses of King Alfred," 89.

and Pratt focus on Asser's political reasons for emphasizing Alfred's illness and his prayerful response: How do such representations of Alfred at prayer help consolidate his power and further his political aims? The most satisfactory answer is Kershaw's: "Asser uses the portrayal of Alfred as a holy supplicant, devout in prayer, to establish Alfred as a king in waiting, mastering his inner drives and establishing his relationship with God through humility and prayer."[13] But what interests me, more precisely, is the way Asser represents prayer and Alfred as a precator. One immediate question has to do with the rhetoric of Asser's account: why does he narrate the passage in this backward way? More centrally, why does he consider petitionary prayer for healing that does not, in the end, seem to work particularly pious? What sort of "relationship with God," to borrow Kershaw's phrasing, does Asser portray? Finally, how are Asser (and Alfred) imagining prayer to work?

The curious qualities of Alfredian piety and of Asser's narration have caught the attention of previous scholars. In "Affective Spirituality: Theory and Practice in Bede and Alfred the Great," Scott DeGregorio examines Alfred's reading practices, arguing that Alfred attempted "a kind of reading experience that would move him, as an individual, to deeper forms of piety and self-knowledge."[14] DeGregorio's larger argument is that the devotional and meditative nature of Alfred's experience places him in a tradition of "textually-directed piety and practice" that is more usually attributed to "a concept of the individual which began to gain currency only in the eleventh century."[15] In connecting Alfred's piety to the development of the individual and to more mystical forms of devotion, DeGregorio's focus extends Allen Frantzen's continued attempts to correct the omission of the Anglo-Saxons from the "grand narratives of devotion and mysticism of the Middle Ages."[16] In fact, Frantzen's article introducing DeGregorio's own essay makes this attempt explicit. While Frantzen's concern is a valid one and DeGregorio's work is a welcome contribution to our understanding of Anglo-Saxon piety, their arguments

13 Kershaw, "Illness, Power, and Prayer," 219.

14 Scott DeGregorio, "Affective Spirituality: Theory and Practice in Bede and Alfred the Great," in *EMS* 22 (2005), 135.

15 DeGregorio, "Affective Spirituality," 135. DeGregorio quotes Hirsch specifically in this passage. "Texts, *Topoi* and the Self" develops closely related ideas.

16 Allen J. Frantzen, "Spirituality and Devotion in the Anglo-Saxon Penitentials," in *EMS* 22 (2005), 117.

necessarily privilege a teleology that leads towards the individual and towards forms of prayer judged more authentic; that is, forms of prayer that would seem to reflect a sense of the inner self of the precator,[17] and also non-petitionary forms judged "purer" because of the lack of self-interest. At the same time, the focus on these types of spirituality ignores forms of devotion that were more normative in and beyond the Anglo-Saxon era.

Despite Asser's extended description of King Alfred at prayer, the *Life of King Alfred* is conspicuously absent from studies of early medieval prayer, even those that deal with the Anglo-Saxon period. Alfred's prayer apparently consists mainly of negotiating for forms of illness that will not render him, as he says, "contemptible" and "useless," petitions that do not strike readers now as very "spiritual." Indeed, Alfred's ritualistic and instrumental prayer, as portrayed by Asser, is exactly the type of prayer often dismissed as less valuable, less "pure," than the more fully spiritual prayer represented by Bede and (especially) Cassian. Significantly, this judgment echoes the criteria used to judge the value of a gift: the most valuable gift, like the "purest" forms of prayer, is sincere and intentional (i.e., not demanded by ritual) and "pure" of ulterior motive – a desire for personal gain. According to this point of view, a sincerely intentional gift is also individually expressive: it reflects the individuality of the giver and respects the individuality of the recipient. Alfred's prayer does not meet these criteria; therefore, when it is considered at all, it is more likely to be studied as part of Alfred's performance of power, or even as symptomatic of his alleged neurosis than within a devotional context. And yet Asser recounts his illness as a marker of Alfred's piety.

Asser's *Life* gives us rare insight into an Anglo-Saxon layman's practice of prayer, not only because he reports (and at some length) this specific instance of prayer, but also because he gives some idea of Alfred's training and habits. Moreover, it is only one of several texts from Alfred's circle that represent prayer. To place the prayer in Asser's *Life* in a larger context, this chapter will examine two of those texts: the prose introductions to the Psalms, which, taken as a guide to prayer, explain how the precator interiorizes and enacts prayer, and the *Soliloquies*, which open with a lengthy prayer that shows how its translator conceptualizes prayer as

17 See Gavin Flood, though, for a critique of a facile identification of "inwardness" with individuality, *The Truth Within: A History of Inwardness in Christianity, Hinduism, and Buddhism* (Oxford: Oxford University Press, 2013), 7–8.

work.[18] In the past, these texts were thought to have been translated by Alfred himself; however, the exact extent of Alfred's involvement is currently debated.

Alfred's famous program to translate "suma bec, þa þe nidbeðyrfesta sien eallum monnum to witanne"[19] (certain books, which are most needful for all to know) from Latin to Old English is usually regarded as the context for a number of works. Traditionally, they fall into two groups. The first group includes those works associated with Alfred's court but not thought to be translated by Alfred himself: Bede's *Historia Ecclesiastica*, Gregory's *Dialogues*, Orosius's *Historiae adversus paganos*, and the *Anglo-Saxon Chronicle*.[20] The texts in the second group are all attributed to Alfred, either in their prefaces or later by William of Malmesbury:[21] Gregory the Great's *Regula pastoralis*, Boethius's *De consolatione philosophiae*, Augustine's *Soliloquia*, the first fifty psalms, and the law code compiled under his name. Yet opinions as to the extent of Alfred's direct involvement with these texts vary. The view that Alfred himself translated

18 There are also several prayers inserted and appended to the *Consolation*. The last is quoted (in part) as the epigraph to this chapter. They develop themes from the *Consolation* as a whole regarding God's creative power and human dependence on him, but they give little context for prayer, and therefore add little to a theory of prayer beyond the texts examined here.

19 Alfred, *King Alfred's West-Saxon Version of Gregory's Pastoral Care*, ed. Henry Sweet (London: N. Trübner, 1871), 6.

20 Bald's Leechbook is also associated with Alfred because of the presence of a number of remedies said to have been sent to Alfred from the Patriarch of Jerusalem, and the Old English *Martyrology* could also have come from Alfred's Program, Keynes and Lapidge, *Alfred the Great*, 34. In addition, the Book of Nunnaminster is thought to have been owned by Alfred's wife Ealhswith because her name is written in it. See Barbara Raw, "Alfredian Piety: The Book of Nunnaminster," in *Alfred the Wise: Studies in Honour of Janet Bately on the Occasion of Her Sixty-Fifth Birthday*, ed. Jane Roberts et al. (Rochester: D.S. Brewer, 1997), 145.

21 Evidence for Alfredian authorship comes from attributions found in the prefaces to the *Pastoral Care*, *Boethius*, and the *Soliloquies*. The Psalms lack any sort of preface. Asser states specifically that Gregory's *Dialogues* were translated by Werferth at the request of Alfred, *Asser's Life*, chapter 77. Later evidence comes from Ælfric, who mentions that Alfred translated books, specifically Bede's *Historia* (see Malcolm Godden, "Did King Alfred Write Anything?" in *Medium Aevum* 76,1 [2007], 3) and William of Malmesbury, who tells us that Alfred had translated the first fifty psalms before he died as well as Orosius, *Pastoral Care*, the *Dialogues*, the *Consolation*, the *Soliloquies*, Bede, and the *Anglo-Saxon Chronicle*; see Allen J. Frantzen, *King Alfred* (Boston: Twayne Publishers, 1986), 8.

them now seems to be falling out of favour. Malcolm Godden argues for the position that seems to be ascendant (although not yet dominant): that Alfred did not actually write or translate anything at all.[22] Yet Janet Bately argues *contra* Godden that Alfred translated the texts typically attributed to him, although probably not on his own.[23] While the question of Alfred's authorship is unsettled, it seems probable that the texts under discussion here all originated under influence of Alfred's translation program. For the purposes of my argument, affinity matters more than authorship; I shall refer to "the translator" of the Psalms and the *Soliloquies*.[24]

22 Godden, in "Did King Alfred Write Anything?", argues that the later evidence attributing texts to Alfred need show nothing more than that he had a reputation for writing and that the works that have come down to us as Alfred's were attributed to him from an early date, and that the internal evidence claiming Alfredian authorship are an example of the practice of one person writing in the name and voice of another, 3–7. Leslie Lockett, who is currently working on an edition of the *Soliloquies* for Dumbarton Oaks, also expresses reservations that Alfred authored that text or the *Boethius* (personal correspondence).

23 Janet Bately, "Did King Alfred Actually Translate Anything? The Integrity of the Alfredian Canon Revisited," in *Medium Aevum* 78.2 (2009), 209. Bately responds to Godden largely on the basis of lexicographical evidence, and she also invokes Pratt's "Problems of Authorship and Audience in the Writings of King Alfred," in *Lay Intellectuals in the Carolingian World*, ed. Patrick Wormald and Janet L. Nelson (Cambridge: Cambridge University Press, 2006), as evidence against Godden's position. Patrick O'Neill, *King Alfred's Old English Prose Translation of the First Fifty Psalms* (Cambridge, MA.: Medieval Academy of America, 2001), and Frantzen, *King Alfred*, also argue for Alfredian authorship. Michael Treschow et al., "King Alfred's Scholarly Writings and the Authorship of the First Fifty Prose Psalms," in *The Heroic Age* 12 (2009), assume that Alfred translated the *Pastoral Care*, *Consolation*, and *Soliloquies*. Their computer-aided stylometric analysis seems to show that the prose paraphrase of the Psalms does not cluster as tightly together as the other three works more usually attributed to Alfred. I have reservations about their methods; for instance, I would like to see how a text entirely outside the Alfredian canon maps onto the textual distribution in their Figure 1. However, the fact that the Psalms, on the graph of their analysis, fall pretty much in between the group of texts usually attributed to Alfred (the *Consolation*, *Soliloquies*, and *Pastoral Care*) and the group usually attributed to the Alfredian circle (Bede, Orosius, the *Dialogues*) seems to indicate that they come from the same milieu, even if it says nothing specific about their authorship. Bately also points to methodological problems with Treschow's analysis.

24 Pratt argues that, at a minimum, Alfred must have been familiar with the contents of the works attributed to him, "Problems of Authorship," 174.

Several features of Alfredian prayer seem to move it towards a more transactional exchange than what we have seen in Bede. The texts do this first by separating the precator's intention from the prayer itself. To some extent, doing so reifies prayer, separating it from the person of the giver and making it a thing that one performs and gives so that God will hear one's intention or desire. The focus on intention returns us to the problem of will: if prayer is centred on human desire, if prayer is an alienable "thing" that precators trade with to get what they want (whether healing or salvation), this is a transactional mindset, a type of commodity exchange that sees God and humans as fundamentally separate and self-interested entities. From this perspective, Alfred desires healing, and so he trades prayer to get what he wants. However, several characteristics of Alfredian prayer work against this type of transactional mindset. As Asser's account demonstrates, the exchange imagined in prayer is "open" – there is not a one-to-one correspondence between the thing desired and the thing received. This openness creates its own set of problems (how does the precator know that God has heard?); however, it also moves prayer into the higher-status gift economy. The lack of correspondence between thing given and thing received creates space for trust, especially for precators to demonstrate their trust in God, as they extend prayer (as it were) on credit, showing through their continued faithful performance that they believe even when no answer is immediately forthcoming.

Furthermore, as this chapter will show, the Alfredian texts present prayer as work. While prayer as work seems to move the model of prayer outside of a gift paradigm, these texts present prayer as labour that cannot be alienated. Thus, the work of prayer is a gift to God; it still carries with it the personhood of the giver, the precator, who does not imagine that God *pays* him for his work so much as that God *rewards* him. More specifically, God rewards the personal qualities, demonstrated through the work performed, of the one who performs it. While Bede presents a strong sense that prayer changes – indeed, transforms – the precator, for Alfred, it is a more difficult question to say whether God rewards the precator for who he *is* or who he *becomes*. As we will see in the discussion of these texts, the work of prayer also has subjective effect as it narrativizes the praying self, acting as guarantee that God will hear the precators' intentions even as it subsumes those intentions into the narrative of the prayers themselves. Thus, these texts represent prayer in a distinctive way that situates it within a higher-status gift economy in which the personal worth of the precator is rewarded, rather than a lower-status transactional economy.

Asser's *Life of Alfred*

Whether Asser's account can be thought of as an accurate representation of Alfred's spirituality specifically has also been the subject of some debate.[25] Alfred Smyth has argued that the hagiographic mode of the *Life* undermines its historicity because it is a tissue of commonplaces mined from other sources.[26] In response, Pratt notes that as Asser wrote when Alfred was still alive, and "royal sanctity was an entirely posthumous phenomenon in Anglo-Saxon England," Asser's representation of Alfred's piety pertains to the sphere of lay devotion rather than hagiography.[27] M.J. Toswell, also responding to the idea of the *Life* as a kind of hagiography, argues that Asser appears to present Alfred as a type of David, noting various Davidic echoes Asser uses to describe Alfred.[28] Yet she says that Asser's use of this model can be taken as evidence of the pervasive influence of the Psalms, both as a narrative model for representing good kingship and as a characteristic of personal piety.[29] Scott DeGregorio has responded to Smyth's claims by troubling the way Smyth conflates textual borrowing with fiction.[30] DeGregorio argues that Alfred himself constructed his own spiritual identity out of the texts he had read: "the self could in part be structured around, and so gain a sense of identity from, a text."[31] Therefore, Asser's *Life* reflects an attitude towards textuality that DeGregorio calls "textualizing the self,"[32] which was shared in common

25 In fact, while Asser's *Life* is generally accepted as genuine, it has a complicated textual history (see Stevenson's introduction), and there are still those who doubt its authenticity (notably, Smyth, as noted above).

26 Smyth: "[M]uch of what the author of his *Life* personally contributes on the *persona* of the king was modelled on a saint's *vita*," *King Alfred the Great*, 200.

27 Pratt, "Illnesses of King Alfred," 40.

28 M.J. Toswell, *The Anglo-Saxon Psalter* (Turnhout: Brepols, 2014), 66–72. Toswell notes, among other things, that Asser includes David in Alfred's genealogy, 8 and 65–6.

29 Toswell: "If the psalms were so important in the life of every pious secular nobleman that they warranted this kind of concentration [as a feature of noble piety], then their very ubiquity in these narratives suggests the absolute importance of the psalms," *Anglo-Saxon Psalter*, 71.

30 DeGregorio: "Alfred's dubious piety is thus explained away [by Smyth] as nothing more than a string of textual fictions that reflect little upon real life and all too much upon conventions of literary representation," "Texts, *Topoi* and the Self," 81.

31 DeGregorio, "Texts, *Topoi* and the Self," 82.

32 DeGregorio, "Texts, *Topoi* and the Self," 82.

by Asser and Alfred. Spiritual *topoi* found in texts were meant to be borrowed in the construction of both a *Life* and a life. As we will see below, the piety that the introductions to the Psalms present is open to all who pray the Psalms. Asser's account may therefore be accepted as a reasonably accurate reflection of the general cast of Alfred's piety.[33]

Alfred clearly expects prayer to be materially efficacious; he prays for healing. We might conclude, then, that prayer that does not result in healing does not work. Prayer that "works" usually means that precators get what they desire. Answered prayer may be taken as proof of the existence of God,[34] and unanswered prayer as proof of the opposite. In Asser's account, Alfred fears he will "incur God's disfavor" by not following God's will, and he objectifies the subjective spiritual efficacy of prayer by desiring a bodily, corporeal effect. Instead of praying that God will take away his carnal desires, he prays for a bodily illness that will enable him to control them. By this standard of efficacy, Alfred's prayer is not fully "successful." In fact, rather than emphasizing the efficacy of Alfred's prayers, Asser's backwards narration calls attention to the fact that Alfred ends up with the very kind of illness he prayed not to have. Yet this does not seem to bother Asser at all: Asser's orientation towards prayer is not whether it works but the kind of work prayer does and the kind of work prayer is. Asser's account of Alfred at prayer shows that, in the end, material efficacy is the least important aspect of prayer, and his use of *ordo praeposterus* (non-chronological narration) only emphasizes this.

Asser's account begins with the illness that afflicts Alfred at his wedding. Many scholars have noticed the confusion caused by the backward narration, although Simon Keynes and Michael Lapidge, in a note to their translation call it "adequately coherent,"[35] and Marie Schütt, in her analysis of Asser's rhetoric, denies that there is confusion at all, if we follow the

---

33 Kershaw, "Illness, Power, and Prayer," and Pratt, "Illnesses of King Alfred," both take Asser's account as reflecting Alfred's understanding of his illness. Kershaw sees no reason to doubt that Alfred really was ill or really prayed for healing, as Asser reports. Although Pratt proposes an alternate reality behind Asser's representation, he also takes Asser's account as a reflection of Alfred's own understanding of his illness and prayer, as, for the early years of Alfred's life, "Asser had to rely primarily on the testimony of others, most notably the king himself, his 'truthful lord,'" 58. Thus, the account of Alfred's illness is likely to reflect Alfred's own understanding and interpretation of those events.

34 This is the central point of John R. Rice's *Prayer: Asking and Receiving* (1942; rprnt. Wheaton: Sword of the Lord, 1945).

35 Keynes and Lapidge, *Alfred the Great*, 255.

chronological sequence.[36] Yet even Schütt does not fully notice the way Asser's narration is driven by a logic in which each subsequent piece of information explains something that went before it. In tracing Asser's logic, we find that his interest lies in clarifying that the first and second illnesses are unrelated and that Alfred did not receive the first as a punishment.[37] After recounting the event, Asser explains that the guests who witnessed Alfred's wedding illness interpreted it in various ways. The only interpretive possibility he forecloses is that Alfred suffered on account of sin, and he does this by simply omitting it from the variety of interpretations that the wedding guests give to explain the illness:

> Multi namque favore et fascinatione circumstantis populi hoc factum esse autumabant; alii diaboli quadam invidia, qui semper bonis invidus existat; alii inusitato quodam genere febris; alii ficum existimabant, quod genus infestissimi doloris etiam ab infantia habuit.[38]
>
> (Many, to be sure, alleged that it had happened through the spells and witchcraft of the people around him; others, through the ill-will of the devil, who is always envious of good men; others, that it was the result of some unfamiliar kind of fever; still others thought that it was due to the piles, because he had suffered this particular kind of agonizing irritation even from his youth.)

Rather than giving the definitive interpretation we might expect, Asser next explains that Alfred no longer suffered from the youthful infirmity at the time of his wedding. To clarify that there is no connection between the two illnesses, Asser regresses to narrate how Alfred was completely healed of the first: when he was young he had been afflicted by an "agonizing" (*infestantis*) illness, but while hunting in Cornwall, Alfred prayed for a substitute that would be less severe, "ea tamen condicione, ut corporaliter exterius illa infirmitas non appareret, ne inutilis et despectus esset"[39] (on the understanding that the new illness would not be outwardly visible on his

36 Marie Schütt, "The Literary Form of Asser's 'Vita Alfredi,'" in *English Historical Review* 72.283 (1957), 215.

37 Pratt, "Illness of King Alfred," argues otherwise. While his conclusions may be sound, medically speaking, they clearly do not reflect the way Alfred's illness was understood at the time. In fact, the whole tenor of Pratt's argument is to figure out what "really" happened and to read Asser's account in light of this reconstructed reality.

38 *Asser's Life*, 55, ll. 12–17; trans. Keynes and Lapidge, 89.

39 *Asser's Life*, 55, ll. 28–30; trans. Keynes and Lapidge, 89.

body, whereby he would be rendered useless and contemptible). Shortly after Alfred finished praying he felt himself to be completely cured, even though "hunc dolorem in primaevo iuventutis suae flore ... nactus fuerat"[40] (he had contracted the malady in the first flowering of his youth).

Asser next offers the story of how Alfred first contracted the illness. In this case he notes his reason for recounting the story; it shows Alfred's disposition towards God: "ut de benevola mentis suae devotione Deo succinctim ac breviter, quamvis praeposterato ordine, loquar"[41] (if I may speak briefly and cursorily – although I go back to the beginning – of the kindly disposition of his mind towards God).[42] Asser then continues to show that the first illness was *not* a punishment for sin but a *munus*, a gift, in exchange for his devotion. Asser then says, "Cumque hoc saepius magna mentis devotione ageret, post aliquantulum intervallum praefatum fici dolorem Dei munere incurrit"[43] (When he had done this frequently with great mental devotion, after some time he contracted the disease of piles through God's gift). That is, Asser takes pains to clarify the second illness is not a recurrence of the first, and the first was not a punishment but a gift. From the beginning, Alfred wanted to please God by controlling his sexual desires. He asked for an illness that would help him do so, on the condition that it be one that he would be able to tolerate, not one that would make him unworthy and useless.

Finally, Asser returns to the wedding affliction: "Sed, proh dolor! eo amoto, alius infestior in nuptiis ... eum arripuit"[44] (But, alas, when it had been removed, another more severe illness seized him at his wedding feast). Again, the new illness is completely separate from the old. This one, Asser says, "eum ... incessabiliter fatigavit" and "quasi inutilem eum, ut ei videtur, in divinis et humanis rebus propemodum effecit"[45] (plagued him remorselessly ... and ... rendered him virtually useless – as it seemed to him – for heavenly and worldly affairs).

---

40 *Asser's Life*, 56, ll. 37–9; trans. Keynes and Lapidge, 89.

41 *Asser's Life*, 56, ll. 39–41; trans. Keynes and Lapidge, 89.

42 Asser uses the rhetorical technique of *ordo praeposterus*, a form of rhetorical embellishment in which events are told out of chronological order. As Geoffrey of Vinsauf indicates in his much later treatise, the "order of art" could be perceived as "more elegant than the natural order, and in excellence far ahead, even though it puts last things first"; *Poetria Nova of Geoffrey of Vinsauf*, trans. Margaret F. Nims (Toronto: Pontifical Institute of Mediaeval Studies, 1967), ll. 98–100.

43 *Asser's Life*, 56, ll. 55–8; trans. Keynes and Lapidge, 90.

44 *Asser's Life*, 57, ll. 60–2; trans. Keynes and Lapidge, 90.

45 *Asser's Life*, 57, ll. 63–4, 68–70; trans. Keynes and Lapidge, 90.

Aside from the method of narration, Asser's account of Alfred's prayer has four notable features. First, while Asser does not expressly state *what* Alfred prayed, he would likely have been praying the Psalms, an especial feature of the night office,[46] and set prayers of the sort Asser says he copied in the enchiridion he carried with him always.[47] Asser tells us that praying the Psalms was a fundamental part of Alfred's devotion, both through memorizing them, which Alfred began to do from a young age, and also through participating in the Divine Office, which runs through the complete *cursus* of the Psalms in a week.[48] Asser's account also fits with what we know of lay piety for high-ranking people following a Carolingian model.[49] Even if Alfred performed the Psalms and other set prayers so that the words did not spontaneously express his individual personality, Alfred specifies his intention (i.e., the thing he is praying for, as differentiated from the specific words he prays) very carefully. Yet the second feature of Alfred's prayer is that both intentions he states are curiously indirect. Rather than praying for continence, Alfred first prays for illness that will bring continence. Alfred next prays for a lighter illness rather than for complete healing. Third, because Asser bookends the chapter with an account of Alfred's public and debilitating illness, he makes it easy to overlook the fact that Alfred's prayers were actually answered.[50] The

46 The Psalms feature in all the hours; however, a greater number of them are sung at night than during the day offices. See J.B.L. Tolhurst, ed., *The Monastic Breviary of Hyde Abbey* (London: Harrison and Sons, 1942), 7–14, for a brief summary of the *opus dei* of Benedict as performed in English monasteries. While Jesse D. Billett, *The Divine Office in Anglo-Saxon England, 597–c. 1000* (London: Boydell, 2014), shows that English monasteries did not regularly follow the Benedictine Office until the reforms of the late tenth century, the Psalms form a central part of prayer in various offices.

47 *Asser's Life*, chapters 24 and 88. Robert Deshman, "The Galba Psalter: Pictures, Texts and Context in an Early Medieval Prayerbook," in *ASE* 26 (1997), reads the Galba Psalter in the context of Alfred's cultural revival (although the Psalter is older, it was modified during the reign of Alfred's son, Edward), comparing it to the description Asser gives of Alfred's enchiridion and describing the importance of the Psalms in Alfred's reforms, 128–36.

48 *Asser's Life*, 24.

49 Pratt, "Illnesses of King Alfred," 40–56; Kershaw, "Illness, Power, and Prayer," 210–13.

50 Or, for some, which prayers were answered. Janet L. Nelson, for instance, makes the second illness a result of Alfred's youthful prayer and says God responded to it with an illness "that would ensure Alfred's humility while not rendering him useless and contemptible," "Monks, Secular Men, and Masculinity," in *Courts, Elites, and Gendered Power in the Early Middle Ages: Charlemagne and Others* (Aldershot: Ashgate, 2007), 136. This is the opposite of the way Alfred himself understands the situation.

two times Alfred prays, his prayer "works": he gets a response, although that response is in excess of what he asked. He wants, first, some illness "quam posset sustinere"[51] (which he would be able to tolerate) to control sexual desire; instead, he receives an agonizing illness as a *munus*, a reward. Next, he asks for a new illness to substitute "stimulos praesentis et infestantis infirmitatis"[52] (for the pangs of the present and agonizing infirmity); instead, he receives complete healing. However, the fourth feature of Alfred's prayer is that even though his request that he might have a lighter illness is answered with healing, in the end, at his wedding, Alfred receives exactly the kind of illness he had asked not to have, an illness that renders him "quasi inutilem"[53] (virtually useless). While his prayers are answered – God is understood to have responded – his intentions are not.

The objective efficacy of Alfred's prayers is clearly what drives Asser's account. Asser's *ordo* makes prominent the issue that even though God answers Alfred's prayers, Alfred's attempts to stipulate the nature of his desired illness are, in the end, unsuccessful. Asser makes no mention at all of Alfred praying for relief from the second illness. Even more surprising, Asser makes no attempt to interpret the cause of Alfred's second illness. The account is peculiarly "open" in that respect; Asser does not seem to be interested in establishing a correspondence between the specific thing requested and the actual answer received.

Thus, even though Alfred prays specifically for healing and expects prayer to be efficacious, readers perhaps assume that efficacy centres on his request for healing; however, Asser's point is not that Alfred prayed for healing (and did not get it), but that he prayed. Both the prayer in the *Soliloquies* and the introductions to the Psalms distinguish intention, the thing requested, from the performance of prayer. That is, while the precators' needs or desires drives them to pray, the prayer itself does not communicate those needs and desires to God. In the *Soliloquies*, intention is the impetus to pray but the prayer itself is understood as a service God rewards. The Psalms can be prayed in the same way; however, the introductions move beyond precators' intentionality: through praying the Psalms, precators enter into the narrative established by David and fulfilled in Christ. Precators adopt, in some fashion, the intentions of David and Christ as they adopt their persona. These texts present prayer itself as

51 *Asser's Life*, 56, ll. 52–3; trans. Keynes and Lapidge, 90.
52 *Asser's Life*, 55, ll. 26–7; trans. Keynes and Lapidge, 89.
53 *Asser's Life*, 57, l. 68; trans. Keynes and Lapidge, 90.

something one *does* – a service, or a work – that God then rewards, but not necessarily with the thing asked for. The Psalm introductions, then, help establish a context in which prayer could be understood as efficacious without actually getting precators what they pray for: rather than assuring those praying that the Psalms will gain them their own desire, the efficacy they assure is that they will be heard by God.

The Introductions to the Psalms

Scholars usually study the introductions to the Psalms within their exegetical traditions; however, the primary use of the Psalms was for prayer, both corporate and personal.[54] If we read the introductions as introductions to prayer, they prove enlightening for a theory of prayer. In one respect, the introductions seem to promise an obvious use: that anyone singing a psalm about a particular thing can apply it to one's own situation. That is, language is almost always instrumental – intended to communicate – and the introductions merely point out what each particular psalm communicates. Because precators use the Psalms as prayers, they are intended to communicate with God.[55] But what do they communicate? Furthermore, in prayer the one petitioned is not present to the senses and the desired end is usually deferred. So in what sense is prayer efficacious? How does one judge efficacy if it is not immediately apparent? The practice of prayer usually demands that the precator perform the Psalms as it were on credit (i.e., believing a gift will be returned), believing that prayer is and will be

54 Frantzen: "[B]y the early Middle Ages they had become a chief form of prayer in monasteries and the most commonly used form of private prayer among the educated nobility," *King Alfred*, 94. One exception to the exegetical approach is Michael S. Driscoll, who mentions that the attributions given by the introductions permit readers to pray the psalms through the persona of the psalmist, "making the psalms more relevant," "The Seven Penitential Psalms: Their Designation and Usages from the Middle Ages Onwards," in *Ecclesia Orans* 17 (2000), 155. See also Toswell, *Anglo-Saxon Psalter*, 23–9, for private versus communal use.

55 Some of the Introductions state more clearly that David's psalms are addressed to God. For instance, the introduction to Psalm 2 says that it is called "David's psalm" "for þi he seofode on þæm sealme and mænde to Drihtne be his feondum, ægðer ge inlendum ge utlendum, and be eallum his earfoðum; and swa deð ælc þæra þe þysne sealm sincgð be his sylfes feondum" (because he lamented in the psalm and complained to the Lord about his enemies, either domestic or foreign, and about all his hardships; and so does each of those who sing this psalm about his own enemies), O'Neill, *King Alfred's Prose Translation*, 100.

efficacious, even if it is not now presently apparent. The same logic underlies the reciprocal gift. Insofar as gifts create "debts," the precator believes that God will make good on his debts. Furthermore, as Godelier shows, the parties are in relation only as long as the gift is not returned or as long as balance is not reached; once the gift is returned, the debt is repaid, and the relationship ends. As with the gift, the space of deferral allows prayer the room to do its work. The psalm introductions form part of the apparatus authorizing the Psalms as prayer, indicating what kind of efficacy they promise and giving a guarantee sufficient that the precator can extend the credit necessary to perform them. At the same time, the Psalms work to authorize precators by guaranteeing their intentions before God: that they do not pray merely to obtain what they want. Thus, the introductions do a little more imaginative work than they seem to at first.

The first fifty psalms[56] consist mainly of prayers of lament attributed to David.[57] In the prose paraphrase, most of these psalms begin with brief introductions[58] taken from those attributed to Bede and now known to be pseudonymous.[59] While the superscriptions to the Psalms themselves attribute psalms 41 through 49 to the Korahites and Asaph, the introductions attribute all fifty psalms to David. They follow a standard Antiochene (and Irish)[60] exegetical model that posits a fourfold interpretation of the basic *argumentum* of a particular psalm: the historical situation in which

56 Following the Vulgate numbering in which Psalms 9 and 10 are combined. Therefore, Alfred's translation goes up to the 51st Psalm in bibles following the Hebrew numbering, as all modern translations do. I will follow Alfred in using the Vulgate numbering.

57 See Kershaw, "Illness, Power, and Prayer," 217–19, for resonances between David and Alfred's stories.

58 Psalms 1, 21, and 26 are missing introductions.

59 O'Neill, *King Alfred's Prose Translation*, 11. The Pseudo-Bede introductions can be found in PL 93, col. 483–1098. O'Neill's article, "The Old English Introductions to the Prose Psalms of the Paris Psalter: Sources, Structure, and Composition," in *Studies in Philology* 78.5 (1981), also concludes that the same person translated both the introductions and the psalm paraphrases, basing them on an Irish four-fold exegetical model, but making his own modifications as he went.

60 The "Antiochene" school of biblical interpretation focused on the literal and historical meaning, in contrast to the Alexandrian school, which focused on allegorical interpretation. On the background see Patrick O'Neill, "Irish Transmission of Late Antique Learning: The Case of Theodore of Mopsuestia's Commentaries on the Psalms," in *Ireland and Europe in the Early Middle Ages: Texts and Transmission*, ed. Próinséas Ní Chatháin and Michael Richter (Portland, OR: Four Courts, 2002). My interest here is not with the exegetical model and its history but rather with the introductions as a model for precators using the Psalms.

David composed the psalm, a second Old Testament application, a moral interpretation applying the theme to anyone who sings the psalm, and a Christological interpretation. As an example, here is the introduction to Psalm 6:

> Dauid sang þysne syxtan sealm be his mettrumnesse and be his earfoðum, and eac be þam ege þæs domes on Domesdæge; *and swa deð ælc þæra þe hine singð*; and swa dyde Crist, þa he on eorðan wæs, he hine sang be his earfoðum; and eac Ezechias be his untrumnesse.[61]

> (David sang the sixth psalm about his illness and about his hardships, and also about the terror of judgment on Judgment Day, *and so does every one of those who sing it*; and so did Christ, when he was on the earth, he sang it about his hardships; and also Hezekiah about his sickness.)

The sense of efficacy the psalm introductions communicate is not so much concerned with the utility of precators getting what they want as it is with moulding their desires and authorizing them as a particular kind of person. In fact, too close a link between the precators' will and what they get (utilitarian efficacy) actually lowers the Psalms' value by situating them within a lower-status trade economy centred on the precators' material desires. If prayer is treated as a commodity exchange, the things gained are the central focus, not the personhood of the giver. Leaving openness in the response to prayer not only acknowledges that humans cannot control God, it also allows prayer, no longer centred on precators' will, to transform and reveal their personal qualities, thereby allowing them to accrue worth or honour. Thus, the Psalms assure a personal efficacy: they assure precators that God hears them. The authorship of David and Christ guarantees this efficacy; they stand as authoritative witnesses to the Psalms' truth. The model recalls the one advanced by Cassian, only it is not so "pure," in that precators do not practice it with the same sort of psychological rigour. It therefore leaves more room for precators' specific desires (one could pray for one's own illness, for instance). The Psalms are also efficacious to authorize the person of the precator by both placing precators within a larger human narrative established by David and Christ, and by crediting the intentions of the psalmist to them.

61 O'Neill, *King Alfred's Prose Translation*, 104.

The majority of the first fifty psalms directly address God.[62] The introductions acknowledge that prayer is not merely an aesthetic performance; one prays because one desires a particular end. The language of the introductions communicates this efficacy using two common formulas: out of forty-three total psalms with introductions containing a moral application, the slim majority use some variant of the *swa deð* formula quoted above: "Dauid sang þysne syxtan sealm be his mettrumnesse ... and swa deð ælc þæra þe hine singð" (David sang the sixth psalm about his illness ... and so does every one of those who sings it). The bulk of the remainder follow a *Dauid witgode* formula. Psalm 32 presents the basic model:

> [Dauid] lærde on þam sealme ealle menn þæt hi sceoldon Gode þancian ealra þæra gooda þe he him dyde; and he witgode eac be Ezechie þæt he sceolde þæt ylce don þonne he alysed wære of his earfoþum; and be ælcum þæra þe þysne sealm singð; and eac be Criste he witgode þæt he sceolde æfter his æriste ealle men þæt ylce læran.[63]

> (David taught all people in this psalm that they should thank God for all the good things which he did for them; and he prophesied also about Hezekiah that he should do the same when he was released from his sufferings; and about each of those who sing this psalm; and also about Christ he prophesied that he would teach the same to all people after his resurrection.)

Typically in this formula, the audience of the psalm becomes the subject of its prophecy as they in turn sing it. In spite of the fact the "swa deð" formula specifies that precators sing any given psalm for their own illnesses or against their own enemies, this formula does not put the needs or desires of the individual precator at the centre of prayer. That is, "swa deð" neither commands people to pray the psalm (it is not: "so *should* everyone do") nor does it state the conditions under which the precator might *want* to pray the psalm. The introduction to Psalm 19, for instance, does not say, "When you want to pray for your king, pray this psalm." Rather, it

62 A number of the psalms cannot strictly be called prayers, as the psalmist addresses his audience directly rather than addressing God. In this case, the introductions state that David "taught" (*læran*) people that they should thank God (32, 33, 46, 47), or give alms (28), or not imitate the evil-minded (36), or not store up wealth (38, 48).

63 O'Neill, *King Alfred's Prose Translation*, 136.

promises that those who do sing it sing it for their kings: David said in this psalm how his people prayed for him in his distress, "and swa doð ealle Cristene men þe þysne sealm singað; hy hine singað for heora kyningas"[64] (and so do all Christians who sing this psalm; they sing it for their kings.) Thus, although it seems that the formula specifies a certain sort of utility (what the psalm is good for), it does not reduce the psalter to some sort of spiritual recipe book one can thumb through to find a prayer appropriate to one's circumstance.[65]

The introductions imagine the recitation of the Psalms as ongoing praxis: the precators are already and habitually singing the Psalms. In a monastic context this is obviously the case: monks living according to the Benedictine Rule would have been reciting the entire psalter every week from the time they entered the monastery. But the Psalms were also the foundation of lay piety for high-ranking people. Although Alfred's practice was not as regular as monastic practice, his formative experience of the Psalms was in reciting them as part of his spiritual discipline, not in response to some particular need or situation. The "swa deð" formula indicates the understanding that the Psalms have an ongoing meaning that precators enter into when they *also* sing the psalm. Thus, the formative experience of the Psalms does not present the personal desires of the precator as primary, but rather the desires embodied in the Psalms, to which the one praying then gives voice. This orientation imagines that the precator's intentions follow those of the psalmist, as the introduction to Psalm 27 states explicitly:

> [O]n þæm sealme [Dauid] wæs cleopiende to Drihtne, wilnode þæt he hine arette and gefriðode wiþ eallum earfoðum, ægðer ge modes ge lichaman, and wið ealle his fynd gescylde, ge wið gesewene ge wið ungesewene ... and þæs ylcan wilnað ælc þe hine singð, oþþe for hine sylfne oððe for oþerne.[66]

64 O'Neill, *King Alfred's Prose Translation*, 121.

65 Which is not to say that the Psalms cannot be used this way. The point is that the introductions are not meant to guide the precator towards a specific psalm to meet a specific moment of need. While there is nothing stopping a person from praying an appropriate psalm at an appropriate moment (and it seems unlikely that they *would not* have been used this way, especially in light of the Carolingian evidence mentioned in chapter 1), such an orientation springs from an entirely different theory of prayer from that advanced by the introductions.

66 O'Neill, *King Alfred's Prose Translation*, 130.

> (In this psalm David was crying out to the Lord; he desired that he refresh and comfort him against all troubles, both of mind or of body, and protect him from all his enemies, both seen and unseen … And anyone who sings it desires the same, either for himself or for another.)

Therefore, the efficacy promised by the Psalms does not privilege the precator's will. In fact, from this perspective, prayer loses value (i.e., it cannot work to bring honour) when the prayer act is too closely tied to objective efficacy, becoming merely about the individual will. However, the praxis represented by the Introductions aims to decentre and retrain the individual precator's will, so that the precator sings "as does" David.

In part, the way the introductions decentre precators' will acknowledges the theological position that humans cannot control God, but as we shall see, the openness between prayer and response also allows prayer to transform the person of the precator. Thus, the Psalms act as guarantee that God will hear the one praying. The introductions imply the basis of the guarantee: every introduction specifies that David sang the particular psalm following, and that Christ also used it in his own circumstances – the Psalms prophetically refer forward to Christ. The Psalms are thus particularly valuable prayers because of their connection to both King David, the "man according to [God's] own heart," and Christ himself.[67] Thus, when the introduction to Psalm 2 says that David "seofode on þæm sealme and mænde to Drihtne be his feondum, ægðer ge inlendum ge utlendum, and be eallum his earfoðum; and swa deð ælc þæra þe þysne sealm sincgð be his sylfes feondum"[68] (lamented in the psalm and complained to the Lord about his enemies, either domestic or foreign, and about all his hardships; and so does each of those who sing this psalm about his own enemies), the point of that "swa deð" does not merely specify what the psalm communicates (its *argumentum*). Rather, it specifies what the psalm communicates *to God*. The authorship of the Psalms stands as authoritative witness that God will hear *this* prayer because the precator prays in God's own words, which are a reflection of God's own heart.

The "Dauid witgode" formula clarifies the way this works, as they say that David prophesied about, for instance, the "guiltlessness of Israel against the Assyrians" and also prophesied about the situation of everyone who sings the psalm: "he sings it about himself and about that which

67 Acts 13:22.

68 O'Neill, *King Alfred's Prose Translation*, 100.

afflicts him guiltlessly."[69] By singing the psalm, the precator enters into the subject of David's prophecy, just like Israel, and just like Christ. By entering into the prophecy, those singing the Psalms enter into the same story, given weight and authority by its continued repetition in the stories of Israel and Hezekiah, and its ultimate fulfilment in Christ.

However, the majority of the "Dauid witgode" psalms use the verb **sculan* to indicate that those coming after David, the subjects of his prophecy, *sceolde* do something. Because **sculan* almost always expresses obligation, it seems initially that the introductions portray David's prophecy as moral instruction: that the psalm is a command that the subject of his prophecy must carry out. For example, Psalm 29:

> Dauid sang þysne … sealm þam Gode þe hine alysde æt his feondum and æt eallum earfoðum; and þæt ylce he witgode be Ezechie: þæt he sceolde þæt ylce don þonne he alysed wære æt Assirium and æt his metrumnesse; and þæt ylce he witegode be ælcum rihtwison men þe þysne sealm singð oþþe for hine sylfne oþþe for oðerne, Gode to þancunge þære blisse þe he þonne hæfð; and eac he witegode on þam sealme be Criste, hu he sceolde alysed beon, ægðer ge fram Iudeum ge of ðy deaðe.[70]

> (David sang this psalm to God who delivered him from his enemies and from all troubles; and he prophesied the same about Hezekiah: that he should [*sceolde*] do the same when he would be delivered from Assyria and from his illness; and he prophesied the same about everyone righteous who sings this psalm either for himself or for another, in thanksgiving to God for the joy which he has; and also he prophesied in the psalm about Christ, how he should [*sceolde*] be delivered, both from the Jews and from death.)

69 Ps. 25: "Dauid sang þisne fif and twentigoðan sealm be his unschyldinesse wið his sunu and wið his geþeahteras þe hine on woh lærdan; and eac he witgode on þam sealme be þære unscyldignesse Israela folces wið Asirie, þa hi hy læddan on hæftnyd to Babilonia; and eac swa ylce ælc rihtwis man þe hine singð: he hine singð be him sylfum and be þam þe hine unscyldigne dreccað; and swa dyde eac Crist be Iudeum" (David sang this twenty-fifth psalm about his innocence towards his son and towards his counselors who wrongly advised him. And also he prophesied in the psalm about the innocence of the people of Israel towards the Assyrians, who led them in captivity to Babylon; and likewise about every righteous person who sings it: he sings it about himself and about those who afflict him though innocent; and so also did Christ concerning the Jews), O'Neill, *King Alfred's Prose Translation*, 127.

70 O'Neill, *King Alfred's Prose Translation*, 132.

While **sculan* is typically translated "shall," "must," "ought," it is clear that it expresses a stronger element of inevitability when paired with *witegian*.[71] That is, David did not prophesy that Hezekiah *must* or *ought to* sing the following psalm to God when he was delivered from Assyria – his prophecy does not operate as a command for Hezekiah – but that he is destined to (he "is to") do the same. David foretells what Hezekiah is to do, just as he prophesies Christ's deliverance in the final clause. The introduction to Psalm 50 (the famous penitential psalm, *Miserere mei*) helps clarify this use of **sculan*, since there "be ælcum rihtwisum men he witgode, hu hy sceoldon syngian and eft hreowsian"[72] (he prophesied about all the righteous, how they are to sin and then repent). David is not prophesying that righteous people *ought* to sin, but that they *will* sin, and then they will repent. In short, this formulation does not express that those singing the Psalms *should* do something in order to make their prayer efficacious, but rather that by singing the psalm, they *are doing* something. Any righteous person who sings the psalm sings, like David (and like Hezekiah, and like Christ), about how God has delivered him from his enemies and all troubles. The "Dauid witgode" introductions complement the "swa deð" introductions; they assure precators that through singing the psalm, they enter into David's subject of prophecy when they in turn sings the Psalms. Like Christ, like Hezekiah, like the nation of Israel, they become part of the same narrative. This narrative structures personal experience.

The way prayer structures experience is a variety of the theory of prayer presented in the more interior monastic model that decentres individual experience. In the monastic *cursus* of the Psalms one enters into a work and an experience larger than oneself, rather than subordinating the Psalms to one's own experience. This model, the one expounded by Cassian, is more radical than the idea that particular psalms can be used to give shape or meaning to personal experience. To state the concept yet another way, one does not pray Psalm 25 because one needs bodily healing: rather, one enters into the human experience of needing healing by praying the psalm. The rationale behind the psalm *cursus* assumes that David sings about general human situations. The precator does not use them in any sort of individually unique situation but instead because, like all humans,

71 See Bruce Mitchell, *Old English Syntax*, vol. 1 (Oxford: Oxford University Press, 1985), sect. 1023. There he gives examples that "suggest that **sculan* and *willan* at times come pretty close to expressing futurity with no undertone of compulsion or volition."
72 O'Neill, *King Alfred's Prose Translation*, 163.

he suffers. By singing the Psalms, he represents his *human* (rather than his personal) need before God and performs a particular *position* in relation to God, regardless of the needs of the present moment, which obviously come and go. Therefore, the *cursus* gives a much more stable sense of the human situation than if the precator's situations and needs were imagined as individually specific and unique, although, paradoxically, the human condition is imagined as unstable, fragile, and needy.

Although the efficacy of the Psalms is guaranteed by their authorship, they do contain wording that might make it seem that efficacy rests, at least in part, on the moral standing of those praying. We see this in the introductions that specify that the following psalm is efficacious when sung by a *welwillende* person (that is, one of good will, as in Psalm 4) or, more usually, *rihtwis* (righteous, just) person.[73] In this case, the promise that God hears the precator's prayer seems guaranteed by the *rihtwisnes* of the one praying rather than by the authorship of the Psalms. While the Psalms contain an element of moral training, the training of the desires or the will comes from the act of reciting the Psalms itself: the Psalms produce or authorize the *rihtwisness* they require. When precators fully enter into the Psalms' prophetic narrative, it produces their correct orientation. It is clear, for instance, that *rihtwis* does not mean that precators are sinless or uniformly virtuous. Here is the introduction to Psalm 50 again, quoted more fully:

> Dauid sang … hreowsiende for ðam ærendum þe Nathan se witga him sæde, þæt wæs, þæt he hæfde gesyngod wið Ureus þone Cyðþiscan, þa he hine beswac for his wifes þingum, þære nama wæs Bersabe; and heac he witgode on þam sealme be Israela folce, hu hy sceoldon hreowsian hyra hæftnyd on Babilonia; and eac be Sancte Paule þam Apostole; and be ælcum rihtwisum men he witgode, hu hy sceoldon syngian and eft hreowsian.[74]
>
> (David sang … repenting on account of the message that Nathan the prophet said to him, that he had sinned against Uriah the Hittite, whom he betrayed on account of his wife whose name was Bathsheba; and also he prophesied in

73 In most cases, the *rihtwisness* of the precator is specified when the psalm is about God's help against the singer's enemies or is a lament for injustice (4, 11, 13, 25, 29, 45, 46), or is in the context of return from exile (14, 25, 26). That is, the precator's *rihtwisness* is in contrast to the evil that surrounds or unjustly oppresses him.

74 O'Neill, *King Alfred's Prose Translation*, 163.

the psalm about the people of israel, how they should repent their captivity in Babylon. And also about St. Paul the Apostle; and also about everyone righteous he prophesied, how they should sin and again repent.)

This introduction does not imagine that the *rihtwis* do not sin but rather that the *rihtwis* are those who, entering into David's prophetic narrative, sin and repent. Thus, *rihtwis* does not mean sinless or uniformly virtuous. *Rihtwis*, most literally, means that a person is oriented correctly; "riht" is "that which is straight."[75] Similarly, *welwillende* means to will or desire well. One is oriented correctly or desires well according to the standard set forth by God, modelled by David, and fulfilled by Christ. Precators do not produce the *rihtwis* orientation; the psalm does. Thus, the introductions promise a dual guarantee to the Psalms' efficacy: that God will hear the precator on the basis of the Psalms' authorship, and also that the Psalms authorize the precator, as they produce the righteousness they require. Several introductions gesture in this direction. Psalm 34, for instance, says,

Dauid sang þysne ... sealm, siofigende to Drihtne his yrmða, tealde his ungelimp and hu he hine gebæd to Gode þæt he him gearode; and eac he witegode on þam ilcan sealme þæt ylce be ælcum rihtwison menn þe þysne sealm sunge, oððe for hine sylfne oþþe for oþerne mann, þæt he sceolde þæs ylcan wilnian; and eac he witgode be Criste þæt he wolde þæt ylce don þonne he come – ma witgiende þonne wyrgende oððe wilniende.[76]

(David sang this psalm, lamenting to the Lord his miseries, recounting his misfortune and how he prayed to God that he honor him; and also he prophesied in the same psalm the same about every righteous person who sings this psalm, either for himself or for another, that he is to desire the same; and also he prophesied about Christ that he would do the same when he come – prophesying rather than condemning or desiring.)

The logic of this introduction is that the singer becomes the object of the prophecy when he sings the psalm; David's prophecy is that the

75 BT, "riht," sense I.

76 O'Neill, *King Alfred's Prose Translation*, 139. The final clause refers back to David and serves to mitigate the opening of the following psalm. That is, David prophesies that God will judge his enemies, rather than condemning them himself or desiring that judgment. See O'Neill's note, 229.

person who sings the psalm will desire "the same" – that God will honour him. And, as we have seen, *sceolde* has a strong element of inevitability when paired with *witegian*. That is, David does not prophesy that the one who sings the psalm *must* or *ought* to desire that God will honour him, but that the singer *will* desire the same. The recitation of the psalm produces the desire.

The "Dauid witgode" introductions promise that anyone who sings the Psalms *does* the same thing that David did. The "swa deð" formula does something similar; however, rather than placing precators within the sacred narrative of the Psalms, it promises a transference of intention from David to those currently singing the psalm. Thus, the efficacy that the Psalms promise is not merely as a guarantee to precators that God will *hear* their prayer; they also guarantee the *person* of the one praying before God. That is, they stand as testimony to his or her worth. In this way, the efficacy that the psalm introductions promise is actually an efficacy of intent: that God extents credit to *rihtwise* precators as David's intentions are credited to those praying the Psalms.[77] At the same time, the authority of David and Christ that guarantees the Psalms allows the precator to extend credit, to perform the Psalms on a sort of credit – to credit or to believe that God hears his prayer and to hope for a response.

---

77 The notion of credit is further reflected in the introductions that state that a psalm can be sung either for the benefit of the precator or for someone else, as in Psalm 37:

> Dauid sang þysne … sealm … andettende Drihtne his scylde, and seofigende his ungelimp þæt he ær mid his scyldum geearnode; and he eac healsode Drihten on ðæm sealme þæt he hine on swylcum earfeðum ne lete his life geendian; and he witegode eac be Ezechie þam kyncge þæt he sceolde þæt ylce don on his earfoðum; and eac be ælcum þæra þe þysne sealm sunge, oþþe for hine sylfne oððe for oðerne man, he witgode þæt he sceolde þæt ilce mænan and eac þæt ylce gemetan; and eac be Criste he witegode, þæt he wolde þæt ylce don. O'Neill, *King Alfred's Prose Translation*, 144–5.
>
> David sang this … psalm, confessing his guilt to the Lord, and repenting his misfortune that he previously earned with his guilt; and he also beseeched the Lord in the psalm that he not let his life end in such distress; and he prophesied also about Hezekiah the king that he should do the same in his troubles; and also about each of those who sang this psalm, either for himself or for another, he prophesied that he should lament the same and also experience the same; and also about Christ he prophesied, that he would do the same.

Here David prophesies that everyone who sings the psalm will lament either his own guilt or someone else's, and that the guilty will experience God's mercy. The wording here touches on the mediatory work of the *opus Dei*, performed by the Church on behalf of the world.

Thus, the psalm Introductions, while they leave room for precators' desires, fundamentally ask them to enter into another narrative, to allow the desires of the Psalms to shape their own desires. They also imagine value not in precators' own language, but in the authoritative language that derives its authority from David and from Christ. Precators pray David's own words in their situations – or not so much David's *words* as David's *heart*. From a utilitarian perspective, prayer that does not bring about the will of the precator does not work. However, if the goal of prayer is to bring about *rihtwisnes*, to orient the person rightly towards God, any prayer that is narrowly intentionalist more clearly does not work: it cannot remake those praying in the image of another.

Alfred's prayer in the *Life* clearly makes more room for individual intention than Cassian's. Asser tells us that Alfred prayed for healing. And Frantzen notes ways that the translator personalizes the psalms as he translates them.[78] Yet Asser also says that Alfred prayed habitually for a long time. Something other than his own natural desire for physical healing clearly informs the intentions of Alfred's prayers; rather, he prays for spiritual healing, which Asser and Alfred understand as being brought about by bodily effect. Thus, Alfred prays for illness, not continence. Asser presents Alfred's prayer as expressing a desire that is understood as the precator following, rather than leading, the will of God.

My conclusion here is similar in some ways to DeGregorio's in "Texts, *Topoi* and the Self: A Reading of Alfredian Spirituality." DeGregorio speaks in terms of "textualizing the self," arguing that Alfred's spirituality "can be understood as one shaped and informed by texts"[79] as he "internalizes" the things he reads.[80] DeGregorio emphasizes the role of contemplation in reading to perform that internalization of texts.[81] But prayer differs from both reading and contemplation in several important ways that make it more accurate to say that prayer *narrativizes* the self. Prayer is other-directed and, as the prayer beginning the *Soliloquies* further demonstrates, understood as an action (and, at times, as a thing); it does not fill the same role as contemplation. Many precators experienced

78 Chiefly, Frantzen notes themes that link the translations of the Psalms to other texts translated by Alfred, such as the need for penance and confession, 101, or Alfred's own need for solitude, 103, *King Alfred*, 101–5.

79 DeGregorio, "Texts, *Topoi* and the Self," 82.

80 DeGregorio, "Texts, *Topoi* and the Self," 86.

81 DeGregorio, "Texts, *Topoi* and the Self," 88–9.

the Psalms as texts for study, but their primary experience – especially for the illiterate, as Asser tells us Alfred initially was – would have been aural and oral.[82] It is therefore, as I have been arguing, more accurate to say that the precator takes on a persona through David's words rather than reciting a text.[83] Furthermore, prayer is not the type of moral or didactic literature that DeGregorio focuses on, and it is not merely a "model for behavior."[84] Prayer *is* behaviour, although that behaviour is enacted, not generated, by the praying self. Through prayer, precators repeat David/Christ's narrative and participate in that persona. The Psalms authenticate the person of precators by placing them in a larger human narrative established by David and Christ and by crediting the intentions of the Psalms to the precators.

The Prayer of the *Soliloquies*

The prayer that begins Book One of the Old English translation of the *Soliloquies* further illuminates the separation between intention and prayer. In this case, the text represents intention more as the cause than the content of prayer. This distinction illuminates an understanding of prayer as work rather than merely communication. God responds to Augustine's prayer as a reward for his labour, not because the prayer clearly communicates his request. Because desire motivates Augustine's prayer, and because the outcomes are largely the same, the distinction is a subtle one to make. Yet embedded within the Old English translation is an economy of prayer that distinctly diverges from the Latin original by presenting prayer as work that God rewards. The prayer itself is a fairly close, although not slavish, translation of the Latin.[85] Augustine's prayer is elaborate, highly

82 Asser, chaps. 87 and 88. Toswell also mentions that "Alfred's engagement with biblical texts was remarkably aural and not visual," *Anglo-Saxon Psalter*, 70.

83 As a result, the *exact* words of prayer permit more variation than something experienced as a text. That is to say, a prayer does not have to be produced with verbatim accuracy to be understood as the same prayer David prayed.

84 DeGregorio, "Texts, *Topoi* and the Self," 93.

85 Frantzen argues that "[w]e can be sure that Alfred did not follow Augustine's pattern closely or translate his work literally. Alfred's aim was less to duplicate Augustine's achievement than to adapt it to his own concerns," *King Alfred*, 71. The translation becomes more free as it progresses; as Thomas Carnicelli says, "the OE text up to 85.16 is essentially a translation of Augustine's *Soliloquies*. After this point, it becomes an anthology of ideas from several sources," Alfred, *King Alfred's Version of St. Augustine's Soliloquies*, ed. Carnicelli (Cambridge, MA: Harvard University Press, 1969), 28.

rhetorical, and fits the prayer formula found in early Christian prayers.[86] Some three columns long in the *PL* (160 lines in the Old English translation), it begins with a complicated invocation, asks for mercy, and then rehearses the other things God has given. Augustine then asks for God to come to his aid before moving into a description of God's character and works, then finally gets down to more requests, all fairly general (hear me, receive me, teach me how to come, convert me to you) and interspersed with reminders of the precator's position before God and why he needs God's help. The prayer is more invocation and praise than petition, and the petitions are general ones, reflecting the thematic context, but in spite of the fact he ostensibly prays for physical health to perform the task at hand, it does not reflect Augustine's particular situation.

As Frantzen notes, the preface to the translation (which Frantzen takes to be written by Alfred), "and the many additions to the text which follow, suggest that Alfred sought to develop a work different in scope and character from Augustine's ... Alfred's aim was less to duplicate Augustine's achievement than to adapt it to his own concerns."[87] The translation is more closely literal as he begins his project than when he ends it, and yet as Frantzen points out, the translator changes the logic of the beginning prayer away from Augustine's Neoplatonism to something more in line with observable reality.[88] The translator also adjusts the language to add

---

86 See Hugh H.G. Houghton, "The Discourse of Prayer in the Major Apocryphal Acts of the Apostles," in *Apocrypha* 15 (2004), 175–81. It is worth noting that the early Christian prayer Houghton describes was adapted from pagan forms of prayer, which were explicitly reciprocal: "Pagan prayers often take the form of a transactional bargain, hence a substantial *pars epica* [the narrative explaining the reason for prayer] in order to persuade the divinity," 176. In Christian prayer, however, "the explicit bargaining element is abstract," 176, and the Christian predication does not name the god in order to specify precisely which god is invoked but to praise him, 177.

87 Frantzen, *King Alfred*, 71.

88 Frantzen, *King Alfred*, 73–4. Alfred also makes some minor changes to the text that arguably reflect his own particular situation. Treschow et al. note that in the section leading up to the prayer, Alfred, unlike Augustine, "did not see the task of thinking deep thoughts as requiring 'utter solitude,'" "King Alfred's Scholarly Writings," §15; he accordingly had *Gesceadwisnes* (Reason) point out that he needed a quiet place *and* "cuðe men and creftige," (wise and skillful men) (*King Alfred's Soliloquies*, ed. Carnicelli, 49, l. 20), to help him. Toward the end of the prayer itself, Alfred again adds reference to his friends, "Ic nat þeah hwes ic þer bydde, hweðer ic bydde nyttes þe unnittes me sylfum," adding the clause: "oððe þam freondum þe ic lufige and me lufiað" (I do not know what I ask, whether I ask for something useful or useless to me, or to the friends which I love and who love me), *King Alfred's Soliloquies*, 55, ll. 25–6. Indeed, the point of this

the idea of earning or meriting (*geearnian*) his request from God. In both cases, (*ge*)*earnian* (the form with the prefix is more common) is a translation of Latin *agere*, far more frequently translated as *don* (to do, perform, act) within the Old English corpus. By choosing *geearnian*, the translator reveals his understanding that it is not the intention of the precator that God credits to him but rather the work: the work that causes the intention to be credited. The *Soliloqiua*'s prayer opens with the petition, "[P]ræsta mihi primum ut bene te rogem, deinde ut me agam dignum quem exaudias, postremo ut liberes"[89] (Give to me first that I may pray to you rightly; next, that I might act as one worthy for you to hear; finally, that you free me). But the translator renders the idea "that I might act as one worthy" as "þæt ic mage geearnian þæt ic si wurðe"[90] (that I may merit that I be worthy). *Geearnian* is repeated again after the prayer, when *Gesceadwisnes* (Reason) observes, "Ic geseo þæt þu þe gebæde. Ac seige nu hwæs þu earnodest, oððe hwæt þu habban woldest"[91] (I see that you have prayed. But say now what you have earned, or what you wish to have). Compare that to Augustine's Latin: after Augustine declares, "Ecce oravi Deum"[92] (See, I have prayed to God), *Ratio* (Reason) asks, "Quid ergo scire vis?" (What therefore do you want to know?).

By means of these small changes, the translator shifts the emphasis towards prayer as work that God rewards. In addition, although Augustine's prayer ostensibly models praying a particular prayer for a particular intention, that intention is represented in many ways as the cause rather than the content of the prayer. In spite of the prayer's length and complexity, really only after the prayer, when *Gesceadwisnes* asks Augustine to say what he has earned, do we get a clear idea of the specific content of Augustine's desire: "ic wolde ongytan eall and witan hwæt ic nu sang"[93] (I wish to understand everything and know what I just recited). *Gesceadwisnes* pushes him to be clearer: "gadera þonne of ðam eallum þe þu ðær embe sunge … and befoh hyt þonne mid feawum wordum …"[94] (then gather up from

section is not to say that prayers *cannot* reflect the intentions of the one praying – they often do – but that whether they do or not is largely immaterial to understanding how prayer works.

89 Augustine, *Soliloquia*, PL 32, col. 869, 1.1.2.

90 Alfred, *King Alfred's Soliloquies*, ed. Carnicelli, 50, ll. 11–12.

91 *King Alfred's Soliloquies*, 56, ll. 12–13.

92 *Soliloquia*, PL 32, col. 872, 1.2.7.

93 *King Alfred's Soliloquies*, 56, l. 14.

94 *King Alfred's Soliloquies*, 56, ll. 15–17.

everything which you just recited ... and put it in a few words ...), to which Augustine responds, "god ic wolde ongytan, and mine agene saule ic wolde witan"[95] (I want to understand God, and I want to know my own soul). The prayer does not fully reflect the *intention* of praying, as *Gesceadwisnes* indicates when she asks for a summary afterwards. Rather, Augustine seems to accrue some sort of merit through the act of praying.

Geearnian can be translated as "to earn" or "to merit." It is typically translated as "to merit" in religious texts; indeed, the *DOE* uses this passage to exemplify sense 2.a, "to merit/deserve something." The difference between the two Modern English concepts, to merit and to earn, bears further thought, specifically as to how they presuppose the roles of the two parties within the exchange – either the payment returned to the one earning, or the reward returned to the meritorious. Modern English "earn" descends from Old English *earnian*, while "merit" enters English through French and can be traced back to the Latin *meritare*.

Geearnian's etymological roots lie in harvest and in field labour, as can be seen from the *OED*'s etymology. The Germanic cognates almost all connect to the idea of harvest,[96] although several of them have the additional sense of payment or reward (i.e., Old Dutch *arnon,* to obtain as a reward for labour; Middle Dutch *arnen* to expiate, pay; Old High German *arnōn,* to harvest, reap, to redeem, redress, to obtain as a reward for labour, to acquire). Finally, the *OED* notes that these words come from the same Germanic root as the Old English *-ern*, found "in the compound *Rugern*, apparently lit. 'rye harvest,' the name of a month, August or September." In this case, then, the word emphasizes the agency, in the form of labour, of the labourer. The harvest is a direct consequence of this

95 *King Alfred's Soliloquies*, 56, ll. 18–19. Although Alfred only slightly shifts the wording, the change in meaning is again significant. In the *Soliloquia*, Augustine wants to know God and "the soul," "Deum et animam scire cupio" (*Soliloquia*, PL 32, col. 872, 1.2.7), while Alfred's Augustine wants to know more specifically his *own* soul.

96 From the *OED*, *earn*: "Middle Low German *ernen* to harvest, reap, Old High German *arnōn* to harvest, reap, to redeem, redress, to obtain as a reward for labour, to acquire (Middle High German *arnen*) < the same Germanic base as Old English *-ern* (in the compound *Rugern*, apparently lit. 'rye harvest,' the name of a month, August or September), Old Frisian *ern, erne, arn, arne*, Middle Dutch *arn, arne*, Middle Low German *ārn, ērn, ārne, ērne, arnde*, Old High German *aran, arn* (Middle High German *arn, ern, erne, ernde*, German *Ernte*), Gothic *asans*, chiefly in senses 'harvest, harvest time, summer,' and probably also Old Icelandic *ǫnn*, Norwegian *ann, onn*, Old Swedish *an, and* (Swedish *and*), all in senses 'labour, field-labour, harvest.'"

labour.[97] Modern English still contains the idea that the return results from the work of the earner, and, in some senses even still contains the idea that the result is a direct, unmediated consequence.[98]

"Merit," on the other hand, comes into English via French. The Latin etymological root, *meritare* (or *merere*), means to earn or gain, or more specifically, to serve for pay.[99] In French the word loses its connection with wages and comes to mean "to reward," and then "to deserve."[100] Thus, in its earliest root, the word gives agency to a returning party in a way that the etymology of "earn" does not. In French, the returning subject, the one rewarding the merit, also gives return on the basis of his or her recognition of the others' desert. "Merit" first enters English as a noun, in a theological sense in the 1200s, where it means "the quality of being entitled to a reward from God."[101] "Merit" also has a connection to honour or worth that "earn" does not and is therefore the higher status word. It involves one party's recognition of worth or desert in another. While a person might show his or her worth through service (or work), "merit," at bottom, recognizes the personal qualities, which are then rewarded. Modern English "merit" recognizes the person, while "earn," which does not imply personal evaluation in the same way, recognizes the work.

Old English *(ge)earnian* makes no distinction between the labour and the person. In many ways, therefore, *geearnian* is closer to "merit" in that the return it indicates is a recognition of the meritorious personal qualities, the honour or worth (*weorþ*), of the one recognized. At the same time, *geearnian* emphasizes the work of the one *geearniende*. Another way of saying this, however, is that the work of *geearnian* is inalienable. Work must necessarily reveal the personal qualities of the one working, and the benefits of that work will (through God's grace) accrue to the worker.[102]

97 To be clear, the harvest is the direct consequence of labour, but labour is not the sole cause of the harvest, which also needs good weather, fertile soil, etc.

98 See *OED*, *earn*, sense 3, "Of a quality or action: to get or result in, as a direct but unintended consequence, (a name, reputation, etc.) for a person or thing," and sense 5, "of money invested ... to be the means of producing (an income, interest, etc.)."

99 Lewis and Short, v. *mereo*.

100 *OED*, *merit*, senses 1 and 5.

101 *OED*, *merit*, sense1b.

102 The vast majority of instances of "geearnian" are in religious contexts. In poetry, it is relatively rare. Aside from one occurrence as the noun *geearnung*, rewards, in Elliott Van Kirk Dobbie, ed., *The Battle of Maldon*, ASPR VI (New York: Columbia University Press, 1942), l. 196, all the poetic occurrences refer specifically to eternal rewards. *Geearnung* also shows up in charters, specifically in contexts where one person has "earned" land from another.

This is nowhere more true than in the practice of prayer, as represented in the Alfredian texts. Practitioners understand prayers as a thing, a gift (or a sacrifice) given to God, while they understand praying as a work, a service, that God rewards. Like the gift, the work of prayer partakes in the personhood of the one praying. In Alfred's *Soliloquies*, Augustine's desire compels him to pray, but he does not understand the act of prayer as mere communication. In fact, prayer is unnecessary to communicate with an all-knowing God; prayer is, rather, work that *geearnað* the precator a reward, although that reward is not necessarily the thing prayed for. The prayer's beauty, its length, and (in the case of the written version)[103] the difficulty of writing it down are all component parts of the prayer as gift. Through the work of prayer Augustine reveals himself to God; however, he also reveals that through language he *cannot* reveal himself; he is only revealed, only known, insofar as God can know him and reveal the nature of his "agene saule" back to himself. Thus, the act of prayer does not merely reveal the personal qualities of the one praying, it also enables the precator to know himself as he is seen in the eyes of God. Self-knowing comes first by narrativizing the self, as we have seen with the Psalms, and by understanding one's own experience through the narrative supplied. Yet significantly, narrativization is an interpretive device applied to one's own circumstances. It is not a process of making prayer more relevant to the life but of making life more relevant to the prayer.

Returning to Alfred's Prayer in Asser

As we return to Asser to consider the theory of prayer represented in his text, several things about his account stand as significant. First, Asser emphasizes the duration and frequency of Alfred's prayer, which, as I have argued, are the set prayers of the Psalms and others like them. Asser says Alfred prayed "for a long time" ("diu in oratione"),[104] "saepius magna mentis devotione"[105] (frequently with great mental devotion), and

103 "Wilna ðe to gode, hælend modes and lichaman, þæt ðu mage þurh þa hele begitan þæt ðæt þu wilnast; and þonne þu ðe gebeden hæbbe, awrit þonne þæt gebed, þi læs þu hit forgyte, þæt þu si ðe werðer þines creftes" (Address yourself to God, healer of mind and body, so that you can through the healing obtain that which you desire; and when you have prayed, then write that prayer lest you forget it, so that you will be the more worthy of your task), Alfred, *King Alfred's Soliloquies*, 50, ll. 4–7.

104 *Asser's Life*, 55, l. 24.

105 *Asser's Life*, 56, ll. 55–6; trans. Keynes and Lapidge, 90.

"saepissime ... diu prostratus"[106] (very often ... lay prostrate a long while). If prayer merely communicates requests, it would seem to be an inefficient means of communication. The conclusion towards which Asser points his readers is that long and frequent prayer marks Alfred's devotion, and that devotion in prayer is part of the work that Alfred does in service, as a gift, to God. We might then understand that when Asser twice tells us that Alfred's prayers were finished (*oratione autem finita* and *oratione facta*),[107] his point is not that Alfred had finished making his request, or that he declared himself done, but that the prayers he was performing and offering were complete in the eyes of God, who then responded to them.

Second, the specificity of Alfred's intention when he offers prayers for healing appears to represent a utilitarian, materially efficacious attitude towards the work prayer does. When he first prays for illness he specifies "aliquam infirmitatem, quam posset sustinere"[108] (some illness which he would be able to tolerate). When he prays for healing, his intention is that God "praesentis et infestantis infirmitatis aliqua qualicunque leviori infirmitate mutaret"[109] (might substitute for the pangs of the present and agonizing infirmity some less severe illness). If Alfred were praying in a pagan context, we might assume that he so carefully spelled out his intention due to the desire to communicate prudently with the god who might not know what his devotee needs, or might too literally grant a carelessly formulated intention, like a genie in a bottle. Christian doctrine, however, teaches that God knows all things and grants prayers for the good of the precator, based on God's omnipotence. Neither Asser nor Alfred could have been unaware of this. Insofar as a Christian precator carefully formulates his intention, such a discipline represents his desires to himself, not God. However, Asser's reportage here informs *readers* of Alfred's intention; Alfred's overwhelming concern with becoming *inutilis* (useless) is a fear repeated three times in the chapter.[110]

106 *Asser's Life*, 56, ll. 47, 49–50; trans. Keynes and Lapidge, 89.
107 *Asser's Life*, 56, l. 33, and 57, l. 60.
108 *Asser's Life*, 56, ll. 52–3; trans. Keynes and Lapidge, 90.
109 *Asser's Life*, 55, ll. 26–8; trans. Keynes and Lapidge, 89.
110 *Asser's Life*, 55, l. 30; 56, l. 54; and 57, l. 68. See Kershaw, "Illness, Power, and Prayer," 210, 221–2; Pratt, "Illnesses of King Alfred," 41, for the connection between Alfred's fear of uselessness and Carolingian rhetoric.

Third, Alfred did not at first pray for healing at all but for illness. Or rather, Alfred prayed for an illness that might help him control his sexual urges – an illness leading to spiritual wholeness. Alfred's experience of prayer thus shows how praying the Psalms led to narrativizing the self, understanding himself *in light of* the Psalms already being prayed. And yet, his prayer does more than this; it also guarantees Alfred's character. Rather than praying for the easy gift, that God would get rid of his sexual urges, the prayer for illness to effect that change guarantees Alfred's worth. He does not ask for whatever is easiest for himself.

Finally, the fact that God did not in fact fully grant Alfred's intentions as stated shows that Asser is not presenting Alfred in the mode of a saint. While we are not told that Alfred prayed to have the final illness removed, he ended up with an illness that "quasi inutilem eum, ut ei videtur, in divinis et humanis rebus propemodum effecit"[111] (rendered him virtually useless – as it seemed to him – for heavenly and worldly affairs). That is, in the end, as far as Alfred could tell, God granted neither of his intentions, although, according to Asser, Alfred's perception was mistaken: he was a very "useful" king. Alfred's prayer shows the distance maintained between cause and effect, which preserves the openness necessary for prayer to keep its value. More importantly, that God did not grant Alfred's intentions shows there is no one-to-one correspondence between what Alfred asks for and what he gets. It is the lack of efficiency, the openness, in the economy of prayer that allows Alfred's prayer to escape pure utility, decentring his individual experience and even need in a way that, in the end, authorizes him before God, bringing him honour.

Narrativizing the self leads Alfred to understand the *ficus* with which he was afflicted as a *munus* rather than as an accident. From a sceptical perspective we might say that Alfred attributes meaning to a meaningless event, and that no matter what he prayed, he would understand whatever happened next as the response to the prayer. But does this matter? Alfred's prayer is not concerned with matters of proof; rather, he has already made the decision to understand the events of his life in accordance with a particular narrative, a narrative which he enters into through the discipline of prayer. To speculate what "really" happened with Alfred's illness, as Pratt

111 *Asser's Life*, 57, ll. 68–70; trans. Keynes and Lapidge, 90.

does,[112] is to adopt an objective perspective on a subjective act. To do so is not an illegitimate approach, but it is one foreign to Alfred's and Asser's own ways of thinking.

Alfred and Lay Piety

I do not intend to generalize from Alfred's example to argue that all Anglo-Saxons understood prayer in the rigorous and learned way outlined in this chapter. In fact, the same prayer text could obviously be performed with different understandings of how that performance worked. Asser's *Life* presents evidence regarding the lay practice of prayer during the age of Alfred. Aside from Alfred's own practice of prayer, he actively encouraged and provided training for those in his household and those who ruled under him. Training in prayer seems to have had a central place in their education. Asser tells us Alfred's youngest son, Æthelweard, "ludis literariae disciplinae ... cum omnibus pene totius regionis nobilibus infantibus et etiam multis ignobilibus, sub diligenti magistrorum cura traditus est"[113] (was given over to training in reading and writing under the attentive care of teachers, in company with all the nobly born children of virtually the entire area, and a good many of lesser birth as well). Furthermore, when Asser goes on to speak of the education of Alfred's second and fourth children, Edward and Ælfthryth, he says, "Nec etiam illi sine liberali disciplina ... otiose et incuriose vivere permittuntur, nam et psalmos et Saxonicos libros et maxime Saxonica carmina studiose didicere"[114] (Nor ... are these two allowed to live idly and indifferently, with no liberal education, for they have attentively learned the Psalms, and books in English, and especially English poems). The place of "English poems" in Edward and Ælfthryth's education has garnered the most critical attention; however, I would like to return our attention to the earlier part of

112 Pratt takes the causality here the other way around, arguing that surely Alfred retrospectively rationalized the events surrounding his first illness, so that it arrived as a response to his prayer rather than forming the source of his devotion, "Illnesses of King Alfred," 63. He argues that Alfred's knowledge of the Psalms must have come when he was older, since he lamented that he remained ignorant of letters as a youth. This is unconvincing. Further, Pratt does not seem to credit that a person could be pious or devout without some affliction to force him to it since he several times mentions Alfred's extreme devotion as a result of his illness; see 64 and 89, for example.

113 *Asser's Life*, 58, ll. 11–15; trans. Keynes and Lapidge, 90.

114 *Asser's Life*, 58–9, ll. 26–30; trans. Keynes and Lapidge, 91.

that sentence in which Asser places learning the Psalms as the cornerstone of a "liberal education."[115] If this is so, Æthelweard, Edward, Ælfthryth, and the other children educated with them would also have learned the Psalms. Furthermore, Alfred's educational ambitions were for the entire ruling class to learn to read – not only his children and household, but all the ealdormen, reeves, and thegns – in order that they could rule justly and wisely.[116] Certainly, from a practical viewpoint, those learning to read need books; psalters would have been among the most common books produced and therefore the most accessible to students.

In addition, Asser tells us in the next chapter that Alfred

> Divina quoque ministeria et missam scilicet cotidie audire, psalmos quosdam et orationes et horas diurnas et nocturnas celebrare, et ecclesias nocturno tempore, ut diximus, orandi causa clam a suis adire solebat et frequentabat.[117]
>
> (was in the invariable habit of listening daily to divine services and Mass, and of participating in certain psalms and prayers and in the day-time and night-time offices, and, at night-time, as I have said, of going [without his household knowing] to various churches in order to pray.)

Keynes and Lapidge note at this point that "Alfred's daily (*cotidie*) participation in the 'day-time and night-time offices' reveals exceptional devotion in a layman."[118] At the same time, the fact that Asser specifies that Alfred participated in prayers at day and night *and also* went to various churches to pray at night without his household knowing implies that they were probably often expected to join him at the prayers and offices first listed. Therefore, while Alfred was exceptionally pious (i.e., he knew the psalter, he prayed by himself at night, and he went out of his way to worship at saints' shrines), it is not out of line to conclude that Alfred

115 Alfred's educational program has connections to Carolingian practices. Donald A. Bullough refers to the liturgy as an "instrument of education" for Alcuin, putting the Psalms at the centre of his educational program, *Alcuin: Achievement and Reputation* (Leiden: Brill, 2004), 176. While Alcuin's program focused on "pueri and clerici," sources such as Dhuoda's *Handbook for Her Warrior Son*, ed. and trans. Marcelle Thiébaux (Cambridge: Cambridge University Press, 1998) also assume lay knowledge of the Psalms (in fact, she quotes Alcuin on the use of the Psalms in Book 11).

116 *Asser's Life*, chapter 106.

117 *Asser's Life*, 59, ll. 12–16; trans. Keynes and Lapidge, 91.

118 Keynes and Lapidge, *Alfred the Great*, 257n134.

desired that the upper ranks should also know the psalter and regularly participate in the hours of prayer. This goal was not out of reach for (at the least) those closest to the king, such as his children and those raised in his household, and Alfred's literacy program also encouraged such familiarity in those who ruled under him. This is a far higher level of spiritual literacy than Ælfric or Wulfstan expect for "every Christian," who should know the Paternoster and the Creed. Alfred's court, then, sets the highest general standard that we can expect for lay piety in his era.

Chapter Four

Ælfric and the Community of Prayer

Eall swa gelice se ðe gelyfð wiglungum
oððe be fugelum . oððe be fnorum .
oððe be horsum . oððe be hundum .
ne bið he na cristen . ac bið for-cuð wiðer-saca .
Ne sceal nan man cepan be dagum
on hwilcum dæge he fare . oððe on hwylcum he gecyrre .
forðan þe god gesceop ealle ða seofan dagas .
þe yrnað on þære wucan oð þysre worulde geendunge .
Ac seðe hwider faran wille . singe his paternoster .
and credan . gif he cunne . and clypige to his dryhten .
and bletsige hine sylfne . and siðige orsorh
þurh godes gescyldnysse . butan ðæra sceoccena wiglunga .

(Also likewise he who trusts in sorceries, either by birds or by sneezings or by horses or by hounds, he is not at all Christian, but is a wicked apostate. Nor should anyone observe according to days, on which day he travel or on which he return; because God made all the seven days which run through the week until this world's end. But he who wishes to travel anywhere should sing his Paternoster and Creed, if he knows them, and call to his Lord, and bless himself, and travel safely through God's protection without devils' sorceries.)

– Ælfric, *De auguriis*[1]

1 *Lives of Saints*, ed. Walter W. Skeat (London: Trübner, 1881–1900) I.17, ll. 88–99.

My initial interest in Anglo-Saxon prayer grew out of the passage quoted above, from Ælfric's famous sermon *De auguriis*. In it, Ælfric preaches against all forms of pagan practice, advocating that his audience turn to God instead.[2] Striking in this passage is the way a sermon *against* sorcery and superstition seems to advocate a superstitious, charm-like use of the Paternoster, Creed, and sign of the cross for protection while travelling. Ælfric seemingly replaces charms with Christian scripts in a way that seems potentially syncretistic and certainly makes concessions to popular religion in a way that neither Bede nor Alfred have done.[3] Central to the perception that these prayers are used like charms is the fact that their content has little relation to their use – the Paternoster is not about safety while travelling; the Creed (technically not a prayer at all) is a doctrinal précis. Indeed, Ælfric seems to be advocating "prayer" of the most objectively efficacious nature, working by formula or gesture alone to confer protection automatically, as long as the words are said or the ritual is performed correctly. But what is ironic – and part of the reason I quote *De auguriis* above at such length – is that in the very passages scholars point to as giving space to syncretism, Ælfric himself preaches adamantly *against* the combining of pagan and Christian systems, insisting that people *not* engage in pagan practices and that one who does "is not at all

2 Since this sermon largely draws from sources by Caesarius of Arles, Martin of Braga, and others, it is somewhat doubtful whether the practices enumerated were practised in Anglo-Saxon England. See Audrey Meaney, "Ælfric's Use of His Sources in His Homily on Auguries," in *English Studies* 66.6 (1985). Meaney believes, however, that "we can accept what he has to say about idolatrous practices as referring to things current in the society that he knew," 495.

3 For a summary of this position and a more nuanced reading of the "syncretism" and learned/popular divine in Anglo-Saxon charms, see Karen Louise Jolly, *Popular Religion in Late Saxon England: Elf Charms in Context*, 2nd ed. (Chapel Hill: University of North Carolina Press, 1996). One of Jolly's major arguments is that we tend to expect the early Christian understanding of the natural world as more rationalistic than it actually was; therefore, both the Christian world and the pagan held many beliefs in common. Practices that now seem non-Christian (and superstitious) to us were features of both systems of belief. Jolly argues that the "construct of a European magical religion" advanced by Keith Thomas in *Religion and the Decline of Magic* (1971; rprnt. London: Penguin Global, 2012), and Valerie I.J. Flint in *The Rise of Magic in Early Medieval Europe* (Princeton: Princeton University Press, 1991), is anachronistic: "it presupposes a distinction between magic and religion (or science) that developed only later," 16. See chapter 1 especially.

Christian" but "apostate." Clearly Ælfric did not consider such uses of the Paternoster as either superstitious or syncretic.

As Ælfric's teachings on prayer show, Ælfric addresses a very different audience than Bede – an audience whose perceived need for protection or healing draws them to pray. Like Bede, Ælfric (c. 950–c. 1010) was one of the most learned men of his day. His large body of work, much of it vernacular sermons, manifests a concern for pastoral care like Bede's, and, like Bede's, Ælfric's works remained influential long after his death.[4] Ælfric's two sermon series, the *Catholic Homilies* I and II, were unusual in their day both in the scope of the collection and in his development of an Old English prose style for preaching.[5] His series were an ambitious

4 In the Old English preface, Ælfric explicitly states his desire that the integrity of his homilies as a collection be preserved through care in the copying and by not mixing them with other homilies, *Catholic Homilies* I, ll.128–31. However, as is often noted, his instructions were ignored. As Jonathan Wilcox argues Ælfric's homilies often circulated as booklets that ended up being combined with other vernacular homilies, "The Use of Ælfric's Homilies," in *A Companion to Ælfric*, ed. Hugh Magennis and Mary Swan (Leiden: Brill, 2009), 351. Furthermore, his homilies were often added to and extracted by later writers; see Elaine M. Treharne, "Making Their Presence Felt: Readers of Ælfric, c. 1050–1350," in *Companion to Ælfric*. Thus, the *CH* as a *series* is something very few people would have experienced. See also Mary Swan, "Ælfric's *Catholic Homilies* in the Twelfth Century," in *Rewriting Old English in the Twelfth Century*, ed. Mary Swan and Elaine M. Treharne (Cambridge: Cambridge University Press, 2000). For an example of his influence following a particular homily (*CH* I.14) see Mary Swan, "Old English Made New: One Catholic Homily and Its Reuses," in *Leeds Studies in English* 28 (1997). Like Bede's homilies, Ælfric's were mixed with and used as sources for other homilies.

5 Ælfric rewrote some of the *Catholic Homilies* over the course of his life. For one example of his types of revisions, see Robert Upchurch's article on the rewriting of *CH* I.17, "A Big Dog Barks: Ælfric of Eynsham's Indictment of the English Pastorate and *Witan*," in *Speculum* 85 (2010). He wrote a further forty or so homilies, printed in *Homilies of Ælfric*, 2 vols., ed. John C. Pope (London: Oxford University Press, 1967–8), and an additional series, *Lives of Saints*, 2 vols., ed. Walter W. Skeat (London: Trübner, 1881–1900). Aaron J Kleist, "Ælfric's Corpus: A Conspectus," in *Florilegium* 18.2 (2001), is a reference work summarizing Ælfric's work and the major editions. Joyce Hill, "Ælfric: His Life and Works," in Magennis and Swan, *A Companion to Ælfric*, situates Ælfric's *oeuvre* within what is known of his life. On the scope of the *Catholic Homilies*, see Milton McC. Gatch: "No one before Ælfric or in the century after him produced or attempted to assemble in the vernaculars a coherent set of exegetical commentaries on the pericopes for the Christian year. Thus Ælfric seems to be *sui generis*, without precursors or followers in his effort to provide a cycle of exegetical addresses *ad populum* for the Temporale," "The Achievement of Ælfric and his Colleagues in European Perspective," in *The Old English Homily and Its Backgrounds*,

undertaking designed to be distributed throughout England to make orthodox teaching available to the unlearned – both those who did not adequately understand Latin and those who could not read in any language. Thus, Ælfric's homilies are largely pitched to a much broader audience than Bede's, not merely to monks and nuns but also to laypeople.[6] Ælfric's teachings on prayer studied in this present chapter are certainly not from the monastic tradition and are addressed to a lay audience.

While much more scholarly attention has been paid to Ælfric's homilies than to Bede's, unlike Bede or Alfred, Ælfric has received almost no attention within spirituality studies or as a devotional writer.[7] One reason for

---

ed. Paul E. Szarmach and Bernard Huppé (Albany: University of New York Press, 1978), 60. On Ælfric's prose style, see Peter Clemoes, "Ælfric," in *Continuations and Beginnings: Studies in Old English Literature*, ed. Eric Gerald Stanley (London: Thomas Nelson, 1966). For a revision of Clemoes's argument, see Bruce Mitchell, "The Relation between Old English Alliterative Verse and Ælfric's Alliterative Prose," in *Latin Learning and English Lore: Studies in Anglo-Saxon Literature for Michael Lapidge*, ed. Katherine O'Brien O'Keeffe and Andy Orchard (Toronto: University of Toronto Press, 2005).

6 For the complicated question of Ælfric's audience, see Malcolm Godden, *Ælfric's Catholic Homilies: Introduction, Commentary, and Glossary* (Oxford: Oxford University Press, 2000), xxi–xxix (hereafter called *Commentary*). While the main audience for the *Catholic Homilies* is the laity, he also anticipated those who could read, xxii. See also Mary Clayton, "Homiliaries and Preaching in Anglo-Saxon England," in *Old English Prose: Basic Readings*, ed. Paul E. Szarmach (New York: Garland, 2000). She argues with Gatch, "Achievement of Ælfric," by emphasizing the monastic aspect of Ælfric's work: "What Ælfric is doing to an ever-increasing degree, therefore, is rendering 'monastic' material into the vernacular," 187. Jonathan Wilcox, "Ælfric in Dorset and the Landscape of Pastoral Care," in *Pastoral Care in Late Anglo-Saxon England*, ed. Francesca Tinti (Woodbridge: Boydell, 2005), imagines the situation on the ground that would have led to the mixed audience Ælfric envisions in his homilies. See Catherine Cubitt, "Ælfric's Lay Patrons," in Magennis and Swan, *A Companion to Ælfric*, for discussion of the lay patrons for whom Ælfric wrote much of his work.

7 Scott DeGregorio includes him in his dissertation, "Explorations of Spirituality in the Writings of the Venerable Bede, King Alfred, and Abbot Ælfric of Eynsham" (PhD diss. University of Toronto, 1999). His article "Ælfric, *Gedwyld*, and Vernacular Hagiography: Sanctity and Spirituality in the Old English Lives of SS Peter and Paul," in *Ælfric's Lives of Canonized Popes*, ed. Donald Scragg (Kalamazoo: MIP, 2001), considers the way Ælfric used the *vita* of saints Peter and Paul to convey "spirituality" to his audience: meaning, how believers should behave and observe the liturgy, 98. Robert Upchurch, "Catechetic Homiletics: Ælfric's Preaching and Teaching During Lent," in Magennis and Swan, *A Companion to Ælfric*, examines Ælfric's Lenten homilies to identify the type of catechesis laypeople would have received, although with a focus on moral instruction and theology rather than subjective aspects of belief. M.J. Toswell

this may be passages like the above, which seem to present prayer as automatically efficacious rather than a spiritual exercise. Another reason may be that Ælfric's teaching on prayer is largely catechetical and shows little monastic influence; he does not present prayer as a regular discipline but as something people engage in as a response to perceived needs, spiritual and material. He therefore does not represent the interiority of prayer in ways that speak directly to the concerns of spirituality studies.

How does Ælfric present prayer? For Ælfric, as we will see, people pray to the god whom they serve. The act of prayer itself declares allegiance and loyalty and claims protection. Ælfric spends a good deal of time convincing his hearers that not only is it the human duty to serve the Christian God, he is also a better object for people's loyalty than the alternative. People want healing, protection, provision. They think their lord has an obligation to provide it for them. If protection, as in the case above, is not forthcoming, prayer's failure potentially risks precators turning to alternate means of getting what they need. This is the central problem of prayer as Ælfric presents it. While both Bede and the Alfredian texts expect the relationship between precators and God to be beneficial to precators, for both prayer has characteristics that decentre the individual will and cause the focus to be on the persons, not the things. In neither case do they idealize aneconomic prayer or the free gift, but neither do they treat prayer as transaction. People do not buy salvation with their prayers or good works, or earn it through alienated labour. In both cases the discipline of prayer transforms precators' will or intention.

For Ælfric, prayer – objective in its effects – has no such safeguard. Emphasis on prayer's material efficacy potentially risks centring prayer on the will of precators, moving it away from reciprocity to transaction and giving a sense that humans have power to compel God to act according to their own will. If God fails to act, if prayer proves inefficacious to gain precators what they want, such a failure can be read as evidence either of God's lack of interest or his lack of power, proving damaging to faith. Yet the way Ælfric presents and contextualizes prayer shows his

---

discusses Ælfric's use of the psalms, but more from the perspective of Ælfric as teacher than as a study of devotional practice, *The Anglo-Saxon Psalter* (Turnhout: Brepols, 2014), 82–92. Although Ælfric does present the allegorical and prophetic link to the Psalms through David as a type of Christ, his statements on the Psalms lack the close identification between precator and David that we find in the Alfredian introductions.

awareness of this problem; foreclosing that possibility threads through his teaching on prayer.

In theoretical terms, the issue Ælfric's presentation of prayer grapples with is the difference between gift and purchase and the question of who controls the gift. Presenting God as a social person inserts him into social obligations. Tying prayer too closely to its result replicates problems in the gift: that is, if a gift expects a return, the lines between gift and various forms of transaction becomes harder to place. In fact, because Mauss (and theorists following him) represents gift giving as a cycle in which the first gift invites a return gift, he is sometimes criticized for reducing the gift to economic exchange.[8] Indeed, once gifts are understood to participate in exchange, and because the language of the gift (that they are voluntary and not reciprocated) does not reflect the practice of gift giving, determining the essential features differentiating gift from other types of exchange becomes both more necessary and more difficult. C.A. Gregory, as I mentioned in the introduction, presents one important way of thinking about the difference: gifts relate persons to one another, while commodities relate things. His is not the only approach, however.[9] Another way to define the boundaries between gift and purchase is to note that return gifts cannot be made either in kind or immediately (and after the initial gift, all subsequent gifts are a return, whichever party gives them). Pierre Bourdieu argues that this delay is what, from the subjective point of view, removes the gift from the economic sphere, creating gift out of transaction: "The interval inserted between the gift and the counter-gift is an instrument of denial which allows a subjective truth and a quite opposite objective truth [the economic function of the gift] to coexist."[10]

Bourdieu's reading reduces everything to economy and capital in the end; however, the gap between the "subjective" and "objective" perspectives that Bourdieu notes and names as "denial" (the gap between the

---

8 Mark Osteen, paraphrasing Rodolphe Gasché, writes: "In figuring the gift as a circle, then, Mauss reduces it to an economic exchange," "Introduction: Questions of the Gift," in *The Question of the Gift: Essays across Disciplines*, ed. Mark Osteen (New York: Routledge, 2002), 7. To counter this, Osteen argues for focusing on a "different set of norms ... a set founded upon spontaneity rather than calculation, upon risk instead of reciprocity, upon altruism in place of autonomy," 7.

9 C.A. Gregory, *Gifts and Commodities* (London: Academic Press, 1982), 41. Discussed above, pp. 42–4.

10 Pierre Bourdieu, "Selections from *The Logic of Practice*," in *The Logic of the Gift: Toward an Ethic of Generosity*, ed. Alan D. Schrift (New York: Routledge, 1997), 200.

discourse and the praxis of the gift) is itself the productive site where the relationship is maintained. The very act of deferral keeps the relationship from balancing and enables it to continue. Furthermore, the terms or expectations of the exchange are not and cannot be clearly spelled out without it degenerating into a type of commodity exchange. The vagueness of the terms of the gift causes each party to rely on the good will and generosity of the other. Thus, the gap between discourse and practice allows the gift to do its work, relating persons to each other in such a way that their orientation towards social behaviour is revealed. Because receiving a gift is an implicit promise of future return, a failure to return gifts can be seen, not merely as a failure in manners, but as a species of deception. As *Maxims I* puts it, "lean sceal, gif we leogan nellað, þam þe us þas lisse geteode"[11] (return must be made, if we do not wish to deceive, to him who granted us these favours). However, insofar as God is imagined as a social person, he also gains social obligations to repay loyalty with protection.

There are certain anxieties and slippages attendant on the gift that religious discourse mutes or amplifies in interesting ways. As intimate and affective as these gift relationships might be (the exact emotional contours of gift relationships vary depending on local ideals and the social nature of the relationship, as I discussed in chapter 2), they are also valuable, economically and socially.[12] The relationship is conceptualized as being good for both parties involved; therefore, gifts are not altruistic but neither are they completely self-interested – generosity rather than altruism is the ideal. Yet the interweaving of personal regard and economic value means that it can be difficult to determine another's motive and intention in a relationship: whether one gives from desire for the person and recognition of his or her value, or whether one gives to get, with a desire to manipulate the other into doing what one wants, or with loyalty that can therefore be bought.

11 George Philip Krapp and Elliott Van Kirk Dobbie, eds., *The Exeter Book*, ASPR III (New York: Columbia University Press, 1936), l. 70.

12 Example: marriage is an example of a relationship that is usually conceptualized as being personal, affective, and intimate but that also has a strong economic component. Because the happiness of one partner generally depends on the happiness of the other, a purely altruistic action in a marriage would be difficult to achieve. Furthermore, for one to claim that one does things altruistically that one is, in fact, obligated to do, to insist on one's freedom of action within a relation of reciprocal obligation, becomes insulting to the recipient.

In addition, there are situations in which people prefer a certain outcome over the openness of the gift. While gift giving builds relationships and contributes to the growth of honour, it is an inefficient way to gain specific things.[13] Furthermore, while in many ways gifts create a social network that should buffer its participants against future calamity, they also introduce uncertainty into the future: one never knows when a return will be expected or exactly what form will be appropriate to it. Finally, gifts are not as predictable as other forms of transfer, such as taxation. Thus, people will often trade the openness of the gift away for the certainty of other types of exchange, while sometimes using the language of one kind of transfer to describe a transaction of a different type altogether.

How then can a teacher such as Ælfric promise his audience that God *will* respond to prayer, without simultaneously creating the expectation that God *must* respond to prayer, thereby creating a transaction out of a gift and undermining the relational aspect of prayer? How does he address the issue of precators' will and intentions? How can he promise God is a good lord without letting his audience determine the standards of that goodness? And what happens when it is God who does not give a return?

To explore the way Ælfric addresses these problems, this chapter examines the four homilies in which Ælfric addresses prayer in a direct and sustained way.[14] Two were written for Rogationtide, the three days before Ascension when a large proportion of the community could be expected in church: *CH* I.18, *In letania maiore*, explains the reason for Rogationtide; I.19, *Feria III de Dominica oratione*, explicates the Paternoster. These homilies situate prayer in the community rather than the individual. Like most homilies on the Paternoster, the middle section of I.19 is a literal line-by-line explication of the seven petitions of the prayer. Ælfric's says almost nothing explicitly about the practice of prayer, and says very little explicitly about a theory of prayer, especially when compared to treatises like Origen's and Cassian's, and even Augustine's commentary. *CH* I.18

13 Economists talk about the "dead-weight loss" of Christmas giving, for instance.

14 Naturally, prayer is mentioned frequently in the homilies, many of which end with brief benedictions or calls to prayer. Outside of the four I focus on particularly in this chapter, *CH* I.3, on the martyrdom of St Stephen, gives the fullest discussion of prayer, where prayer is listed among the types of gifts humans give to God. In *CH* II.20, the stories appended to the sermon on Fursey speak to the efficacy of prayer for the dead and of the Mass.

is an amalgamation of many different elements. In the first part of the sermon, Ælfric explains the origins of Rogationtide, which itself incorporates two different traditions, beating the bounds and penitential practices intended to ward off natural disasters. As Stephen J. Harris notes, this context lends greater emphasis to the efficacious nature of prayer and the liturgy, as the occasion "sought to assuage terrestrial suffering by removing the spiritual causes of that suffering."[15] In the second part of the homily Ælfric adapts two Augustinian sermons[16] to explicate the pericope for the day, Luke 11:5–13, on God's willingness to grant requests. Similarly, the coda to *CH* I.31, *Passio sancti Bartholomei apostoli*, addresses prayers for healing to clarify that people should turn to God, not devils, for help. While *CH* I.18 and 19 both reflect Augustinian sources, *CH* I.10, *Dominica in quinquagessima*, a Lenten homily, uses a Gregorian source that places prayer in a penitential, and thus more personal, context.[17] One might therefore assume that *CH* I.10 might present prayer with more emphasis on the individual and on purity, and perhaps give a greater sense of prayer's subjective efficacy. However, while Gregory's homily focuses on the subjective efficacy of perseverance in prayer to enlighten the mind, in Ælfric's homily prayer works through the direct intervention of God in response to precators' requests. In addition, this chapter will examine the way *CH* I.1, *De initio creaturae*, an extra-liturgical homily with which he begins his sermon series, provides the cosmological context for prayer by recounting the story of the fall of angels and humans.

While Ælfric's explicit teachings on prayer derive primarily from Augustine and Gregory, he makes consistent and systematic changes to his sources that move the theory of prayer away from an idea of the discipline of prayer's subjective effect and away from Neoplatonic abstractions towards a more concretely social idea of God. He presents prayer as a way for humans to petition for God's aid in their times of need, material as

15 Stephen J. Harris, "The Liturgical Context of Ælfric's Homilies for Rogation," in *The Old English Homily: Precedent, Practice, and Appropriation*, ed. Aaron J Kleist (Turnhout: Brepols, 2007), 147.

16 Sermon 61 (which is on the parallel passage in Matthew 7:7–11), in *Sermones in Matthaeum*, CCSL 41Aa, ed. P.-P. Verbraken et al. (Turnhout: Brepols, 2008), and Sermon 105, in PL 38, cols 618–25.

17 See Godden, for the relationship between Ælfric's homily and Gregory's, *Commentary*, 77.

well as spiritual. As I.1 and I.19 clearly show, his homilies place his congregation in a cosmological order in which all humans are subject to either God or the devil, who are imagined as rival lords, protecting (or not) and providing for (or afflicting) those who serve them. In so doing, he includes God in social structures of obligation to a much greater extent than Bede and the Alfredian texts have. In addition, Ælfric emphasizes the human duty to obey God, rather than invoking gift and gratitude through the concept of *gratia* (OE *gifu*), Ælfric's account of the Fall grapples with the related theological conundrum of free will.[18] The repeated theme through the first part of *CH* I.1 is that angels and humans were both given "agen cyre" (own choice), the Old English translation of *liberum arbitrium*: free will. *Liber* emphasizes the existential freedom of the will; *agen* emphasizes that the choice is one's own responsibility, but it means that humans have something to give back to God. Thus, Ælfric's emphases increase the sense that God owes something to humans for their service and potentially makes the efficacy of prayer into evidence of God's ability or his interest in helping his followers.

But Ælfric counteracts a transactional economy of salvation by creating a three-way exchange between humans and God as the rich give to those in need and the poor pray for the rich, creating a gift cycle that disrupts a sense of transactional accounting and moves the emphasis away from material goods to the spiritual. Furthermore, in the coda at the end of *CH* I.31 Ælfric uses unanswered prayer to create an economy of honour, in which people gain honour by serving God without direct immediate reward. The theory of prayer we see emerging within these homilies is one in which prayer enacts a cosmological order that puts all things into right relationship with each other. In this relationship gifts serve to strengthen the bonds between God and his people: God's gifts, of creation and salvation, and the human return of prayer, almsgiving, and other good works.[19]

18 Upchurch, "Catechetic Homiletics," notes the importance of free will to Ælfric's catechesis generally.

19 *CH* I.3, 204, ll.164–6: "Ure gastlican lac sint ure gebedu. 7 lofsang. 7 huselhalgung 7 gehwilce oðre lac þe we gode offriað. þa we sceolun mid gesibsumere heortan. 7 broðorlicere lufe gode betæcan" (Our spiritual offerings are our prayers and hymns and attendance at mass and whatever other offerings that we give to God, which we should entrust to God with peaceful hearts and brotherly love).

God us fet ... deofol us wile ofslean: *Catholic Homilies* I.1 and I.19

Two Lords

Like Bede, Ælfric situates prayer within a reciprocal relationship between humans and God, in which humans cooperate with God's grace for their own salvation.[20] And, like Bede, Ælfric begins his own sermon series by clarifying the relationship between humans and God. While Bede does so by focusing his Advent homilies on the figure of Mary as a model of one who receives and uses God's gifts, Ælfric does so by including an "extra" homily outside of the liturgical cycle that begins with an account of creation and gives a brief summary of human history up to Christ. In so doing, he establishes a cosmology in which God and the devil are rival lords, each characterized by different kinds of exchange, which humans must choose between. He then situates his explication of the Paternoster within this rivalry. Who people pray to is a key expression of this choice.

The tension between God and the devil that Ælfric's account of the fall establishes is informed by the doctrine of the ransom theory of atonement.[21] The patristic apologist Irenaeus developed ransom theory in the second century to combat Gnostic beliefs in the absolute duality of good and evil. Briefly summarized, he taught that because Adam obeyed the devil by eating the forbidden fruit instead of obeying God, his sin put humankind under the devil's power, giving the devil legitimate claim to

20 See Aaron J Kleist, *Striving with Grace: Views of Free Will in Anglo-Saxon England* (Toronto: University of Toronto Press, 2008), chapter 7, for Ælfric's position on the doctrinal question.

21 See Gustaf Aulén, *Christus Victor: An Historical Study of the Three Main Types of the Idea of Atonement*, 13th printing (1931; New York: Macmillan, 1967). Ransom theory was never doctrinally codified the way that substitutionary atonement later was; hence, it may be most usefully seen as the dominant metaphor for salvation in the early church. Substitutionary atonement is also a metaphor, but by the time of Calvin (and hence in modern theology), its metaphorical element was mostly lost; it is now usually seen as a literal explanation of Christ's salvific act. Additionally, see Jeffrey Burton Russell's study, *Lucifer: The Devil in the Middle Ages* (Ithaca: Cornell University Press, 1984), for a summary of Anglo-Saxon diabology, including Ælfric's specifically, although he conflates Ælfric's presentations of devils with the Devil (Satan), chapter 6. William C. Marx, *The Devil's Rights and the Redemption in the Literature of Medieval England* (Cambridge: D.S. Brewer, 1995), emphasizes the continuity in soteriological models through Anselm and afterward to argue that appearances of the ransom theory in late medieval English literature are not anachronisms.

human souls. Christ broke the devil's domination when he gave himself as a ransom paid to the devil to free humankind.[22]

As doctrine forged in apologetic fires tends to do, ransom theory ends up retaining the structures of the heresy it was developed against. Thus, this model gives the devil a much more prominent role in humanity's destruction and in God's salvific work than does the later soteriological model, substitutionary atonement, developed by Anselm.[23] Essentially, ransom theory makes God and the devil into rival lords. Gregory the Great further popularized ransom theory,[24] and we can see specific references to it throughout the Anglo-Saxon corpus. We saw this view reflected briefly in Bede's Homily 1.22, and it perhaps underlies the attribution of Alfred's second illness to the envy of devils; but in neither Bede nor Alfred does the devil as God's opposite gain the prominence that he does in Ælfric. *CH* I.1 establishes the nature of Lucifer's rebellion, thus showing Ælfric's audience what manner of lords they have to choose between and, in the process, what they themselves are: subjects of God, recipients of his gifts, obliged to obey him, and through fulfilment of that obligation they will earn the vacated seats of the fallen angels.

Rather than prayer being a subjectively efficacious means of attaining purity, through prayer precators enact their choice of lords. Gustaf Aulén's summary of the difference between the objective nature of ransom

---

22 Irenaeus, *Adversus Haereses*, PG 7, ed. Jacques-Paul Migne (Paris: Garnier Fratres, 1882), 5.1.1.

23 Ransom theory was the predominant metaphor of salvation for the first thousand years of Christianity until Anselm developed the doctrine of substitutionary atonement in the twelfth century. Substitutionary atonement removes the devil from the equation, so that man's sin is no longer conceptualized as placing him in thrall to the devil, and Christ's sacrifice is no longer imagined as ransoming humanity from the devil's just claims. Rather, man's sin is seen as an affront to God's honour; the debt he owes is owed to God, and Christ's sacrifice pays humanity's debt to God. Substitutionary atonement also conceptualizes God as a lord, but the model used for sin and debt is legal rather than the more personally relational model of ransom theory. In this case, good deeds and other gifts are understood as the payment of a debt rather than gifts that express a dependent relationship upon God. Anselm did not develop substitutionary atonement out of whole cloth; rather, he made use of two models already available within Christian practice: the substitutionary sacrifice re-enacted in the Eucharist, and the practice of penance.

24 For instance, in his Homily 25, *Homiliae in evangelia*, ed. R. Étaix, CCSL 141 (Turnhout: Brepols, 1999), 213, ll. 226–48, for Easter Day.

theory contrasted with Anselm's later doctrine of substitutionary atonement helpfully highlights the difference:

> [I]t scarcely needs to be said that this "dramatic" type [of soteriology] stands in sharp contrast with the "subjective" type of view. It does not set forth only or chiefly a change taking place in men; it describes a complete change in the situation, a change in the relation between God and the world, and a change also in God's own attitude. The idea is, indeed, thoroughly "objective"; and its objectivity is further emphasised by the fact that the Atonement is not regarded as affecting men primarily as individuals, but is set forth as a drama of a world's salvation.[25]

Most notably, the ransom theory predisposes people to think in terms of God as a lord, and of salvation as a matter of allegiance to one lord or another predicated upon which lord one obeys. In these terms, obedience is not a matter of learning to purify one's inner eye or training the desires. Nor does it focus on a change in the inner disposition from unwillingness and inability to please God, but rather on a choice of right action and of the lord to whom one prays. Obedience brings about release from a prior condition of bondage and makes humans free to serve their rightful Lord. Within this structure, however, Ælfric systematically undermines any sense of closeness or reward attendant upon following the devil, or any sense of communal belonging that results from following the devil. Being a child of God implies a close relationship; being a child of the devil does not, because the devil "us wile ofslean gif he mot"[26] (will kill us if he can), whether "we" are God's followers or his own.

Ælfric's emphasis on God's power shows that God is a stronger lord than the devil, and his emphasis on God as creator shows the legitimacy of his rule. Although God's punishment of the rebellious angels is swift and the penalty promised Adam for breaking the "lytle bebod"[27] (little commandment) severe, the weight falls not on God's power to punish and destroy but on his creative, life-giving power and his ability to protect. As lord, Ælfric thus characterizes God as one who creates and one who gives.

---

25 Aulén, *Christus Victor*, 6.

26 *CH* I.19, 331, ll. 180–1.

27 *CH* I.1, 181, l. 82.

In contrast, the devil "[n]e mæg ... nane gesceafta gescyppan. for ðan ðe he nis na scyppend"[28] (can create no creatures, for he is not a creator). The devil therefore falls through his attempt to take power and keep it for himself: "habban anweald 7 rice ongean gode ælmihtigum" (to have power and dominion against God almighty). In this formulation there are thus two types of lord: one who creates and gives, and one who cannot create and who takes for himself.

Ælfric's opening statements emphasize the supremacy and self-sustaining nature of God: "An angin is ealra þinga þæt is god ælmihtig. he is ordfruma 7 ende; He is ordfruma for ði þe he wæs æfre; he is ęnde buton ælcere geendunge. for ðon þe he bið æfre ungeendod"[29] (There is one source of all things, that is God Almighty. He is beginning and end. He is beginning because he always was; he is end without any ending because he will always be endless). Ælfric emphasizes that as the originator of all things, God's design contains all things, and that while God contains both beginning and end, he himself has no beginning or end and is therefore outside of and encompasses all things. They depend on him for existence, but his being is separate from that which he has brought forth. Within the frame of gift economy, Ælfric's narrative presents God as the only truly independent actor. God owes no one anything, and so everything he gives is completely voluntary.[30] He creates solely out of his own will; once he creates the universe, he sustains it out of his own will, against which "mæg nan þinc ... wiðstandan"[31] (nothing can resist). God is an individual

28 *CH* I.1, 183, ll. 118–19.

29 *CH* I.1, 178, ll. 6–8. Crossed þ has been silently expanded to *þæt* throughout.

30 Georg Simmel states the idea of moral obligation this way: "Once we have received something good from another person, once he has preceded us with his action ["*vorgeleistet*"], we no longer can make up for it completely, no matter how much our own return gift or service may objectively or legally surpass his own. The reason is that his gift, because it was first, has a voluntary character which no return gift can have. For, to return the benefit we are obliged ethically; we operate under a coercion which, though neither social nor legal but moral, is still a coercion. The first gift is given in full spontaneity; it has a freedom without any duty, even without the duty of gratitude," "Faithfulness and Gratitude," in *The Sociology of Georg Simmel*, ed. and trans. Kurt H. Wolff (Toronto: The Free Press, 1950), 392. Brackets are original to the translation.

31 *CH* I.1, 178, ll. 12–13.

independent of either the obligation to give or receive gifts, who need answer to no one. He is essentially non-social, in that he is independent of gift bonds,[32] yet by his act of creation he chooses sociability. Thus, God is not just the origin of all things, but also the original giver of all things.

Maurice Godelier's work in *The Enigma of the Gift* helps bring into focus the ideals invoked at the beginning of *CH* I.1 by taking seriously the cultural role often accorded to the spirit world in ratifying gift exchange among humans.[33] Godelier's work is on the Baruya of Papua New Guinea, but he establishes several generalizable principles: because the gods are the originators of all things, they are the owners of all things. Therefore, in gifts involving the spirit world, the primary claim is not the one that humans hold over the gods, but the one that the gods hold over humans. The hierarchy is unshakable and absolute. The fact that all first gifts come from the gods creates the human obligation to give back to the gods and to give on to other humans. Thus gifts become central to the production of social order and the reproduction of cultural identity into the next generation. Godelier here speaks specifically of cultic objects believed to originate with the gods, and these objects create a much more defined and limited sense of group identity than anything we see in Ælfric. However, Ælfric invokes God as the origin of all things, and then later invokes the "brotherhood" of all believers – potentially a universal human identity – as a result of God's creative fatherhood. Thus, for Ælfric, God's gifts establish a right social order, an imperative to return the gift by giving back and giving on, and a sense of human identity.

---

32 This is what Louis Dumont's definition of an individual is getting at: an "independent, autonomous, and thus essentially nonsocial moral being," *Essays on Individualism: Modern Ideology in Anthropological Perspective* (Chicago: Chicago University Press, 1986), 25, someone who exists outside of the "normal" (for a gift society) bonds of reciprocity.

33 Maurice Godelier, *The Enigma of the Gift*, trans. Nora Scott (Cambridge: Polity, 1999). Although sacrifice is often approached as the same species of exchange as gifts between humans, without much attention to the role of the gods in human exchange, many theorists do think about the nature of sacrifice, gifts from humans to gods. See, for instance, Marcel Mauss's own essay with Henri Hubert, *Sacrifice: Its Nature and Function*, trans. W.D. Halls (Chicago: Chicago University Press, 1964), and Dennis King Keenan, *The Question of Sacrifice* (Bloomington: Indiana University Press, 2005). Jeffrey Carter, ed., *Understanding Religious Sacrifice* (London: Continuum, 2003), compiles selections from many of the classic works on the topic.

In contrast, Lucifer resists reciprocity with God, struggling to create an independent identity and to keep for himself.[34] He reaches for autonomy from God through his attempt to claim an identity for himself outside of God's gift and to withhold gratitude (although Ælfric does not call it that) from God. Lucifer first begins to imagine "þæt he mihte beon þam ælmihtigum gode gelic"[35] (that he could be like the Almighty God). However, he recasts the idea of what likeness ("gelic") means. Whereas God is defined by his limitlessness, his self-generated creativity, and by his choice to be social, Lucifer reduces divinity to independence and mere dominance. These become the objects of his desire. The nature of Lucifer's concept of "likeness" to God is the more striking as he meditates ways to "dælan rice wið god"[36] (share power with God). It seems that he wants to be equal ("gelic") to God and share ("dælan") rulership with him, yet he really desires to dominate, to take, and to keep.

The primary sense of *dælan* is "to divide" or "to separate," with (often) a secondary sense "to distribute (the parts),"[37] but the implication of this distribution can be various: it can mean a willing sharing, giving out (as treasure or alms), or dividing and handing over (as in land in charters). This dividing is usually done by someone who has the right or at least the ability to do it.[38] What *dælan* does not mean is *to take* – and this is what Lucifer actually proposes to do, not to *share* power with God, as

34 The story of the struggle between God and Lucifer easily lends itself to being cast in heroic language. Two Old English poems, *Genesis* and *Christ and Satan*, do just that, imaging Satan as a rebellious thegn and overtly invoking the norms of reciprocity and loyalty that should obtain between a lord and his retainers. In comparison, Ælfric's account is notable for the way it avoids heroic language. For more on the comparison between Ælfric's *oeuvre* and heroic poetry, see Jocelyn Wogan-Browne, "The Hero in Christian Reception: Ælfric and Heroic Poetry," in *Old English Literature: Critical Essays*, ed. Roy M. Liuzza (New Haven: Yale University Press, 2002). She examines the ways that Ælfric's rhetorical forms and concerns might overlap with heroic literature, examining especially Ælfric's presentation of martial themes, but she concludes, "In tenth and eleventh-century social structures there is, then, a version of the lord and retainer bond central to heroic verse, but it is a Christian society's system of obligation and its terms of loyalty are common to legal and doctrinal discourses and to social history, rather than a prerogative of heroic poetry," 219 [*sic*].

35 *CH* I.1, 180, l. 40.

36 *CH* I.1, 180, l. 42–3.

37 *DOE* "dælan."

38 In the *DOE*, sense 2, the only example of an inferior doing the dividing is this passage in *CH* I.1.

though Lucifer had any right to do the *dælende*, but to take it. In fact, in spite of the potential slippage in *gelic* and *dælan*, Lucifer does not want to be equal to God or share power, acting as co-ruler in the north part of heaven. Rather, he wants to separate himself from God, to have "anweald 7 rice *ongean* gode ælmihtigum"[39] (authority and a kingdom *against* God Almighty), to be the one to do the *dælende*. Lucifer does not want any power that God hands over willingly. To assert independence from God, his power has to be taken by force.

Lucifer faces a difficult bid for independence: he cannot reject God's gifts, as one of them is his very existence and because all he has is given him by God (and all that exists was made by God). To keep these things is to keep his identity as God's servant, and yet he has no way of refusing them and nothing that he can return except his own obedience. Thus, he cannot even challenge God through agonistic exchange of gifts. Andrew Cowell in *The Medieval Warrior Aristocracy* situates Godelier and Annette Weiner's theories[40] of inalienable possessions in a medieval context in his examination of agonistic gift manoeuvres in literary and historical sources in the eleventh and twelfth centuries. He points to various historical and literary instances of people refusing gifts, giving splendid counter-gifts, and attempting to claim and keep symbolic property for themselves (or their families), independent of a lord's bestowal, as part of a strategy to declare or keep their autonomy when threatened by a lord of equal or greater power. Those who have the power and social position to give gifts while not receiving them (except in certain clearly defined instances), or to outgive someone who gives gifts to them (and, most importantly, to claim property of their own safe from the demands of a gift economy) are able to function outside the normal social bonds restricting autonomy.[41] That Lucifer has not even the ability to challenge God in this way belies his claim to equality.

Instead, Lucifer takes and attempts to keep: he refuses to give, to give back. Lucifer roots his pride in his sense of preeminent singularity, defining

39 *CH* I.1, 179, ll. 33–4. Italics mine.

40 Annette Weiner, *Inalienable Possessions: The Paradox of Keeping-While-Giving* (Berkeley: University of California Press, 1992), provides the essential insight regarding a category of possessions that are central to identity and thus kept that Godelier's *Enigma of the Gift* builds on.

41 Andrew Cowell, *The Medieval Warrior Aristocracy: Gifts, Violence, Performance, and the Sacred* (Cambridge: D.S. Brewer, 2007), 87–101.

himself in something that sets him apart from the rest of the communion of angels. As Ælfric says, he was

> swiðe fæger 7 wlitig gesceapen. swa þæt he wæs gehaten leohtberend. þa began he to modigeanne for ðære fægernysse. *þe he hæfde*. and cwæð on his heortan. þæt he wolde 7 eaðe mihte beon his scyppende gelic.[42]
>
> (created very fair and beautiful, so that he was called Lucifer. Then he became prideful because of the fairness *that he had*, and said in his heart that he would and easily could be like his Creator.)

By claiming something that "he hæfde" as his own, ostensibly independent of God's gift, Lucifer is able to understand himself as independent of God, precipitating his desire to usurp God's place. There is a sort of incoherent madness to his claim. Beauty is specular; it can only exist in the eyes of those seeing it (especially in the days before high quality mirrors!) – those who named him Lucifer on account of his beauty ("he *wæs gehaten* leohtberend"). Lucifer therefore claims as his own peculiar property the thing that individuates him, something that was given him in the first place and that requires a social context for its value. Able to imagine himself as independent on the basis of his own singular beauty, he asserts this independence by seeking to "deal" in power.

Significantly, in Ælfric's sermon, God first reacts to Lucifer's rebellion by changing all the rebel angels "of ðam fægeran hiwe þe hi on gescapene wæron. to laðlicum deoflum"[43] (from the fair forms in which they were created to loathly devils), attacking the source of Lucifer's pride. Ælfric emphasizes the fitness of this punishment: "And swiðe rihtlice him swa getimode. þa ða he wolde mid modinysse beon betera þonne he gesceapen wæs"[44] (And very rightly it so befell him, when he wished with pride to be better than he was created). Lucifer, understanding his beauty as his own to keep, had plotted how he might take a kingdom for himself as well; God's actions respond to both these attempts at independence and then at dominance:

42 *CH* I.1, 179, ll. 29–32. Italics mine.

43 *CH* I.1, 180, ll. 37–8.

44 *CH* I.1, 180, ll. 38–40.

> hwile þe he smeade hu he mihte dælan rice wið god. þa hwile gearcode se ælmihtiga scyppend him 7 his geferan hellewite. 7 hi ealle adræfde of heofenan rices myrihðe. 7 let befeallan on ðæt ece fyr þe him gegearcod wæs for heora ofermettum.[45]
>
> (while he considered how he could share power with God, the Almighty Creator prepared hell torments for him and his companions, and drove them all out of the joy of the heavenly kingdom and let them fall into the eternal fire which was made for them for their pride.)

God removes the beauty Lucifer had taken for his essential attribute and prepares a place for all the fallen angels so that even in their punishment they cannot escape being in a God-created place. At this point, Ælfric also switches from considering Lucifer as an individual to grouping him with the rest of the devils who fell.

Gratitude, as Georg Simmel points out, can have the taste of bondage if the desired state is independence.[46] Lucifer's fundamental problem is that he does not want the relationship with God that comes from accepting his gifts. For Lucifer the exchange is not even agonistic – he attempts to give nothing back. Rather, for Lucifer, the whole relationship is antagonistic. As Simmel shows, the point at which gift exchange engenders antagonism is often when the recipient feels himself to be equal or near equal to the giver.[47] In this case, the giver's generosity threatens the recipient's own self-conception. Ælfric's account of Lucifer's fall reveals the false nature of Lucifer's claims, in that God gave Lucifer all he had. Lucifer's failure of gratitude is a moral failure, a refusal of the ideals of reciprocity. He insists

45 *CH* I.1, 180, ll. 42–5.

46 Simmel: "This, perhaps, is the reason why some people do not like to accept, and try to avoid as much as possible, being given gifts ... these people act on the instinct, perhaps, that the return gift cannot possibly contain the decisive element of the original, namely, freedom; and that, in accepting it, therefore, they would contract an irredeemable obligation. As a rule, such people have a strong impulse to independence and individuality; and this suggests that the condition of gratitude easily has a taste of bondage ...
A service, a sacrifice, a benefit, once accepted, may engender an inner relation which can never be eliminated completely, because gratitude is perhaps the only feeling which, under all circumstances, can be morally demanded and rendered," "Faithfulness and Gratitude," 48. Cowell, *Medieval Warrior Aristocracy*, makes a similar point in his account of aristocratic manipulation of gift exchanges to claim or maintain independence.

47 Indeed, Simmel's essay presupposes social equality between parties exchanging gifts.

on casting his relationship with God in terms of power (his own) rather than of love,[48] thus reducing God's gifts to dominance instead of understanding them as markers of personal affection. In an ironic twist, in the end Lucifer's focus on power and dominance means that he cannot even imagine conditions of full autonomy; what Lucifer takes as autonomy is really a warped dependence. By setting himself up in relational opposition to God ("ongean")[49] he locks himself into being God's opposite, never able to truly break free. The devil operates in the world of humans as God's opposite, a wicked lord in contrast to a good one, and he bequeaths to his followers a satanic gift: the desire for independence. Humans can thus choose to be like the devil, atomized individuals who take rather than receive, whose focus is on their own will. Or they can choose to be like God, who chooses sociability by giving the gifts of life and whose lordship leads to communal wholeness through reciprocity.

Agen Cyre

Adam and Eve's situation does not parallel Lucifer's. As an alternate (false) god, Lucifer makes claims to power and independence that are closed to humans. Unlike the angels, Adam and Eve are given a specific, "eaðlic"[50] (easy) command to follow. Their choice is between obeying God or obeying the devil. Identity for them never holds the promise of independence, but this command, through which they exercise *agen cyre*, enables them

48 I choose the word "love" here for its affective resonance, but the concept is loyalty and faithfulness sourced in both duty and affection – the very response that the gift ideally calls forth. In Fred C. Robinson's analysis of *The Battle of Maldon*, he argues that the central conflict of that poem is over loyalty, a concept central to Anglo-Saxon social organization: "the interlocking bonds of loyalty were the principle on which Anglo-Saxon civilization rested, the only bulwark against primitive chaos and anarchy," "God, Death, and Loyalty in The Battle of Maldon," in *J.R.R. Tolkien, Scholar and Story-Teller: Essays in Memoriam*, ed. Mary Sau and Robert T. Farrell (Ithaca: Cornell University Press, 1979), 95. Within a study of a heroic poem, this might seem to be somewhat of a poetical take on more complex social realities. However, Alice Sheppard, *Families of the King: Writing Identity in the Anglo-Saxon Chronicle* (Toronto: University of Toronto Press, 2004), argues similarly for the *Anglo-Saxon Chronicle*'s presentation of the importance of loyalty in lordship, although she is careful not to claim that this is more than a literary construct here, either.

49 *CH* I.1, 179, l. 33.

50 *CH* I, 181, l. 80.

to define and know themselves.[51] In his fieldwork among the Baruya (who are animists), Godelier noticed that there are classes of objects that are not given or traded away but simply kept. These objects, originally from the gods, are sacred, and are central to group identity, the production of social order, and the reproduction of a cultural identity into the next generation.[52] While Adam and Eve are not given a thing to keep, for them the "sacred kept" upon which their identity is constructed is the command not to eat of the fruit of the tree, given so that they might know who they are.

As Katherine O'Brien O'Keeffe argues, for Ælfric *agen cyre*, exercised within obedience, gives humans some form of moral agency that allows responsibility for good or evil works. As she puts it, for Ælfric "the deeds of men are their own because they are free to choose good behavior or bad."[53] Aaron J Kleist, too, notes the way Ælfric's discussion of free will invokes merit – the ability to choose the good enables humans to be rewarded for it.[54] Indeed, that the deeds of men are their own gives Adam and Eve something to give back to God, allowing them to enter into a reciprocal relationship with him that then reveals their identity. As Ælfric states,

> hu mihte adam tocnawan hwæt he wære. buton he wære gehyrsum on sumum þincge his hlaforde; swilce god cwæde to him; Nast ðu þæt ic eom þin hlaford and þæt ðu eart min þeowa buton ðu do þæt ic ðe hate. 7 forgang þæt ic þe forbeode.[55]

---

51 Lucifer and the angels also had free will: "Næs him gesceapen fram gode. ne he næs genedd þæt he sceolde godes bebod tobrecan. ac god hine let frigne. 7 sealde him agenne cyre. swa he wære gehyrsum. swa he wære ungehyrsum" (He was not created thus by God, nor was he compelled to break God's command, but God allowed him freedom, and gave him "own choice," whether he would be obedient, or he would be disobedient), *CH* I.1, 184, ll. 155–7.

52 While medieval Christianity was clearly invested in cultic objects, which attested to the power and presence of God and often contributed to a sense of social identity, they were not, of course, used in the same way as the Baruya cultic objects. However, some of Godelier's insights about gift exchange and religion are generalizable, with all due allowance for their culturally specific realizations. As mentioned above, Cowell, *Medieval Warrior Aristocracy*, applies the concept as he considers the importance of kept objects to aristocratic identity in the eleventh and twelfth centuries.

53 Katherine O'Brien O'Keeffe, *Stealing Obedience: Narratives of Agency and Identity in Later Anglo-Saxon England* (Toronto: University of Toronto Press, 2012), 25–6.

54 Kleist, *Striving with Grace*, 183–203. As Kleist notes, Ælfric seems to follow a "Gregorian rather than Augustinian view of the will," 211. Upchurch, in "Catechetic Homilies," 230–2, also considers the issue of human will in Ælfric's homilies for Lent as allowing humans to earn victory in the afterlife.

55 *CH* I.1, 181, ll. 75–8. The question was originally posed by Augustine.

(how might Adam know what he was unless he were obedient in one thing to his Lord? As if God said to him: "You do not know that I am your lord and that you are my servant unless you do what I command you and avoid that which I forbid you.")

Thus, *agen cyre* and the command on which to exercise it allows Adam (and Eve) to recognize their place in the cosmological order. O'Brien O'Keeffe notes that this passage "makes obedience central to the fashioning of human identity."[56] God's command also creates them as a subject in an economy. Adam and Eve have received everything from God and therefore have nothing to give back to God except obedience.

Adam and Eve cannot obey where there is no distinction between human will and divine will. God's command thus allows humans to recognize difference between human volition and God's volition, creating a sense of *ego* and *alter*. Differentiating between the two creates an economy, giving Adam and Eve the means to enter into reciprocity with God as they choose whether to obey him. As they choose to obey God by not eating from the forbidden tree, God intends that "mid þære eaðelican gehyrsumnysse. þu geearnast heofenan rices myrhðe. 7 þone stede þe se deofol of afeoll þurh ungehyrsumnesse"[57] (with that easy obedience you will earn the joy of the heavenly kingdom and the position that the devil fell from through disobedience). Adam and Eve's chosen obedience relates them to God, creating an economy in which God gives and God promises to reward their obedience to him. Their ability to choose to obey, their *agen cyre*, gives obedience meaning and constitutes them as subjects within the divine economy by giving them something to give back, as giving selves separate from but dependent on God.

When Adam and Eve choose to listen to the devil rather than to God, they give up this marker of his identity, their status as God's servants, and any claims to God's protection. In so doing, however, they do not become free (not even in the negative sense of lordless); they instead become dependents of the devil, the one they listened to: "He wearð þa deofle gehyrsum. 7 gode ungehyrsum. 7 wearð betæht he 7 eal mancynn æfter ðisum life into hellewite. mid þam deofle ðe hine forlærde."[58] (He became obedient to the devil and disobedient to God, and he and all mankind were

56 O'Brien O'Keeffe, *Stealing Obedience*, 28.
57 *CH* I.1, 181, ll. 80–2.
58 *CH* I.1, 184, ll. 157–9.

given up after this life to hell torments with the devil who led him astray). The tragedy is that, like Lucifer, who chose to take something he already had – authority – in obeying the devil, Adam and Eve also reach for something they were going to be given: the vacated seats of the fallen angels. In so doing, they lose their place as dependents of God, creator and life giver, falling into the disorder that results from being dependents of the devil.

God's command imparts self-knowledge; the tree itself cannot. The devil promises that the fruit will give Adam and Eve knowledge of good and evil, making them like the angels: "gif ge of ðam treowe geetað. þonne beoð eowere eagan geopenode. 7 ge magon geseon 7 tocnawan ægðer ge god. ge yfel. 7 ge beoð englum gelice"[59] (if you eat from the tree your eyes will be opened, and you will see and know both good and evil, and you will be like the angels). In *CH* I.1, God does not name the tree from which they are forbidden to eat, and the only consequence he gives for disobedience is death, the complete negation of gifts. The tree holds no promise of knowledge in itself. Thus, in her transgression, Eve mistakes the fruit of the tree for the thing itself – knowledge of good and evil – rather than as the symbolic object it is, a marker of humanity's relationship with God, the *not* eating of which brings the knowledge they need – an understanding of their relationship with God.

Given Ælfric's conception of *agen cyre* as constructed around giving and keeping, it does not really matter that Eve's disobedience was occasioned by deception. While deception leads to questions of culpability within the context of free will (how free a choice does a person make who is deceived?), it does not matter one way or another if a person is deceived into giving up something she knew she was supposed to keep, since it is the status of the kept thing that is important rather than the conditions of turning it over. In the rest of Ælfric's corpus this is a significant point, since people are often deceived into worshiping idols.[60] Of course, after the Fall, before Jesus's coming, the human situation is reversed, in that

59 *CH* I.1, 183, ll. 134–6.

60 Within this homily, for example, after the Tower of Babel, people make idols who become inhabited by demons who then claim that they are gods. The people "weorðodon hi. 7 him lac ofredon … 7 þæt beswicone mennisc feoll on cneowum to þam anlicnyssum and cwædon ge sind ure godas …" (worshiped them and offered them offerings … and that deceived race fell on their knees before the idols and said, "You are our gods"), *CH* I.1, 186, ll. 215–16, 217–19.

they are in thrall to the devil, and all the human choice in the world cannot change this fact.[61]

Ure Fæder

CH I.19 further develops the way petition happens within the cosmological tension between God and the devil, the two great lords that humanity can serve. Compared to other explications of the Paternoster, Ælfric introduces the devil in a much more structured and pervasive way, emphasizing his role as counter-lord to God.[62] People petition and listen to the one whom they acknowledge as lord. To pray to God is to acknowledge him as lord, whereas to pray to devils is to renounce God and claim the devil as lord. Ælfric's exposition of the prayer establishes the devil as a rival to God by mentioning him in the explication of seven of the eight phrases of the prayer. The devil's prominence has the effect of clarifying that humans must make a choice between serving God or serving the devil. Like Adam and Eve's choice, human choice to serve God, expressed through obedience and prayer, gives them something to return within a reciprocal relationship.

In the homily, the connection between humans and the devil is not formed in the same way as the connection to God. Ælfric builds on the terminology of the Paternoster – God as father – to establish God's lordship

61 Kleist says, "By presenting freedom of choice … as a defining characteristic of the righteousness of God, Ælfric argues that what mankind had at creation is still available to fallen people today," *Striving with Grace*, 183. But the Church taught that in the period between the Fall and Christ's coming, all humans went to Hell, and that Jesus rescued them from Hell after his death and before his resurrection in an event known as the Harrowing of Hell.

62 See discussion in chapter 1. In addition, this homily is one of the few on the Paternoster *not* addressed to catechumens and, aside from a translation of the prayer and a brief encouragement to pray it by Wulfstan, it is the only extant Old English homily on the Paternoster. In Bethurum VII, *De fide catholica*, Wulfstan uses the Paternoster to introduce an explication of the Creed, *The Homilies of Wulfstan*, ed. Dorothy Bethurum (Oxford: Clarendon, 1957). Every Christian should know both texts, he says, and he mentions that the Paternoster contains seven petitions for everything needful that people can pray privately to God. But then he asks how a man can pray inwardly to God if he does not believe truly, and he goes from there into an explication of the Creed. The following "sermon," VIIa, gives a translation of the Paternoster and the Creed, although it might be noted that Wulfstan's translation of the prayer is very odd if he really intends this to be the version that Christians should pray. While highly alliterative and ornate, it is not the most literal of translations.

and a familial relationship, based on his creative power and reaffirmed by the care he shows his children:

> [W]e men sind godes bearn for þan ðe he us geworhte. 7 eft þa ða we forwyrhte wæron he asende his agen bearn us to alysednysse; Nu sind we godes bearn. 7 crist is ure broðor gif we þam fæder on riht gehyrsumiað 7 mid eallum mode hine wurþiað.[63]
>
> (We are God's children because he made us, and then, when we were ruined, he sent his own son to free us. Now we are God's children, and Christ is our brother, if we rightly obey the Father and honor him with all our mind.)

Those who honour God are his children three times over: by creation, by redemption, and, as their return, by obedience. Ælfric then contrasts the situation of the children of God to those who are children of the devil:

> [W]itodlice se man þe deofle geefenlæcð. se bið deofles bearn. na þurh gecynde. oððe þurh gesceapennysse. ac þurh ða geefenlæcunge. 7 yfelum geearnungum; And se man þe gode gecwemð he bið godes bearn. na gecyndelice ac þurh gesceapenysse. 7 þurh godum geearnungum.[64]
>
> (Truly, the one who imitates the devil, he is the devil's child, not in the natural way or through creation but through imitation and evil deeds. But the man

63 *CH* I.19, 326, ll. 23–7.

64 *CH* I.19, 326, ll. 34–8. As Godden, *Commentary*, 468, points out, this idea is similar to one found in Augustine's *Tract.*, 42.15.11–14, 37, which Ælfric uses in *CH* II.13: "Et ex Deo sunt, et ex Deo non sunt; natura ex Deo sunt, vitio non sunt ex Deo: natura enim bona quae ex Deo est, peccavit voluntate, credendo quod diabolus persuasit, et vitiata est ... imitando diabolum, filii diaboli facti erant" (They [the Jews] are both of God, and not of God. By nature they are of God: by depravity they are not of God; for the good nature which is of God sinned voluntarily by believing the persuasive words of the devil, and was corrupted ... imitating the devil, they had become the children of the devil); trans. John Gibb and James Innes, *Homilies on the Gospel of John*, NPNF, First Series, vol. 7, sect. 15. Jerome also links the idea of sonship and obedience in his commentary on Matthew, right before the Paternoster section: "*Vt sitis filii Patris uestri qui in caelis est.* Si Dei praecepta custodiens filius quis efficitur Dei, ergo non est natura filius sed arbitrio suo" ("So that you may be sons of your Father who is in heaven." If one becomes a son of God by keeping God's commands, then he is not a son by nature

who serves God he is God's child, not in the natural way, but through creation and through good deeds.)

Imitating the devil (*geefenlæcan*, to emulate, to make equal), does not invoke the obligation attendant on generation or creation. While God as father clearly cares about his creation, *geefenlæcan* does not suggest that the devil recognizes or rewards human imitation. Without a head that recognizes the parts, the parts are all individuated; there is no sense of sociability in the devil's "family." Ælfric does not imply any particular mutual obligation or relationship resulting from that imitation. In contrast, good deeds put one in a position of "gecwemende" (pleasing, serving) God, which implies that God recognizes those who please him.

Ælfric continues the depersonalization of the "relationship" between the devil and his followers in the discussion of the sixth petition. Here, God abandons those who sin to the power of the devil: "Se man þe wile gelomlice syngian. 7 gelomlice betan. he gremað god; And swa he swiðor syngað. swa he deofle. gewyldra bið. 7 hine þonne god forlæt. 7 he færð swa him deofol wissað"[65] (The one who often sins and often amends, he angers God. And the more he sins, the more he will be in the power of the devil, and God will abandon him and he will go as the devil directs). Yet those who follow the devil's direction ("wissian") are not rendering service to him; rather, they have fallen under his influence, an influence that carries with it no inherent promise of protection or reward. According to this logic, if humans imitate the devil, God abandons them to his lordship. The devil's domination does not bring promises of closeness or reward; his is rather an atomized, dysfunctional family. On the contrary, those who serve God become members of an orderly family in which obedience is rewarded with protection and sustenance, and further belonging.

Ælfric ends the explication of the prayer with its final phrase, "deliver us from evil," by contrasting the lordship of each:

---

but by his own choice), *Commentariorum in Matheum*, ed. D. Hurst and M. Adriaen, CCSL 77 (Turnhout: Brepols, 1967), 34, ll. 706–8. In neither case is the correspondence especially close. Augustine's explication is much longer and focuses on explaining why Jesus called the Pharisees children of the devil. Jerome's context is closer to Ælfric's, but in Ælfric the idea of being a son by one's own choice is buried within the concept of making oneself acceptable to God ("se man þe gode gecwemð," *CH* I.19, 346, l. 36).

65 *CH* I.19, 331, ll. 160–3.

Alys us fram deofle 7 fram eallum his syrwungum; God lufað us. 7 deofol us hatað; God us fet 7 gefrefrað. 7 deofol us wile ofslean gif he mot … for þi we sceolon forbugan 7 forseon þone lyþran deofol mid eallum his lotwrencum. for þan ðe him ne gebyrað naht to us. 7 we sceolon lufian 7 fyligan urum drihtne. se þe us læt to þam ecan life.[66]

(Deliver us from the devil and from all his tricks. God loves us, and the devil hates us. God feeds and comforts us, and the devil will kill us if he can … Therefore, we should flee from and reject the wicked devil with all his deceits, because he is of no concern to us at all, and we must love and follow our Lord, he who leads us to the eternal life.)

God's nature as creator and life sustainer creates the obligation for humans to return love and follow him. In so doing they are protected by a lord who loves them and leads them to fuller life. For Ælfric, then, praying the Paternoster and the Creed for protection while travelling, as he advises in *De auguriis*, are both acts that state the precator's allegiance to God rather than the devil, and in so doing, call upon God to protect his own.

Only small steps separate such a use of the Paternoster for protection from devils from praying over medicinal herbs (as Ælfric advocates in *CH* I.31),[67] from singing the Paternoster and Creed in the course of a healing charm.[68] In both *De auguriis* and in *CH* I.31 the major difference for Ælfric between prayer and *wiglung* (sorcery) is whose power the precator invokes. However, in all three uses of the Paternoster just given, the words and performance of the prayer are believed to have objective effect. Thus, a further marker that separates prayer from *galdor* (charm, incantation, magic) is the intention of the performer: as an act of submission to God and an expression of loyalty, or as an attempt to invoke the power of God to gain material blessing. Lori Ann Garner, in "Anglo-Saxon Charms in Performance," makes the point that it is important to consider the performance context of charms as we examine the way they represent the

66 *CH* I.19, 331–2, ll. 179–85.

67 "Ne sceal nan man mid galdre wyrte besingan ac mid godes wordum hi gebletsian 7 swa þicgan" (No one may enchant herbs with charms but with God's words bless them and so partake), *CH* I.31, 450, ll. 323–5.

68 As, for instance, in the charm against a wen quoted by Lori Ann Garner, which involves singing the Paternoster and Creed while fetching water, "Anglo-Saxon Charms in Performance," in *Oral Tradition* 19.1 (2004), 32.

world for Anglo-Saxons,[69] but even that can tell little about performers' understanding of themselves before God. Orthodox prayer lacks some of the performative markers of magic,[70] but as uses of the Paternoster show, the difference between prayer as Ælfric defines it and magic could lie in the intention of the performer as much as in the performance context. The promise of prayer's protective efficacy could easily be understood as promising whatever the precator needs and could create a sense that God is obliged to help precators in the way they think they need it, centring prayer on human will. To foreclose such a (mis)understanding, Ælfric emphasizes obedience as the source of human identity and the means by which humans enter God's family. He also takes pains to show that serving the devil is not a good choice: the devil is deceitful and shows no loyalty to those who follow him.

Cristes Broðorræden: *Catholic Homilies* I.19 and I.18

Ælfric also undercuts a sense of transactionality through the way he situates prayer within community both in his explication of the Paternoster and in his discussion of prayer and almsgiving in *CH* I.18. Stephen Harris notes the way that I.18 seems to shift suddenly from prayer to poverty and almsgiving, but the connection between prayer and almsgiving is a standard feature of patristic teaching on prayer, and the collocation ultimately originates from the context of the Paternoster in Matthew 6.[71] For most early writers on prayer both almsgiving and prayer operate on the same plane of action, because both are good works performed for salvation. In

69 Garner, "Anglo-Saxon Charms," 42.

70 There is a robust body of literature on the lines between prayers and charms, and the relationship between words and actions in all sorts of ritualized communications with the supernatural world. One of the classic articles on the topic is Stanley J. Tambiah, "The Magical Power of Words," in *Man* n.s. 3.2 (1968). He briefly touches on the artificial opposition between prayers and spells, 176.

71 Harris, "Liturgical Context," 154. Harris makes the point that these themes are also present in the Rogationtide liturgy. See Harris for the liturgical context of Ælfric's Rogationtide sermons (of which he wrote nine in total) and the way the liturgy is reflected in Ælfric's themes. Matthew 6 begins by stating that almsgiving should be done in secret rather than for the praise of men (6:1–4) and moves to prayer, which should be private and brief (6:5–8). At this point the Paternoster is given (9–13), followed by instructions on fasting (16–18) and further teaching on the correct relationship to material wealth (19–34).

this way prayer is tied closely to almsgiving as parts of the same reciprocal cycle. Ælfric uses this idea to interrupt a transactional *do ut des* sense that prayer is a means for humans to get what they want. God's gifts create the responsibility to give back to God in obedience and to give on to others, creating a sense of communal identity, the *broðorræden* of Christ.[72]

CH I.19 has no particular source; however, Malcolm Godden identifies some affinities to Augustine's commentary on the Paternoster in *De sermone Domini in monte*,[73] which is Augustine's most detailed commentary on the prayer. Ælfric's sermon is certainly influenced by Augustine – one might even say it is broadly Augustinian – but the differences in emphasis are quite striking when one compares it to Augustine's commentary or even to his sermons to catechumens. For *CH* I.18 Ælfric uses multiple sources, but the section of greatest interest here is his explication of Luke 11:5–13, found towards the end of the sermon. In this passage Jesus gives two parables. In the first, a man asks his neighbour for bread, and persistence in asking is the main point of the story.[74] In the second, Jesus likens prayer to a child asking his father for food, assuring his hearers of God's good intentions towards them.

Ælfric again bases his exposition on Augustinian sermons.[75] In both cases, Augustine's focus throws Ælfric's preoccupations into relief and shows the marked ways he differs from explications that are more strictly Augustinian. In Augustine's commentary on the Paternoster in *De sermone*

---

72 "[W]e magon cuðlice to him clypian swa swa to urum breþer. gif we þa broðerrædene swa healdað … þæt is þæt we ne sceolon na geþafian. þæt deofol mid ænigum unþeawum us geweme fram cristes broþorrædene" (we may familiarly cry to him as to our brother, if we so observe our brotherhood … that is, that we should not allow the devil with any evil practices to seduce us from the brotherhood of Christ), *CH* I.19, 326, ll. 30–3.

73 According to Godden: "Förster suggested that Ælfric was drawing on Augustine's sermons *ad competentes*, numbers 55–9 [*sic*], as well as material traditionally used in teaching in the monastic schools. The sermons do contain similar material, but the same points are made more fully in Augustine's commentary on the Sermon on the Mount, which includes some passages very close to Ælfric … Occasional similarities of phrasing in the sermons, especially 59, suggest that Ælfric may have known those too, but the debt could be indirect … There remains much however for which no source is yet in evidence," *Commentary*, 154 (Augustine's sermons *ad competentes* are actually numbers 56–9).

74 Kleist discusses Ælfric's explication of this parable in *CH* I.18 in the context of Ælfric's ideas on faith and human nature, *Striving with Grace*, 172–6.

75 See above, n. 16.

Domini, he sidesteps a potentially transactional understanding of prayer by focusing on the cleansing of the heart through prayer and almsgiving leading to purity.[76] In contrast, Ælfric, in stressing community over the individual, emphasizes a sense of communal wholeness. In addition, while *De sermone Domini's* concern with purity avoids suggesting that alms are traded for salvation, in Augustine's homiletic treatments of the same passage (partial sources for I.18), alms are explicitly given to "get" justice from God. For Augustine, the central relationship in almsgiving is dyadic, between each person and God. But in Ælfric's discussion of almsgiving in *CH* I.18, he deepens the communal orientation of prayer presented in *CH* I.19 through presenting prayer – the petition for salvation – as a three-way gift cycle involving the community and God. Such a cycle undermines a sense of *do ut des* as it creates a non-commensurate gift exchange involving multiple parties each acting in the other's interests. Thus, even though traditional teaching underlies all aspects of Ælfric's homilies, he reworks his sermons to reflect a relationship imagined between God and humans built on obedience and protection, and he places his explication within a different complex of concerns, namely those of the praying community.[77] Through all of this, Ælfric largely excises Augustine's conception of purity as detachment from the material world and replaces it with a vision of a reciprocal community made whole through prayer and almsgiving.

76 Matt. 6:22, "lucerna corporis est oculus si fuerit oculus tuus simplex totum corpus tuum lucidum erit" (The light of thy body is thy eye. If thy eye be single, thy whole body shall be lightsome) is the idea that Augustine uses to begin his discussion (as seen in the quote given below), and it governs his discussion of the passage.

77 To some extent, Augustine's and Ælfric's different emphases come from their different preaching contexts. As Godden notes, Ælfric's themes of brotherhood are appropriate for Rogationtide, when the whole community might be expected to gather in church: "The opening and closing sections [of *CH* I.19] draw out the general implications of the prayer to stress ideas of community and the equality of all ranks before God. Possibly this was felt to be an appropriate theme for Rogationtide when the whole populace might be present," *Commentary*, 154. Augustine's relation of purity to prayer comes as much from the typical context for teaching on the Paternoster in baptismal catechesis and for praying it in the Mass as it does from the contextualizing passage in Matthew, which does not introduce the idea of purity that Augustine uses to start his discussion until verse 22 (furthermore, the theme of purity need not necessarily govern the discussion on the passage. Compare, for instance, Jerome's commentary on Matthew). When Augustine states, regarding the "eye" of the heart through which God is seen,

Purity Versus Community: CH I.19

Augustine focuses on the person as set apart, while Ælfric concentrates on the necessity of the whole community. Augustine situates prayer in the heart, creating a private space where the self is in relation to God alone. We might think of this theory of prayer as founded on an idea of the holy as separate, *sanctus*: the precator is imagined as individually set apart from the world, acting solely in the eyes of God.[78] While both Augustine and Ælfric teach, as the prayer opens, that God's name needs to be hallowed by everyone, Augustine says "ut sanctum habeatur ab hominibus, id est ita illis innotescat deus, ut non existiment aliquid sanctius, quod magis offendere timeant"[79] (that people may hallow it, that is, so that God may be so well known to them that they would not consider anything else more hallowed which they would more dare to offend). In sermon 56 Augustine defines "hallowed" more specifically for his congregation: "Quid est *sanctificetur*? Sanctum habeatur, non contemnatur"[80] (What does "hallowed be" mean? May it be treated as holy [*sanctus*], not disdained). Augustine's idea of *sanctificatio* situates the concept within the context of taboo/sacred, that which a person fears to defile or transgress, and thus shows proper respect to. His teaching correspondingly focuses on set-apartness, on purity, on detachment from the material world.

"Huic autem oculo magna ex parte mundato difficile est non subripere sordes aliquas" (But it is difficult for this eye, which has been mostly purified, to avoid the incursion of certain impurities), *De sermone Domini in monte*, ed. Almut Mutzenbecher, CCSL 35 (Turnhout: Brepols, 1967), 91, ll. 7–8; trans. Michael G. Campbell, "The Lord's Sermon on the Mount," WSA I/15 (New York: New City Press, 2014), 69, the reference echoes the function of baptism that cleanses the catechumen of all his sins and then the daily praying of the Paternoster that cleanses the precator from the small defilements that creep over him. This idea is found in all Augustine's sermons on the Paternoster, but for example in Sermon 58: "[R]emissio peccatorum est una quae semel datur in sancto baptismate, alia quae quamdiu uiuimus hic datur dominica oratione" (There is one forgiveness of sins that is given only once in holy baptism; another which, as long as we live here, is given in the Lord's Prayer), CCSL 41Aa, 204, ll. 123–5; trans. Edmund Hill, *Sermons* WSA III/3 (Brooklyn: New City Press), 121, 6.

78 Latin *sanctus* is part of a family of words meaning to render sacred, consecrate, make inviolable (see Lewis and Short, *sancio*). For the Indo-European root, see *sak-* (to sanctify) in the *American Heritage Dictionary Online*, Appendix I (Houghton Mifflin Harcourt, 2016), https://ahdictionary.com/word/indoeurop.html#IR094600. Thus, something that is *sanctus* is set apart, separated from that which could contaminate it.

79 CCSL 35, 109, ll. 412–15; WSA I/15, 78.

80 CCSL 41Aa, 157, ll. 96–7; trans. WSA III/3, 97, 5.

In contrast, Ælfric presents an idea of the *halig*, the holy, as that which is whole,[81] as opposed to that which is set apart. In *CH* I.19, he says:

> Ac þis word is swa to understandenne þæt his nama sy on us gehalgod. 7 he us þæs getiþige þæt we moton his naman mid urum muþe gebletsian. 7 he us þæs getiþige þæt we moton his naman mid urum muþe gebletsian. 7 he us sylle þæt geþanc. þæt we magon understandan þæt nan þing nis swa halig swa his nama.[82]

> (But this word should so be understood that his name be hallowed in us, and he grants to us that we may bless his name with our mouth, and he gives us that thought that we can understand that nothing is so holy as his name.)

Ælfric's teaching notably situates the idea of holiness in a more positive context, associating it, not with fear of offending God, but with blessing him. Furthermore, the ability both to bless God and to understand his holiness is read within this context as a gift from God. Rather than something to be feared, Ælfric sees the holy as something to be praised and notes that holiness comes from God to man: "he us ealle gebletsað and gehalgað"[83] (he blesses and hallows all of us), and then is returned from man to God as people strive to live holiness and to speak blessings back to God.

Ælfric's presentation of a unified, peaceful Christian community constituted by whom they turn to in prayer reflects the same ideas of wholeness: "we magon cuðlice to him clypian swa swa to urum breþer. gif we þa broðerrædene swa healdað"[84] (we may familiarly cry to him as to our brother, if we so observe our brotherhood). His ideal community is one that exists in a cycle of gift and return gift, being blessed and blessing. For Ælfric, the identity conferred upon Christians as children of God creates peace and unity between them:

---

81 Old English *halig*, holy, is part of a complex of words related to the ideal of wholeness: *hal* (whole, well, safe), *hælu* (health, safety, salvation), see BT. For the Indo-European root, see *kailo-* (whole, uninjured, of good omen) in the *American Heritage Dictionary*, Appendix I.

82 *CH* I.19, 328, ll. 76–9.

83 *CH* I.19, 328, ll. 75–6.

84 *CH* I.19, 326, ll. 30–1.

on eallum þingum we sceolon healdan sibbe and annysse. gif we wyllað habban þa micclan geþincþe. þæt we beon godes bearn se þe on heofenum is: on þære he rixað mid eallum his halgum. on eallra worulda woruld. AMEN.[85]

(in all things we should hold peace/kinship and unity if we wish to have the great privilege that we be God's children, he who is in heaven where he rules with all his saints through all ages. Amen.)

Here, Ælfric emphasizes the particular relationship between Christians and God that is manifested through prayer and enacted as people cry out to Christ as brother and to God as father. Certain obligations go along with belonging to this community, both to obey God and to realize one's fundamental equality with other believers and thus one's obligations towards them. In fact, this relationship has, for Ælfric, real social implications for the members of a community constituted by and built upon the continual reiteration of the central Christian prayer:

ealle cristene men ægðer ge rice. ge heane. ge æþelborene ge unæþelborene. 7 se hlaford 7 se þeowa ealle hi sind gebroðra … Nis se welega na betera on þysum naman þonne se þearfa; Ealswa bealdlice mot se þeowa clypian god him to fæder ealswa se cyning; ealle we sind gelice ætforan gode."[86]

(all Christians, whether rich or poor, noble-born or common, the lord and the slave, all are brothers … The wealthy is not better for this sake than the needy. The slave can just as boldly call God his father as the king. We are all alike before God.)

In contrast, in Augustine's explication of Matthew 6 in *De sermone Domini* he primarily focuses on the cleansing of the heart through prayer and almsgiving, and situates prayer within the privacy of a person's heart.[87] Augustine defines cleansing of the heart as what happens as one's motives become rightly aligned, when one does what one does for the praise of God rather than other people:

---

85 *CH* I.19, 334, ll. 240–3.

86 *CH* I.19, 326, ll. 40–5.

87 "VOS AVTEM CVM ORATIS, *inquit, INTROITE IN CVBICVLA VESTRA.* Quae sunt ista cubicula nisi ipsa corda" (*But when you pray*, he says, *go into your bedrooms.* What are those bedrooms if not our very hearts?), CCSL 35, 101, ll. 233–4; trans. WSA I/15, 74.

> Pertinet ergo ad oculum mundum non intueri in recte faciendo laudes hominum et ad eas referre quod recte facis, id est propterea recte facere aliquid, ut hominibus placeas. Sic enim etiam simulare bonum libebit, si non adtenditur nisi ut homo laudet, qui quoniam uidere cor non potest, potest etiam falsa laudare. Quod qui faciunt, id est qui bonitatem simulant, duplici corde sunt. Non ergo habet simplex cor, id est mundum cor, nisi qui transcendit humanas laudes et illum solum intuetur, cum recte uiuit, et ei placere nititur qui conscientiae solus inspector est.[88]
>
> (It pertains to the pure eye, then, to disregard people's praises in doing what is right and not to draw their attention to the good that you do, in other words, to do something so as to win people's approval. For even the pretence of doing good will be appealing when all that is sought is the praise of a person who, because he is unable to look into the heart, can even praise things that are false. Those who behave in this manner, by feigning goodness, have a divided heart. And so no one possesses an undivided heart, that is, a pure heart, unless he transcends human praise, fixes his gaze on him alone when he leads an upright life, and endeavors to please him who alone scrutinizes the conscience.)

For Augustine, the secrecy of spiritual practice clarifies motive, but it also creates the self in relationship to God alone, as the one "looks at him only." The inward nature of the heart and incorporeal nature of desire give it natural affinity with the spiritual realm. Through these associations, he links the sacred with the private and interior parts of the person.[89] The theory of prayer presented forms a self imagined as open to the Divine gaze in the privacy of its heart. Although in this passage Augustine assumes social agreement on the "good," he faults people whose sense of the "good"

---

88 CCSL 35, 92, ll. 24–33; trans. WSA I/15, 69.

89 "Parum est intrare in cubicula, si ostium pateat inportunis, per quod ostium ea quae foris sunt inprobe se inmergunt et interiora nostra appetunt … Claudendum est ergo ostium, id est carnali sensui resistendum est, ut oratio spiritalis dirigatur ad patrem, quae fit in intimis cordis, ubi oratur pater in abscondito" (It is of little consequence to go into bedrooms if the door is left open for intruders, for the things on the outside burst through the door with abandon and seek out our innermost recesses … The door must therefore be kept closed – that is, we must resist the fleshly senses so that a spiritual prayer which comes into being in the inner recesses of the heart, where we pray to the Father in secret, may be directed to the Father), CCSL 35, 101–2, ll. 237–40, 243–6; WSA I/15, 74.

is formed by communal praise. Thus, he creates room for people to develop a sense of "goodness" apart from communal norms, although the new norms are not understood as a product of the individual. Augustine emphasizes prayer's subjective efficacy upon the individual precator as the discipline of praying retrains desire.[90]

Augustine does explicate "Our Father," the opening words of the Paternoster, to teach that all Christians should treat each other as brothers.[91]

90 "Fit ergo in oratione conuersio cordis ad eum qui semper dare paratus est, si nos capiamus quod dederit, et in ipsa conuersione purgatio interioris oculi" (A movement of the heart, therefore, takes place in prayer towards the one who is always prepared to give, provided that we are disposed to receive what he gives, and within that very movement there occurs a purification of the inner eye), CCSL 35, 104, ll. 290–2; trans. WSA I/15, 75.

91 "Admonentur hic etiam diuites uel genere nobiles secundum saeculum, cum christiani facti fuerint, non superbire aduersus pauperes et ignobiles, quoniam simul dicunt deo: pater noster, quod non possunt uere ac pie dicere, nisi se fratres esse cognoscant" (The rich and those who are wellborn are warned here [in the salutation], once they have become Christians, not to behave arrogantly to the poor and those of lowly birth, because they all say *our Father* together, which they cannot honestly and piously say if they do not recognize one another as brothers), CCSL 35, 107, ll. 358–62; trans. WSA I/15, 76–7. Augustine's commentary is, in fact, the earliest one that contains the idea as fully formulated as this, although Cyprian discusses the meaning of the plural pronoun used throughout the prayer (more on this later). The same idea is found in two of Augustine's sermons, neither of which give the weight to it that Ælfric does: Sermo 58: "Dicimus autem communiter: *Pater noster.* Quanta dignatio! Hoc dicit imperator, hoc dicit mendicus; hoc dicit seruus, hoc dicit dominus eius. Simul dicunt: *Pater noster, qui es in caelis.* Intellegant ergo se esse fratres, quando unum habent patrem. Sed non dedignetur fratrem habere seruum suum dominus eius, quem fratrem uoluit habere Dominus Christus" (Now we say *Our Father* all together; what all-embracing generosity! The emperor says it, the beggar says it; the slave says it, his master says it. They all say together, *Our Father who art in heaven*. So they must realize that they are brothers, since they all have one Father. The master must not scorn to have as a brother the slave of his whom the Lord Christ was willing to have as a brother), CCSL 41Aa, 200, ll. 22–8; trans. Hill, WSA III/3, 118, 2. Sermo 59: "Ad magnum genus pertinere coepistis. Sub isto Patre fratres sunt diues et pauper, sub isto Patre fratres sunt dominus et seruus, sub isto Patre fratres sunt imperator et miles. Omnes christiani fideles diuersos in terra habent patres, alii nobiles, alii ignobiles; unum uero Patrem inuocant, qui est in caelis" (You have begun to belong to a huge family. Under this Father rich and poor are brothers; under this Father master and slave are brothers; under this Father emperor and private soldier are brothers. Christian believers all have different fathers on earth, some aristocrats, some commoners. But they all call upon one Father who is in heaven), CCSL 41Aa, 2, ll. 14–18; trans. *Sermons*, 9.2.

In so doing, he echoes Cyprian's earlier explication of the Paternoster in his treatise on the prayer. Cyprian presents the Paternoster as a "public and common" prayer on the basis of the plural pronouns used throughout. Ælfric also builds on this idea; however, he uses it to bracket the homily with an appeal to "sibb" (peace, family bonds) dependent on God as father and Christ as brother of all. Ælfric says: "Ne cwyð na on þam gebede. min fæder. þu ðe eart on heofonum. ac cwyþ ure fæder ... On þam is geswutelod hu swiðe god lufað annysse. 7 geþwærnysse on his folce"[92] (It is not said in the prayer, "My Father, you who are in heaven," but it is said, "Our Father" ... In this is revealed how much God loves unity and concord in his people). While Cyprian follows the passage above with a catena of biblical quotations developing this theme, Ælfric moves on into the metaphor of the human body from I Corinthians 12: "Æfter godes gesetnysse ealle cristene men sceoldon beon swa geþwære. swilce hit an man wære"[93] (According to God's decree all Christians should be so united as though they were one man).

Thus Ælfric begins and ends the homily with an appeal to brotherhood and a statement that all Christians need each other; the rich especially need the poor.[94] The universality of God's fatherhood creates a communal identity encompassing all strata of society, and it creates an obligation to give on as well as give back. The brotherly bond has radical implications for the way different members of society treat each other, so that "ælc oþerne lufige swa swa hine sylfne. 7 nanum ne gebeode þæt he nelle þæt man him gebeode"[95] (each loves the other just as himself, and commands no one anything that he does not wish someone command him). Although Ælfric

92 *CH* I.19, 333, ll. 215–19. Cyprian: Non dicimus: *Pater meus, qui es in caelis* ... Publica est nobis et communis oratio, et quando oramus, non pro uno sed pro populo toto rogamus, quia totus populus unum sumus. Deus pacis et concordiae magister qui docuit unitatem, sic orare unum pro omnibus uoluit, quomodo in uno omnes ipse portauit" (For we say not "My Father, which art in heaven"... Our prayer is public and common; and when we pray, we pray not for one, but for the whole people, because we the whole people are one. The God of peace and the Teacher of concord, who taught unity, willed that one should thus pray for all, even as He Himself bore us all in one), *De dominica oratione*, in *Opera, pars II*, ed. C. Moreschini, CCSL 3A, 93, 8, ll. 103–9; trans. Ernest Wallis, "On the Lord's Prayer," ANF 5, 449, 8.

93 *CH* I.19, 333, ll. 219–21.

94 Godden, *Commentary*, points out that this passage owes nothing to Augustine.

95 *CH* I.19, 327, 49–51.

speaks of a fundamental equality of all Christians, clearly he does not envision a levelling of social roles. Rather, invoking God as father creates a stable identity, transmitted from one to another as people act towards each other with "soþan sibbe"[96] (true peace, but with the idea of peace based on kinship), enacting true kinship bonds that, as we will see in *CH* I.18, he characterizes through the mutual exchange of gifts and services.

Alms: CH I.18

In the context of *CH* I.18 prayer is connected to almsgiving in a fundamental way, but not in its standard association with the reorientation of desire as found in Augustinian teaching. Rather than making precators pure, prayer functions to place the precators in a particular relationship to God, his dependents and subordinates, who then enact that dependency and subordination through their persistence in turning to God with their petitions. The rich give alms to the poor, recognizing that they themselves are in the same dependent position upon God, modelling the treatment they would like to be shown. Prayer – the prayer of the poor for the rich – transforms the almsgiving relationship into a reciprocal one in which each party is essential for the salvation of the other. As people enact generosity towards each other in almsgiving and prayer, they in turn give back to God within a complex cycle of exchange, enacting a faith for which God will eventually give them eternal life. Almsgiving and prayer are not a personal matter between the petitioner and God in Ælfric's teaching, but rather a social matter binding together rich and poor in a community-wide statement of belief and a petition for salvation that moves a community towards wholeness.

Theorists of the gift often use alms (gifts given to help the poor) as an example of the free gift that proves there are no free gifts. Donors give alms out of no obligation to recipients with whom they have no particular ties[97] and from whom they expect no return. In fact, alms are as embedded

96 *CH* I.19, 327, l. 49.

97 That is, "charity" cannot be extended from a parent to a child (say), because the parent has an obligation to provide for the child. "Charity" given to friends usually termed by some other transaction (a gift, or a loan), given with the fiction (if not the fact) that it will be returned or the favour will be repaid.

in the economy as any other type of gift.[98] The giver often feels some sort of social pressure or obligation (even though it is not legal, relational, or enforceable) towards generosity. He gains in social capital[99] for this generosity, or (if the almsgiving is secret) at the least he gains the warm feeling of a deed well done to which so many modern-day charities appeal for donations.[100] On the recipient's side, there are often strings attached: that he be worthy of the charity he has been given (for instance, in a modern context, that he show willingness to work), and that he use well what he is given (no drugs!). Donors want to know their money is going to a worthy recipient, that it is "doing some good," or at least that it is not funding vice.[101]

Expressing a common sentiment in Western treatments of charity, Jonathan Parry says, "The unreciprocated gift debases the recipient."[102] But Parry misses the fact that this can only be so if the recipient is not "debased" to begin with. The recipient can only be debased if alms call attention to a pretence to equality or independence that is not, in fact, true, and if equality and independence is the desired state.[103] In some ways almsgiving most perfectly represents the relationship between God and humans:

---

98 As Jacques Derrida points, at the very least, donors expect gratitude, and perhaps social approbation, or at least a subjective sense of their own largesse or goodness in return, *Given Time I: Counterfeit Money*, trans. Peggy Kamuf (Chicago: University of Chicago Press, 1994), 11–14. In addition, in the case of direct donation there is always a "danger" (to the freeness of the gift) that a relationship will result; the recipient will come to expect alms; the donor will feel obliged to give them.

99 The term is from Bourdieu, *Logic of Practice*. As I noted in the introduction, I find problematic the way he subsumes all exchange back into the logic of markets and commodities through postulating different forms of "capital."

100 For Derrida the donor's self-acknowledgment returns to himself a "symbolic equivalent" of the gift, making the gift impossible, *Given Time*, 13.

101 Boniface Ramsey considers who the proper recipients of alms were in early Christian thinking, "Almsgiving in the Latin Church: The Late Fourth and Early Fifth Centuries," in *Theological Studies* 43.1 (1982), 230–3. The Christian position came to be that alms were to be given to all the needy on the basis of their humanity, although in practice some of the poor were seen as more worthy (or perhaps more needy) than others.

102 Jonathan Parry, "The Gift, the Indian Gift and the 'Indian Gift,'" in *Man* 21.3 (1986), 458.

103 That modern recipients of handouts are often ungrateful when they receive it illustrates Parry's point in "The Gift, the Indian Gift," that charity wounds the recipient. We all imagine ourselves equals, and charity – in its recognition that you, the recipient, do not need to pay me back (because you cannot) – challenges that fiction.

all gifts come freely from God to humans who have nothing. Humans have nothing with which to reciprocate since all they have (including life itself) comes from God. Humans are therefore God's beggars, his *mendici*,[104] his *þearfan*,[105] dependent on his charity but in no way able to approach intimacy of relationship with him. In fact, alms negate reciprocity and the relationship that ensues by calling attention to the disparity in situations between the donor and the recipient. In practice, the hierarchy alms establish between donor and needy calls attention to the inequality that exists between them. No return is expected because none can be made. Alms are *more* debasing to the recipient in a situation in which the recipient feels the social distance between the donor and himself is closer than the act of almsgiving implies. In a firmly hierarchical society, where the poor have no expectations of becoming the social peers of the rich, the inequality that alms call attention to is already accepted. If recipients already know themselves to be needy, and dependence carries no particular stigma, alms merely acknowledge recognized need. Yet almsgiving is an understanding of the relationship between God and humans that Anglo-Saxon teaching on prayer tends to resist. Because of *gratia* in Bede and the closely related concept of *agen cyre* and *gehyrsumness* in Ælfric, humans are able to enter into a reciprocal relationship with God in which they give God gifts for which he rewards them. But Ælfric's preaching on almsgiving also resists unidirectionality in the alms the rich give to the poor; he makes the poor full participants in reciprocity.

Alms not only feature in human social relationships, they also participate in the economy of salvation. As Boniface Ramsey's account of early almsgiving makes clear,[106] teaching on almsgiving in the early church rarely appealed to altruism (thus, it is not a "pure" gift), and it was quickly subsumed into a *do ut des* exchange in which alms are sacrificed to God (via the poor) for the cleansing of sins and salvation of the donor.[107] That is, the transaction that takes place can be seen as one essentially between the donor and God in which the poor are instrumental rather than essential partners. A passage from Augustine, which will be discussed more

104 Sermo 61, CCSL 41Aa, 268, l. 82.
105 *CH* I.18, 323, l. 179.
106 Ramsey, "Almsgiving."
107 Almsgiving could also be seen as the repayment of a debt to God. Ramsey quotes Augustine in this regard, "Almsgiving," 238.

fully momentarily, illustrates: "Magis eroga pecuniam, ut habeas iustitiam"[108] (disburse money in order to get justice). The "get" (*habeas*, have) is telling: the donor disburses to get, rather than disbursing to give justice.[109] However, expressing the Christian ideal of human equality, early Christian teachings on prayer often emphasize the way that the poor can also give alms, either to those less fortunate than themselves or through acts of service to the wealthy, such as helping stranded travellers.[110] This levels some of the hierarchy built into almsgiving, although the primary exchange is still between the donor and God.

Again, the contrast between Augustine's approach to almsgiving in the sources Ælfric uses helps bring Ælfric's concerns into focus. For Augustine both prayer and almsgiving bring the practitioner to the purity necessary for salvation. Almsgiving, then, is essentially a matter between the one giving alms and God, but it is not a *do ut des* relationship, nor are alms conceptualized relationally. Rather, almsgiving is subsumed into the same concern for purity manifest in Augustine's teaching on prayer: giving alms for the praise of God rather than men leads to cleansing of the heart. Almsgiving is an important part of this cleansing: through almsgiving the individual demonstrates (and perhaps helps bring about) his detachment from the material world – a conception of the holy formed by ideas of *sanctus*. In *De sermone Domini* Augustine asks: "Simplex autem quomodo erit, si duobus dominis seruit, nec una intentione rerum aeternarum purificat aciem suam, sed eam mortalium quoque fragiliumque rerum amore obnubilat?"[111] (For how can [the heart] be undivided if it serves two masters and does not purify its vision by concentrating solely on eternal realities but instead obscures it with the love of those that are mortal and fragile?) Through giving secretly, as the Gospel commands, the one giving demonstrates his detachment both from material things and from the praise of

108 Sermo 61, CCSL 41Aa, 268, l. 80; trans. Hill, WSA III/3, 144, 4.

109 Arnold Angenendt et al. note the "much lamented medieval 'egotism of salvation': alms were given not out of love for the poor but out of a desire to assure oneself a place in heaven," "Counting Piety in the Early and High Middle Ages," in *Ordering Medieval Society: Perspectives on Intellectual and Practical Modes of Shaping Social Relations*, ed. Bernhard Jussen, trans. Pamela Selwyn (Philadelphia: University of Pennsylvania Press, 2001), 20. Note that this critique is brought by those within a modern economy who tend to understand reciprocity as transaction.

110 See Ramsey, "Almsgiving," 240.

111 CCSL 35, 100 , ll. 209–11; WSA I/15, 73.

men. Almsgiving shows that the one giving alms is not ruled by his own possessions, and it acts as a purificatory practice in training the eye of the heart to be single. In the end, what is given to God (if anything) is not the alms, but the purity.

Augustine's idea of alms thus resonates faintly with Derrida's idea of the pure gift.[112] In Derrida's thinking, a pure gift is one from which the giver gains nothing, not even praise or her own satisfied feeling. The main difference between alms in this passage and Derrida's pure gift[113] is that for Augustine detachment transfers the function of the alms from the mundane to the spiritual economy. Within the gift theories of sacrifice, this sort of transference is usually what differentiates a gift from a sacrifice.[114] However, for Augustine, the gift transferred to the spiritual realm has no function there. One does not, in this passage, give alms as a gift to God in return for purity or for salvation; one gives alms to people as a means of purification, which is understood to be as much a loss as it is a gain. The gift disappears, and all that is left is the pure eye of the heart (as Augustine puts it), an achieved state of affinity with or likeness to God, *ego* subsumed back into *Ego*. Thus, almsgiving brings about a change in the giver that leads to further ability to see God, but the alms themselves have no relational function binding together donor and recipient or even the giver and God. Augustine's treatment of alms is also is unlike anything Ælfric does.

In sermon 61 Augustine considers at some length the relationship Christians ought to have to material possessions: "Est ergo bonum quod faciat bonum; et est bonum unde facias bonum. Bonum quod facit, Deus est"[115] (So there is a good that can make good, and there's a good with which you can do good. The good that makes good is God). He then continues to develop a metaphor of trading one's goods for justice:

112 Perhaps because Augustine is thinking more in terms of Neoplatonic purity than in terms of exchange.

113 Aside from the fact that Augustine's alms would have some effect on the recipient, even if given in perfect secrecy.

114 Mauss, *The Gift: The Form and Reason for Exchange in Archaic Societies*, trans. W.D. Halls (New York: W.W. Norton, 1990), and Hubert and Mauss, *Sacrifice*, see sacrifice as essentially the same as the gift. The major difference is that it takes place within the unalterable hierarchy between gods and humans, and that certain procedures are necessary to transfer the thing given from the human realm into the divine.

115 Sermo 61, CCSL 41Aa, 266, ll. 49–50; trans. Hill, WSA III/3, 143, 61.3.

Magis eroga pecuniam, ut habeas iustitiam. A quo enim habebis iustitiam, nisi a Deo, fonte iustitiae? Ergo, si uis habere iustitiam, esto mendicus Dei, qui te paulo ante ex euangelio ut peteres, quaereres, pulsares monebat.[116]

(Rather, I'm telling you, disburse money in order to get justice. After all, whom will you get justice from if not from God the fountain of justice? So if you want to get some justice, be a beggar to God, who a little while ago was advising you in the gospel to ask, to seek, to knock.)

In Augustine's explication, almsgiving is primarily a matter between the giver and God; he emphasizes the ethical responsibility of the wealthy to care for the poor, but as far as righteousness (*iustitia*) is concerned, the goods given to the poor become part of an exchange between the wealthy and God.

Ælfric follows Augustine's major points fairly closely; however, as in *CH* I.19, he reorients the alms-mediated relationship between people. The poor become essential partners in the exchange. Although Ælfric does not use the term "ælmesse" in this homily, the rich giving to the needy is a central concept. As we have seen, alms are an important part of petitionary practice; sometimes, as in Augustine's commentary, they are associated with purificatory practices, and sometimes, as here, they are presented as part of an exchange relationship with God. But Ælfric's explication of Luke 11:5–13 primarily emphasizes the unidirectionality of God's gifts. While in both parables the petitioner asks within a pre-existing relationship, in both cases the petitioner asks his *ben* (petition) without apparently appealing to or offering anything in return. Ælfric emphasizes this: "þy he cwæð na for freondrædene. for ðan þe nan mann nære wurðe ne ðæs geleafan. ne ðæs ecan lifes gif godes mildheortnys nære ðe mare. ofer mancynne"[117] (So he says, "Not for friendship," because no one is worthy of the faith nor eternal life if God's mercy were not the greater over mankind). Ælfric uses the unidirectionality of God's gifts to make the point that "Ealle we sind godes þearfan"[118] (We are all God's needy). That is, because God's gifts are unidirectional rather than reciprocal, the relationship between humans and God is one in which humans are dependent upon

116 CCSL 41Aa, 268, ll. 80–3; trans. Hill, WSA III/3, 144, 4.
117 *CH* I.18, 320, ll. 89–92.
118 *CH* I.18, 323, l. 179.

God's alms as beggars, having no particular claim upon him and able to offer him nothing in exchange. Every gift springs from God's unconstrained generosity – an appropriately Augustinian idea for a sermon based on Augustinian sources.

Yet Ælfric presents a model of exchange, again following Augustine, in which humans *do* return gifts to God, through almsgiving and prayer. Ælfric uses the point that "we are all God's needy" to remind the wealthy that they are obliged to hear the petitions of the poor who ask of them, if they want God to hear their own petitions: "Uton for ðy oncnawan þa þearfan þe us biddað: þæt god oncnawe us. þonne we hine biddað ure neode"[119] (Let us therefore acknowledge the needy who petition us so that God may acknowledge us when we ask him for our needs). In this model of almsgiving Ælfric does not appeal to any idea of purification or disassociation from the material world;[120] instead he appeals to the sense of brotherhood, and reminds his hearers that because God gives in response to prayer, they should also give: "Hu mihtu for sceame. æniges þinges æt gode biddan: gif ðu forwyrnst þinum gelican. þæs þe ðu foreaðelice him getiðian miht"[121] (How can you for shame ask anything from God if you refuse those like you that which you could easily grant them?).

Augustine solves the potential problem of transactionality in prayer by downplaying any return on the part of the needy. In so doing, he avoids suggesting that the poor could therefore give anything to God that would predispose his favour through the analogy that the poor are like all humans,

119 *CH* I.18, 323, ll. 179–81. Augustine says, "Mendici enim Dei sumus: ut agnoscat ille mendicos suos, agnoscamus et nos nostros" (We are God's beggars, remember; for him to take notice of his beggars, we in our turn must take notice of ours), Sermo 61, CCSL 41Aa, 270, ll. 130–1; trans. Hill, WSA III/3, 145, 8.

120 Ælfric quotes Augustine on attitudes towards wealth later: "Oþer is þæt hwa rice beo. gif his yldran him æhta becwædon: oðer is gif hwa þurh gitsunge. rice gewurðe; Ðises mannes gitsung is gewreht wið gode: Na þæs oðres æht" (It is one thing that one is rich if his parents left him possessions; it is another thing if one becomes rich through greed. This person's greed is accused before God, not the other's possessions), *CH* I.18, 324, ll. 196–9. For both Augustine and Ælfric, greed is sinful, not wealth. For Augustine, the condemnation of greed furthers the goal of material disengagement. For Ælfric, the imperative to give is created because it is disgraceful to hoard possessions. In neither case do they appeal to "pure" love for the poor. Human need is an assumed constant, something that all the giving in the world will never fully eradicate; therefore, the emphasis is on not keeping or consuming more than one ought rather than on eradicating poverty. See Ramsey, "Almsgiving," 255.

121 *CH* I.18, 323, ll. 184–5.

the rich like God. That his metaphor is not perfect in the details can be seen in comparison with the non-personal way he imagines alms functioning in *De sermone Domini*, discussed above. Furthermore, the exchange metaphor involves a little finessing on Augustine's part to clarify that he is not suggesting that people can buy justice from God. This can be seen in the way he switches the terms of the exchange in the passage above: justice comes from begging God for it – a petition in which the precator himself has nothing to offer– not, ultimately, from giving away one's goods.[122]

Ælfric, however, addresses the problem of transactionality by turning the mundane economy of its head: the prayers of the poor are worth more than the alms of the rich. In so doing, he does not present the needy as having nothing of their own to offer the rich in return for their alms. Rather,

> Se rica 7 se þearfa sind him betwynan nydbehefe; se welega is geworht for ðan þearfan. 7 se þearfa for ðam welegan. þam spedigum gedafenaþ þæt he spende 7 dæle. þam wædlan gedafenað þæt he gebidde for ðam dælere; Se earma is se weig. þe læt us to godes rice. Mare sylð se þearfa þam rican: þonne he æt him nime.[123]
>
> (The rich and the needy are necessary to each other. The wealthy is made for the needy, and the needy for the wealthy. It is fitting for the prosperous that he give and distribute; for the poor it is fitting that he pray for the giver. The poor man is the road that allows us into God's kingdom. The needy gives more to the rich than he takes from him.)[124]

---

122 Here one can see clearly the way that almsgiving and prayer are often collapsed into essentially the same thing. Although Augustine's sermon does not put almsgiving into the clear context of purity, as he does in his *Tractatus* 3 on John, the same idea of lessening one's attachment to material possessions still underlies his discussion. The *Tractates*, in fact, reflect much more obviously Neoplatonic terminology and ways of thinking in common with much of Augustine's early work. In Augustine's later work, the concept of *iustitia* (justice, justification) gains in importance. See Alister E. McGrath, *Iustitia Dei: A History of the Christian Doctrine of Justification*, 3rd ed. (Cambridge: Cambridge University Press, 2005), 39. All *iustitia* comes ultimately from God.

123 *CH* I.18, 324, ll. 205–9.

124 Jonathan Wilcox, "Rewriting Ælfric: An Alternative Ending of a Rogationtide Homily," in *Leeds Studies in English* n.s. 37 (2006), looks at a marginal notation to this homily in MS Cambridge, Trinity College, B. 15. 34, that he argues is an alternative ending that softens Ælfric's call that the rich should redistribute their wealth.

Ælfric's choice of pronoun ("us") reflects his perspective (or that of his congregation) as among those who give.[125] The poor for Ælfric are not merely recipients of goods in a transaction that does not fundamentally involve them. Instead, they reciprocate by praying for the wealthy – an action Ælfric calls more valuable than the material provision. In this way, the poor are set up as intercessors for the rich to petition on their behalf for entry to the kingdom.[126] They are essential participants in the gift cycle instead of (as in Augustine's teaching) instruments in the relationship between the rich and God.

Ælfric's idea of the righteousness or goodness that almsgiving brings has little in common with Augustine's idea of purity, or even with Augustine's ideas of almsgiving as laid out in these sermons; rather, as in *CH* I.19, he envisions goodness as a sort of communal wholeness, a right use of goods to create and maintain relationships, where every person has a role to play in ensuring the welfare, both material and spiritual of his "equals," those "like him" (i.e., human). This shifts the emphasis from Augustine's sermons, in which the central relationship is God and the wealthy almsgiver.[127] For Augustine, the acts of generosity the almsgiver performs are

---

125 Yet it should not be assumed that Ælfric himself was from the highest levels of society, as Wilcox notes, in "Use of Ælfric's Homilies," 367. Furthermore, congregations for preaching would have been composed of "just about everybody," people from all walks of life, 367. It is possible that Ælfric's language reflects that of his source, but it is also possible that Ælfric wants all Christians to think of themselves as "rich," having something to give. Indeed, Augustine makes just this point (see Ramsey, "Almsgiving," 235), and Ælfric, in *CH* II.7, a Lenten homily on almsgiving, states specifically, "Nis nan ðearfa fram ælmesdædum ascyred" (no one poor is freed from almsdeeds), 64, ll. 115–16. Because almsdeeds "wash away" the sins of the givers, Ælfric's statement that even the poor can give them is intended to be reassuring and to give value even to small gifts.

126 This idea is not found in Augustine, but it can be found in Paulinus of Nola and a sermon by Maximus; see Ramsey, "Almsgiving," 248–9. It is also in some Greek sources that Ælfric is unlikely to have known, namely, the Shepherd of Hermas and Clement's *Stromata*. See Origen, *Origen's Treatise on Prayer*, trans. Eric George Jay (rprnt. Eugene, OR: Wipf and Stock, 2010), 12.

127 *CH* II. 7 also gives an extended discussion of almsgiving within the context of Lenten fasting. In that homily (largely adapted from a pseudo-Augustinian sermon, although the ideas are quite standard for teaching on alms, as Ramsey's article, "Almsgiving," makes clear) Ælfric largely concentrates on the dyadic exchange relationship between the giver and God, focusing on the reasons to give and the rewards for giving. However, he reorients the hierarchy: in his homily the poor are closer to God, who calls them "my poor" ("mine ðearfan," 63, l. 82); Ælfric also quotes Christ saying that those who help the poor help him (adapting Matthew 25), 63. The rich are entrusted with

done essentially in the sight of God, whereas for Ælfric, the prayers of the poor serve as testimony to the deeds of the rich. Their prayers mediate the good deeds of the rich, in the process adding meaning to them.

In addition to bonding people together, however, the cyclical nature of the exchange creates a deferral that keeps gifts separate from commodities: the rich do not trade their wealth to God for salvation, nor do the poor trade their prayers. Rather, the gift binds everyone together within a web of reciprocal generosity and the joy of the gift. Because gifts and return gifts are never fully commensurate and equal, the gift cycle creates imbalances of debt and obligation rather than the zero-sum balance found in either commodity exchange or the free gift that dissolves relationships. At the same time, everyone has something to give. All are God's *þearfan* (needy, beggars), but none are quite destitute in the human economy. The non-commensurate nature of gift exchange, where the things given are never quite the same as the things received in return, creates productive space between gift and counter-gift in which relationships can form through ties of mutual obligation and gratitude. Because of this, the whole human community is necessary to one another, moving together towards salvation.

Prayer and the Person: *Catholic Homily* I.10

Catholic Homilies I.18 and I.19 both use Augustinian sources, both teach about prayer within the context of the praying community, and Ælfric wrote both for a time of year when a large lay congregation would have been present. In contrast, in *CH* I.10 Ælfric uses a Gregorian source that places prayer in a penitential context, and wrote it for the season just before Lent.[128] *CH* I.10, then, might presumably present prayer with more emphasis on the individual and on purity, and perhaps give a greater sense

wealth in order to distribute it (62, ll. 70–1) and to test them, and as I noted above, each Christian is to think of himself or herself as having something to give. Furthermore, Ælfric appeals to the fact that all things are God's and given by God as creating the moral imperative to give on (62–3, ll. 72–82).

128 See Godden, *Commentary*, 77. He notes that Ælfric follows Gregory's development but seems to have occasionally found the wording in an adaptation by Haymo of Auxerre helpful. It is also possible that he is using a lost Anglo-Saxon adaptation of Gregory's sermon. In comparing Ælfric to Gregory, I am not arguing that Ælfric's adaptations are fully original; rather, that a comparison between the two helps their differing preoccupations stand out the more clearly.

of prayer's subjective efficacy. Thus, in depicting a penitent person praying for God's help, *CH* I.10 is in some ways Ælfric's counterpart to Bede's Homily 1.22.[129] However, in this homily, while Gregory preaches on the subjective efficacy of perseverance in prayer to enlighten the mind, Ælfric emphasizes prayer's objective ability to catch Jesus's attention and cause him to drive temptation from the mind. For Ælfric, prayer's efficacy does not reside in its disciplinary practice, which reforms the human heart. Rather, it works through the direct intervention of God in response to the precators' request. Although he uses the imagery of blindness and light from Gregory's homily, he does so in a way that disrupts the Neoplatonic imagery Gregory develops, replacing it with a more concrete sense of life as exile from the kingdom of heaven. Thus, Ælfric's homily presents a much more concretely relational view of prayer.

The source, Gregory's Homily 2,[130] is on Luke 18:35–43. The passage begins with Jesus foretelling his death and resurrection to his disciples, but then continues to tell of a blind man healed as they travel on the road to Jericho. Gregory allegorizes the passage in such a way that the blind man becomes a pattern for penitential Christian prayer. The homilies interact closely with the passage, so I quote it here:

> Factum est autem cum adpropinquaret Hiericho caecus quidam sedebat secus viam mendicans. Et cum audiret turbam praetereuntem interrogabat quid hoc esset. Dixerunt autem ei quod Iesus Nazarenus transiret. Et clamavit dicens, Iesu Fili David miserere mei. Et qui praeibant increpabant eum ut taceret ipse vero multo magis clamabat: Fili David miserere mei. Stans autem Iesus iussit illum adduci ad se, et cum adpropinquasset interrogavit illum dicens, quid tibi vis faciam? At ille dixit, Domine ut videam. Et Iesus dixit, illi respice fides tua te salvum fecit. Et confestim vidit et sequebatur illum magnificans Deum. Et omnis plebs ut vidit dedit laudem Deo.[131]
>
> (Now it came to pass, when he drew nigh to Jericho, that a certain blind man sat by the way side, begging. And when he heard the multitude passing by, he asked what this meant. And they told him that Jesus of Nazareth was passing

129 Ælfric also has a homily on the gentile woman who asks for healing of her demon-possessed daughter, but it is not Bedan and does not deal with prayer.

130 CCSL 141, 12–19; trans. as Homily 13 by David Hurst, *Gregory the Great: Forty Gospel Homilies* (Kalamazoo: Cistercian Publications, 1990).

131 Luke 18:35–43.

by. And he cried out, saying: Jesus, son of David, have mercy on me. And they that went before, rebuked him, that he should hold his peace: but he cried out much more: Son of David, have mercy on me. And Jesus standing, commanded him to be brought unto him. And when he was come near, he asked him, saying: What wilt thou that I do to thee? But he said: Lord, that I may see. And Jesus said to him: Receive thy sight: thy faith hath made thee whole. And immediately he saw, and followed him, glorifying God. And all the people, when they saw it, gave praise to God.)

Gregory interprets the blind man as the human race, blinded by sin. The crowd that tries to silence him are those of the "desideriorum carnalium"[132] (bodily desires) and "vitia" (vices) that "voces cordis in oratione perturbant" (confuse what we say in our hearts as we pray). Gregory, of course, spiritualizes Jesus's healing of the blind man: he is made able to participate in the "eternal light."

Gregory's treatment of prayer and penance is much more psychological than is usually found in explications of the Paternoster or in Ælfric's other treatments of prayer. Like Augustine's *Tractatus*, discussed in chapter 2 as one of Bede's sources, Neoplatonic patterns and symbolism clearly influence it, in this case through the opposition of the visible/material/transitory versus the invisible/spiritual/eternal and through the imagery of light and sight.[133] Gregory's homily also shows interest in the interior work of penitential prayer. Key to this prayer's efficacy is persistence,

132 CCSL 141, 14, l. 41. Unattributed translations of Gregory's homilies in this chapter are my own.

133 For instance: " … dum diuinitas defectum nostrae carnis suscepit, humanum genus lumen quod amiserat recepit. Vnde enim Deus humana patitur, inde homo ad diuina subleuatur" (… when a divine person undertook the weakness of the body the human race recovered the light that it had lost. God suffered as a human being, and humans are raised up to divinity), CCSL 141, 13, ll. 25–7; trans. Hurst, 95. And "haec ipsa quae sentit non per corpus sed per animam cogitat … Ex inuisibili anima uisibile regitur corpus. Si auferatur quod est inuisibile, protinus corruit hoc quod uisibile stare uidebatur. Ex inuisibili ergo substantia in hac uita uisibili uiuitur" (There are things we understand by reflecting on them not through the body but through the soul … Our visible body is ruled by an invisible soul. If what is invisible be taken away, what was visible and appeared to be lasting immediately perishes. We live in this visible life on account of an invisible substance), CCSL 141, 17, ll. 116–21; trans. Hurst, 98. And, "quia rerum corporalium delectatione a gaudio interno cecidimus, cum qua amaritudine illuc redeatur ostendit" (Because we had fallen away from inner joy by our delight in material things, he showed with what bitterness we must return to it), CCSL 141, 18, ll. 145–7; trans. Hurst, 99.

which overcomes the crowds of "desideriorum carnalium"[134] (bodily desires) that disturb the thoughts and muddle the words in the precator's heart as he prays. Gregory presents the penitential self as potentially divided, desiring to "be converted," but bothered by the images of sin:

> Saepe namque dum conuerti ad Deum post perpetrata uitia uolumus, dum contra haec eadem exorare uitia quae perpetrauimus conamur, occurrunt cordi phantasmata peccatorum quae fecimus, mentis nostrae aciem reuerberant, confundunt animum et uocem nostrae deprecationis premunt ... in ipsa nos nostra oratione conturbant.[135]
>
> (We often wish to be converted to the Lord when we have committed some wrong. When we try to pray earnestly against the wrongs we have committed, images of our sins come into our hearts. They obscure our inner vision, they disturb our minds and overwhelm the sound of our petition ... and throw us into confusion in the very act of praying.)

Persistence eventually brings it about that "ad orationis opus conuertimur"[136] (we are turned to the work of prayer), when the vices the precator used to enjoy now seem burdensome. Persisting in prayer performs the work of prayer by fixing Christ in the heart of the one praying: "Cum uero orationi uehementer insistimus, stat Iesus ... quia Deus in corde figitur ..."[137] (when we persist ardently in prayer, Jesus stands, because God is fixed in the heart). Once Christ is fixed in the heart, he can then be followed or imitated. This adds up to an understanding of the work of prayer that associates the spiritual realm with the unchanging divine and the material realm with the changeable human. Perseverance is thus, for Gregory,

---

134 CCSL 141, 14, l. 41.

135 CCSL 141, 14, ll. 44–9, 51–2; trans. Hurst, 96. Also, Gregory later presents a potential objection "our unspiritual mind" might make to the prominence he gives the soul, as though people have spiritual minds through which they understand the truth, and unspiritual minds that lead to confused objections, 98.

136 CCSL 141, 15, l. 64.

137 CCSL 141, 15, ll. 73–4. Additionally: "Ecce quem turba increpat ut taceat magis ac magis clamabat, quia quanto grauiori tumultu cogitationum carnalium premimur, tanto orationi insistere ardentius debemus" (Lo, how the one the crowd rebuked that he be silent cried out the more, because the more we are pressed by the burdensome tumult of our fleshly thoughts, the more we must ardently persist in prayer), CCSL 141, 14, ll. 54–7.

an essential part of prayer's work insofar as it enables the precator to "fix" Christ in his heart, stabilizing the heart and allowing it to take part in the unchangeable nature of the divine.

For Gregory, the governing tension between the permanence and immutability of the divine/spiritual versus the transitory nature of the mundane world can also be seen when he considers the significance of Jesus's passing by the blind man on the way to Jericho and his standing still to heal him. As Gregory explicates it, Jesus's passing is his taking on of human flesh, thereby entering into this transitory world. The fact that Jesus took on human flesh allows him to hear the cry of the blind man and have pity on him. But Jesus's standing still represents the immutable nature of his divine power through which he is able to heal the blind and bring about spiritual sight of the eternal light.

In Gregory's homily, prayer and the struggle it potentially involves occurs within the heart, as though the heart is its own kind of space that can be occupied either by vices or by Jesus; that is, it can be aligned either with the physical world or with the spiritual. The heart has a voice, and this "uox cordis" used in persistent prayer partially determines who eventually occupies the heart. But the agency portrayed is ambiguous. Gregory presents the precator as active, needing to firmly persist in prayer to overcome the clamorous crowds of vices. In this sense, prayer seems to be subjectively efficacious; the discipline of prayer itself reforms the one praying, in part because this persistence repudiates the changeableness of the human condition and replicates the stability of the spiritual world the precator aims for.

But Gregory also recognizes that people need help outside themselves to be converted to the spiritual condition; they need to be "conuerti ad Deum" (converted, or turned to God). This mixed agency is portrayed in the active/passive combination of verbs: "dum ab hoc mundo animum ad Deum mutamus, dum ad orationis opus conuertimur"[138] (when we remove the soul from this world to God, then we are turned to the work of prayer). "We" actively change or move the soul from this world to God, but then "we" are passively turned to prayer. Within that *mutans* Gregory emphasizes the nature of human mutability accompanying mortality, both through the necessity of change resulting from the human condition and the need to change to a more spiritual (hence, stable) condition.

138 CCSL 141, 15, 4, ll. 63–4.

Changeableness constrains humans; they can turn to God, but (because of their mortality) they cannot fix themselves in this turning; they must turn their minds to God, but they must also be fixed.[139] They can persist, but Christ must come into their hearts: "Sed cum in oratione nostra uehementer insistimus, transeuntem Iesum figimus[140] (But when in our prayers we earnestly pursue Jesus, who is passing by, we fix him [in place]). Elsewhere in the homily, Gregory refers to this as "homo ad diuina subleuatur"[141] (humans are raised to divinity). Thus, for Gregory, prayer must be "of the heart." His emphasis here is not on sincerity, or even on a particular type of emotional affect, but on the heart's potential affinity with the spiritual realm. Prayer – true, efficacious prayer – for Gregory, then, is "of the heart"; it communicates with the spiritual realm because it potentially partakes in those same spiritual characteristics.

Ælfric's homily closely follows Gregory's structure and adopts much of his language. However, he consistently makes small shifts to Gregory's ideas so that the Neoplatonic contrasts that organize Gregory's homily become residual rather than central.[142] Ælfric uses the passage of Jesus standing still, but without attaching it to the idea of fixing God in the heart, a concept he drops entirely. He disassociates the material world and the vices and moves the "location" of prayer from the heart to the voice. He also makes the precator more active in praying for Christ's help, and Christ's aid in overcoming temptation more direct. As part of this, he once again adds the devil to his discussion of prayer.[143]

---

139 This is in line with Gregory's view of grace and human will, which is more active than the Augustinian view. See Kleist, *Striving with Grace*, chapter 2.

140 CCSL 141, 15, ll. 69–70.

141 "quia dum diuinitas defectum nostrae carnis suscepit, humanum genus lumen quod amiserat recepit. Vnde enim Deus humana patitur, inde homo ad diuina subleuatur" (because when divinity took up the weakness of our flesh the human race received the light which it had lost. When God shares in humanity, then humans are raised to divinity), CCSL 141, 13, ll. 25–7.

142 See, for instance, the passages explaining Christ's passing and his standing still, the relationship between the soul and the body, and the nature of the spiritual light. Each of these reproduces Gregory fairly faithfully but without connecting the smaller parts into a greater whole.

143 It is not that Gregory excludes the devil on principle. According to Aulén, "In Gregory the Great the classic idea of the Atonement [ransom theory] finds vigorous expression. He pictures the drama of redemption in lurid colours. Many realistic and even grotesque images had been employed in the previous centuries to illustrate this theme, but Gregory outdoes all his predecessors," *Christus Victor*, 40–1. An example

Consequently, Ælfric's idea of prayer is not informed by the same framework as Gregory's. So, for instance, rather than moving from the significance of the name Jericho to the idea of divinization, as Gregory does, Ælfric entirely drops the idea. Later on in the homily, Gregory states "et quia rerum corporalium delectatione a gaudio interno cecidimus, cum qua amaritudine illuc redeatur ostendit"[144] (And because we were cut off from internal joy by delight in corporeal things, he showed with what bitterness we should return to it). Ælfric instead says, "Nis þeos woruld na ure ęþel: ac is ure wræcsið; for ði ne sceole we na besettan urne hiht on ðisum swicelum life: Ac sceolon efstan mid godum geearnungum to urum eðele. þær we to gesceapene wæron. þæt is to heofonanrice"[145] (This world is not our homeland, but it is our exile. Therefore, we should not set our hope in this deceitful life, but we must with good deeds return to our homeland for which we were created, that is, to the heavenly kingdom), thereby replacing the tension between material and spiritual with the idea of exile and the desire to return home.[146]

Thus, when we move to the passage on the psychology of temptation, we are not quite moving within the same cosmology as in Gregory's sermon. This is evident immediately when Ælfric replaces Gregory's "desideriorum carnalium" and "tumultus vitiorum"[147] (bodily desires and crowds of vices) with "unlustas" and "leahtras"[148] (evil pleasures and crimes), moving away from the association of the fleshly with evil to that which is more generally forbidden (*un-*). The heart is involved but does not fill the same role as the site of communication with the spiritual realm. For Ælfric, the vices occupy the heart; Jesus never promises to do so. For Gregory, Jesus is the eventual occupant; the crowds of vices do not occupy the heart itself, but their images disturb it (obscure its inner vision, disturb the mind). Gregory's vices interfere with the words of prayer; Ælfric's interfere with

of Gregory's treatment of the ransom theory can be found in Homily 25, CCSL 141, for Easter Day. He also has passages considering the devil's role in the psychology of temptation. See, for instance, the *Moralia in Iob, Libri I–X*, ed. M. Adriaen, CCSL 143, 4.27.49.

144 CCSL 141, 18, ll. 145–7.

145 *CH* I.10, 264, ll. 161–4.

146 Blickling II also does this. By this point in Ælfric's homily he has moved further away from Gregory. The idea of this life as exile is also patristic; the point here, however, is Ælfric's selection of ideas.

147 CCSL 141, 14, ll. 41–2.

148 *CH* I.10, 260, l. 69.

zealousness in prayer. Whereas Gregory's soul "conuertimur" (is turned) to the work of prayer, Ælfric's precator *wishes* to turn: he "wyle yfeles geswican: 7 his synna gebetan. 7 mid eallum mode to gode gecyrran"[149] (wishes to cease from evil and amend his sins, and with all his mind to turn to God). Christ responds to this desire more directly: "we scolon hryman swiðor 7 swiðor to ðam hælende þæt he todræfe þa yfelan costnunga fram ure heortan"[150] (we should cry more and more to the Savior, that he drive the evil temptations from our hearts). Through such changes Ælfric excises Gregory's theme of transitory versus stable, instead imagining a precator who directly calls on God for help, to whom God actively responds.

Ælfric's passage also contains the idea of perseverance, but his precators are more often told to "hryman swiðor" (cry more) to the Saviour. In Gregory's case, persistence in prayer matters; for Ælfric, it is something like volume. The change fits with the pattern in which Ælfric emphasizes the voice while Gregory emphasizes the heart. Furthermore, in Ælfric, the vices "gedrefað his mood 7 willað gestillan his stemne: þæt he to gode ne clypige"[151] (trouble his mind and wish to still his voice so that he cannot call to God), a more direct appeal to God's aid than in Gregory, who, at the same point, emphasizes the act of praying that the vices crowd out: "uocem nostrae deprecationis premunt"[152] (crowd out the voice of our petition).

Ælfric also introduces the devil as the agent of trouble, setting him up as Jesus's opponent. He says his hearers should cry out for help like the blind man "gif us deoful drecce mid mænigfealdum geþohtum. 7 costnungum"[153] (if the devil afflicts us with manifold thoughts and temptations). Jesus's aid at once gains victory for him over the devil, and victory for the precator over the thoughts and temptations that trouble him. Thus, prayer more directly appeals to God – loudly appeals – who will "todræfe þa yfelan costnunga fram ure heortan"[154] (drive the evil temptations from our hearts). God responds by rescuing the precator, playing a more active and direct role than in Gregory, for whom the discipline of prayer itself seems to be an integral part, as it trains the heart in persistence, aligning it with spiritual stability.

149 *CH* I.10, 260, ll. 72–3.
150 *CH* I.10, 261, ll. 78–80.
151 *CH* I.10, 260–1, ll. 74–5.
152 CCSL 141, 14, ll. 48–9.
153 *CH* I.10, 261, ll. 77–8.
154 *CH* I.10, 261, ll. 79–80.

Still, Ælfric does leave room for the reorienting process of prayer. At the end of the passage, he says, "Gif we þonne þurhwuniað on urum gebedum. þonne mage we gedon mid urum hreame þæt se hælend stent"[155] (If we then persevere in our prayers we may bring about with our cry that the Savior stands), although once again, he focuses on the sound of the cries: Jesus "wyle gehyran ure clypunge"[156] (will hear our crying). Later, when he discusses why Jesus asked the blind man what he wanted, even though Jesus, being divine, already knew, Ælfric gives the standard Augustinian answer: "þurh þa gebedu. bið ure heorte onbryrd:· 7 gewend to gode"[157] (through prayer our heart is moved and turned to God). Gregory's answer is clearly in the same tradition and it shows the same shift in focus – "ad hoc requirit ut cor ad orationem excitet"[158] (to this end he questions, that the heart might be roused to prayer) – but one can see each authors' differing preoccupations again. Whereas Gregory emphasizes the process of prayer itself, Ælfric emphasizes turning directly to God: the relationship rather than the discipline.

Finally, Ælfric follows Gregory in noting that the way to heaven is difficult, although each develops this point differently. For Gregory that difficulty is the necessity of suffering as Christ suffered: "Quid itaque homo pro se pati debet, si tanta Deus pro hominibus pertulit?"[159] (What therefore ought humans suffer for themselves, if God bore so much for humans?) Ælfric chooses to discuss the "sticolan weig"[160] (narrow way) that leads to life, emphasizing first not what one must leave behind but the positive virtues the narrow way entails (mercy, chastity, and so forth).[161] While Ælfric presents the narrow way as difficult, he does not present it within the same penitential, purificatory framework that Gregory does, of needing to suffer on our own behalf to gain the kingdom. Ælfric focuses on following Christ in difficulty more than imitating him in suffering. Ælfric ends with a call to penitence and confession.

Within this treatment of prayer, then, we can see ways in which Ælfric de-emphasizes or removes the alignment Gregory sets up between the

155 *CH* I.10, 261, ll. 80–2.
156 *CH* I.10, 261, l. 82.
157 *CH* I.10, 262, l. 104.
158 CCSL 141, 16, ll. 97–8.
159 CCSL 141, 18, ll. 147–8.
160 *CH* I.10, 265, l. 184.
161 *CH* I.10, 264, ll. 170–5.

spiritual/invisible/eternal and the mundane/visible/temporary. Ælfric's precator is more active in praying for Jesus's help, and Jesus gives his help more directly. Rather than adopting Gregory's focus on more abstract suffering, Ælfric teaches the necessity of following, creating a more personally relational connection between the precator and Jesus. Because of these changes, Ælfric's conception of prayer is consistently more objective; prayer communicates one's need to Jesus, causing him to intervene rather than reforming the one praying through the discipline of prayer itself. Yet Ælfric's understanding of prayer also presents the relationship between the precator and Jesus as a close one, in which precators follow rather than lead.

Unanswered Prayer: *Catholic Homily* I.31

At the end of *CH* I.31, the *Passio sancti Bartholomei apostoli*, Ælfric addresses most directly the problem that humans might view prayer to God as a transactional means to get what they want. The *passio* itself tells the story of Bartholomew taking the Gospel to India,[162] where devil-inhabited idols run a sort of healing racket in which they pretend to heal illnesses that they also (secretly) cause. When Bartholomew arrives, he brings true healing to the people as they turn to belief in God. But Ælfric seems wary of the *passio's* potential implication that loyalty to God implies physical benefits, creating a relationship beneficial to humans on their own terms, subordinating God's power to human will. In addition, Ælfric notes that human experience shows that a great many prayers to God go, in fact, unanswered. To address this, he ends the homily with an independent seventy-line reflection on unanswered prayers to God,[163] and he addresses the point that God causes as many illnesses as he heals. As Ælfric does this, he tears apart any close cause-and-effect between prayer and response. In meditating on the possible meanings of unanswered prayer, he also makes the meaning difficult to determine. By doing these things, he disrupts an

---

162 Ælfric's version of Bartholomew's passio is quite faithful to its Latin source, which dates to the sixth century. See Frederick M. Biggs, ed., *The Apocrypha* (Kalamazoo: MIP, 2007), for further information on the Latin passio. See Godden's *Commentary*, 257, for the relationship of Ælfric's translation to its source.

163 Godden, *Commentary*, 257. "Independent" does not mean fully original; Ælfric draws on the biblical story of Job, a type of patient suffering under affliction, and various biblical passages, which Godden gives at pp. 264–6.

economy of prayer that could lead to a sense that material well-being can be bought by loyalty, and that loyalty can be abandoned if people do not get what they bargained for.

In *Given Time*, as I said in the Introduction to this book, Derrida shows that the gift stands at the centre of anxieties about communication. Chris Wickham, addressing human gift giving, gives examples of the varying interpretations given to gifts in the early Middle Ages: "But the problem was always that gifts could be read in different ways, and one had to both be careful about misreadings and, if one could, control the semiological content: how the gift was read, and/or was reported to have been read."[164] The gift manifests the same need to control meaning as does any other form of communication, so that it can never be subverted into anything other than what it should be. Yet, as Derrida's argument indicates, although perhaps by accident,[165] ambiguity, because it allows for freedom, is an essential feature of the gift. People, modern or medieval, do not tend to be very comfortable with ambiguities that cede so much control; they therefore often try to lock down meaning and to find ways to guarantee intention. Done too explicitly, this destroys the gift: a gift with its obligations clearly defined, where everyone knows that patrons always tip 15 per cent regardless of service, is no longer gratuitous.[166] Therefore, the rules that govern the gift are mostly unspoken (i.e., the discourse differs from the practice). Still, there are rules, and as Derrida's larger point makes clear, any symbolic system is open to counterfeit[167] – the rules that seek to guarantee value/meaning make the counterfeit possible.

164 Chris Wickham, "Conclusion," in *The Languages of Gift in the Early Middle Ages*, ed. Wendy Davies and Paul Fouracre (Cambridge: Cambridge University Press, 2010), 240.

165 That is, he does not say this explicitly. Derrida is interested in the instability of language and in the way it shares this instability in common with the gift, not in considering the way the indeterminate nature of the gift is actually necessary to its function.

166 The fact that an American tip of 15 per cent is essentially an obligation explains the inflation of tipping percentages: if 15 per cent is standard (and we are assured by the service industry that it is *not*; 20 per cent is "standard"), a generous tip must now be 20 per cent, and when 20 per cent becomes standard, generosity must be signalled by tipping 25 per cent, since generosity must always go beyond the expected.

167 Although one might say that Derrida's system of meaning is not itself based on the gold standard.

The desire to gain something of value for something worthless motivates counterfeit. The falseness of the currency distinguishes counterfeit from the desire to get a good deal, to get something for less value than it is worth. Rules for currency are designed to guarantee its value; the rules for gift exchange are designed to guarantee a certain sort of person. Because society arbitrates generosity – the giver does not determine his own generosity – the giver must actually behave generously to be seen as generous. Thus, it is not so much in the *giving* that the potential to counterfeit slips in, but rather in the intentions behind the gift, which can, by a clever enough giver, be masked. Because, Derrida aside, the gift, to be a gift, is *necessarily* intentional, bad intentions – the desire to dominate, to receive more than is given, to get a bargain through giving a gift – can counterfeit good intentions.

In Bartholomew's *passio*, healing from God is contrasted with healing from devils, and both use different exchange paradigms. The terms of the exchange between humans and devils are so explicit as to turn it into a type of purchase: when the Indians give their offerings (*lac*) to the devils, the devils give healing. However, the devils are masking their true intentions: when they give healing, they gain the precators' souls. Thus, they counterfeit the gift by disguising a bargain or a purchase as a higher-status gift exchange that is supposed to guarantee *persons*, not results. As Ælfric's uneasiness shows, exchange with the Christian God runs the risk of the same problems: because it is not altruistic (it is supposed to benefit humans, and God expects obedience), and because anything humans give is always of less value than gifts God has given, Christian exchange runs the risk of producing counterfeit humans when humans counterfeit the actions intended to guarantee a certain sort of person but with an eye towards getting God to give them what they want.[168] Ælfric's coda to Bartholomew's *passio* addresses exactly this impulse to control the exchange. Within the circle made by the gift cycle is space wherein the relationship can develop.

At the beginning of the coda, Ælfric first underlines the moral that turning to sources other than God is forbidden: "We magon niman bysne be ðære apostolican lare. þæt nan cristen man ne sceal his hæle gefeccan buton æt þam ælmihtigum scyppende"[169] (We can take example from the apostolic

168 Augustine also calls it "counterfeit goodness" ("bonitatem simulant," in *De sermone Domini*, quoted above, p. 243) when humans produce good actions for the sake of other people's praise rather than to please God.

169 *CH* I. 31, 448, ll. 244–5.

teaching that no Christian may seek his healing except from the almighty Creator). As the *passio* itself has already clarified, this is because asking for favours is an expression of a particular intention: that is, loyalty. But from there, he turns to a central problem that the *passio* introduces: through the figure of Bartholomew, loyalty to God seems to promise physical healing. That God might choose to heal through a saint is not the problem; he later tells his audience to turn to saints' shrines to pray for healing;[170] rather, it is the expectation that God *must* heal, and that humans have any way to force God to heal through *lac* or fervency of prayer or good behaviour, or even to determine what healing or lack thereof might mean.

Ælfric's coda thus introduces an interesting series of problems. First, there is no one-to-one correspondence between an illness and its meaning:

> [F]or mislicum intingum beoð cristene men geuntrumode:· hwilon for heora synnum. hwilon for fandunge:· hwilon for godes wundrum. hwilon for gehealdsumnysse goddra drohtnunga:· þæt hi þy eadmoddran beon:· ac on eallum þysum þingum is geþyld nydbehefe; Hwilon eac þurh godes wrace becymð þam arleasan men swiðe egeslic yfel. swa þæt his wite onginð on þyssere worulde.[171]
>
> (For various causes are Christians made sick, sometimes because of their sins, sometimes for testing, sometimes for God's miracles, sometimes for preservation of good conduct, that they be the humbler. But in all these things patience is necessary. Sometimes also through God's wrath very terrible evil comes upon the wicked, so that his punishment begins in this world …)

In Ælfric's coda the openness of what illness might mean disrupts any easy ability to determine its meaning. In fact, even though prayer makes meaning within a system that attributes meaning to anything that follows it, whether healing or non-healing (as we saw in chapter 3), Ælfric gives multiple ways of interpreting non-healing without giving any particular key to applying those interpretations to personal circumstance.

Both the good and the wicked fall ill, Ælfric says, and both devils and God inflict disease upon people. While the devils afflict people in order to entrap their souls, God "beswincð mid untrumnyssum his gecorenan

170 *CH* I. 31, 450, l. 311. Ælfric also claimed to witness some of the healings at St Swithun's shrine in his *LS* 21, *Natale Sancti Swyðuni, Episcopi*, ll. 262–4.

171 *CH* I. 31, 448, ll. 250–6.

swa swa he sylf cwæð; þa ðe ic lufie ða ic þreage 7 beswinge"[172] (afflicts his chosen with illness, just as he himself said: "Those whom I love, those I correct and afflict"). Ælfric lists various reasons (quoted above) why God might choose to do this, but his major point is that sickness could come to the sinful or to the righteous. This leads to a revelation that might be surprising to people with a utilitarian, prophylactic understanding of prayer: a life loyally lived in service to God is no guaranteed protection against illness. In that case, what use is loyalty?

Ælfric responds, following the usual theology, that God's non-responsiveness to prayers for physical healing is a result of his concern for spiritual healing: "And þeah ðe hit hefityme sy þam ðrowiendum þeahhwæðere wyle se goda læce to ecere hælðe hine gelacnian"[173] (And although it be grievous to the sufferer, nevertheless, the good doctor wants to heal him to eternal health). Affliction patiently endured can work for the eventual salvation of the sufferer. God's gift is thus the opposite of counterfeit in that it substitutes the more-valuable spiritual healing for the less-valuable physical healing.

All of this may be true, but it is a third-person omniscient perspective on things that is perhaps more objective and cold-blooded than is necessarily a comfort to the ill or dying. For someone in the midst of suffering a devastating illness, there is another way of looking at the dynamic Ælfric notes: human souls are owned either way, whether by devils or by God. Devils give an immediate end to pain and suffering. God gives salvation eventually, but only after the sufferer dies. That is, Ælfric's answer abstracts the need for healing from real-life concerns and defers God's response so far into the future that his response to those who show him allegiance through prayer could easily be seen as no response at all.

Those who turn to God for healing are promised no response: whether the precator is sinful or righteous, God might not heal him. Healing, a gift as a physical thing or benefit that God might give in return for service, disappears. However, it is the "disappearing gift" that restores space between the gift and its return and allows for the teasing out of intention and the revelation of character. If God does not heal on demand, then to gain nothing from God and yet still believe and serve him shows the truest service of all because it proves one trusts and recognizes the honour due

172 *CH* I. 31, 448, ll. 249–50.
173 *CH* I. 31, 448, ll. 273–4.

God. However, this response in turn brings honour to the one serving (in this case, by suffering patiently through affliction): "gif he rihtwis bið," says Ælfric, "he hæfð þonne maran geþincðe þurh his brocunge gif he geþyldig bið"[174] (if he is righteous, he has the greater honour through his sickness, if he is patient). Consequently, and paradoxically, God's non-gift allows Christians to earn the honour that comes from serving someone honourable just because they recognize his value. In a value system in which a person's worth is measured by loyalty, his or her own honourableness is recognized by the reward of eternal salvation – a moment when the faithful are allowed through the gates and seated at the high table of the eternal feast.

In the *passio*, the devilish healing is counterfeit in two ways. As mentioned, devils substitute a fraud for true healing. But it is also counterfeit because, although *lac* is supposed to signify the intention for a loyalty relationship, neither party is interested in the relationship created but rather in the goods exchanged. Healing is important to the afflicted; souls are important to devils. A *lac* is worth a healing; a healing is worth a soul. The terms of the exchange are carefully spelled out with an explicitness that expresses mistrust – or, at least, allows no room for generosity. It is a proto-contract governing a commodity exchange rather than an expression of an intention for a relationship that acknowledges the personal qualities of both parties. In contrast, in the relationship between God and humans, the promised benefit of the relationship is deferred so far into the future that it restores the gap between discourse and praxis, which gives the necessary room for generosity to be manifest and trust to be displayed. Rather than debasing the coinage, the "disappearing gift" secures the standard: the relationship is essentially based on loyalty; lack-of-healing allows God's devotees to prove loyalty because devotion and motives are clearest when there is nothing presently to be gained.

Complicating things still more: gift language is slippery. People use exchange terminology loosely, calling gifts purchases and purchases gifts. Givers pretend that the recipient has already done something to "earn" a gift in order to avoid invoking debt. Businesses pretend that nothing need be done to receive a "gift" except, perhaps, signing up for a credit card. "Free gifts" are usually conditional on a purchase. Similar slippage occurred in prior eras; we saw in chapter 2 the way Augustine, who certainly

174 *CH* I. 31, 448, ll. 262–3.

did not think salvation was purchased, used purchase metaphors to talk about salvation. There is often something to be gained by calling one type of exchange by another name; that something is called a gift (or a purchase) does not always mean it is one.[175]

In the coda, Ælfric uses purchase language figuratively to describe the exchange between humans and gods in a way that reveals the different logic behind each exchange. He warns his congregation that the sick should not "beceapie na þurh æninne deofles cræft mid his sawle þæs lichaman gesundfulnysse,"[176] (buy with his soul, through the devil's skill, the healing of the body). Later on he says that the apostles and martyrs "mid heora agenum feore þæt heofonlice rice beceapodon"[177] (bought the heavenly kingdom with their own lives). While he uses the same word, *beceapian*, to express each exchange, and while both exchanges involve credit (one part of the transaction is given immediately, the other will be given later), in the second case the notion of credit embedded in the exchange is reversed. The first is like a purchase on credit in which the benefit (physical healing) is immediate and the price (the soul) will be fully paid later. This exchange might seem like a good deal, not only because people tend to value the present and discount the future, but also because one might bet that the full price will never come due, if, say, there is no such thing as a soul or if devils turn out to be uninterested in it. In this exchange, humans receive the present benefit and pay (or not) the future price.

In the second exchange, humans pay the price up front and expect the benefit later. In this case the exchange is made on trust that the purchase price will be honoured. If it is not honoured – if no salvation is forthcoming – the purchaser has lost everything with no hope of restoration. Thus, even though mortal life is worth less than eternal life, the exchange is still not a bargain; the giver gives up everything he has. In addition, it is a price that is hard to counterfeit; giving one's life on the hope of return expresses trust that the other party will come through. It also is not exactly "buying" – the risk on return is too great, and the difference in status between the two parties too insurmountable for the giver to ever see justice if his trust is misplaced. The apostles and martyrs thus lend credit (Latin *credo*)

175 The gift is the more meaningful form of exchange: more intimate in the modern era, more honourable in the medieval. Because exchanges have meaning, there is usually some social reason for representing an exchange in a particular way.

176 *CH* I. 31, 450, ll. 309–10.

177 *CH* I. 31, 450, l. 328.

to God. The value of using the language of purchase is that "beceapian" expresses, in the first example, that the price will be demanded – healing from devils is not such a good deal as it may seem – in the second, that the return will be made; God is trustworthy.

In these homilies, the theory of prayer that Ælfric presents is focused on protection and healing. The way he removes the relationship between human and God from Neoplatonic abstraction and concerns of purity in his sources presents prayer as being about communication, not subjective transformation. One prays to whom one serves. Prayer, then, is often prophylactic, or the precator expects a materially efficacious response. However, by situating prayer within the community, Ælfric is careful not to tie the response to prayer too closely to individual will and to show that small gifts cannot be used to purchase big gifts. While God responds to prayer, prayer is not automatically efficacious and cannot be used to compel him to do the precator's will. From one perspective, Ælfric's teaching reflects the lesson of experience: prayer is not always physically efficacious. Ælfric's concern, however, is not with prayer's efficacy as proof that God exists – he accepts that as a given. Rather, his concern is that humans do not try to "buy" God with small gifts, accepting thereby a counterfeit of true healing. As people serve God they can prove loyalty and gain honour by serving even when they suffer, extending to him the credit that he will, in the end, save.

Conclusion

God sceal mon ærest hergan
fægre, fæder userne, forþon þe he us æt frymþe geteode
lif ond lænne willan; he usic wile þara leana gemonian.

(God must first and properly be praised, our Father, for in the beginning he granted us life and lent us will; he wishes to remind us of those loans.)

–*Maxims I*[1]

What do Anglo-Saxons think they do when they pray? Too often, in the study of prayer, the answer to this question is assumed: prayer communicates with God. Everyone prays. Even birds pray, to paraphrase Tertullian. The very ubiquity of the prayer leads us to assume we understand its basic contours. But birds (to adopt Tertullian's flight of fancy for a moment) surely do not pray in the same way angels pray.[2] In examining prayer and

1 George Philip Krapp and Elliott Van Kirk Dobbie, eds., *The Exeter Book*, ASPR III (New York: Columbia University Press, 1936), ll. 4b–6.

2 From the final paragraph of *De oratione liber*, although I suspect Tertullian did not mean this as merely a poetic image: "orant etiam angeli omnes, orat omnis creatura. orant pecudes et ferae et genua declinant, et egredientes de stabulis et speluncis ad caelum non otiosi ore suspiciunt vibrantes spiritum suo more. sed et aves nunc exsurgentes eriguntur ad caelum, et alarum crucem pro manibus expandunt et dicunt aliquid quod oratio videatur. quid ergo amplius de officio orationis? etiam ipse dominus oravit:

the gift, this book argues that one of the major factors influencing how people imagine prayer is the economic structures they use to imagine it. Forms of economy predispose people to imagine the relationship between themselves and others and to objects in certain ways. Transactional language in early medieval prayer has gained more attention than the language of the gift precisely because such language (and the egoistic selfhood that accompanies it) is largely seen as inappropriate today in a religious context. However, as I argued in the introduction, some of the exchanges we understand as transactional are actually reciprocal: the gift exchange, rather than being focused on the things exchanged, serves instead to bind together the people who make the exchange. Similarly, people use transactional language metaphorically to describe other forms of exchange. Thus, even when people across different eras use gift language to describe prayer, the same understanding or ideals of the gift are not stable over time.

What does it mean for our Anglo-Saxon authors that prayer is a gift? I began this study by considering the different expectations invoked by "gift." Those who idealize the free gift often understand the reciprocal gift as a transaction, a corrupted or at least lesser form of the gift. Economists speak of the dead-weight loss of the gift, an inefficient and economically irrational method of transferring property between people. Rather than asking what is lost in such an inefficient mode of transfer, we might ask, as gift theorists have done, what is gained. Gift giving creates or maintains relationships between the parties involved. The openness characteristic of the gift creates economic inefficiency, but it also creates the conditions in which people can trust each other enough to transact business, arrange marriages, conclude peace treaties, and compete for status without violence, or it helps to maintain the good will that sustains both intimate and public relationships. Another way of putting it: the inefficiency of the mode of transfer creates openness that is then transformed into something else: friendship, social and personal identity, honour.

---

cui sit honor et virtus in saecula saeculorum" (Even the angels pray, all of them. The whole creation prays. Cattle and wild beasts pray, and bend their knees, and in coming forth from their stalls and lairs look up to heaven, their mouth not idle, making the spirit move in their own fashion. Moreover the birds now arising are lifting themselves up to heaven and instead of hands are spreading out the cross of their wings, while saying something which may be supposed to be a prayer. What more then of the obligation of prayer? Even the Lord himself prayed: to him be honour and power for ever and ever), ed. and trans. Ernest Evans (London: S.P.C.K., 1953), 41.

Like the gift, prayer is inescapably economic. Many scholars, such as Mayke de Jong, Megan McLaughlin, and Barbara Rosenwein,[3] have studied the socioeconomics of prayer – the way medieval prayer circulates between people to create and maintain relationships, hierarchies, and networks of power. But until now very little attention has been given to the circulations and exchanges, the types of economic structures people imagine in their teachings on prayer. When we examine what they say, we see a complex system of circulation and meaning making. Humans pray from a position of dependency and need, because they want something from the god to whom they pray. Like the gift, prayer is an inefficient means of getting material goods or benefits. As with material transactions, people often want a certain outcome: contract or purchase, not gift; magic, not prayer; a means to compel God, to bind him, not openness or transformation. But, like the gift, it is that inefficiency, the distance between what precators want and what they get, the space of deferral, that allows prayer to do the work the Anglo-Saxon authors attribute to it, decentring the individual precator's will.

The Anglo-Saxon authors conceptualize prayer as essentially petitionary, consisting of the performance of formal, set prayers. *Reverberations*, the website of the Social Science Research Council's New Directions in the Study of Prayer initiative, calls a focus on petitionary prayer "narrow," situating the project in the tradition of William James:

> James, summarizing in 1902 the state of scientific research on prayer, noted its narrow focus on petitionary prayer – on whether prayer can, say, heal the sick, or sway the weather ... Leapfrogging a century, the narrowness that James identified persists: the full range of prayer practices, implications, and effects remains under-studied by scholars and under-covered by journalists.[4]

---

3 Mayke de Jong, "Carolingian Monasticism: The Power of Prayer," in *The New Cambridge Medieval History*, vol. 2, ed. Rosamond McKitterick (Cambridge: Cambridge University Press, 1995); Megan McLaughlin, *Consorting with Saints: Prayer for the Dead in Early Medieval France* (Ithaca: Cornell University Press, 1994); Barbara H. Rosenwein, *To Be the Neighbor of Saint Peter: The Social Meaning of Cluny's Property, 909–1049* (Ithaca: Cornell University Press, 2006).

4 Social Science Research Council, *Reverberations: New Directions in the Study of Prayer*, accessed 1 July 2016, http://forums.ssrc.org/ndsp/category/prayer-in-wider-perspective/.

The Social Science Research Council, speaking specifically to social science research, seeks to widen the prayer phenomena social science researchers study. However, broadening the focus, while entirely necessary, runs the risk of simplifying or flattening petitionary prayer, making it seem like it is only ever a transaction, a means for precators to get what they want, in which prayer's efficacy is judged by how closely it conforms to what the precators pray for. That is not how the Anglo-Saxon authors present it. Even though they understand prayer as essentially petitionary, consisting of the performance of formal, set prayers, they imagine the exchange embedded in prayer as personal. This is not to say that other types of prayer exchange do not exist (such as the proxy prayers of commuted penances or prayers for healing made to saints), only that when Anglo-Saxons imagine prayer as something done between the person and God, they imagine it as fundamentally personal, contributing to and even forming personal identity. Thus, as Bede and the Alfredian texts show, prayer understood as petition can contain sophisticated theories of how such prayer works. Even Ælfric finds ways to decentre human will as prayer becomes an expression of loyalty and unanswered prayer brings precators honour. The Anglo-Saxon authors we have looked at understood humans to be in a gift economy with God, but they each work out the implications of that economy in different ways.

Chapter 1 contextualized Anglo-Saxon teachings on prayer within the prayer tradition that came before it, which they inherited in a partial way, and presented Anglo-Saxon innovations in prayer technologies – breviate psalters and prayerbooks. In that chapter I noted that John Cassian's teaching on prayer in *Conlatio* 9 has received the most attention in spirituality studies. In the early tradition, his is the only one that gives any extended representation of the mind at work, of gaining skill in the discipline of prayer. However, because his teaching on *preces ignates* (fiery prayers) fits within studies of mysticism and spirituality, the aneconomy of that form of prayer has tended to overshadow the text-based nature of Cassian's own presentation of the discipline of prayer in *Conlatio* 10 and has been used to read other forms of early medieval prayer, such as Bede's, that are more embedded in economy.

As we saw in chapter 2, Bede imagines prayer within an intimate lord/retainer relationship with God, in which precators return God's gifts by using them. He understands prayer as a discipline that pervades one's whole life, giving little value to prayer's material efficacy. While Bede's understanding of prayer leaves room for the will of the precator (indeed, relies for its efficacy on that will), the human will is used in cooperation with the divine will, creating an economy of excess that transforms "dogs" to "sheep," bringing those outside the divine economy inside it as friends. Identity, for Bede, is identity given, and then received and returned to God through the gift economy of prayer. As a monk preaching to monks, it is perhaps no surprise that his theory of prayer would be rigorously spiritualized and reflect an ongoing discipline of prayer.

It is perhaps more surprising to find a similar approach in the Alfredian evidence examined in chapter 3, which gives an extended picture of a layman's understanding of prayer, although it is the prayer of a well-educated and pious layman. In Asser's discussion of Alfred's prayer, it seems at first that Alfred's practice might be closer to the sort of automatic efficacy Ælfric later seems to preach, where efficacy is predicated more on correct ritual performance than on the disposition of the precator and is judged by the extent to which the response to prayer is in line with the precator's expectations and desires. Indeed, Asser's account shows Alfred praying for healing, and the "swa deð" (so does) formula in the Psalms seems at a glance to confirm a sort of automatic efficacy for prayer – that the precator repeats David's words when he wants to pray for healing, the death of his enemies, or whatever use a person might imagine for the Psalms, which are especially powerful to get what the precator wants. However, on further study, it becomes obvious that the understanding of prayer from Alfred's circle also reflects a learned ecclesiastical perspective that similarly decentres the will of the precator. Both Bede's and Alfred's precators build a sense of personal identity by performing the ritual forms of prayer, although Bede's prayer emphasizes internalization and awareness of the presence of God as giver and a sense of self formed through gifts, while Alfred's prayer emphasizes prayer as work that God honours and rewards. The identity built through Alfred's theory of prayer is made as one interprets one's life through the narrative presented in the Psalms and the prayers of the Church.

Ælfric's theory of prayer, in chapter 4, is accessible to an audience with less time to meditate on the nuances of Christian texts. In large part, he expects his congregation to be concerned with the need for healing, good weather, and productive crops. His precators pray the Paternoster and Creed and perhaps participate in the prayers of the Mass. However, Ælfric does not preach the Anglo-Saxon version of a prosperity gospel; he, too, presents the praying subject as subject to God's will. Thus, the Ælfrician passages on prayer for safety while travelling, or praying over herbs while picking them, should be situated within the larger context of Ælfric's teaching. In this context, it becomes clear that in Ælfric's view, prayer to

God is a promise of loyalty, and that prophylactic prayers (such as reciting the Paternoster while travelling) lay claim to God's protection, reminding all who hear – God, devils, and perhaps precators themselves – that the one praying is under the protection of God.

And yet, openness in prayer – that the result not be too closely linked to the precator's will – is still crucially important to Ælfric's understanding of the work prayer does. As his meditation on unanswered prayer at the end of Bartholomew's *passio* shows, the economic inefficiency of prayer is what allows for the precator to gain in honour, and that honour is recognized in the eternal kingdom. Reciprocity in prayer, like reciprocity in gift giving, does not make that prayer purely self-interested. Bede, Alfred, and Ælfric do not conceptualize prayer as contest of wills – that is, they did not see prayer as taking place between two self-interested entities each seeking to get the best deal – but as a series of non-agonistic gift exchanges in which there are no winners or losers because the interests of the two parties are not seen to be at odds with one another, even when precators do not get what they want.

For each author, then, prayer as a gift from God gives or confers some aspect of human identity. Prayer as a gift in return to God gives some aspect of the self, although each author imagines that differently. Bede imagines that the self is a gift from God to be enacted and interiorized through the words of prayer, and thus given back to God. The prayer beginning the *Soliloquies* imagines prayer as work, as unalienated labour, for which God rewards the precator. The introductions to the Psalms show further the authority of the prayers: their creation by David and (typologically) by Christ guarantees the efficacy of the prayers – that the precator will be heard – but also authorizes the precator before God as he identifies with David and with Christ by adopting their narrative as his own. Thus, in Asser's account of Alfred at prayer, Alfred's prayer guarantees his worth. For Ælfric, the act of praying to God performs allegiance; the present act of prayer for protection, for healing, or for any need is therefore a promise for the future of the precator's submission to God. In this case, answered prayer – prayer that gains precators what they want – would seem to be proof of God's power, but Ælfric undermines a sense that humans can control God through prayer, compel him to act according to their wishes by opening up the prayer economy, first by creating a three-way exchange that involves all members of the community giving and receiving from each other and, in turn, receiving from God; and, second, by interpreting unanswered prayer as a means to gain honour by serving loyally, even when one is not immediately rewarded for doing so, thereby demonstrating trust.

While it is tempting to read the changes between Bede, the Alfredian circle, and Ælfric's conceptions of prayer as chronological progression, the three mostly represent practices of prayer performed by different groups of people. Monastic and lay prayer each have distinctive traditions before the Anglo-Saxon period. Bede represents monastic practice informed by monastic rules, and with some connection to the type of prayer represented in Cassian. As detailed in chapter 1, monastic practices of prayer – namely, praying the psalter – began to influence high-ranking laypeople in the Carolingian period; Alfred represents these developments and shows us the type of understanding of prayer available to high-ranking laypeople. Ælfric clearly addresses his teachings on prayer to ordinary laypeople, those whose expectations for prayer are prophylactic and materially efficacious.

Study of prayer as gift in the teachings of Bede and Ælfric and in the Alfredian texts shows how important it is to be aware of the way particular forms of selfhood are embedded in particular economic structures, and how religious contexts show authors working through economic issues of selfhood and community. Examining how Anglo-Saxons imagine exchange with God also allows us to see ways that particular forms of belief in God have real effects on human conceptions of self and community. Furthermore, careful study of economic language in teachings on and the presentation of prayer gives one way to see continuity and change across time. This allows us to address the difficulty inherent in the spirituality-studies approach: the dearth of creative, affective, or mystical devotion in most Anglo-Saxon texts. In shifting our focus, we can see that the period is itself situated at a pivotal point for the study of prayer. Not only did it produce new prayer technologies, which alerts us to potential shifts in the theory of prayer, these authors also show the use the English made of texts written in the late antique period, under other economic conditions and in a different language (in the case of the Alfredian text and Ælfric). Through influential figures such as Bede, Alfred, and Ælfric, late antique sources were digested and disseminated, gaining influence beyond Anglo-Saxon England.

The present study has focused mostly on the gift because that is the dominant structure of exchange in Anglo-Saxon teachings on prayer. However, further study could be done on exchange language more generally in early Christian and later medieval prayer, paying close attention to the way language is used and whether the language of exchange matches the phenomenology of exchange. It is interesting to note, for instance, the presence of "purchase"[5] and gift in an apophatic text like the late medieval *Cloud of Unknowing*, because apophatic prayer is one of the least economic forms of prayer. It is also suggestive that major shifts in prayer theories seem to co-occur with economic and cultural shifts: not only do the Anglo-Saxons adjust economic metaphors in their translations and adaptations of Latin writings, but Anselm's meditative prayer and the major disruptions to ritualized prayer that occur with Protestantism's rejection of the liturgy also co-occur with times of socioeconomic change.

For the authors studied here, the work of prayer is to produce certain kinds of persons, not (necessarily) particular practical results. The work it does is imaginative: as precators imagine the god who sees them and receives their prayers, that imagination is turned back on themselves, so that they imagine themselves as seen in the eyes of God, which leaves intention and motive open to self-scrutiny. In the monastic tradition of Bede, and reflected to some extent in Alfred, precators respond by adopting as their own the intentions presented in the prayers they pray. In the lay tradition, represented also in Alfred and especially in Ælfric, precators may pray for specific and material things. By allowing openness in the response, taking whatever comes as from the hand of God and for the precators' good, they are able to increase merit or honour and thereby win the heavenly kingdom as a reward for their personal characteristics. All of the Anglo-Saxon authors emphasize the gift in prayer. That is, they picture the relationship between humans and God as open, generous, and honour based. Thus, the Anglo-Saxons imagine that prayer is made to a God who cannot be compelled by gifts to give but whose great and manifold gifts compel a return, bringing God and man together. What seems to be the human reaching out towards God is understood in the end as God reaching out to humans.

5 "[L]o! here mowe men see what a privé love put may purchase of oure Lorde, before alle other werkes that man may think," ll. 807–8, ed. Patrick J. Gallacher, TEAMS Middle English Text Series Online, http://d.lib.rochester.edu/teams/text/gallacher-cloud-of-unknowing. However, it is also worth considering the way that the language of love in the twelfth century and beyond (and certainly how it is used in texts like the *Cloud*) picks up some of the conceptual questions of the gift; namely, in the way people think about altruism and freedom versus duty in love.

Bibliography

Abbreviations

ANF	Ante-Nicene Fathers
ASE	Anglo-Saxon England
ASPR	G.P. Krapp and E.V.K Dobbie, eds., The Anglo-Saxon Poetic Records, 6 vols. (New York: Columbia University Press, 1931–42).
BT	Joseph Bosworth, *An Anglo-Saxon Dictionary, Based on the Manuscript Collections of the Late Joseph Bosworth Toller*, ed. and enlarged by T. Northcote Toller. (Oxford: Clarendon Press, 1882).
CH I	Peter Clemoes, ed., *Ælfric's Catholic Homilies: The First Series, Text*, EETS s.s. 17 (Oxford: Oxford University Press, 1997).
CH II	Malcolm Godden, ed., *Ælfric's Catholic Homilies: The Second Series, Text*, EETS s.s. 5 (Oxford: Oxford University Press, 1979).
CCSL	Corpus Christianorum Series Latina
CSEL	Corpus Scriptorum Ecclesiasticorum Latinorum
DOE	Dictionary of Old English
EETS	Early English Texts Society
EME	Early Medieval Europe
EMS	Essays in Medieval Studies
Gneuss and Lapidge	Helmut Gneuss and Michael Lapidge, *Anglo-Saxon Manuscripts: A Bibliographical Handlist of Manuscripts and Manuscript Fragments Written or Owned in England up to 1100* (Toronto: University of Toronto Press, 2014).
Lewis and Short	Charleton T. Lewis and Charles Short, *A Latin Dictionary* (Oxford: Clarendon, 1879). Web. http://www.perseus.tufts.edu.

LS	Walter W. Skeat, *Lives of Saints*, 2 vols., EETS 76, 82, 94, 114 (London: Trübner, 1881–1900).
MGH	Monumenta Germaniae Historica
MIP	Medieval Institute Publications
NPNF	Nicene and Post Nicene Fathers
OED	Oxford English Dictionary
PG	Patrologiae cursus completus, series Graeca, ed. Jacques-Paul Migne (Paris: Garnier Fratres).
PL	Patrologiae cursus completus, series Latina, ed. Jacques-Paul Migne (Paris: Garnier Fratres, 1844–1891).
WSA	The Works of Saint Augustine: A Translation for the 21st Century (New York: New City Press, 1990–2014).

Ælfric. *Ælfric's Catholic Homilies: The First Series*. Edited by Peter Clemoes. EETS s.s. 17. London: Oxford University Press, 1997.

– *Ælfric's Catholic Homilies: The Second Series*. Edited by Malcolm Godden. EETS s.s. 5. London: Oxford University Press, 1979.

– *Homilies of Ælfric: A Supplementary Collection*. 2 vols. Edited by John C. Pope. EETS 259, 260. London: Oxford University Press, 1967–8.

– *Ælfric's Lives of Saints*. Edited by Walter W. Skeat. 2 vols. EETS 76, 82, 94, 114. London: Trübner, 1881–1900.

Alcuin. "Beatus igitur David." PL 101, cols. 509–10a.

– *De laude Dei*. Staatsbibliothek Bamberg Msc.Patr. 17, fols. 133r–157r. http://digital.bib-bvb.de/view/bvbmets/viewer.0.5.jsp?folder_id=0&dvs=1466027054424~523&pid=7078628&locale=en&usePid1=true&usePid2=true.

– Preface to *De psalmorum usu*. PL 101, cols. 465b–68a.

Alfred, King of England. *King Alfred's Old English Version of Boethius,* De Consolatione Philosophiae. Edited by Walter John Sedgefield. Oxford: Clarendon, 1899.

– *King Alfred's Version of St. Augustine's* Soliloquies. Edited by Thomas A. Carnicelli. Cambridge, MA: Harvard University Press, 1969.

– *King Alfred's West-Saxon Version of Gregory's Pastoral Care*. Edited by Henry Sweet. EETS 45. London: N. Trübner, 1871.

Algazi, Gadi, Valentin Groebner, and Bernhard Jussen, eds. *Negotiating the Gift: Pre-Modern Figurations of Exchange*. Veröffentlichungen Des Max-Planck-Instituts Für Geschichte 188. Göttingen: Vandenhoeck & Ruprecht, 2003.

American Heritage Dictionary Online, Appendix I. Houghton Mifflin Harcourt, 2016. https://ahdictionary.com/word/indoeurop.html#IR094600.

Angenendt, Arnold. "*Donationes pro anima*: Gift and Countergift in the Early Medieval Liturgy." In *The Long Morning of Medieval Europe: New Directions in Early Medieval Studies*, edited by Jennifer R. Davis and Michael McCormick, 131–54. Aldershot: Ashgate, 2008.

– "Sacrifice, Gifts, and Prayers in Latin Christianity." In *Early Medieval Christianities, c. 600–c. 1100*, edited by Thomas F.X. Noble and Julie M.H. Smith, 453–71. The Cambridge History of Christianity 3. Cambridge: Cambridge University Press, 2008.

Angenendt, Arnold, Thomas Braucks, Rolf Busch, and Hubertus Lutterbach. "Counting Piety in the Early and High Middle Ages." In *Ordering Medieval Society: Perspectives on Intellectual and Practical Modes of Shaping Social Relations*, edited by Bernhard Jussen, 15–54. Translated by Pamela Selwyn. Philadelphia: University of Pennsylvania Press, 2001.

Asser. *Asser's Life of King Alfred Together with the Annals of Saint Neots Erroneously Ascribed to Asser*. Edited by William Henry Stevenson. 1904. Reprint, Oxford: Clarendon, 1959.

– *Alfred the Great: Asser's Life of King Alfred and Other Contemporary Sources.* Translated by Simon Keynes and Michael Lapidge. London: Penguin, 1983.

Augustine of Hippo. *De dono perseverantiae*. PL 45. cols. 993–1034.

– *De sermone Domini in monte.* Edited by Almut Mutzenbecher. CCSL 35. Turnhout: Brepols, 1967.

– *Enarrationes in psalmos, I–L*. Edited by D.E. Dekkers and J. Fraipont. CCSL 38. Turnhout: Brepols, 1956.

– *Enarrationes in psalmos, LI–C*. Edited by D.E. Dekkers and J. Fraipont. CCSL 39. Turnhout: Brepols, 1956.

– *Epistola 130, Ad Probam*. CCSL 31B. Edited by Klaus Daur. Turnhout: Brepols, 2009. 212–37.

– *Homilies on the Gospel of John; Homilies on the First Epistle of John; Soliloquies.* Translated by John Gibb and James Innes. NPNF, First Series, vol. 7. Grand Rapids, MI: Wm. B. Eerdmans Publishing Company, 1888. http://www.ccel.org/ccel/schaff/npnf107.html.

– *In Ioannis evangelium tractatus*. Edited by R. Willems. CCSL 36. Turnhout: Brepols, 1954.

– "Letter 130, to Proba." WSA, II/2: Letters 100–55. Edited by Boniface Ramsey. Translated by Roland Teske, 183–91. New York: New City Press, 2003.

– "The Lord's Sermon on the Mount." *New Testament I and II*. Edited by Boniface Ramsey. Translated by Michael G. Campbell. WSA I/15. New York: New City Press, 2014.

– *Sermo 80*. PL 38, cols. 493–8.

– *Sermones in Matthaeum*. Edited by P.-P. Verbraken L. De Coninck, B. Coppieters 't Wallant, R. Demeulenaere, F. Dolbeau. CCSL 41Aa. Turnhout: Brepols, 2008.

– *Sermons*. Translated by Edmund Hill. WSA, vol. III/3. Brooklyn: New City Press, 1991.

– *Soliloquia*. PL 32. cols. 869–904.

Aulén, Gustaf. *Christus Victor: An Historical Study of the Three Main Types of the Idea of Atonement*. 1931. 13th printing. New York: Macmillan, 1967.

Baker, Peter S. *Honour, Exchange and Violence in "Beowulf"*. Cambridge: D.S. Brewer, 2013.

Bately, Janet. "Did King Alfred Actually Translate Anything? The Integrity of the Alfredian Canon Revisited." *Medium Aevum* 78.2 (2009): 189–215.

Bazelmans, Jos. "Beyond Power: Ceremonial Exchange in *Beowulf*." In *Rituals of Power: From Late Antiquity to the Early Middle Ages*, edited by Frans Theuws and Janet L. Nelson, 311–75. Leiden: Brill, 2000.

– *By Weapons Made Worthy: Lords, Retainers, and Their Relationship in "Beowulf"*. Amsterdam: Amsterdam University Press, 1999.

– "One for All, All for One: The Old English *Beowulf* and the Ritual and Cosmological Character of the Relationship between Lord and Warrior-follower in Germanic Societies." In *Method and Theory in Historical Archaeology: Papers of the Medieval Europe Brugge 1997 Conference*, edited by Guy De Boe and Frans Verhaeghe, 51–3. Zellik: Instituut voor het Archeologisch Patrimonium, 1997.

Bede. *Bede the Venerable: Homilies on the Gospels*. Translated by Lawrence T. Martin and David Hurst. 2 vols. Kalamazoo, MI: Cistercian Publications, 1991.

– *The Ecclesiastical History of the English People*. Translated by Judith McClure and Roger Collins. Oxford: Oxford University Press, 1994.

– *Historia ecclesiastica gentis Anglorum*. 3 vols. Edited by Michael Lapidge. Paris: Les Éditions du Cerf, 2005.

– "Epistola ad Ecgbertum Episcopum." In *Opera Historica*, edited by Charles Plummer, 405–23. Oxford: Clarendon, 1896.

– "In Lucae evangelium expositio." *Opera. Pars II, Opera exegetica.* Edited by D. Hurst, 1–425. CCSL 120. Turnhout: Brepols, 1960.

– *Opera. Pars III, Opera homiletica. Pars IV, Opera rhythmica*. Edited by David Hurst and J. Fraipont. CCSL 122. Turnhout: Brepols, 1955.

Bellah, Robert Neelly. "To Kill and Survive or Die and Become." In *The Robert Bellah Reader*, edited by Steven M. Tipton, 81–106. Durham: Duke University Press, 2006.

Benedict of Nursia. *RB 1980: The Rule of Saint Benedict in Latin and English with Notes*. Edited by Timothy Fry et al. Collegeville, MN: Liturgical Press, 1981.

– *Regula*. Edited by R. Hanslik. CSEL 75. Vienna: Hölder-Pichler-Tempsky, 1977.

Benson, Bruce Ellis, and Norman Wirzba, eds. *The Phenomenology of Prayer.* Perspectives in Continental Philosophy 46. New York: Fordham University Press, 2005.

Bequette, John. "Bede's Advent Homily on the Gospel of Mark: An Exercise in Rhetorical Theology." *American Benedictine Review* 57 (2006): 249–66.

Bestul, Thomas H. "Continental Sources of Anglo-Saxon Devotional Writing." In *Sources of Anglo-Saxon Culture*, edited by Paul E. Szarmach and Virginia Darrow Oggins, 103–26. Kalamazoo, MI: MIP, 1986.

– "St. Anselm and the Continuity of Anglo-Saxon Devotional Traditions." *Annuale Mediaevale* 18 (1977): 20–41.

– "St. Anselm, the Monastic Community at Canterbury and Devotional Writing in Late Anglo-Saxon England." *Anselm Studies* 1 (1983): 185–98.

Bethurum, Dorothy, ed. *The Homilies of Wulfstan.* Oxford: Clarendon, 1957.

Biggs, Frederick M., ed. *The Apocrypha.* Instrumenta Anglistica Mediaevalia 1. Kalamazoo, MI: MIP, 2007.

– "Bede's Use of Augustine: Echoes from Some Sermons?" *Revue Bénédictine* 108.3–4 (1998): 201–13.

Bijsterveld, Arnoud-Jan. *Do ut des: Gift Giving, Memoria, and Conflict Management in the Medieval Low Countries.* Hilversum: Uitgeverij Verloren, 2007.

– "Gift Exchange, Landed Property, and Eternity: The Foundation and Endowment of the Premonstratensian Priory of Postel (1128/1138–1179)." In *Land and Ancestors: Cultural Dynamics in the Urnfield Period and the Middle Ages in the Southern Netherlands*, edited by Frans Theuws and Nico Roymans, 309–48. Amsterdam Archaeological Studies 4. Amsterdam: Amsterdam University Press, 2004.

Billett, Jesse D. *The Divine Office in Anglo-Saxon England, 597–c. 1000.* Henry Bradshaw Society, Subsidia 7. London: Boydell, 2014.

Birch, Walter de Gray. *An Ancient Manuscript of the Eighth or Ninth Century: Formerly Belonging to St. Mary's Abbey, or Nunnaminster, Winchester.* 1889. Reprint from the Collections of the University of California Libraries.

Bjork, Robert E. "Speech as Gift in Beowulf." *Speculum* 69 (1994): 993–1022.

Black, Jonathan. "Psalm Uses in Carolingian Prayerbooks: Alcuin and the Preface to *De psalmorum usu.*" *Mediaeval Studies* 64 (2002): 1–60.

– "Psalm Uses in Carolingian Prayerbooks: Alcuin's *Confessio peccatorum pura* and the Seven Penitential Psalms (Use 1)." *Mediaeval Studies* 65 (2003): 1–56.

– Review of *Alcuins Gebetbuch für Karl den Grossen* by Stephan Waldhoff. *Speculum* 83.3 (2008): 772–4.

Blair, Peter Hunter. *The World of Bede.* 1970. Reprint. Cambridge: Cambridge University Press, 1990.

Bliss, Alan, and Allen J. Frantzen. "The Integrity of *Resignation.*" *Review of English Studies* 27 (1976): 385–402.

Bonner, Gerald. "The Christian Life in the Thought of the Venerable Bede." *Durham University Journal* 63.1 (1970): 39–55.

Bosworth, James, and T. Northcote Toller. *An Anglo-Saxon Dictionary*. Oxford: Clarendon, 1930.

Bourdieu, Pierre. *The Logic of Practice*. Translated by Richard Nice. Stanford, CA: Stanford University Press, 1990.

– "Selections from *The Logic of Practice*." In Schrift, *The Logic of the Gift*, 190–230.

Boynton, Susan. "Libelli Precum in the Central Middle Ages." In Hammerling, *A History of Prayer*, 255–318.

Bradshaw, Paul F. "From Word to Action: The Changing Role of Psalmody in Early Christianity." In *Like a Two-Edged Sword: The Word of God in Liturgy and History*, edited by Martin Dudley, 21–37. Norwich: Canterbury Press, 1995.

– *The Search for the Origins of Christian Worship: Sources and Methods for the Study of Early Liturgy*. 2nd ed. Oxford: Oxford University Press, 2002.

Brakke, David, Michael L. Satlow, and Steven Weitzman, eds. *Religion and the Self in Antiquity*. Bloomington, IN: Indiana University Press, 2005.

Branch, Lori. "The Rejection of the Liturgy, the Rise of Free Prayer, and Modern Religious Subjectivity." *Restoration* 29.1 (2005): 1–28.

Bravo, A. "Prayer as a Literary Device in *The Battle of Maldon* and in *The Poem of the Cid*." *SELIM* 2 (1992): 31–46.

Brown, George Hardin. *A Companion to Bede*. Anglo-Saxon Studies 12. Woodbridge, Suffolk: Boydell, 2009.

– *Bede the Venerable*. Boston: Twayne Publishers, 1987.

Brown, Michelle P. *The Book of Cerne: Prayer, Patronage and Power in Ninth-Century England*. The British Library Studies in Medieval Culture. London: British Library, 1996.

Bullough, Donald A. *Alcuin: Achievement and Reputation: Being Part of the Ford Lectures Delivered in Oxford in Hilary Term 1980*. Leiden; Boston: Brill, 2004.

– "Alcuin and the Kingdom of Heaven: Liturgy, Theology, and the Carolingian Age." *Carolingian Essays: Andrew W. Mellon Lectures in Early Christian Studies*. Washington, DC: Catholic University of America Press, 1983. 1–69.

Burton, P.H., J. Balserak, H.A.G. Houghton, and D.C. Parker, eds. *Vetus Latina Iohannes.* The Verbum Project, April 2015. http://www.iohannes.com/vetuslatina/.

Bynum, Caroline Walker. *Jesus as Mother: Studies in the Spirituality of the High Middle Ages*. Berkeley: University of California Press, 1984.

Byzdl, Donald G. "Prayer in Old English Narratives." *Medium Ævum* 51.2 (1982): 135–51.

Caesarius of Arles. *Sancti Caesari Arelatensis Sermones*. Edited by D.G. Morin. CCSL 103. Turnhout: Brepols, 1953. 235–40.

Caillé, Alain. "The Double Inconceivability of the Pure Gift." *Angelaki* 6.2 (2001): 23–39.

Calkins, Mary Whiton. "The Nature of Prayer." *The Harvard Theological Review* 4.4 (1911): 489–500.

Caputo, John D. *The Prayers and Tears of Jacques Derrida: Religion without Religion*. Bloomington: Indiana University Press, 1997.

– "The Time of Giving, the Time of Forgiving." In *The Enigma of Gift and Sacrifice*, edited by Edith Wyschogrod, Jean-Joseph Goux, and Eric Boynton, 117–47. New York: Fordham University Press, 2002.

Carrier, James G. *Gifts and Commodities: Exchange and Western Capitalism since 1700*. New York: Routledge, 1995.

Carroll, M.T.A. *The Venerable Bede: His Spiritual Teachings*. The Catholic University of America Studies in Medieval History 9. Washington, DC: Catholic University of America Press, 1946.

Carruthers, Mary. *The Craft of Thought: Meditation, Rhetoric, and the Making of Images, 400–1200*. Cambridge Studies in Medieval Literature 34. Cambridge: Cambridge University Press, 1998.

Carter, Jeffrey, ed. *Understanding Religious Sacrifice: A Reader*. London: Continuum, 2003.

Cassian, John. *The Conferences*. Translated by Boniface Ramsey. Ancient Christian Writers 57. New York: Newman Press, 1997.

– *Conlationes XXIIII*. Edited by Michael Petschenig. CSEL 13. Vienna: Verlag der Österreichischen Akademie der Wissenschaften, 2004.

Cherniss, Michael D. *Ingeld and Christ: Heroic Concepts and Values in Old English Christian Poetry*. Studies in English Literature 74. The Hague: Mouton, 1972.

Clarke, Catherine A.M. *Writing Power in Anglo-Saxon England: Texts, Hierarchies, Economies*. Woodbridge, Suffolk: Boydell & Brewer, 2012.

Clayton, Mary. *The Cult of the Virgin Mary in Anglo-Saxon England*. Cambridge Studies in Anglo-Saxon England 2. Cambridge: Cambridge University Press, 1990.

– "Homiliaries and Preaching in Anglo-Saxon England." In *Old English Prose: Basic Readings*, edited by Paul E. Szarmach, 151–98. New York: Garland Publishing, 2000.

Clement of Alexandria. *The Stromata*. Edited by Kevin Knight. Translated by William Wilson. ANF 2. Buffalo, NY: Christian Literature Publishing, 1885. Reprint. Web. http://www.newadvent.org/fathers/0210.htm.

Clemoes, Peter. "Ælfric." In *Continuations and Beginnings: Studies in Old English Literature*, edited by Eric Gerald Stanley, 176–209. London: Thomas Nelson, 1966.

Cloud of Unknowing, The. Edited by Patrick J. Gallacher. TEAMS Middle English Text Series Online, 1997. http://d.lib.rochester.edu/teams/text/gallacher-cloud-of-unknowing.

Constantinescu, Radu. "Alcuin et les 'Libelli Precum' de l'epoque carolingienne." *Revue d'histoire de la spiritualité* 50 (1974): 17–56.

Cowell, Andrew. *The Medieval Warrior Aristocracy: Gifts, Violence, Performance, and the Sacred.* Gallica 6. Cambridge: D.S. Brewer, 2007.

Coy, Ruth Louise. "The Gift in Old English Literature: *Genesis A*, *Christ II*, and *Beowulf*." PhD diss., University of Illinois, 1977.

Cross, J.E. "The Influence of Irish Texts and Traditions on the 'Old English Martyrology.'" *Proceedings of the Royal Irish Academy* 81C (1981): 173–92.

Cubitt, Catherine. "Ælfric's Lay Patrons." In Magennis and Swan, *A Companion to Ælfric*, 165–92.

– "Bishops, Priests and Penance in Late Saxon England." *EME* 14.1 (2006): 41–63.

– "Pastoral Care and Conciliar Canons: The Provisions of the 747 Council at Clovesho." In *Pastoral Care before the Parish*, edited by John Blair and Richard Sharpe, 193–211. Leicester: Leicester University Press, 1992.

Curta, Florin. "Merovingian and Carolingian Gift Giving." *Speculum* 81:3 (2006): 671–99.

Cyprian of Carthage. "De dominica oratione." In *Opera*, edited by C. Moreschini, 87–113. CCSL 3A. Turnhout: Brepols, 1976.

– "On the Lord's Prayer." Edited by Alexander Roberts and James Donaldson. Translated by Ernest Wallis. ANF 5. Grand Rapids, MI: Wm. B. Eerdmans, 447–57. Web. http://www.ccel.org/ccel/schaff/anf05.iv.v.iv.html.

Davies, Wendy, and Paul Fouracre, eds. *The Languages of Gift in the Early Middle Ages.* Cambridge: Cambridge University Press, 2010.

De Jong, Mayke. "Carolingian Monasticism: The Power of Prayer." In *The New Cambridge Medieval History, c. 700–900*, 2 vols., edited by Rosamond McKitterick, 2:622–53. Cambridge: Cambridge University Press, 1995.

DeGregorio, Scott. "Ælfric, *Gedwyld*, and Vernacular Hagiography: Sanctity and Spirituality in the Old English Lives of SS Peter and Paul." In *Ælfric's Lives of Canonized Popes*, edited by Donald Scragg, 75–98. Old English Newsletter Subsidia 30. Kalamazoo: MIP, 2001.

– "Affective Spirituality: Theory and Practice in Bede and Alfred the Great." *EMS* 22 (2005): 129–39.

– "Explorations of Spirituality in the Writings of the Venerable Bede, King Alfred, and Abbot Ælfric of Eynsham." PhD diss., University of Toronto, 1999.
– "Footsteps of His Own: Bede's Commentary on Ezra-Nehemiah." In DeGregorio, *Innovation and Tradition in the Writings of the Venerable Bede*, 143–68.
– ed. *Innovation and Tradition in the Writings of the Venerable Bede*. Medieval European Studies 6. Morgantown, WV: West Virginia University Press, 2006.
– "Texts, *Topoi* and the Self: A Reading of Alfredian Spirituality." *EME* 13.1 (2005): 79–96.
– "The Venerable Bede on Prayer and Contemplation." *Traditio* 54 (1999): 1–39.
Del Giacco, Eric Jay. "Exegesis and Sermon: A Comparison of Bede's Commentary and Homilies on Luke." *Medieval Sermon Studies Newsletter* 50 (2006): 9–29.
Derrida, Jacques. *The Gift of Death*. Translated by David Wills. Chicago: University of Chicago Press, 1996.
– *Given Time I: Counterfeit Money*. Translated by Peggy Kamuf. Chicago: University of Chicago Press, 1994.
Deshman, Robert. "The Galba Psalter: Pictures, Texts and Context in an Early Medieval Prayerbook." *ASE* 26 (1997): 109–38.
Dhuoda. *Dhuoda, Handbook for Her Warrior Son: Liber Manualis*. Edited and translated by Marcelle Thiébaux. Cambridge Medieval Classics 8. Cambridge: Cambridge University Press, 1998.
Dictionary of Old English: A to H online. Edited by Angus Cameron, Ashley Crandell Amos, Antonette diPaolo Healey, et al. Toronto: Dictionary of Old English Project, 2016.
Dobbie, Elliott Van Kirk, ed. *The Battle of Maldon*. ASPR VI. New York: Columbia University Press, 1942. 7–16.
Donahue, Charles. "Potlatch and Charity: Notes on the Heroic in *Beowulf*." *Anglo-Saxon Poetry: Essays in Appreciation for John C. McGalliard*, edited by Lewis E. Nicholson and Dolores Warwick Frese, 23–40. Notre Dame, IN: University of Notre Dame Press, 1975.
Driscoll, Michael S. "The *precum libelli* and Carolingian Spirituality." In *Proceedings of the North American Academy of Liturgy Annual Meeting*, 68–76. Valparaiso, IN, 1990.
– "The Seven Penitential Psalms: Their Designation and Usages from the Middle Ages Onwards." *Ecclesia Orans* 17 (2000): 153–201.
Duby, Georges. *The Early Growth of the European Economy: Warriors and Peasants from the Seventh to the Twelfth Century*. Translated by Howard B. Clarke. Ithaca: Cornell University Press, 1974.

– *History Continues*. Translated by Arthur Goldhammer. Chicago: University of Chicago Press, 1994.

Dumont, Louis. *Essays on Individualism: Modern Ideology in Anthropological Perspective*. Chicago: Chicago University Press, 1986.

Dumville, David N. "Liturgical Drama and Panegyric Responsory from the 8th Century: A Re-examination of the Origin and Contents of the 9th-Century Section of the Book of Cerne." *Journal of Theological Studies* n.s. 23.2 (1972): 374–406.

Dupont, Anthony. Gratia *in Augustine's* Sermones ad populum *during the Pelagian Controversy: Do Different Contexts Furnish Different Insights?* Brill's Series in Church History 9. Leiden: Brill, 2013.

Enright, Michael J. "Lady with a Mead-Cup: Ritual, Group Cohesion and Hierarchy in the Germanic Warband." *Frühmittelalterliche Studien* 22 (1988): 170–220.

Flint, Valerie I.J. *The Rise of Magic in Early Medieval Europe*. Princeton, NJ: Princeton University Press, 1991.

Flood, Gavin. *The Truth Within: A History of Inwardness in Christianity, Hinduism, and Buddhism*. Oxford: Oxford University Press, 2013.

Foot, Sarah. "Parochial Ministry in Early Anglo-Saxon England: The Role of Monastic Communities." *Studies in Church History* 27 (1989): 43–54.

Frantzen, Allen J. *Anglo-Saxon Keywords*. Malden, MA: Wiley-Blackwell, 2012.

– *King Alfred*. Boston: Twayne Publishers, 1986.

– *The Literature of Penance in Anglo-Saxon England*. New Brunswick, NJ: Rutgers University Press, 1983.

– "Spirituality and Devotion in the Anglo-Saxon Penitentials." *EMS* 22 (2005): 117–28.

Froehlich, Karlfried. "The Lord's Prayer in Patristic Literature." In Hammerling, *A History of Prayer*, 59–78.

Fulton, Rachel. "Praying with Anselm at Admont." *Speculum* 81 (2006): 700–33.

Gameson, Richard. *The Scribe Speaks? Colophons in Early English Manuscripts*. Cambridge: Cambridge University Department of Anglo-Saxon, Norse, and Celtic, 2002.

Ganz, David. "Giving to God in the Mass: The Experience of the Offertory." In Davies and Fouracre, *The Languages of Gift in the Early Middle Ages*, 18–32.

– "Le *De laude Dei* d'Alcuin." *Annales de Bretagne et Des Pays de l'Ouest* 111 (2004): 387–92.

Garner, Lori Ann. "Anglo-Saxon Charms in Performance." *Oral Tradition* 19.1 (2004): 20–42.

Gatch, Milton McC. "The Achievement of Ælfric and his Colleagues in European Perspective." In *The Old English Homily and Its Backgrounds*, edited by Paul E. Szarmach and Bernard Huppé, 43–73. Albany: University of New York Press, 1978.

– "The Anglo-Saxon Tradition." In Jones, Wainwright, and Yarnold, *The Study of Spirituality*, 225–34.

Geoffrey of Vinsauf. *Poetria Nova of Geoffrey of Vinsauf*. Translated by Margaret F. Nims. Mediaeval Sources in Translation 6. Toronto: Pontifical Institute of Mediaeval Studies, 1967.

Gneuss, Helmut, and Michael Lapidge. *Anglo-Saxon Manuscripts: A Bibliographical Handlist of Manuscripts and Manuscript Fragments Written or Owned in England up to 1100*. Toronto Anglo-Saxon Series. Toronto: University of Toronto Press, 2014.

Godbout, Jacques. *The World of the Gift*. Montreal, Canada: McGill-Queen's University Press, 1998.

Godden, Malcolm. *Ælfric's Catholic Homilies: Introduction, Commentary, and Glossary*. EETS s.s. 18. Oxford: Oxford University Press, 2000.

– "Did King Alfred Write Anything?" *Medium Aevum* 76.1 (2007): 1–23.

Godelier, Maurice. *The Enigma of the Gift*. Translated by Nora Scott. Cambridge: Polity Press, 1999.

– "Some Things You Give, Some Things You Sell, but Some Things You Must Keep for Yourselves: What Mauss Did Not Say about Sacred Objects." In *The Enigma of Gift and Sacrifice*, edited by Edith Wyschogrod, Jean-Joseph Goux, and Eric Boynton, 19–37. New York: Fordham University Press, 2002.

Gregory, C.A. *Gifts and Commodities*. Studies in Political Economy. London: Academic Press, 1982.

Gregory the Great. *Gregory the Great: Forty Gospel Homilies*. Translated by David Hurst. Kalamazoo, MI: Cistercian Publications, 1990.

– *Homiliae in evangelia*. Edited by Raymond Étaix. CCSL 141. Turnhout: Brepols, 1999.

– *Moralia in Iob, Libri I–X*. Edited by M. Adriaen. CCSL 143. Turnhout: Brepols, 1979.

Grønbech, Vilhelm. *The Culture of the Teutons*. 2 vols. Translated by W.J. Alexander Worster. London: Oxford University Press, 1932.

Günzel, Beate, ed. *Ælfwine's Prayerbook*. Henry Bradshaw Society 108. London: Boydell Press, 1993.

Gurevich, Aaron Yakovlevich. *The Origins of European Individualism*. The Making of Europe. Oxford: Blackwell, 1995.

– "Wealth and Gift Bestowal among the Ancient Scandinavians." In *Historical Anthropology of the Middle Ages*, edited by Jana Howlett, 177–89. Chicago: University of Chicago Press, 1992.

Haas, David C. "Prayer: A Neurological Inquiry." *CSI. The Committee for Skeptical Inquiry*, April 2007. Web. http://www.csicop.org/si/show/prayer_a_neurological_inquiry/.

Haddan, Arthur West, William Stubbs, and David Wilkins, eds. *Councils and Ecclesiastical Documents Relating to Great Britain and Ireland*, vol. 3. Oxford: Clarendon, 1964.

Hall, Thomas N. "The Early English Manuscripts of Gregory the Great's *Homilies on the Gospel* and *Homilies on Ezechiel*: A Preliminary Survey." In *Rome and the North: The Early Reception of Gregory the Great in Germanic Europe*, edited by Rolf H. Bremmer Jr., Kees Dekker, and David F. Johnson, 115–36. Paris: Peeters, 2001.

Hamilton, Sarah. *The Practice of Penance, 900–1050*. Woodbridge, Suffolk: Boydell, 2001.

Hammerling, Roy, ed. *A History of Prayer: The First to the Fifteenth Century*. Leiden: Brill, 2008.

Hammerling, Roy. "Introduction." In Hammerling, *A History of Prayer*, 1–27.

– "The Lord's Prayer: A Cornerstone of Early Baptismal Education." In Hammerling, *A History of Prayer*, 167–82.

– "The Lord's Prayer in Early Christian Polemics in the Eighth Century." In Hammerling, *A History of Prayer*, 223–41.

Hand, Thomas A. *St. Augustine on Prayer*, Westminster, MD: Newman Press, 1963.

Härke, Heinrich. "The Circulation of Weapons in Anglo-Saxon Society." In *Rituals of Power: From Late Antiquity to the Early Middle Ages*, edited by Frans Theuws and Janet L. Nelson, 377–99. Leiden: Brill, 2000.

Harris, Stephen J. "The Liturgical Context of Ælfric's Homilies for Rogation." In *The Old English Homily: Precedent, Practice, and Appropriation*, edited by Aaron J Kleist, 143–69. Studies in the Early Middle Ages 17. Turnhout: Brepols, 2007.

Harrison, James R. *Paul's Language of Grace in Its Graeco-Roman Context*. Wissenschaftliche Untersuchungen Zum Neuen Testament 2. Reihe 172. Tübingen: Paul Mohr Verlag, 2003.

Heckman, Christina M. "*Imitatio* in Early Medieval Spirituality: The Dream of the Rood, Anselm, and Militant Christology." *Essays in Medieval Studies* 22.1 (2005): 141–53.

Heiler, Friedrich. *Prayer: A Study in the History and Psychology of Religion*. Translated by Samuel McComb. New York: Oxford University Press, 1958.

Originally published as *Das Gebet: eine religionsgeschichtliche und religions-psychologische Untersuchung*. München: Verlag von Ernst Reinholdt, 1919.
Heisey, Daniel J. "Mary and Mysticism in Bede's Homilies." *American Benedictine Review* 64.1 (2013): 3–16.
Herz, Martin. *Sacrum Commercium: Eine begriffsgeschichtliche Studie zur Theologie der Römischen Liturgiesprache*. München: Kommissionsverlag Karl Zink, 1985.
Hill, John M. *The Cultural World in "Beowulf"*. Toronto: University of Toronto Press, 1995.
– "Beowulf and the Danish Succession: Gift Giving as an Occasion for Complex Gesture." *Medievalia et Humanistica* 11 (1982): 177–97.
Hill, Joyce. "Ælfric: His Life and Works." In Magennis and Swan, *A Companion to Ælfric*, 35–65.
– "Carolingian Perspectives on the Authority of Bede." In DeGregorio, *Innovation and Tradition in the Writings of the Venerable Bede*, 227–49.
– Rev. of *The Cambridge History of Medieval English Literature* by David Wallace, ed. *The Review of English Studies* n.s. 51.201 (2000): 101–5.
Hill, Thomas D. "Beowulf as Seldguma: *Beowulf*, lines 247–51." *Neophilologus* 74 (1990): 236–9.
Holsinger, Bruce, and Rachel Fulton. "Introduction: Medieval Communities and the Matter of Person." In *History in the Comic Mode: Medieval Communities and the Matter of Person*, edited by Rachel Fulton and Bruce W. Holsinger, 1–11. New York: Columbia University Press, 2007.
Holy Bible Douay-Rheims Version, The. American Edition, 1899. Web. BibleGateway.com.
Houghton, Hugh A.G. "The Discourse of Prayer in the Major Apocryphal Acts of the Apostles." *Apocrypha* 15 (2004): 171–200.
Hubert, Henri, and Marcel Mauss. *Sacrifice: Its Nature and Function*. Translated by W.D. Halls. Chicago: University of Chicago Press, 1964.
Hughes, Anselm, ed. *The Portiforium of Saint Wulstan (Corpus Christi College, Cambridge, MS. 391)*. 2 vols. Henry Bradshaw Society 89. London: Henry Bradshaw Society, 1958.
Hwang, Alexander Y., Brian J. Matz, and Augustine Casiday, eds. *Grace for Grace: The Debates after Augustine and Pelagius*. Washington, DC: Catholic University of America Press, 2014.
Irenaeus. *Adversus Haereses*. PG 7. Edited by Jacques-Paul Migne. Paris: Garnier Fratres, 1882.
James, William. *The Varieties of Religious Experience: A Study in Human Nature*. 1902. Foreword Jacques Barzun. New York: Mentor, 1958.

Jamroziak, Emilia. "Making and Breaking the Bonds: Yorkshire Cistercians and Their Neighbours." In *Perspectives for an Architecture of Solitude: Essays on Cistercians, Art and Architecture in Honour of Peter Fergusson*, edited by Terry N. Kinder, 63–70. Turnhout: Brepols, 2004.

Jerome. *Commentariorum in Matheum*. Edited by D. Hurst and M. Adriaen. CCSL 77. Turnhout: Brepols, 1969.

Jolly, Karen Louise. *Popular Religion in Late Saxon England: Elf Charms in Context*. 2nd ed. Chapel Hill: University of North Carolina Press, 1996.

Jolly, Karen Louise, Catherine E. Karkov, and Sarah Larratt Keefer, eds. *Cross and Culture in Anglo-Saxon England: Studies in Honor of George Hardin Brown*. Morgantown, WV: West Virginia University Press, 2007.

Jones, Cheslyn, Geoffrey Wainwright, and Edward Yarnold, eds. *The Study of Spirituality*. New York: Oxford University Press, 1986.

Jussen, Bernhard. "Religious Discourses of the Gift in the Middle Ages: Semantic Evidences (Second to Twelfth Centuries)." In Algazi, Groebner, and Jussen, *Negotiating the Gift*, 173–92.

Keenan, Dennis King. *The Question of Sacrifice*. Studies in Continental Thought. Bloomington: Indiana University Press, 2005.

Kelly, Henry Ansgar. *The Devil at Baptism: Ritual, Theology, and Drama*. Ithaca, NY: Cornell University Press, 1985.

Kershaw, Paul. "Illness, Power, and Prayer in Asser's Life of King Alfred." *EME* 10 (2001): 201–24.

Klauser, Theodore. *A Short History of the Western Liturgy: An Account and Some Reflections*. Translated by John Halliburton. London: Oxford University Press, 1969.

Kleist, Aaron J. "Ælfric's Corpus: A Conspectus." *Florilegium* 18.2 (2001): 113–64.

– *Striving with Grace: Views of Free Will in Anglo-Saxon England*. Toronto: University of Toronto Press, 2008.

Krapp, George Philip. *The Vercelli Book*. ASPR II. New York: Columbia University Press, 1932.

Krapp, George Philip, and Elliott Van Kirk Dobbie, eds. *The Exeter Book*. ASPR III. New York: Columbia University Press, 1936.

Kuypers, Arthur Benedict. *The Prayer Book of Aedeluald the Bishop, Commonly Called the Book of Cerne*. Cambridge: Cambridge University Press, 1902.

Laidlaw, James. "A Free Gift Makes No Friends." *The Journal of the Royal Anthropological Institute of Great Britain and Ireland* 6.4 (2000): 617–34.

Lake, Stephen. "Knowledge of the Writings of John Cassian in Early Anglo-Saxon England." *ASE* 32 (2003): 27–42.

Lapidge, Michael. "Catalogue of Classical and Patristic Authors and Works Composed before AD 700 and Known in Anglo-Saxon England." *The Anglo-Saxon Library*. Oxford: Oxford University Press, 2005. 275–342.

Leclercq, Jean. *The Love of Learning and the Desire for God: A Study of Monastic Culture*. Translated by Catharine Misrahi. New York: Fordham University Press, 1982.

Lee, Alvin A. *The Guest-Hall of Eden: Four Essays on the Design of Old English Poetry*. New Haven: Yale University Press, 1972.

Leisi, Ernst. "Gold und Manneswert im *Beowulf*." *Anglia* 71 (1952–3): 259–73.

Lévi-Strauss, Claude. *The Elementary Structures of Kinship*. Edited and translated by Robert Needham. Translated by James Harle Bell and John Richard von Sturmer. Rev. ed. Boston: Beacon Press, 1969.

Lewis, Charlton T., and Charles Short. *A Latin Dictionary*. Oxford. Clarendon. 1879. Web. http://www.perseus.tufts.edu.

Liebersohn, Harry. *The Return of the Gift: The European History of a Global Idea*. Cambridge: Cambridge University Press, 2011.

Lockett, Leslie. "The Role of Grendel's Arm in Feud, Law, and the Narrative Strategy of *Beowulf*." In *Latin Learning and English Lore: Studies in Anglo-Saxon Literature for Michael Lapidge*, 2 vols., edited by Katherine O'Brien O'Keeffe and Andy Orchard, 1:368–88. Toronto: University of Toronto Press, 2005.

Love, Rosalind. "Bede and John Chrysostom." *Journal of Medieval Latin* 17 (2007): 72–86.

Magennis, Hugh. *Images of Community in Old English Poetry*. Cambridge: Cambridge University Press, 1996.

Magennis, Hugh, and Mary Swan, eds. *A Companion to Ælfric*. Leiden: Brill, 2009.

Magnani, Eliana. "Almsgiving, *Donatio pro anima* and Eucharistic Offering in the Early Middle Ages of Western Europe (4th–9th century)." In *Charity and Giving in Monotheistic Religions*, edited by Miriam Frenkel and Yaakov Lev, 111–21. Berlin: Walter de Gruyter, 2009.

Martin, Lawrence T. "Bede and Preaching." In *The Cambridge Companion to Bede*, edited by Scott DeGregorio, 156–96. Cambridge: Cambridge University Press, 2010.

– "Bede's Originality in His Use of the Book of Wisdom in His Homilies on the Gospels." In DeGregorio, *Innovation and Tradition in the Writings of the Venerable Bede*, 189–202.

– "Introduction." In Martin and Hurst, trans., *Bede the Venerable: Homilies on the Gospels*, 1:xi–xxiii.

– "The Two Worlds in Bede's Homilies: The Biblical Event and the Listeners' Experience." In *De Ore Domini: Preacher and Word in the Middle Ages*, edited by Thomas L. Amos, Eugene A. Green, and Beverly Mayne Kienzle, 27–40. Kalamazoo, MI: MIP, 1989.

Martin, Lawrence T., and David Hurst, trans. *Bede the Venerable: Homilies on the Gospels*. 2 vols. Kalamazoo, MI: Cistercian Publications, 1991.

Marx, C. William. *The Devil's Rights and the Redemption in the Literature of Medieval England*. Cambridge: D.S. Brewer, 1995.

Mason, Mary Elizabeth. *The Active Life and Contemplative Life: A Study of the Concepts from Plato to the Present*. Milwaukee, WI: Marquette University Press, 1961.

Masters, Kevin S., Glen I. Spielmans, and Jason T. Goodson. "Are There Demonstrable Effects of Distant Intercessory Prayer? A Meta-Analytic Review." *Annals of Behavioral Medicine* 32.1 (2006): 21–6.

Mauss, Marcel. "Gift, Gift." In Schrift, *The Logic of the Gift*, 28–32, translated by Koen Decoster.

– *The Gift: The Form and Reason for Exchange in Archaic Societies*. Translated by W.D. Halls. New York: W.W. Norton, 1990. Originally published as "Essai sur le don, forme et raison de l'échange dans les sociétés archaïques," *L'Année Sociologique* 1 (1925): 30–186.

– *On Prayer*. Edited by W.S.F. Pickering. Translated by Susan Leslie. New York: Durkheim Press/Berghahn Books, 2003.

Mayr-Harting, Henry. *The Coming of Christianity to Anglo-Saxon England*. 3rd ed. London: Batsford, 1991.

McGrath, Alister E. *Iustitia Dei: A History of the Christian Doctrine of Justification*. 3rd ed. Cambridge: Cambridge University Press, 2005.

McLaughlin, Megan. *Consorting with Saints: Prayer for the Dead in Early Medieval France*. Ithaca, NY: Cornell University Press, 1994.

McNeill, John T., and Helena M. Gamer. *Medieval Handbooks of Penance: A Translation of the Principal* Libri Poenitentiales. Records of Western Civilization. New York: Columbia University Press, 1938.

Meaney, Audrey. "Ælfric's Use of His Sources in His Homily on Auguries." *English Studies* 66.6 (1985): 477–95.

Miller, William Ian. *Bloodtaking and Peacemaking: Feud, Law, and Society in Saga Iceland*. Chicago: University of Chicago Press, 1990.

– "Gift, Sale, Payment, Raid: Case Studies in the Negotiation and Classification of Exchange in Medieval Iceland." *Speculum* 61.1 (1986): 18–50.

Mitchell, Bruce. *Old English Syntax, Volume I: Concord, the Parts of Speech, and the Sentence*. Oxford: Oxford University Press, 1985.

– "The Relation between Old English Alliterative Verse and Aelfric's Alliterative Prose." In *Latin Learning and English Lore: Studies in Anglo-Saxon Literature for Michael Lapidge*, 2 vols., edited by Katherine O'Brien O'Keeffe and Andy Orchard, 2:349–62. Toronto: University of Toronto Press, 2005.

Morris, Colin. *The Discovery of the Individual, 1050–1200*. New York: Harper and Row, 1972.

Moussy, Claude. *Gratia et sa famille*. Paris: Presses Universitaires Blaise Pascal, Clermont-Ferrand, 1966.

Muir, Bernard J. *A Pre-Conquest English Prayer-Book [BL MSS Cotton Galba A.xiv and Nero A.ii (ff. 3–13)]*. Henry Bradshaw Society. Woodbridge, Suffolk; Wolfeboro, NH: Boydell Press, 1988.

Mullally, Erin. "The Cross-Gendered Gift: Weaponry in the Old English Judith." *Exemplaria* 17 (2005): 255–84.

Mursell, Gordon. *English Spirituality: From Earliest Times to 1700*. Westminster: John Knox Press, 2001.

Nelson, Janet L. "Monks, Secular Men, and Masculinity." *Courts, Elites, and Gendered Power in the Early Middle Ages: Charlemagne and Others*. Variorum Collected Studies Series. Aldershot, UK: Ashgate, 2007. 121–42.

O'Brien O'Keeffe, Katherine. *Stealing Obedience: Narratives of Agency and Identity in Later Anglo-Saxon England*. Toronto: University of Toronto Press, 2012.

Ó Carragáin, Éamon. *Ritual and the Rood: Liturgical Images and the Old English Poems of the Dream of the Rood Tradition*. Toronto: University of Toronto Press, 2005.

O'Neill, Patrick P. "Irish Transmission of Late Antique Learning: The Case of Theodore of Mopsuestia's Commentaries on the Psalms." In *Ireland and Europe in the Early Middle Ages: Texts and Transmission*, edited by Próinséas Ní Chatháin and Michael Richter, 68–77. Portland, OR: Four Courts Press, 2002.

– ed. *King Alfred's Old English Prose Translation of the First Fifty Psalms*. Medieval Academy Books 104. Cambridge, Mass: Medieval Academy of America, 2001.

– "The Old English Introductions to the Prose Psalms of the Paris Psalter: Sources, Structure, and Composition." *Studies in Philology* 78.5 (1981): 20–38.

Origen. *Origen's Treatise on Prayer*. Translated by Eric George Jay. Reprint. Eugene, OR: Wipf and Stock Publishers, 2010.

Osteen, Mark. "Introduction: Questions of the Gift." *The Question of the Gift: Essays across Disciplines*. Edited by Mark Osteen. New York: Routledge, 2002.

Parry, Jonathan. "The Gift, the Indian Gift and the 'Indian Gift.'" *Man* 21.3 (1986): 453–73.

Pelikan, Jaroslav. *The Christian Tradition: A History of the Development of Doctrine*, vol. 1. *The Emergence of the Catholic Tradition.* Chicago: University of Chicago Press, 1975.

Plummer, Charles. *The Life and Times of Alfred the Great: With an Appendix.* Oxford: Clarendon, 1902.

Pratt, David. "Problems of Authorship and Audience in the Writings of King Alfred the Great." In *Lay Intellectuals in the Carolingian World*, edited by Patrick Wormald and Janet L. Nelson, 162–91. Cambridge: Cambridge University Press, 2006.

– "The Illnesses of King Alfred the Great." *ASE* 30 (2001): 39–90.

Pseudo-Augustine. *Sermo 268, De auguriis*. PL 39, cols. 2268–71.

Pseudo-Bede. *In Psalmorum libro exegesis*. PL 93, cols. 477–1098.

Pulleyn, Simon. *Prayer in Greek Religion*. Oxford: Clarendon, 1997.

Pulsiano, Phillip. "Prayers, Glosses and Glossaries." *A Companion to Anglo-Saxon Literature*. Blackwell Companions to Literature and Culture 11. Oxford: Blackwell, 2001. 208–30.

– "Psalters." In *The Liturgical Books of Anglo-Saxon England*, edited by Richard W. Pfaff, 61–85. Old English Newsletter Subsidia 23. Kalamazoo, MI: MIP, 1995.

Ramsey, Boniface. "Almsgiving in the Latin Church: The Late Fourth and Early Fifth Centuries." *Theological Studies* 43.1 (1982): 226–59.

Raw, Barbara. "Alfredian Piety: The Book of Nunnaminster." In *Alfred the Wise: Studies in Honour of Janet Bately on the Occasion of Her Sixty-Fifth Birthday*, edited by Jane Roberts, Janet L. Nelson, and Malcolm Godden, 145–53. Rochester, NY: D.S. Brewer, 1997.

– *The Art and Background of Old English Poetry*. London: Edward Arnold, 1978.

Ray, Roger. "Who Did Bede Think He Was?" In DeGregorio, *Innovation and Tradition in the Writings of the Venerable Bede*, 11–35.

Reuter, Timothy. "Gifts and Simony." In *Medieval Transformations: Texts, Power, and Gifts in Context*, edited by Esther Cohen and Mayke B. de Jong, 157–68. Cultures, Beliefs and Traditions: Medieval and Early Modern Peoples 11. Leiden: Brill, 2001.

Rice, John R. *Prayer: Asking and Receiving*. 1942. 4th printing. Wheaton, IL: Sword of the Lord Publishers, 1945.

Robinson, Fred C. "God, Death, and Loyalty in The Battle of Maldon." In *J.R.R. Tolkien, Scholar and Story-Teller: Essays in Memoriam*, edited by Mary Sau and Robert T. Farrell, 76–98. Ithaca: Cornell University Press, 1979. Reprinted in *Old English Poetry: Critical Essays*, edited by Roy Liuzza, 425–44. New Haven: Yale University Press, 2002.

Rondeau, Marie-Josèphe. *Les Commentaires patristiques du Psautier (IIIe-Ve siècles)*. 2 vol. *Exégèse prosopologique el théologie*. Orientalia Christiana Analecta 220. Rome: Pont. Institutum Studiorum Orientalium, 1985.

Rosenwein, Barbara H. *To Be the Neighbor of Saint Peter: The Social Meaning of Cluny's Property, 909–1049*. Ithaca: Cornell University Press, 2006.

Rüpke, Jörg. *Religion of the Romans*. Translated by Richard Gordon. Cambridge: Polity Press, 2007.

Russell, Jeffrey Burton. *Lucifer: The Devil in the Middle Ages*. Ithaca, NY: Cornell University Press, 1984.

Sahlins, Marshall. "The Spirit of the Gift." In Schrift, *The Logic of the Gift*, 70–99.

– *Stone Age Economics*. Hawthorne, NY: Aldine de Gruyter, 1974.

Saller, Richard P. *Personal Patronage under the Early Empire*. Cambridge: Cambridge University Press, 1982.

Sawyer, Peter. *The Wealth of Anglo-Saxon England*. Oxford: Oxford University Press, 2013.

Satlow, Michael, ed. *The Gift in Antiquity*. Hoboken, NJ: Wiley-Blackwell, 2013.

Schnurr, K.B. *Hören und Handeln: Lateinische Auslegungen des Vaterunsers in der Alten Kirche bis zum fünften Jahrhundert*. Freiburger Theologische Studien 132. Freiburg: Herder, 1985.

Schrift, Alan D., ed. *The Logic of the Gift: Toward an Ethic of Generosity*. New York: Routledge, 1997.

Schütt, Marie. "The Literary Form of Asser's 'Vita Alfredi.'" *The English Historical Review* 72.283 (1957): 209–20.

Seligman, Adam B., Robert P. Weller, Michael J. Puett, and Bennett Simon. *Ritual and Its Consequences: An Essay on the Limits of Sincerity*. Oxford: Oxford University Press, 2008.

Shadowlands. Dir. Richard Attenborough. Perf. Anthony Hopkins, Debra Winger, and Julian Fellows. Savoy Pictures, 1993.

Shepherd, Geoffrey. "English Versions of the Scriptures before Wyclif." In *Cambridge History of the Bible*, vol. 2, edited by Peter R. Ackroyd, C.F. Evans, G.W.H. Lampe, and S.L. Greenslade, 362–86. Cambridge: Cambridge University Press, 1969.

Sheppard, Alice. *Families of the King: Writing Identity in the Anglo-Saxon Chronicle*. Toronto: University of Toronto Press, 2004.

Simmel, Georg. "Faithfulness and Gratitude." In *The Sociology of Georg Simmel*, edited and translated by Kurt H. Wolff, 379–95. Toronto: The Free Press, 1950.

Sims-Williams, Patrick. *Religion and Literature in Western England, 600–800*. Cambridge: Cambridge University Press, 1990.

– "Thought, Word, and Deed: An Irish Triad." *Eriu* 29 (1978): 78–111.

Skoglund, John E. "Free Prayer." *Studia Liturgica* 10 (1974): 151–66.

Smetana, Cyril L. "Paul the Deacon's Patristic Anthology." In *The Old English Homily and Its Backgrounds*, edited by Paul E. Szarmach and Bernard F. Huppé, 75–97. Albany, NY: State University of New York Press, 1978.

Smith, Wilfred Cantwell. *The Meaning and End of Religion: A New Approach to the Religious Traditions of Mankind.* New York: Macmillan, 1963.

Smyth, Alfred P. *King Alfred the Great.* New York: Oxford University Press, 1995.

Social Science Research Council. *Reverberations: New Directions in the Study of Prayer*. Accessed July 1, 2016. http://forums.ssrc.org/ndsp/category/prayer-in-wider-perspective/.

Southern, R.W. *The Making of the Middle Ages.* New Haven: Yale University Press, 1953.

Stanley, E.G. *In the Foreground: "Beowulf."* Woodbridge, Suffolk: D.S. Brewer, 1994.

Stewart, Columba. *Cassian the Monk*. New York: Oxford University Press, 1998.

Strathern, Marilyn. *The Gender of the Gift: Problems with Women and Problems with Society in Melanesia.* Berkeley: University of California Press, 1988.

Surber-Meyer, Nida-Louise. *Gift and Exchange in the Anglo-Saxon Poetic Corpus: A Contribution towards the Representation of Wealth.* Geneva: Slatkine, 1994.

Swan, Mary. "Ælfric's *Catholic Homilies* in the Twelfth Century." *Rewriting Old English in the Twelfth Century*, edited by Mary Swan and Elaine M. Treharne, 62–82. Cambridge Studies in Anglo-Saxon England 30. Cambridge: Cambridge University Press, 2000.

– "Old English Made New: One Catholic Homily and Its Reuses." *Leeds Studies in English* 28 (1997): 1–18.

Tambiah, Stanley Jeyaraja. *Magic, Science, Religion, and the Scope of Rationality.* Lewis Henry Morgan Lectures. Cambridge: Cambridge University Press, 1990.

– "The Magical Power of Words." *Man* n.s. 3.2 (1968): 175–208.

Tertullian. "De oratione." *Opera.* Edited by G.F. Diercks, 255–74. CCSL 1. Turnhout: Brepols, 1954.

– *De oratione liber. Tertullian's Tract on the Prayer*. Edited and translated by Ernest Evans. London: S.P.C.K., 1953.

– *De paenitentia*. Edited by J.G. Ph. Borleffs, 319–40. CCSL 1. Turnhout: Brepols, 1954.

– *On Repentance*. Translated by S. Thelwall. Christian Classics Electronic Library, 1998. Web. http://www.tertullian.org/anf/anf03/anf03-47.htm#P11261_3190842.

TeSelle, Eugene. "The Background: Augustine and the Pelagian Controversy." In *Grace for Grace: The Debates after Augustine and Pelagius*, edited by Alexander Y. Hwang, Brian J. Matz, and Augustine Casiday, 1–13. Washington, DC: Catholic University of America Press, 2014.

Thacker, Alan. "Monks, Preaching, and Pastoral Care in Early Anglo-Saxon England." In *Pastoral Care before the Parish*, edited by John Blair and Richard Sharpe, 137–70. Leicester: Leicester University Press, 1992.

Theodulf of Orleans. "Carmen LXIII, Ad Gislam." MGH, Poetarum Latinorum Medii Aevi, Tomus I: Poetae Latini aevi Carolini. Berlin: Weidmanns, 1881.

Thieme, Adelheid L.J. "Gift Giving as a Vital Element of Salvation in *The Dream of the Rood*." *South Atlantic Review* 63.2 (1998): 108–23.

– "The Gift in *Beowulf*: Forging the Continuity of Past and Present." *Michigan Germanic Studies* 22.2 (1996): 126–43.

Thomas, Kate Heulwen. "The Meaning, Practice and Context of Private Prayer in Late Anglo-Saxon England." PhD diss., University of York, 2011.

Thomas, Keith. *Religion and the Decline of Magic*. 1971. Reprint. London: Penguin Global, 2012.

Tolhurst, J.B.L., ed. *The Monastic Breviary of Hyde Abbey, Winchester*. Henry Bradshaw Society 6. London: Harrison and Sons, 1942.

Toswell, M.J. *The Anglo-Saxon Psalter*. Medieval Church Studies 10. Turnhout: Brepols, 2014.

Treharne, Elaine M. "Making Their Presence Felt: Readers of Ælfric, c. 1050–1350." In Magennis and Swan, *A Companion to Ælfric*, 399–422.

Treschow, Michael, Paramjit Gill, and Tim B. Swartz. "King Alfred's Scholarly Writings and the Authorship of the First Fifty Prose Psalms." *The Heroic Age* 12 (2009). Web.

Ulanov, Ann, and Barry Ulanov. "Prayer and Personality: Prayer as Primary Speech." In Jones, Wainwright, and Yarnold, *The Study of Spirituality*, 24–33.

Underhill, Evelyn. *Mysticism: A Study in the Nature and Development of Man's Spiritual Consciousness*. New York: Dutton, 1911.

Upchurch, Robert K. "A Big Dog Barks: Ælfric of Eynsham's Indictment of the English Pastorate and *Witan*," *Speculum* 85 (2010): 505–33.

– "Catechetic Homiletics: Ælfric's Preaching and Teaching During Lent." In Magennis and Swan, *A Companion to Ælfric*, 217–46.

van der Walt, A.G.P. "Reflections of the Benedictine Rule in Bede's Homiliary." *Journal of Ecclesiastical History* 37.3 (1986): 367–76.

Walde, Alois, and J.B. Hofmann. *Lateinisches etymologisches Wörterbuch*, vol. 2. Heidelberg: Carl Winter Universitätsverlag, 1954. Web. archive.org.

Waldhoff, Stephan. *Alcuins Gebetbuch für Karl den Grossen: Seine Rekonstruktion und seine Stellung in der Frümittelalterlichen Geschichte der* libelli precum.

Liturgiewissenschaftliche Quellen und Forschungen 89. Münster: Aschendorff, 2003.

Ward, Benedicta. "Bede and the Psalter." Jarrow Lecture. Newcastle upon Tyne, England: Saint Paul's Parish Church Council, 1991.

– *High King of Heaven: Aspects of Early English Spirituality*. Cistercian Studies Series 181. Kalamazoo, MI: Cistercian Publications, 1999.

Warren, F.E., ed. *The Antiphonary of Bangor: An Early Irish Manuscript in the Ambrosian Library at Milan*. 2 vols. Henry Bradshaw Society. Woodbridge, Suffolk: Boydell & Brewer, 1895. Reprint.

Weiner, Annette B. *Inalienable Possessions: The Paradox of Keeping-While-Giving*. Berkeley: University of California Press, 1992.

Wickham, Chris. "Compulsory Gift Exchange in Lombard Italy, 650–1150." In Davies and Fouracre, *The Languages of Gift in the Early Middle Ages*, 193–216.

– "Conclusion." In Davies and Fouracre, *The Languages of Gift in the Early Middle Ages*, 238–61.

Wilcox, Jonathan. "Ælfric in Dorset and the Landscape of Pastoral Care." In *Pastoral Care in Late Anglo-Saxon England*, edited by Francesca Tinti, 52–62. Woodbridge, Suffolk: Boydell, 2005.

– "Rewriting Ælfric: An Alternative Ending of a Rogationtide Homily." *Leeds Studies in English* n.s. 37 (2006): 229–39.

– "The Use of Ælfric's Homilies: MSS Oxford, Bodleian Library, Junius 85 and 86 in the Field." In Magennis and Swan, *A Companion to Ælfric*, 345–68.

Wilkins, John. *A Discourse Concerning the Gift of Prayer, Shewing What it is, wherein it Consists, and how far it is Attainable by Industry*. London, 1704.

Wogan-Browne, Jocelyn. "The Hero in Christian Reception: Ælfric and Heroic Poetry." In *Old English Literature: Critical Essays*, edited by Roy M. Liuzza, 215–35. New Haven: Yale University Press, 2002.

Woolfenden, Graham W. "The Use of the Psalter by Early Monastic Communities." *Studia Patristica* 26 (1993): 88–94.

Workman, Roy. "Ælfwine's Gifts." *Suffolk Review* 4 (1979): 280–2.

Zaret, David. *The Heavenly Contract: Ideology and Organization in Pre-Revolutionary Puritanism*. Chicago: University of Chicago Press, 1985.

Index

Toronto Anglo-Saxon Series

1 *Preaching the Converted: The Style and Rhetoric of the Vercelli Book Homilies*, Samantha Zacher
2 *Say What I Am Called: The Old English Riddles of the Exeter Book and the Anglo-Latin Riddle Tradition*, Dieter Bitterli
3 *The Aesthetics of Nostalgia: Historical Representation in Anglo-Saxon Verse*, Renée Trilling
4 *New Readings in the Vercelli Book*, edited by Samantha Zacher and Andy Orchard
5 *Authors, Audiences, and Old English Verse*, Thomas A. Bredehoft
6 *On Aesthetics in* Beowulf *and Other Old English Poems*, edited by John M. Hill
7 *Old English Metre: An Introduction*, Jun Terasawa
8 *Anglo-Saxon Psychologies in the Vernacular and Latin Traditions*, Leslie Lockett
9 *The Body Legal in Barbarian Law*, Lisi Oliver
10 *Old English Literature and the Old Testament*, edited by Michael Fox and Manish Sharma
11 *Stealing Obedience: Narratives of Agency and Identity in Later Anglo-Saxon England*, Katherine O'Brien O'Keeffe
12 *Traditional Subjectivities: The Old English Poetics of Mentality*, Britt Mize
13 *Land and Book: Literature and Land Tenure in Anglo-Saxon England*, Scott T. Smith
14 *Writing Women Saints in Anglo-Saxon England*, edited by Paul E. Szarmach
15 *Anglo-Saxon Manuscripts: A Bibliographical Handlist of Manuscripts and Manuscript Fragments Written or Owned in England up to 1100*, Helmut Gneuss and Michael Lapidge
16 *The King's Body: Burial and Succession in Anglo-Saxon England*, Nicole Marafioti

17 *From Lawmen to Plowmen: Anglo-Saxon Legal Tradition and the School of Langland*, Stephen Yeager
18 *The Politics of Language: Byrhtferth, Ælfric, and the Multilingual Identity of the Benedictine Reform*, Rebecca Stephenson
19 *Weaving Words and Binding Bodies: The Poetics of Human Experience in Old English Literature*, Megan Cavell
20 *Joinings: Compound Words in Old English Literature*, Jonathan Davis-Secord
21 *Imagining the Jew in Anglo-Saxon Literature and Culture*, edited by Samantha Zacher
22 *Latinity and Identity in Anglo-Saxon Literature*, edited by Rebecca Stephenson and Emily Thornbury
23 *Inhabited Spaces: Anglo-Saxon Constructions of Place*, Nicole Guenther Discenza
24 *England in Europe: English Royal Women and Literary Patronage, c.1000 – c.1150*, Elizabeth M. Tyler
25 *Undoing Babel: The Tower of Babel in Anglo-Saxon Literature*, Tristan Major
26 *Compelling God: Theories of Prayer in Anglo-Saxon England*, Stephanie Clark
27 *Biblical Epics in Late Antiquity and Anglo-Saxon England:* Divina in Laude Voluntus, Patrick McBrine

www.ingramcontent.com/pod-product-compliance
Lightning Source LLC
LaVergne TN
LVHW090150080826
844660LV00013B/752/J